# Reinventing Europe

# Reinventing Europe

## The History of the European Union, 1945 to the Present

*Edited by*
*Brigitte Leucht, Katja Seidel and*
*Laurent Warlouzet*

BLOOMSBURY ACADEMIC
LONDON • NEW YORK • OXFORD • NEW DELHI • SYDNEY

BLOOMSBURY ACADEMIC
Bloomsbury Publishing Plc
50 Bedford Square, London, WC1B 3DP, UK
1385 Broadway, New York, NY 10018, USA
29 Earlsfort Terrace, Dublin 2, Ireland

BLOOMSBURY, BLOOMSBURY ACADEMIC and the Diana logo are
trademarks of Bloomsbury Publishing Plc

First published in Great Britain 2023

Designer: Akihiro Nakayama Urban art commenting on Brexit, as the star representing the
UK is chipped away from the EU flag. The political mural greets traffic in Dover. (© Banksy)

A catalogue record for this book is available from the British Library.

A catalog record for this book is available from the Library of Congress.

ISBN: HB: 978-1-3502-1308-1
PB: 978-1-3502-1307-4
ePDF: 978-1-3502-1309-8
eBook: 978-1-3502-1311-1

Typeset by Newgen KnowledgeWorks Pvt. Ltd., Chennai, India
Printed and bound in Great Britain

To find out more about our authors and books visit www.bloomsbury.com
and sign up for our newsletters.

# CONTENTS

## Part II Institutions and Policies

### Institutions

### Policies

# ILLUSTRATIONS

Tables

# CONTRIBUTORS

**Bill Davies** is Associate Professor in the School of Public Affairs, American University, Washington, DC. His research interests include the history of European integration, the Court of Justice of the European Union and the development of European law. His published works are: *Resisting the European Court of Justice: Germany's Confrontation with European Law 1949–1979* (2012), *European Law Stories: Critical and Contextual Histories of European Law* (co-edited with Fernanda Nicola; 2017), *The History of European Law: The Battle over the Constitutional Practice, 1950 to 1993* (co-edited with Morten Rasmussen; 2022) and *The Education of a Federal Judge: Timothy B. Dyk* (with Tim Dyk; 2022).

**Alexis Drach** is Lecturer in Modern Economic History at Paris 8 Vincennes-Saint Denis University. He holds a PhD in history from the European University Institute in Florence and has been Research Associate in International Economic History at Glasgow University. His interests lie in the history of banking regulation and supervision, banks' internationalization, European integration, globalization and expertise. He has co-edited, with Youssef Cassis, the book *Financial Deregulation: A Historical Perspective* (2021). His first monograph, *Liberté surveillée: supervision bancaire et globalisation financière au Comité de Bâle, 1974–1988*, was published in February 2022.

**Magdalena Frennhoff Larsén** is a Senior Lecturer at the University of Westminster, where she teaches EU studies. Her research interests are in the areas of EU external relations, with a particular focus on the EU as an international negotiator, and she has published widely on the topic. She is also a regular media commentator on the EU and on Brexit for media outlets both in the UK and overseas.

**Carine Germond** is Professor of European Studies at the Norwegian University of Science and Technology in the Department of Historical and Classical Studies. Her research focuses on key areas of the diplomatic and political history of twentieth-century Europe and transnational history with an emphasis on societal actors in European Union (EU) policymaking processes. She has published on post-war Franco-German relations, the EU's common agricultural policy and the European Parliament. Her most recent book is *The European Ambition: The Group of the European People's Party and European Integration* (2020).

**Mathias Haeussler** is Assistant Professor of Modern European History (nineteenth and twentieth centuries) at Regensburg University. He was previously Lumley Research Fellow at Magdalene College University of Cambridge, where he also completed his PhD. His recent publications include *Inventing Elvis: An American Icon in a Cold War World* (2021) and *Helmut Schmidt and British-German Relations: A European Misunderstanding* (2019).

**Ferenc Laczó** is Assistant Professor with tenure in History at Maastricht University. He received his PhD from the Central European University in 2011 and was previously a postdoctoral researcher at the Imre Kertész Kolleg Jena. He is the author or editor of eleven books on Hungarian, Jewish, German, European and global themes. His most recent publication, co-edited with Bálint Varga, is *Magyarország globális története 1869–2022* (*A Global History of Hungary 1869–2022*).

**Brigitte Leucht** is Reader in International History and Politics at the University of Portsmouth. The focus of her research is the history of European integration and transatlantic relations. Her work has focused on explaining the origins and outcomes of policy and decision-making processes through highlighting the impact of transnational and transatlantic networks of actors. Recent publications on the political and legal dimensions of European market integration include the book: *Cassis de Dijon: Forty Years On* (with Catherine Barnard and Albertina Albors-Llorens; 2021).

**Jan-Henrik Meyer** is a senior researcher at the Max Planck Institute for Legal History and Legal Theory, Frankfurt, and an associate researcher at the Leibniz Centre for Contemporary History, Potsdam. His interdisciplinary research interests include the history, law and politics of European integration; transnational public spheres and social movements; international organizations; environmental and energy history. He is currently writing a history of EU environmental law. Recent publications include the book: *Engaging the Atom: The History of Nuclear Energy and Society in Europe* (with Arne Kaijser et al.; 2021).

**Simone Paoli** is Assistant Professor in History of International Relations at the University of Pisa. He is coordinating a university research project on 'Moscow and Brussels from 1985 to 1994' and a Jean Monnet Project on 'Mobility, Migrations and European Integration'. His research interests focus on the history of European integration and cooperation, with an emphasis on educational, cultural, social and migration dimensions. He has published *Frontiera Sud* (2018) and co-edited *Peoples and Borders* (with E. Calandri and A. Varsori; 2017) and *Child Migration and Biopolitics* (with B. Scutaru; 2021).

**Christian Salm** is a policy researcher and advisor at the Foundation for European Progressive Studies (FEPS). Before joining FEPS, he worked as a historian and policy analyst at the European Parliamentary Research Service of the European Parliament. He obtained his PhD from the European Centre for European and International Studies Research at the University of Portsmouth. He has published on several issues pertaining to European transnational history, political parties in European integration, EU policymaking and the history of the European Parliament, including the article 'Diffusing Democracy in Europe? The European Parliament and Southern European Community Enlargement, 1974 to 1979' in the *Journal of European Integration History* (2021).

**Vera Scepanovic** is Lecturer in International Relations and European Studies at Leiden University. She was previously a postdoctoral Max Weber Fellow at European University Institute in Florence and a visiting lecturer at the Central European University in Budapest. She has published many book reviews, articles and chapters in books such as *New Frontier of the Automobile Industry* (2020) and *Successes & Failures in EU Cohesion Policy* (2020).

**Katja Seidel** is Senior Lecturer in History at the University of Westminster. Her research interests include the history of European integration, transatlantic relations and international organizations. She has published widely on the emergence of European common policies and of European administrations. Her publications include: *The Process of Politics in Europe: The Rise of European Elites and Supranational Institutions* (2010) and she is currently working on a biography of the US diplomat and scholar Miriam Camps.

**Laurent Warlouzet** is Professor of History at Sorbonne University. A former postdoctoral fellow at the London School of Economics (LSE), he has published a volume titled *Governing Europe in a Globalizing World: Neoliberalism and Its Alternatives following the 1973 Oil Crisis* (2018; reviewed in *Foreign Affairs*). More recently, he has published a book on the history of European economic policies from 1945 to 2021: *Europe contre Europe: Entre liberté, solidarité et puissance* (2022; reviewed in *Le Monde* and on the LSE blog).

# ABBREVIATIONS

| | |
|---|---|
| AASM | Associated African States and Madagascar |
| ACP | African, Caribbean and Pacific Group of States |
| AfD | Alternative für Deutschland Party |
| BBQ | British Budgetary Question |
| BEUC | European Consumer Organization/Bureau Européen des Unions des Consommateurs |
| CAP | Common Agricultural Policy |
| CDU | Christlich Demokratische Union |
| CEEC | Central and Eastern European Countries |
| CEEP | European Centre of Public Enterprises |
| CFSP | Common Foreign and Security Policy |
| CJEU | Court of Justice of the European Union |
| COMECON | Council for Mutual Economic Assistance |
| COPA | Comité des organisations professionnelles agricoles/ Committee of Professional Agricultural Organizations |
| COREPER | Comité européen des représentants permanents/ Committee of Permanent Representatives |
| CSCE | Conference on Security and Cooperation in Europe |
| DG | Directorate-General |
| DTEU | Draft Treaty on European Union |
| EAGGF | European Agricultural Guidance and Guarantee Fund |
| EC | European Community |
| ECB | European Central Bank |
| ECJ | European Court of Justice |
| ECSC | European Coal and Steel Community |
| EDC | European Defence Community |
| EDF | European Development Fund |
| EEB | European Environmental Bureau |
| EEC | European Economic Community |
| EFSI | European Fund for Strategic Investment |
| EFTA | European Free Trade Association |
| EMS | European Monetary System |
| EMU | Economic and Monetary Union |
| EP | European Parliament |
| EPA | European Parliamentary Assembly |
| EPC | European Political Community |

| | |
|---|---|
| EPC | European Political Cooperation |
| EPP | European People's Party |
| EPU | European Payments Union |
| ERDF | European Regional Development Fund |
| ERM | Exchange Rate Mechanism |
| ERP | European Recovery Programme (Marshall Plan) |
| ERT | European Round Table of Industrialists |
| ESA | European Space Agency |
| ESDP | European Security and Defence Policy |
| ESF | European Social Fund |
| ESM | European Stability Mechanism |
| ESPRIT | European Strategic Program on Research in Information Technology |
| ETUC | European Trade Union Confederation |
| EUI | European University Institute |
| Euratom | European Atomic Energy Community |
| FIDE | Fédération internationale pour le droit européen/ International Federation of European Law |
| FRG | Federal Republic of Germany |
| G7 | Group of Seven |
| GATT | General Agreement on Tariffs and Trade |
| GDP | Gross Domestic Product |
| GMO | Genetically Modified Organism |
| IGC | Intergovernmental conference |
| ILO | International Labour Organization |
| IMF | International Monetary Fund |
| IO | International Organization |
| ITL | Integration Through Law |
| MCAs | Monetary Compensatory Amounts |
| MEP | Member of the European Parliament |
| MLF | Multilateral Force |
| NAT | North Atlantic Treaty |
| NATO | North Atlantic Treaty Organization |
| OCT | Overseas Countries and Territories |
| OECD | Organization for Economic Cooperation and Development |
| OEEC | Organization for European Economic Cooperation |
| OLAF | Office européen de lutte antifraude/European Anti-Fraud Office |
| PCF | Parti Communiste Français |
| PHARE | Poland and Hungary Assistance for the Restructuring of the Economy |
| PSPP | Public Sector Purchase Programme |
| QMV | Qualified majority voting |
| RN | French National Rally |

| | |
|---|---|
| **S&D** | Progressive Alliance of Socialists and Democrats |
| **SEA** | Single European Act |
| **SEPC** | Service for the Environment and Consumer Protection |
| **SGCI** | Secrétariat général du Comité interministériel pour les questions de coopération économique européenne |
| **SGP** | Stability and Growth Pact |
| **SPD** | Sozialdemokratische Partei Deutschlands |
| **SRM** | Single Resolution Mechanism |
| **SSM** | Single Supervisory Mechanism |
| **TEU** | Treaty on European Union |
| **TFEU** | Treaty on the Functioning of the European Union |
| **UEF** | Union of European Federalists |
| **UEM** | United Europe Movement |
| **UN** | United Nations |
| **UNICE** | Union of Industrial and Employers' Confederations of Europe |
| **VAT** | Value-added tax |
| **WEU** | Western European Union |

# Introduction

## Brigitte Leucht, Katja Seidel and Laurent Warlouzet

The European Union (EU) has considerable influence on the politics, economies and societies of its member states and, directly or indirectly, on European citizens' lives. From focusing primarily on market integration in the 1960s, today's EU manages one of the largest economic markets in the world, including a European currency, the euro. As a trading block and a participant in multilateral negotiations such as the COP climate change conferences, the EU's influence reaches beyond its borders. The Union drives an ambitious environmental policy agenda and runs regional and agricultural policies. Its member states cooperate in foreign policy, defence and justice and home affairs, and increasingly so as the 2022 Ukraine war has shown. Through the 'Horizon' research programme, the EU distributes billions of euros, fostering transnational research and innovation in areas such as biomedical sciences, technology, social sciences and humanities. From originally six member states, it has grown to encompass twenty-seven countries – the twenty-eighth, the UK, left the EU in January 2020. Within the EU, and beyond its borders, European integration has solicited a range of reactions, from ardent euro-enthusiasm to Euroscepticism. Yet most people know very little about the EU, how it functions, how it has evolved over time and why it has taken the shape that it has today. *Reinventing Europe* presents this history in an accessible manner.

# Rationale

This volume aims to present the history of how European integration contributed to 'reinventing Europe' after the Second World War. After two destructive wars that originated among European states and empires, Europeans decided to reshape their relationship in an innovative way. While this book examines the history of the EU and its forerunners, it also considers the plethora of other post-war European organizations starting with the Organization for European Economic Co-operation (OEEC), set up in 1948 to administer the Marshall Plan. The chapters in this book embed the history of the EU into the wider context of European history by linking it to the history of the Cold War, transatlantic relations, decolonization, domestic policy choices and capitalism. In doing so, they demonstrate that the story of European integration is an integral part of European political, economic, social and cultural history. The volume thus inserts European integration into the broader narrative of European and global dynamics, including globalization and nationalism, imperialism and decolonization, technological innovations and environmental challenges, and ideological and social upheavals. It does so by assessing various historical constraints, path dependencies, the impact of global trends and phenomena, ideologies as well as individual agency on the formation and development of the EU, its institutions and policies. The book conceives of 'Europe' as more than Cold War Western Europe by including Central and Eastern European states, while also considering the interaction between European integration and citizens of the EU. It thus aims to present a rich and multifaceted history of Europe and European integration.

It is often forgotten that the current EU is rooted in more than seven decades of history, and nearly a century of negotiations on the institutionalization of European cooperation. Hence, in this volume, each chapter, except for the chronological chapters in Part I, covers the development of EU institutions and policies from 1945, or earlier, up to the present day. Such a historically rooted perspective on the EU also allows readers to understand the unique path Europe has taken with European integration, and assess the strengths and weaknesses of the EU. The chapters in this volume aim to cast an honest and critical perspective on the EU and its history, one that explains the roots of current issues by highlighting historical constraints, diverging interests, weak compromises, missed opportunities and path dependencies.

One example is Brexit. Why did Britain's voting public opt for leaving the EU in a referendum in June 2016? To understand this, the chapter on Britain and Europe explores Britain's historically difficult and volatile relationship with European integration right up to the Brexit vote, while also highlighting the important contribution Britain made to European integration. Other issues the textbook explores in a long-term perspective include the questions of: why France and Germany are often seen as 'engines' of European integration; why the EU has become an important actor in global environmental initiatives and agreements; the extent to which the eurozone crisis was rooted in earlier decisions; and why the EU has ended up with an agricultural policy that is widely seen as wasteful and lacking transparency? Our book shows that the answers to these questions are to be found in a deep and complex set of historical constraints, opportunity structures and decisions.

History is made by people and European integration is the result of ideas, initiatives and tough bargaining. This volume aims to demonstrate that European integration was the result of decisions taken by individuals – and not only prominent political leaders such as Winston Churchill, Charles de Gaulle, Margaret Thatcher and Angela Merkel but also civil servants, jurists, economists, bankers, scientists, trade unionists, entrepreneurs and individual citizen activists. The chapters in this volume aim to bring those individual actors into the story as well as the interests and ideas they advanced.

# Structure of the book

This volume features both a chronological and a thematic approach. Part I covers the chronological development of European integration from 1945 to the present day in four chapters. These are introductory chapters that highlight the main developments during the period. The remaining chapters are thematic and arranged in Parts II and III. Part II deals with institutions and policies. It explores the history of three of the EU's main institutions – the European Commission, the Court of Justice of the EU and the European Parliament – and presents a selection of the EU's most salient policy areas. The book makes no claim to completeness, but we took care to include a range of long-standing and important policies such as the single market, economic and monetary union and the common agricultural policy as well as newer policies such as environmental and consumer policies. Part III focuses on themes and geographical spaces. It includes a chapter on the history of the European idea, which shows how this has at times shaped European integration, as well as a chapter on Euroscepticism, which innovatively explores alternative and anti-European ideas and trends in a long-term perspective. It also contains a comprehensive chapter on the historiography of European integration. The chapters on different geographical spaces were equally guided by the concern of being relevant and exemplary. Due to Britain's varied relationship with European integration and the country's decision to leave the EU, this was an important chapter to include. Another important region the volume covers is Central and Eastern Europe in a chapter that offers a unique insight into the history of the region and its relationship with Western Europe both during and after the period of Communism, an issue that is usually absent from surveys on EU history. Another country chapter focuses on the Franco-German relationship in the EU showing how a bilateral relationship can impact a multilateral institution, while the chapter on the EU as a global power delves into the variegated relationships the organization has had with its major trading partners, for instance, the United States.

# How to use the book

Readers can use this volume in a flexible manner. While it can be read cover to cover as an up-to-date synthesis of the history of European integration, it is also possible to read chapters individually to gain a better understanding of an issue or use a chapter as a point of departure for further research. The chronological chapters in Part I, introducing information comprehensively but at the basic level, are supplemented with the thematic chapters providing more background to an issue. All chapters contain cross-references to other chapters in the volume where a topic is explored in more depth.

The chapters encompass a range of useful pedagogical features, including timelines, extracts from primary sources, photographs, cartoons, statistics, textboxes and short biographies of key personalities. These features are used to illustrate and clarify certain issues discussed in the chapters. Each chapter ends with five key questions, inviting readers to reflect on the main arguments of the chapter. Students can use those questions independently to test their understanding of the issues discussed in the chapter. Each chapter also contains ten key readings that readers can use as a point of departure to delve deeper into the subject matter. The volume also features a substantial chapter on the historiography of the EU, including a guide to web resources, a chronology as well as a glossary. The editors and authors are historians and political scientists experienced in researching and teaching EU history and have taught courses whose designs have inspired this book. They are based at institutions across the EU and beyond. When we started teaching courses on EU history, there was no textbook as such available that could be used to structure an entire course. We hope that this book fills this gap.

# A note on terminology

The EU is notorious for its jungle of acronyms. For clarity, in this volume, we are referring to the European Economic Community (EEC) when discussing institutions, policies and events that have their origins in the Treaty of Rome of 1957. In 1993 the Maastricht Treaty came into force, creating the EU which also incorporated the EEC. When discussing events from 1993 onwards the chapters therefore refer to the EU and no longer to the EEC. Unless stated otherwise, treaty articles refer to the original EEC Treaty of Rome.

# PART I

# Chronology

# 1

# The formation of the European Coal and Steel Community, the European Economic Community and Euratom, 1945–58

## *Brigitte Leucht*

## Introduction

On 8 May 1945 the Wehrmacht capitulated signalling the end of the Second World War in Europe. Almost to the day five years later – on 9 May 1950 – French Foreign Minister Robert Schuman stunned the world with a proposal for Franco-German cooperation. France and West Germany were to pool their resources in coal and steel and put them under the control of a joint 'high authority'. Following the interstate negotiations on the Schuman Plan, in which France and Germany, the Benelux countries and Italy participated, the treaty establishing the European Coal and Steel Community (ECSC) was signed in Paris on 18 April 1951. Thus, the foundation for the integration of the 'core Europe' of the Six was laid, and in 1952, the institutions of the ECSC, including a High Authority, a Common Assembly, a Court of Justice and a Special Council of Ministers, began operating.

There is a fascinating puzzle lurking behind this apparently straightforward historical account: how can we explain the French proposal of 1950 to collaborate with the newly established West German state only five years

following the end of the Second World War? This chapter will take this
puzzle as a point of departure, and its first part will examine the origins of
the ECSC as a response to the two world wars, the emergence of a bipolar
world order and the demise of European empires. The chapter's first section
will also assess how the ECSC differed from other, earlier attempts at
fostering European cooperation in the post-45 period, on the one hand, and
from previous collaboration in the heavy industries, on the other.

The second part of the chapter focuses on unpacking the move from
integration in coal and steel to promoting the integration of the entire
economies of the Six through the establishment of a common market. Sectoral
integration continued in nuclear energy and resulted in the formation of the
European Atomic Energy Community (Euratom). But it was the European
Economic Community (EEC) Treaty, which established the institutions
(in particular the European Commission and the Court of Justice of
the European Union (CJEU)) and policies (including agriculture, trade,
competition and the free movement of goods, services, capital and labour),
that would unfold their full potential against the backdrop of the political
and economic governance crises of the 1970s and the end of the Cold War in
Europe. Again, there is a puzzle informing this account of the development
from the ECSC to the EEC in the second part of the chapter: how can we
account for the continuing integration of the core Europe of the Six – first,
in light of setbacks in advancing European integration, most importantly
the failure of the European Political and Defence Communities in 1954;
second, in the context of competing and overlapping institutions promoting
European international cooperation, including the Council of Europe and
the Organization for European Economic Cooperation (OEEC); and third,
in the framework of the Cold War and progressive decolonization?

# 1. International collaboration in post-1945 Europe and the Schuman Plan

## Transatlantic and European organizations advancing European integration

Following the end of the Second World War, leading politicians and
policymakers in Europe and the United States shared a belief in the importance
of cooperation to avoid the economic and political instability of the interwar
period. European leaders cooperated with the Harry S. Truman government
of the United States in their pursuit of economic recovery, exchange rate
coordination and tariff reduction; and they began cooperating with each
other in laying new foundations for European collaboration. This course
of action for a (Western) European liberal democratic order was supported
by voters at the polls. Two countries with strong Communist parties and

therefore the potential for closer alignment with the Soviet Union were France and Italy. In France's first elections following the end of the Second World War, the Parti Communiste Français (PCF) won around 25 per cent of the vote enabling it to take part in the Fourth Republic's first government. Following the dismissal of the Communists from the cabinet in 1947, however, the PCF did not participate in any Fourth Republic administration. In Italy, the 1948 elections, the first free elections since 1922, were decided against the Communists and in favour of the Christian Democratic Party and its Western course.

(Western) European governments agreed with the US government on the need for cooperation and integration. They had different ideas, however, for establishing organizations that would address urgent economic challenges while ensuring stability and peace in Europe in the long run. Of crucial importance in safeguarding the dual objective of achieving economic reconstruction and safeguarding peace was the 'German question', that is, the issue of how to deal with a potentially powerful Germany at the centre of Europe. Approaches by Western European and the US governments to resolving the German question and promoting the establishment of European organizations were shaped by two wider international developments: the emerging Cold War and the increasing challenge to European colonial rule.

It is helpful to imagine the emergence of the core Europe of the Six within a triangle, the corners of which consist of: the German question, the superpower pre-eminence and the future of European empires. Against this backdrop, the graph and timeline shown in Figure 1.1 introduce important developments and turning points from 1945 to 1952, which are discussed below.

An important attempt to institutionalize European integration was the proposal of the Marshall Plan by the US government on 5 June 1947. This initiative for a US-supported European Recovery Programme (ERP, 1948–52) responded to American fears about the collapse of Europe's economies and Europe's dollar shortage. US foreign-policy makers worried Europe's dire economic situation could be exploited by the Soviet Union that had already extended its sphere of influence far into Eastern and Central Europe, including Poland, where a Communist government was installed in 1947. The Marshall Plan encouraged European governments to cooperate and made it a prerequisite for them to formulate a joint economic programme to be eligible for US aid. This condition reflected the idea that economic cooperation between European states would create interdependency and therefore foster economic *and* political stability, which informed the US preference for (Western) European political and market integration. The states eventually receiving aid through the ERP met the US government's requirement by establishing the OEEC (1948). The organization administered the US programme in Western Europe and facilitated limited trade liberalization (1949–58) and a payments union (1950–8).

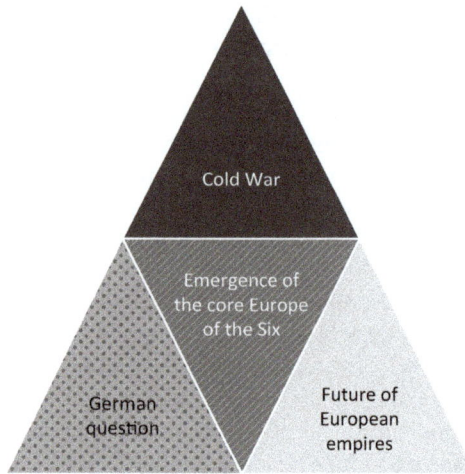

| 1946 | | French War in Indochina (–1954) |
| 1947 | | Independence of India and Pakistan and establishment of the Commonwealth of Nations |
| 1947 | | European Christian Democrats meet in Geneva Circle and Nouvelles Equipes Internationales |
| 5 June 1947 | | US government proposes the Marshall Plan |
| 16 April 1948 | | Establishment of the OEEC |
| 1948 | | European Recovery Program (–1952) |
| 1949 | | Communist victory in China |
| | | Establishment of the Union française |
| 4 April 1949 | | Establishment of the Council of Europe |
| 9 May 1950 | | Schuman Plan declaration |
| 24 June 1950 | | Outbreak of the Korean War |
| 23 July 1952 | | ECSC Treaty enters into force (–2002) |

FIGURE 1.1 *The emergence of the core Europe of the Six, 1945–52.*

Regarding the eventual integration of the core Europe of the Six, the Marshall Plan was important for embracing a regional Western European rather than a global solution for safeguarding peace and stability in Europe. The failed devaluation of the British pound sterling in the summer of 1947 and the inability of the British government to establish the sterling as a reserve currency represented a decisive step away from the global world economic order envisaged by the Bretton Woods system (Milward 1984; Asbeek Brusse 1997). It had become clear that Western European economic reconstruction could only happen based on regional solutions that shielded the fragile European economies from American competition. The recipient states of Marshall Plan aid encompassed a wider geographical scope than the future ECSC, also including (occupied) Austria, Denmark, Sweden, Norway, Iceland, the UK and Ireland, Portugal, Greece, Turkey and, for a period, Trieste. The inclusion of West Germany, which originally joined as the Anglo-American Bi-zone plus the French zone of occupation, was as significant in accelerating the division of Europe in the early Cold War as the (self-)exclusion of the Soviet Union and its Central and Eastern European satellites (Hitchcock 2010). Furthermore, the Marshall Plan formed the point of departure for the founding of the North Atlantic Treaty Organization (NATO) in 1949. The Norwegian historian Geir Lundestad (1998) has portrayed NATO as the result of a 'spillover' from political and economic integration in the Marshall Plan into security and defence.

At the same time, intra-European debates on facilitating the cooperation and integration of European states led to the establishment of another important organization, the Council of Europe (Wassenberg 2013; see also Chapter 13). Against the backdrop of surging public support for a more integrated Europe with deep inroads in the strong Christian Democratic parties in continental Europe, the governments of France, the emerging West German state, the Benelux countries and Italy promoted the creation of a political organization aimed at uniting Europe (Kaiser 2007). This initiative failed in the Council of Europe Assembly in 1948 due to political resistance and cultural reservations from Britain and the Nordic countries. The British government also found it difficult to square the circle between the emergence of a Western European organized economy and the Commonwealth in the negotiations over the economic reconstruction of Western Europe in the OEEC. As a result of the experiences of only limited progress at political and economic integration made in the Council of Europe and the OEEC, the governments of the six continental European countries were gradually coming to terms with the fact that the British government would not provide the political leadership expected. For the very same reason, the US government reacted favourably when the French Christian Democratic government rather than the UK government took the lead and proposed a new initiative promoting Franco-German cooperation in the spring of 1950: the Schuman Plan.

## The Schuman Plan: Between continuity and new beginnings

Wolfram Kaiser has demonstrated that the transnational collaboration of Christian Democrats – in 1950 in government in all the future member states of the ECSC – was essential for the successful launch of the Schuman Plan proposal as well as its political realization and the ratification of the

ECSC Treaty. French Foreign Minister Robert Schuman and West German Chancellor Konrad Adenauer were among the leading Christian Democratic politicians who had met informally to prepare Franco-German rapprochement in the Nouvelles Equipes Internationales, a distant forerunner of the European People's Party (see Chapter 7), and secret high-level meetings in the so-called Geneva Circle. From 1947 to 1950 European Christian Democrats established political consensus on advancing European integration through Franco-German co-operation in the coal and steel sectors and without the participation of the UK (Kaiser 2007). The core principle underpinning the Schuman Plan was its supranational approach, which distinguished the initiative from other attempts at institutionalizing European integration after 1945, including intergovernmental co-operation in the Council of Europe and the OEEC. In these organizations it had become clear that the UK government was reluctant to go beyond intergovernmental cooperation, and the supranational dimension of the Schuman Plan thus provoked the self-exclusion of the UK from the core European project. What is more, the British Labour government (1945–51) would not agree on accepting foreign interference in two sectors of the economy ready for nationalization.

The supranational approach – the delegation of authority from the national to the European level – promoted by Christian Democrats was not new. To the contrary, it owed to the political concept of supranationality, which shared similarities with the organization of the Catholic Church and its 'supranational' centre in Rome. Supranationality was also tied to the idea that European integration would serve as a tool to restore 'Western civilization' within the boundaries of the Carolingian Empire but on democratic foundations. Lastly, the delegation of authority from the national to the supranational European level matched the principle of subsidiarity derived from Catholic social teaching, which embraced the dispersion of authority across different societal levels (Kaiser 2007). Crucially, the idea of going beyond purely intergovernmental cooperation matched the US foreign policy preference for (Western) European political and market integration. In the context of the emerging Cold War, an endorsement by the US government was necessary for any initiative at European integration to be realized.

The text of the Schuman Plan declaration of 9 May 1950 was developed under the auspices of Jean Monnet (Box 1.1), the director of the French Planning Commission, which was responsible for implementing the French national programme for reconstruction (1947–52). At the core of the Schuman Plan was a supranational high authority with independent powers which would integrate the French and German coal and steel sectors. The issue of coal and steel represented a major obstacle to Franco-German reconciliation. Coal served as Europe's primary energy source and steel as a core material for industrial production (depending on coal to manufacture it). West Germany's Ruhr area, where coal deposits were located, was subjected to Allied restrictions on production, ownership and sale of coal and steel, however. France wanted to control and access Ruhr coal to meet both its own steel industry's need for raw materials and the objective of modernizing the heavy industries. In this context, the proposed organization promised a common and balanced organization of two crucial sectors of the economy that traditionally had been at the heart of the military machinery. For West Germany, it also offered the status of an equal partner within an international organization. The coal and steel pool, therefore, was an economic peace treaty between France and Germany (Milward 1984) and a solution to the German question, the first of the three corners of our imagined triangle.

## BOX 1.1  BIOGRAPHY OF JEAN MONNET

| 1888 | (Cognac, France)–1979 (Houjarray, France) |
|---|---|
| 1916–18 | French representation at the Inter-Allied Supply Committee in London |
| 1919–23 | Deputy secretary general to the League of Nations |
| 1923–38 | Trader and investment banker (including collaborating with the New York investment bank firm Blair and Company) |
| 1938–45 | Senior French and then Allied official (including for the British Supply Council in Washington) and member of the French Committee for National Liberation |
| 1945–52 | First commissioner of the French Plan |
| 1952–5 | First president of the ECSC High Authority |
| 1955–75 | Founder and later president of the Action Committee for the United States of Europe |

The Schuman Plan declaration paid homage to the (French) Briand Plan of 1930 (see Chapter 13), but it also connected to the interwar period via the idea of improving Franco-German relations through the creation of a coal and steel pool. As early as 1923, at the height of the crisis between France and Germany over the Ruhr, Konrad Adenauer, then mayor of British-occupied Cologne, proposed the establishment of a 'Rhenisch Republic' within a heavily decentralized Germany (Köhler 1986). At the time, Adenauer argued that peace between France and Germany relied on Western European industrial integration (Schwarz 1995). According to this view and reflecting the prevalent approach during the interwar period, the problem of European integration required economic rather than legal tools and concepts. Indeed, in 1926, the twofold notion of industrial cooperation and Franco-German reconciliation materialized when European steel industrialists from Germany, France, Belgium and Luxembourg formed the International Steel Cartel (ISC) following an initiative of the Luxembourg industrialist Emile Mayrisch (Nocken 1989). The ISC attempted to solve the problem of balancing the basic industries between France and Germany after the latter had lost sovereignty over Alsace-Lorraine and temporarily the Saar because of the Versailles peace settlement. The cartel set an important precedent for the transnational cooperation of industrialists in the heavy industries, for example, between French steel producers and the South German steel-consuming industry (Gillingham 1986).

The experience of the ISC resonated in the post-45 period in two ways. On the one hand, Chancellor Adenauer galvanized the crucial support of the concerned industries for the advancement of relations with France through industrial co-operation, when he encouraged the German industrialist Günter Henle to develop a proposal for Franco-German collaboration in 1948 (Bührer 1986). Through his attempt to get a leading industrialist on board of pooling the heavy industries and by advocating the idea of a Franco-German union, including in two interviews with an American news agency in the spring of 1950, Adenauer attempted to prepare the ground for the Schuman Plan's endorsement in West Germany (Kaiser 2007). On the other hand, the notion of powerful industrialists establishing cartels was problematic in post-1945 Western Europe, where the US government pushed for the establishment of liberal market economies. US foreign-policy planners and liberally minded European policymakers and experts argued that cartels could facilitate the rise of autocratic and totalitarian systems. According to this argument, an intimate economic, political and moral link had existed between the cartelization of the European heavy industries in the interwar period and the rise of the nationalist right in both Germany and France. Cartels indeed had grown rapidly during the years of the French Vichy and the German National Socialist regimes, and representatives of the heavy industries in both countries had collaborated with these regimes.

Not surprisingly, the initial reaction of the US government to the Schuman Plan was sceptical. The proposal was in line with the US policy preference for supranational European integration but seemed to counter their other core preference for a free, competitive market economy. When they were presented with the Schuman Plan initiative prior to its launch on 9 May 1950, US Secretary of State Dean Acheson and David Bruce, formerly the head of the Marshall Plan administration in France (1948–9) and at the time the US ambassador to Paris, were very concerned that the proposal would establish an international cartel. It was only due to reassurances provided by Jean Monnet and John McCloy, the US high commissioner for Germany, that Acheson and Bruce could be won for the plan in high-level talks before Schuman went public with it (Acheson 1969). This episode demonstrates that the day-to-day cooperation between the French Planning Commission and the US Marshall Plan administration was instrumental in safeguarding crucial American support for the Schuman Plan initiative in the emerging superpower conflict (Leucht 2009), the second corner of our imagined triangle.

Having sketched the development of organizations fostering European integration and the Schuman Plan in relation to two of the corners of the triangle – the German question and the early Cold War – the following section will proceed to address its third corner: the future of European empires.

## The Schuman Plan and Eurafrica

The colonial dimension is a relatively recent focus in research on the origins of European integration (see also Chapter 14). Peo Hansen and Stefan Jonsson's book *Eurafrica* (2014) argues that European integration represented nothing less but an attempt to 'rescue' the declining European empires. After all, three of the founding member states of the ECSC – France, the Netherlands and Belgium – had colonial possessions at the time of the Schuman Plan declaration. France was also fighting a brutal colonial war in Indochina (1946–54), followed by Algeria (1954–62). Moreover, following the independence of India and Pakistan in 1947, Britain established the Commonwealth of Nations, and in 1949, France created the Union française, signalling attempts by European empires to reorganize their relations with the (former) colonies, while retaining control (Pasture 2018). To be sure, the colonial dimension became more important *after* the conclusion of the ECSC Treaty, due to the changing dynamics of the Cold War. However, the Schuman Plan declaration itself linked to Europe's colonial heritage and articulated aspirations beyond Europe, when it stated that 'Europe, with new means at her disposal, will be able to pursue the realisation of one of its essential tasks: the development of the African continent' (The Schuman Declaration 1950).

This statement is noteworthy for alluding to the concept of Eurafrica in the Schuman Plan. The idea of unity between Europe and Africa was particularly popular in the interwar period, as is also discussed regarding the Pan-European movement in Chapter 13. After 1945, Eurafrica was re-established and adjusted to meet the challenges of the emerging Cold War. Asserting their influence over Africa became a vehicle for European powers, especially for Britain and France, to contribute to shaping the new Cold War world order in the face of superpower pre-eminence. Asia quickly turned from a site of colonial conflict to the major theatre of the early Cold War, with the Communist victory in China in 1949 and the outbreak of the Korean War in 1950, which led Britain and France to focus their colonial aspirations on Africa. There were attempts to institutionalize Eurafrica in both the OEEC and the Council of Europe. The OEEC included an overseas territories working group to promote European cooperation in colonial questions, and the Council of Europe identified colonial cooperation in Africa as one of its priorities (Hansen and Jonsson 2014).

Furthermore, the Schuman Plan's reference to 'the development of the African continent' as an 'essential task' reflects a commitment to modernization and enhancing the technical infrastructure in Africa. Commentators at the time widely regarded this investment in the African continent as a first step leading to the exploitation of raw materials and providing further access to markets for finished European products as well as additional space for Europe's populations (Hansen and Jonsson 2014).

## The legacy of the Schuman Plan

Returning to our puzzle of accounting for the Schuman Plan of 1950, only five years following the end of the war against Nazi Germany, we can recapitulate that this was possible because of a combination of the transnational cooperation of Christian Democrats, the pressing need of the French economy to access the Ruhr's coal resources, crucial US support for supranational European integration and the potential European integration represented for rescuing European empires.

The Schuman Plan shaped European integration beyond 1952. The ECSC Treaty created important path dependencies, which would resonate beyond coal and steel and even beyond the formative period of European integration. The treaty, which was negotiated by the governments of the Six (1950–1) and entered into force on 23 July 1952, established a powerful, supranational executive, the High Authority, with extensive competencies and legislative powers. From its outline in the Schuman Plan proposal, this institution was designed to operate independently of the influence of national governments and interest groups. The choice for independence was supposed to facilitate the efficiency of the new community. At the same time, the independence of the High Authority needed to be balanced with some degree of accountability. In the ECSC Treaty, the dilemma of independence and efficiency, on the one hand, and accountability, on the other, was resolved by adding an institutional ensemble that comprised a Special Council of Ministers, a Common Assembly and a Court of Justice (Leucht 2010). This solution only partly resolved the perceived lack of representation and the concerns about the democratic quality of core Europe, however, and created one important path dependency for the process of European integration.

Another path dependency was created by codifying tensions between different economic approaches to integrating the coal and steel sectors, which would resonate beyond these sectors. The ECSC Treaty combined liberal with interventionist elements and laid the foundation for 'a moderate liberal economic order' (Ophüls 1951, 381). The clearest expression of the treaty's commitment to market liberalization can be found in its antitrust provisions, which were drafted with informal American input behind the scenes of the interstate negotiations on the Schuman Plan (Leucht 2009). These provisions provided *one* important model for the competition rules of the EEC (Leucht and Seidel 2008), which ultimately played a crucial role in the construction of the Community's Common Market.

Finally, as the community came into operation, the coal and steel markets developed differently from what had been projected in the detailed policy prescriptions in the ECSC Treaty. As a result, both the concerned industries and national governments resisted attempts by the High Authority to execute the treaty. Institutionally this meant that the Council often blocked the High Authority. The High Authority also crucially failed to enforce the de-cartelization of the coal and steel industries, envisaged by its antitrust provisions (Witschke 2009). Despite these difficulties in the operation of Europe's first supranational community, the Six continued expressing ambitions for further integration, which will be discussed in the second part of this chapter.

# 2. From coal and steel to the common market for the Six

## Beyond sectoral integration in core Europe

In the first half of the 1950s, the ECSC was seen as only one organization among several that established an ambitious constitutional and institutional framework for European integration. A significant development in the early days of the interstate negotiations on the Schuman Plan – the outbreak of the Korean War in June 1950 – had resulted in plans for further sectoral integration by the Six. The Korean War catapulted the crucial question of the rearmament of West Germany to the top of the US foreign policy agenda. The US government embraced West German rearmament within the framework of committing US troops to Europe, organizing an integrated command structure for the Atlantic alliance, integrating West German military units into the alliance and raising the limits of German steel production (Gillingham 1991). Importantly for purposes of addressing this chapter's second puzzle of accounting for the continuing integration of the core Europe of the Six, the governments taking part in the Schuman Plan conference developed plans for establishing a European army to deal with German rearmament. France was reluctant to accept a German army integrated into NATO indicating the ongoing tensions associated with the German question. The plans for a European Defence Community (EDC) and a European Political Community (EPC) failed to achieve the necessary backing in the French National Assembly in August 1954. The composition of the French parliament had changed to the disadvantage of the pro-European

Christian Democrats (Parsons 2003). Sectoral and supranational integration did not seem to hold the key to further European integration. Abandoned and alone, the ECSC did not seem to have a bright political future in the mid-1950s; rather it looked increasingly like a purely technical organization (Griffiths 2000; Poidevin and Spierenburg 1993).

For the Benelux countries, the failure of the ambitious EDC/EPC plans represented a potential return to the Franco-German commercial bilateralism of the interwar period (Fischer 2012). To counter this unwelcome prospect, the Benelux foreign ministers launched a double pitch, including a Belgian proposal for a nuclear energy community (Euratom), developed under the auspices of the first president of the High Authority, Jean Monnet (Figure 1.2), and a Dutch proposal for creating a common market based on a customs union. This proposal built on the 'Beyen Plan', named after the Dutch Foreign Minister Johan Willem Beyen, which was first put forward in the context of the EPC negotiations in 1952–3. The Beyen Plan and its 1955 rearticulation represented a clear commitment to continuing the integration of the core Europe of the Six. This commitment was remarkable given the mixed record of the High Authority in operation, the failure of the EDC/EPC initiative and ongoing discussions of alternative plans for wider Western European integration. A case in point for alternative plans is provided by the idea of establishing a free trade zone, including the UK and the Scandinavian countries, which Belgian Minister for Foreign Trade Victor Larock introduced in the OEEC in November 1954. Larock's proposal was far from unique, and it matched, for example, the preference of German Economics Minister Ludwig Erhard – the architect of the German economic miracle – for establishing a wider Western free trade area (Segers 2020). So how can we explain the triumph of the core Europe idea, which would provide the foundation for the Benelux Memorandum of 18 May 1955, over competing plans for advancing European integration in the OEEC and beyond?

Crucial to the success of the core Europe idea was Beyen's forging of a coalition with Belgian Foreign Minister Paul-Henri Spaak, a socialist, previously the first president of the Consultative Assembly of the Council of Europe (1949–51) and the president of the ECSC Common Assembly (1952–4). Spaak was a proponent of further sectoral integration and, starting in 1954, he liaised with Monnet and leading officials in the High Authority in preparing the initiative for transport and atomic energy integration. It was Spaak who convinced Monnet that the combination of sectoral integration with the common market proposal was key to launching the Benelux initiative successfully. In the meeting of the ECSC Common Assembly in Strasbourg, on 9 May 1955, Monnet as well as the vice president of the High Authority, the German Christian Democrat Franz Etzel, lent their support to the Benelux initiative (Segers 2020). The Benelux Memorandum therefore had the important endorsement of the existing core Europe institutions.

FIGURE 1.2 *Jean Monnet (front, left), first president of the High Authority, with Robert Schuman on the third anniversary of the Schuman Plan, Luxembourg, 9 May 1953; Monnet's collaborator Etienne Hirsch is seen in the back to the left.* Courtesy of Théo Mey/Photothèque de la ville de Luxembourg. *Source*: Fondation Jean Monnet, Lausanne, Fonds Jean Monnet, JM 9/30/52.

# From the Benelux Memorandum to the Treaties of Rome

From 1 to 3 June 1955, the foreign ministers of the Six met in Messina, Sicily (Figure 1.3), to discuss the Benelux Memorandum. At first, it looked highly unlikely that this proposal would be able to reinvigorate European integration. The UK government, which had been invited to the meeting, was somewhat relieved that the plan seemed overambitious. If the proposals were not realized, the British would not have to decide on whether to participate or not; they therefore quickly withdrew from the intergovernmental 'Spaak committee' established to flesh out the proposals. The problems were multiple. Firstly, the wave of sympathy for the federal cause had lost steam both at the popular level and in government circles. It was clear that the French government would only be able to accept a more functional economic version of European integration with a limited and less overt political ambition. Secondly, the interest of member-state governments in the two proposals was limited and conditional. In West

Germany, the pro-Europeans in the Foreign Ministry under the leadership of Secretary of State (and future first President of the European Commission) Walter Hallstein supported the plans. The German Economics Ministry was divided with Minister Erhard opposing the plan, while a group of officials, including the future EEC commissioner for competition policy Hans von der Groeben, was in favour of the common market. Other ministers and ministries opposed both Euratom *and* the common market; and Chancellor Adenauer prioritized dealing with the position of the Federal Republic in the Cold War in 1955–6 over yet another round of difficult European

FIGURE 1.3 *The Messina conference of the foreign ministers of the Six, 1 June 1955.* Left to right: Joseph Bech (L), Paul-Henri Spaak (B) and Johan Beyen (NL). *Courtesy of European Communities, 1955.*

negotiations (Segers 2020). In France, Euratom was supported across the political spectrum because of the notion that this may help finance the plans for a French nuclear strike force. But the plans for a common market looked hopeless. In a situation where an increasingly costly war was being conducted in Algeria (since 1954), the stagnating French economy was not ready for liberalization.

Moreover, French parliamentary support for a common market seemed highly unlikely. Other governments generally supported the initiative for broad political reasons, even if concrete plans were not always particularly interesting to all parties. Furthermore, in contrast to earlier integration proposals by the Six, the US government's reaction to the relaunch was lukewarm reflecting the failure of the EDC project, which had enjoyed much public support by US President Dwight Eisenhower personally, on the one hand, and increasing criticism of the ECSC's cartel for steel exports, on the other. The Eisenhower government initially favoured the Euratom initiative over the common market proposal and only endorsed the latter following the intergovernmental Venice conference, 29–30 May 1956, held by the Six (Winand 1993).

A specific constellation of domestic and international forces in the second half of 1956 and early 1957 first endangered the negotiations over Euratom and the common market but, in the end, brought them to a successful conclusion. In France, a pro-European socialist government under Guy Mollet came into power in early 1956 and pursued not only the Euratom Treaty but also a deal on the common market. This deal took French interests on welfare and farmers into account, and it integrated a colonial dimension into the new economic treaty for core Europe. In the preparation of the Venice conference, in May 1956, the Ministry for Overseas France proposed to include French and Belgian Africa into the common market negotiations. On the first day of the conference, French Foreign Minister Christian Pineau added the item of the colonies to the agenda of the Six providing the planned European common market with a Eurafrican dimension (Hansen and Jonsson 2014).

From the summer of 1956, moreover, the common market negotiations intersected with the Suez crisis. Importantly, the Suez crisis highlights the significance of both the Cold War and the challenge to European colonial rule in accounting for the continuing integration of the core Europe of the Six. The crisis emerged when Egyptian President Gamal Abdel Nasser, supported by Soviet arms and money, nationalized the Suez Canal, which was controlled by French and British interests. The Eisenhower administration was concerned about an outbreak of hostilities between its NATO Allies and attempted to broker a diplomatic settlement of the British-French-Egyptian dispute. Crucially, for the common market negotiations, the foreign ministers of France and Belgium immediately agreed that there was a link between the Suez crisis and Egypt, on the one hand, and France's ongoing war in Algeria, on the other. Much to the distaste of the United

States, France had already transferred most of its NATO troops to Algeria from 1955, linking the Cold War to colonial rule and Eurafrica. The Suez crisis reinforced this connection. Summarizing the French perspective, Foreign Minister Pineau stated: 'If Egypt's action remained without a response, it would be useless to pursue the struggle in Algeria' (Hansen and Jonsson 2014, 157).

Furthermore, the height of the Suez crisis in late October 1956, when Israeli armed forces advanced into Egypt, coincided with the temporary breakdown of the negotiations on the common market treaty. At the core of the dispute was the question of integrating the colonies, or 'associated countries', into the common market. The problem was how to establish a customs union, that is, introducing a common external tariff for the Six, while maintaining preferential links between France and its overseas countries and territories (OCT). The treaty negotiations almost derailed when German Economics Minister Erhard refused to accept Franco-Belgian proposals for Eurafrica and the possible involvement of the OCT in the common market. Erhard was generally sceptical of the regional common market and French economic proposals, which, he argued, conflicted with basic German economic preferences. In the context of the Suez crisis, however, Chancellor Adenauer decided to overrule Erhard and to concede to French demands. Moreover, Adenauer lent moral support to France's intervention in Egypt and confirmed France's right to keep Algeria (Hansen and Jonsson 2014). The West German chancellor prioritized the acquisition of nuclear arms as he was fearful that the United States would withdraw its troops partially from continental Europe – a daunting prospect also in face of the intervention of the Soviet Union in Hungary in early November 1956. For Adenauer, Suez corroborated that Franco-German cooperation could provide a viable alternative to transatlantic cooperation. The new European communities seemed the fastest option towards the development of an independent European political force that might acquire a nuclear deterrent independent of the United States. The French government secretly acquiesced to this and signed an armament agreement with West Germany in January 1957, which included nuclear weapons. Ironically, Charles de Gaulle immediately annulled this decisive concession to Adenauer when he became president of France in 1958.

The negotiations on the common market treaty and discussion of the Franco-Belgian proposal for Eurafrica resumed in November 1956. Final agreement on the arrangements for the association of the OCT was only reached by the meeting of the heads of state and government of the Six in Paris, 19–20 February 1957. The agreement, codified in the Treaty of Rome's part IV, expressed a commitment to associating the OCT, to invest in them and further their development, and detailed the financial contribution of each member state for a period of five years. It also contained a special application for Algeria (part VI of the treaty) resolving the contested issues of the extent to which the common market's agricultural provisions and the free movement of workers would apply to Algeria (Hansen and Jonsson 2014).

## The legacy of Rome

Returning to the puzzle of accounting for the continuing integration of the core Europe of the Six, this development responded to the dynamics of the Cold War and attempts by European states to sustain their colonial influence over Africa. As in the early period of core Europe integration in 1950–1, Franco-German cooperation proved important in achieving a workable solution to the question of including the OCT. At the same time, it is not possible to tell the story of the Treaties of Rome as a story of Christian Democratic plotting in the same way as in the case of the Schuman Plan. A similar observation applies to the role of the US government in the relaunch of European integration (1955–7). Clearly, the US government was important through its role in the Cold War – and 1956 represented a crucial year in the Cold War, evidenced by the Suez crisis as well as the Soviet intervention in Hungary. But the Eisenhower administration was no longer invested in European integration. In addition to the reasons for this discussed above, once the Treaties of Rome came into force, the United States would be faced with an economic competitor. Initially, this competitive relationship evolved around the EEC's common agricultural policy, which erected protective tariffs, shielding the European agricultural sector and making it difficult for US firms to penetrate the EEC markets. Later, competition policy, another supranational policy established by the EEC Treaty, would specify the conditions for US multinational corporations to trade on European markets. Without doubt, the EEC Treaty changed transatlantic economic relations, which will be further discussed in Chapter 14 on the EU in international politics and trade.

In contrast to its predecessor, the ECSC, the EEC fulfilled its potential and eventually established a common market and a political European Union. The institutions for this political union were already developed in 1956–7. When negotiating the Treaties of Rome, the governments of the Six tried learning from the pitfalls of the ECSC Treaty, especially from the difficulties of the High Authority in enforcing the treaty. As a result, the powers of the supranational executive were reduced. This more pragmatic approach to the institutional set-up also had the advantage that it would make it easier for the French government to secure treaty ratification by its National Assembly.

However, while the two new Treaties of Rome represented a pragmatic approach to cooperation institutionally and politically, more in line with classical international law, the legal experts drafting the treaties and designing the court system developed and enhanced certain constitutional elements in subtle ways. Most importantly, a system of preliminary reference from national courts to the CJEU was developed, which would fuel the development of the community's legal system after 1958 (Boerger 2012). Moreover, the common market established an extremely broad scope for cooperation. While the two new treaties therefore at first appeared institutionally and politically less ambitious than the ECSC, the integration of the entire economies of the Six through a customs union and a common market carried with it important political potential. In essence, the institutional and legal design of the Treaties of Rome reflected the centrality of member-state governments in the European integration process, but the manner in which the two new communities would develop specifically was left relatively open. It may be that the treaties were designed to create two communities of international law, as argued in the ratification debate by Luxembourg Foreign Minister Joseph Bech, but there were sufficient legal provisions in the treaties to argue that they could form the basis for a genuine European public law, which is further discussed in Chapter 6.

As regards Euratom, the contemporary fascination with nuclear energy as the future source of energy did not prove a durable basis for European integration, reflecting the experience with integration through coal and steel. Consequently, both the ECSC and Euratom would wane in influence already in the 1960s. Instead, it was the ugly duckling of the common market, including agriculture, that provided the societal foundations for lasting European cooperation. The combination of controlled trade liberalization in the framework of the OEEC and the rise of the West German market economy in the 1950s had shown that export-led growth to a regionally organized European market was an ideal basis for growth, employment and the financing of welfare states. The further liberalization in a customs union after 1958, which included West Germany, rapidly modernized the French and Italian economies.

# Five key questions

1.  How can it be argued that the origins of European integration are to be found in the interwar period?
2.  What was the role of the 'German question' in accounting for the establishment of the ECSC?
3.  How can we explain the commitment to further integration in core Europe after the failure of the EDC/EPC initiative?
4.  How important were challenges to colonial rule in the formation of the three 'core' European communities?
5.  To what extent can it be argued that the early Cold War triggered European integration?

# Ten key readings

Boerger, A. (2012), 'Negotiating the Foundations of European Law, 1950–
    1957: The Legal History of the Treaties of Paris and Rome', *Contemporary
    European History*, 21 (3): 339–56.
Gillingham, J. (1991), *Coal, Steel, and the Rebirth of Europe, 1945–55: The
    Germans and the French from Ruhr Conflict to Economic Community*,
    New York: Cambridge University Press.
Hansen, P., and S. Jonsson (2014), *Eurafrica: The Untold History of European
    Integration*, London: Bloomsbury Academic.
Kaiser, W. (2007), *Christian Democracy and the Origins of European Union*,
    Cambridge: Cambridge University Press.
Leucht, B. (2009), 'Transatlantic Policy Networks in the Creation of the First
    European Anti-trust Law: Mediating between American Anti-trust and German
    Ordo-liberalism', in W. Kaiser, B. Leucht and M. Rasmussen (eds), *The History
    of the European Union: Origins of a Supranational Polity 1950–72*, 56–73,
    Abingdon: Routledge.
Leucht, B. (2010), 'Expertise and the Creation of a Constitutional Core
    Europe: Transatlantic Policy Networks in the Schuman Plan Negotiations', in
    M. Gehler, W. Kaiser and B. Leucht (eds), *Transnational Networks in Regional
    Integration: Governing Europe, 1945–83*, 18–37, Basingstoke: Palgrave
    Macmillan.
Lundestad, G. (1998), *'Empire' by Integration: The United States and European
    Integration, 1945–1997*, Oxford: Oxford University Press.
Milward, A. S. (1984), *The Reconstruction of Western Europe*, London: Routledge.
Pasture, P. (2018). 'The EC/EU between the Art of Forgetting and the Palimpsest of
    Empire', *European Review*, 26(3): 545–81.
Winand, P. (1993), *Eisenhower, Kennedy, and the United States of Europe*,
    New York: St Martin's.

# 2

# From the early Common Market to the crises of the 1960s, 1958–68

## *Katja Seidel*

## Introduction

When the European Economic Community (EEC) was created in 1957, it entered a crowded field. It became one of many European organizations that had been founded after the Second World War. These included the Organization for European Economic Cooperation (OEEC), an intergovernmental body set up in 1948 to manage the Marshall Plan and deal with trade liberalization, and the Strasbourg-based Council of Europe founded in 1949, another intergovernmental organization with a broad remit, including human rights. Then there were the other 'supranational' organizations: the European Coal and Steel Community (ECSC) dating back to 1951 (Chapter 1), and the European Atomic Energy Community (Euratom) founded in 1957.

The signing of the Treaties of Rome on 25 March 1957 by Belgium, France, Germany, Italy, Luxembourg and the Netherlands (also known as 'the Six') creating the EEC and Euratom was thus firmly in the tradition of post-war international cooperation, but it was also a new start. The EEC provided opportunities for closer integration in a range of policy areas that went to the heart of national sovereignty such as trade policy, economic and monetary policy and agricultural policy. Euratom was first hailed by some as the more important of the two new communities, reflecting the significance of nuclear technology in the early Cold War, but in the end it did not play a very important role in the history of European integration.

The founding of the EEC solidified the division of Western Europe into the inner core of the Six, experimenting with closer economic and even political integration, and the 'periphery', with the other OEEC members – the UK, Austria, Denmark, Greece, Iceland, Ireland, Norway, Portugal, Spain, Sweden, Switzerland and Turkey – remaining outside the EEC. Some of them sought further free trade arrangements in the form of the European Free Trade Association (EFTA), founded in 1960. Others, such as Turkey and Greece in 1961, negotiated association agreements with the EEC.

This chapter focuses mainly on the EEC in the ten years from 1958, when it started to function, to 1968, when the customs union was completed. In this eventful first decade the EEC had to prove its usefulness to its members, take important decisions on its policies, build up its institutions and establish a functioning relationship between them. It also had to forge a relationship with other international organizations, particularly the OEEC in the exploration of a free trade area (FTA) and within the General Agreement on Tariffs and Trade (GATT), as well as with non-member countries. In the course of the 1960s, the EEC emerged to become the most prominent and powerful among the plethora of European organizations it initially competed with.

However, neither was the EEC's success guaranteed nor was its eventual pre-eminence over other European integration organizations a foregone conclusion (Patel 2013). Indeed, the 1960s was a decade of trial and error, of conflicts and crises resulting from differing ideas about the balance of power between Community institutions and the member states as well as the issue of membership of the UK in the EEC. This chapter is divided into three chronological parts: the first focusing on the 'honeymoon' years 1958–62, the second covering the crises of 1963–6 and the concluding part the remaining two years. The first part also contains thematic sections, crucial for the understanding of this period. These sections focus on the institutions of the EEC, the FTA negotiations, the advances in policies during the 1960s, the EEC's budding external role and 'grand designs'.

# 1. Honeymoon, 1958–62

The beginnings of the EEC were rather precarious. In 1958 the member states had not been able to agree on a city to accommodate the new organization. The ECSC had its seat in Luxembourg, and the issue of where the EEC would be located was highly political as many member states wanted to host the new organization. As a result, European institutions were spread out across three cities: Brussels, Luxembourg and Strasbourg. The Parliamentary Assembly held its plenary sessions in Strasbourg but had its offices in Luxembourg and its committee meetings in Brussels. The Court of Justice had its seat in Luxembourg, where it also served the ECSC. The EEC Commission and the Council of Ministers took offices in Brussels. In 1965 the member states officially sanctioned this absurd arrangement (but until 1992 only provisionally) and failed to consolidate all Community institutions in one city.

Another potentially more disruptive factor was the return to power in France of General Charles de Gaulle in May 1958. De Gaulle had been a critic of the kind of supranational integration his compatriot Jean Monnet had promoted with the ECSC. However, to the surprise and relief of the other member states, de Gaulle did not withdraw France from the EEC. Instead, he felt it could be beneficial for French economic modernization, and he appreciated the prospect of a common agricultural policy (CAP) to support French agriculture (Warlouzet 2011). In spite of the unresolved question of the seat and the uncertainty surrounding de Gaulle's return, the first four years of the Community are often seen as the 'honeymoon' period (Marjolin 1986). This refers both to the progress made in certain areas of the treaty as well as the optimism that reigned in institutions such as the Council, the Parliamentary Assembly and the Commission.

## The Community institutions

The EEC had four core institutions: the Council of Ministers, the Commission, the Parliamentary Assembly (European Parliament) and the Court of Justice. An Economic and Social Committee was also created to give a voice to societal actors such as industry and trade unions, but it had a purely consultative role.

The Council of Ministers was the main decision-making organ of the EEC. Initially it took most decisions unanimously, but the treaty foresaw the increased use of qualified majority voting from January 1966. The Council of Ministers met at least once a month with different ministers attending meetings in Brussels, depending on the subject matter that was under negotiation. The Council presidency was assumed by a member state for six months, on a rolling basis. To help provide continuity and coordinate their efforts on a more permanent basis, the member states appointed permanent representatives, the equivalent of ambassadors, in Brussels. These representatives met weekly in the Committee of Permanent Representatives, abbreviated as Coreper. Van Middelaar succinctly summarized the Coreper's special status: 'the ambassadors represented national interests in Brussels and, conversely, community interests in their capitals' (2013: 46). They prepared the Council meetings and were often able to anticipate and iron out conflicts. Senior Commission officials participated in the weekly Coreper meetings to discuss policy proposals and gauge the mood in the member states' capitals before a proposal would go to the Council of Ministers for decision.

The Commission of the EEC represented the Community interests vis-à-vis the member states (Chapter 5). The term 'Commission' applied to both the institution and the college of Commissioners heading the institution. Its most important prerogative was its 'right of initiative' to propose legislation to the Council of Ministers. The Council could amend a proposal from the Commission only if it decided to do so unanimously. The Commission's second important role was that of being the 'guardian of the treaty' in that it had to ensure the provisions of the treaty and the decisions taken on the basis of it were applied. The Commissioners were meant to act independently of the member states and, in this role of impartial arbiter, often facilitated compromise and agreement during Council negotiations. The Commission was also tasked with overseeing the implementation of Community legislation. During the 1960s the Commission had nine members who were appointed by member-state governments. The German Walter Hallstein, a law professor and state secretary in the German Foreign Ministry, became the first president of the Commission. Hallstein, a fervent pro-European, had far-reaching aims for further European integration and the leading role he felt the Commission and the European Parliament (EP) should play in the development of the EEC (Schönwald 2017).

It was not until 1979 that European citizens were able to elect parliamentarians to the Parliamentary Assembly. Before that, parliamentarians were delegated from member-state parliaments to serve on this body (Chapter 7). To underscore their Europeanness, these delegates decided not to sit according to their nationality but according to political party lines. In March 1962 the parliamentarians voted to rename the assembly European Parliament. This was a political statement but one that expressed the aspirations of the institution more than its real influence. The powers of the EP were limited to scrutinizing draft legislation, drafting opinions and holding the Commission and the Council of Ministers to account. The EP was only obliged to meet once a year, but it decided to meet more often. It established parliamentary commissions and became very active in scrutinizing legislation and monitoring the activities of the Commission and the Council. The Commission, made up of unelected bureaucrats, saw the EP as an opportunity to increase the democratic credentials of the EEC. Both institutions pressed for direct elections of the EP and the expansion of its powers.

The Court of Justice consisted of nine judges (Chapter 6). Like the Commission it was the 'guardian of the treaty', with Article 164 specifying that the Court 'shall ensure observance of law and justice in the interpretation and application of this Treaty'. The question was whether with its judgements the Court would strengthen the Community institutions or confirm member states' sovereignty. Generally speaking, the former was the case. From the early 1960s the Court's rulings tended to support a supranational reading of the EEC Treaty. Its first landmark case was *Van Gend en Loos* in 1963 where the Court advised that 'the Community constitutes a new legal order of international law for the benefit of which the states have limited their sovereign rights, albeit within limited fields, and the subjects of which comprise not only member states but also their nationals'. In a second landmark case in 1964, *Costa vs ENEL*, the Court decided that EEC law had primacy over national laws. With its interpretations of the EEC Treaty and Community legislation, the Court contributed to the emergence of a European legal order that existed independently of the member states. Some scholars have termed this development of European integration through court rulings 'the quiet revolution' (Weiler 1994).

## Common Market versus free trade area

Even before the EEC began its work in January 1958, negotiations had been under way since 1957 to establish an FTA among OEEC members (Ellison 2000a; Kaiser 1996; Milward 2002; Warlouzet 2018b). The initiative had been launched by the UK government, which had ruled out participation in the closer-knit EEC but wanted to reap the advantages of free trade in Europe. Many EEC members, such as the Benelux countries and part of the German political elite, were in favour of adding a wider FTA to the customs union of the Six for economic reasons, and also to maintain a close relationship with Britain. France, on the other hand, was sceptical about the benefits of an FTA. Both the French government and French industry feared the competition a larger FTA would bring to its relatively weak industrial sector and how harmful that could be for France's economic reconstruction.

The second point of contention for the French, but not only for them, was the fact that an FTA did not require its members to adopt a common external tariff and a common trade policy (see Table 2.1). France feared that this would lead to distortion of competition and diversion of trade to countries with lower external tariffs from where the goods could travel freely to any country within the FTA. Thirdly, many saw the FTA proposal as an attempt by Britain to dilute the EEC and its customs union. The negotiations went to the core of the question about what kind of integration or cooperation there should be in Europe: closer integration that went beyond the issue of trade and that involved stronger institutions and the acceptance that member states would give up some of their sovereignty, or a more loosely integrated group of states limiting themselves to cooperating on trade.

France and the Commission were of the opinion that tariff reductions should be negotiated in the GATT and that OEEC members were free to seek membership of the EEC. The US government, perhaps surprisingly, supported the Commission and France in their view that the EEC needed to be developed first. They accepted the EEC and the potential economic disadvantages the United States as a third country would incur through the customs union, because the EEC had a political as well as an economic goal. With a European FTA, the United States was bound to lose out on trade

**Table 2.1** *Characteristics of a free trade area, a customs union and a common market*

| Free trade area | Customs union | Common market |
| --- | --- | --- |
| Reduces tariffs and quotas to zero between members. | Reduces tariffs and quotas to zero between members. | Reduces tariffs and quotas to zero between members. |
| Each member decides on the tariffs they want to maintain vis-à-vis third countries. | Establishes a common external tariff vis-à-vis non-members. | Establishes a common external tariff vis-à-vis non-members. |
| No common commercial policy necessary. | Requires members to adopt a common commercial policy vis-à-vis third countries. | Requires members to adopt a common commercial policy vis-à-vis third countries. |
| | | Goes even further than a customs union by removing other, non-tariff, barriers to trade, e.g. by harmonizing product standards or agreeing to recognize each other's standards. |
| | | EEC Common Market aims to establish four freedoms: free movement of goods, services, capital and labour. |
| | | Other policies to regulate trade and the behaviour of economic actors become necessary: e.g. a common competition policy. |

without there being any political advantages. Negotiations regarding the FTA broke down in the summer of 1958 after de Gaulle came to power and committed France to the EEC (Warlouzet 2011).

Britain and six other countries – Austria, Denmark, Norway, Portugal, Sweden and Switzerland – then founded EFTA on 3 May 1960 (Kaiser 1997). EFTA was mainly formed as a response to the EEC's Common

Market and to improve the bargaining position of EFTA's members with the EEC. Britain's interest in trade with the other EFTA countries was certainly limited, and it was only a matter of time until the British government had to seek an arrangement with the economically stronger EEC countries.

## Advancements in policy areas: Steps towards a Common Market

The EEC Treaty decreed that the Common Market 'shall be progressively established during a transition period of twelve years' (Article 8). The core of the Common Market was the customs union, an internal free trade area to be created through the progressive reduction and finally removal of customs duties and quotas, that is, limits on the quantities of imported products (quantitative restrictions), as well as the establishment of a common external tariff due on imports of industrial and agricultural products from third countries. The treaty provided a timetable for these gradual reductions: each stage was to last four years, and it imposed a schedule for the reduction in customs duties in the first stage (1958–61) and the second stage (1962–5) and a complete removal of customs duties by 31 December 1969. The first reduction of 10 per cent in customs duties and a 20 per cent increase in quotas were due only one year after the treaty had come into force, on 1 January 1959 (see Figure 2.1).

The economic context was propitious as the EEC member states were still riding high on the post-war economic boom and experienced a period of political stability. In spite of the increased competition they were facing, businesses adapted surprisingly well to the changes. Business leaders were thus in favour of accelerating the timetable for the creation of the customs union, and farmers' unions were keen on seeing a CAP established. Both industrial leaders and farmers' unions created European-level lobby organizations: Union des industries de la Communauté Européenne (UNICE) for industry and Comité des organisations professionnelles agricoles (COPA) for farmers. Other interest groups followed, establishing offices in Brussels. This network of contacts between Community officials, government ministers, national civil servants and non-governmental organizations would become denser over time, facilitating information exchange and increasing efficiency of the EEC institutions. Ultimately, this Brussels 'comitology', as the vast and complex networks of meetings and committees is known, also facilitated the creation of a European polity (Kaiser, Leucht, Rasmussen 2009).

On 12 May 1960 the Council of Ministers took the decision to accelerate the move towards the customs union by deciding to abolish the quota system and reduce customs duties by an additional 10 per cent on 31 December 1961, the starting date for the second stage. The negotiations to agree on the transition to the second stage in December 1961 were anticipated with

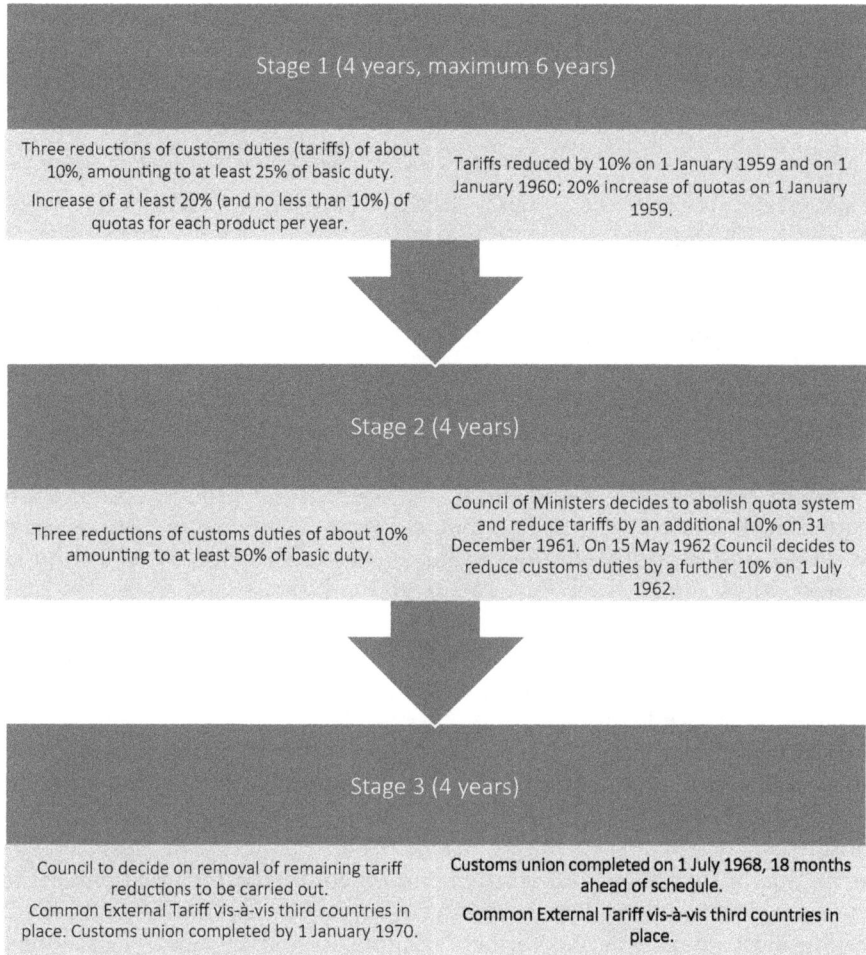

**Stage 1 (4 years, maximum 6 years)**

Three reductions of customs duties (tariffs) of about 10%, amounting to at least 25% of basic duty.
Increase of at least 20% (and no less than 10%) of quotas for each product per year.

Tariffs reduced by 10% on 1 January 1959 and on 1 January 1960; 20% increase of quotas on 1 January 1959.

**Stage 2 (4 years)**

Three reductions of customs duties of about 10% amounting to at least 50% of basic duty.

Council of Ministers decides to abolish quota system and reduce tariffs by an additional 10% on 31 December 1961. On 15 May 1962 Council decides to reduce customs duties by a further 10% on 1 July 1962.

**Stage 3 (4 years)**

Council to decide on removal of remaining tariff reductions to be carried out.
Common External Tariff vis-à-vis third countries in place. Customs union completed by 1 January 1970.

Customs union completed on 1 July 1968, 18 months ahead of schedule.
Common External Tariff vis-à-vis third countries in place.

FIGURE 2.1 *Achieving the customs union in three stages. The column on the left shows the schedule to create the customs union as outlined in the EEC treaty, and the column on the right shows the realization of these steps as well as the acceleration of this schedule by the Council of Ministers. Source: Author's compilation.*

trepidation by France's partners who felt they were a litmus test of de Gaulle's commitment to the EEC. The French government, but also other member states, linked their agreement to the transition decision to progress on other issues. While France demanded that the CAP be agreed on at the same time as the decision to move to the second stage, Germany wanted an agreement on regulating competition in the Common Market. Decisions on different issues were thus tied together and eventually agreed on after a marathon negotiation round that lasted from mid-December to 14 January 1962. The deadline of 31 December was not met, but instead of breaking off the negotiations, ministers decided to stop the clock and continue the discussions. This Council meeting inaugurated three traditions for negotiations in the Community: tying different issues together to form a package deal from which every member state could take away an advantage, the custom of stopping the clock to allow negotiations to continue if a deadline was not met and marathon sessions often lasting several days. The Council took another decision to accelerate the move to the customs union on 15 May 1962, agreeing to reduce customs duties by a further 10 per cent by July 1962.

At the insistence of mainly France and the Netherlands, the CAP was developed in parallel with the customs union. In European integration research the idea is widespread that there was a trade-off between France and Germany: the former benefitting from the CAP and the latter benefiting from free trade in the Common Market. However, French industry also profited from trade liberalization, and the CAP allowed Germany to continue subsidizing its inefficient farm sector through the generous and stable farm prices it provided. While the CAP was hailed as a great success at the time – a success for European integration generally and testament to the ability of the Council of Ministers to take difficult decisions – it had inbuilt flaws. Prices for agricultural products were generally set at a fairly high level, well above world market prices. This incentivized farmers to produce more, leading to costly overproduction (Chapter 9).

In terms of the development of other Community policies, the EEC tackled some areas covered by the treaty, but by no means all of them. Driven mainly by German interest in the issue, competition policy became an important area, seen as vital to regulate economic behaviour in the Common Market (Chapter 8). Robert Marjolin, Commission vice-president in charge of economic and monetary affairs, laid the foundations for closer coordination of member states' economic and monetary policy. However, the treaty did not give the Commission much margin for initiatives, not least as since 1944 the Bretton Woods system had provided a stable monetary framework for Western capitalist countries. The member states therefore at first lacked urgency in developing joint approaches to economic and monetary policy. This changed when US balance of payments problems and inflationary pressures affected the EEC economies and exchange rate adjustments by individual member states threatened to undermine the unity of the Common Market. In 1964 member states agreed to consult each other prior to exchange rate adjustments. A Monetary Policy Committee had already been provided for in the EEC Treaty (Article 107), and the Commission proposed adding a Committee of Governors of Central Banks. In the longer term, the regular meetings of central bankers, civil servants from finance ministries and the Commission helped to foster an international group of financial experts that was then better able to tackle the monetary difficulties the Community encountered in the late 1960s and 1970s. They would also play a crucial role working towards economic and monetary union in the 1980s and 1990s (James 2012).

# The EEC in a Cold War world: External relations, GATT, developing countries and the Cold War

In the 1960s the EEC took the first tentative steps on the international stage. The Common Market, which included a common external tariff, required the EEC to establish a common commercial policy vis-à-vis third countries. The Commission represented the EEC in external trade negotiations using negotiation briefs agreed in the Council of Ministers. Trade liberalization negotiations took place within GATT. In the GATT the EEC had to prove, particularly to the United States, but also its European partners in the OEEC, that it was not creating a protectionist bloc but was prepared to play its part in the liberalization of trade. In the GATT Dillon Round of 1961–2 the EEC agreed to reduce tariffs by 20 per cent on 560 industrial goods, and the United States agreed to do the same for 575 products. However, this was not yet the big breakthrough in trade liberalization. More important was the GATT Kennedy Round that lasted from May 1964 to May 1967. Named after US President John F. Kennedy, the round resulted in the EEC reducing import duties by about 35 per cent on industrial products and up to 50 per cent on individual products such as cars. This was reciprocated by the United States. While the Kennedy Round was a success in reducing tariffs on industrial goods, it also demonstrated to the Americans and other agricultural exporters that the EEC would be protectionist in trade with agricultural products (Coppolaro 2016). Though hard-pressed by the US government, the Community did not agree to change the CAP, and the Americans were not prepared to negotiate on their own farm support system.

The other important area of the EEC's engagement with third countries was in development policy (Chapter 14). When the EEC was founded, France and Belgium were still colonial powers. The EEC's venture into development policy was thus at least at first a way to ensure continued close relations between France and Belgium and their colonies in Africa (Migani 2013; Dimier 2014). The treaty provided for a five-year association of these colonies with the EEC as well as a European Development Fund (EDF). After five years, the association agreement expired and, since most of these colonies had obtained independence in the meantime, a follow-on association agreement was negotiated between the six EEC members and 18 Associated African States and Madagascar (AASM). This was the Yaoundé I Agreement, signed on 20 July 1963. It was renewed in 1969 for another five years (Yaoundé II). The agreements included funding from the EDF and an FTA between the EEC and the AASM countries. The EEC's development policy was not uncontested. Germany and the Netherlands, in particular, were not comfortable with it as in their view it fell to them, as net payers into the EEC budget, to fund Belgium and France's special relationship with their former colonies.

# Grand designs

Two plans for the further development of European integration within the Western alliance dominated the early 1960s. One was about developing the transatlantic relationship between the EEC and the United States in the form of an 'Atlantic partnership'. The other was aiming to move further away from a close relationship with the United States by developing Western Europe into a powerful and politically united bloc. Both proposals were a reaction to the Cold War: the United States required a strong European military ally and a reliable trading partner. De Gaulle's plans aimed at creating a strong and independent Europe that could stand on its own in the global Cold War and did not need to rely on the United States for its defence.

# The Fouchet Plans, 1961–2

Even though de Gaulle had accepted the EEC and recognized its advantages for the French economy, he continued to develop his own far-reaching plans for European unity (Ludlow 2006; Trachtenberg 2012). De Gaulle's 'grand design' involved creating a political union in Europe, not by developing the supranational elements of the EEC, the Commission and the European Parliament, which he despised, but by proposing a confederation of sovereign European nations. These should develop a strong bond, leading to a political, economic, military and cultural unit. De Gaulle, a critic of the North Atlantic Treaty Organization (NATO) and US dominance in this military alliance, aimed at more autonomy of Europe vis-à-vis the United States, particularly in terms of security and defence. The closest the Six came to agreeing on a political Europe was in the Fouchet Plans in the early 1960s. In a press conference in September 1960 the French president outlined what he had in mind:

> Ensuring a regular cooperation of Western Europe is what France considers desirable, possible and practical in the political, economic and cultural domains as well as in defence. This includes regular meetings by participating governments and also the work of specialized agencies in each of these areas. These agencies will be subordinate to the governments. (De Gaulle 1960)

The crux was de Gaulle's mention of 'specialized agencies' to be set up to manage economic, political, cultural and defence cooperation. For the other five member states this smacked of an assault on the EEC which already dealt with economic integration. At a summit meeting in February 1961 the Six nevertheless agreed to set up a study group for political cooperation, the so-called Fouchet Committee, named after Christian Fouchet, a French diplomat. The Committee proposed regular consultations of the heads of

state and government of the Six to formulate common policies and pledged
to strengthen the Atlantic alliance and develop the existing Communities.
Based on these agreements, the French presented two draft treaties, one in
late 1961 and the other in early 1962 (Fouchet I and II). In the end, no
agreement was achieved. The gulf between the different positions could not
be overcome, not least because de Gaulle moved the goalpost and retracted
a concession he had made to include a commitment to strengthening the
transatlantic alliance and maintaining the EEC.

The failed plans for political cooperation exposed rifts between member
states and raised important questions: Who was in charge in Europe? The
sovereign nation states or European institutions? For de Gaulle it had to
be the former. For him the Commission could not be a 'political' entity,
and he wanted to downgrade it to a technical secretariat at the service of
the member states. Other member states objected to a weakening of the
supranational institution, not least as the smaller member states feared
that this would result in the dominance of the larger states, France and
Germany. Belgium, the Netherlands and Luxembourg had come to value
the influence they were able to have in the institutional interplay of the
EEC where, it is true, nothing could happen against the wishes of the large
member states, but where small member states were represented as equals.
They also wanted Britain to participate in such a political union, something
de Gaulle opposed. Finally the proposals also challenged the Six to position
themselves in the debate over NATO: would they go down the path of de
Gaulle's European defence cooperation or would they maintain a close
relationship with NATO and the United States? The other member states
and even the German government, usually supportive of de Gaulle, firmly
supported NATO and a close alliance with the United States. They were in
no doubt that France's weak nuclear deterrent did not offer any credible
alternative to US protection against a potential Soviet threat.

## The Atlantic partnership: John F. Kennedy's grand design

The US government was deeply sceptical about de Gaulle's aims, which it
feared would divide the Western alliance and only benefit the Soviet Union.
In spite of these tensions, plans for an Atlantic partnership peaked during
the Kennedy presidency (1960–3) (Giauque 2002; Winand 1993). On 4
July 1962, American Independence Day, Kennedy gave a speech proposing
'interdependence' to its Western European partners. Reiterating US support
for European Integration, he offered Europeans closer political and economic
cooperation on equal terms:

I will say here and now, on this Day of Independence, that the United
States will be ready for a Declaration of Interdependence, that we will be

FIGURE 2.2 *Hallstein meets with Kennedy at the White House, 4 March 1963.*
Photo courtesy of Benjamin E. 'Gene' Forte/CNP/Getty Images.

prepared to discuss with a united Europe the ways and means of forming
a concrete Atlantic partnership, a mutually beneficial partnership between
the new union now emerging in Europe and the old American Union
founded here 175 years ago. (Kennedy 1962b).

What was behind this proposal? In spite of the lofty rhetoric and the
friendly attitude towards the new European institutions and its leaders (see
Figure 2.2), the Atlantic partnership proposal was responding to specific
US problems and aims. These included strengthening the EEC as a reliable
partner in the Cold War and maintaining and expanding US economic
opportunities in Europe. The Kennedy administration also expected the UK
to become a member of the EEC in the short term. British membership
would keep the EEC firmly on side with the United States and committed
to NATO. The United States was experiencing slower economic growth
and balance of payments problems. The Kennedy administration was thus
concerned about the EEC's emergence as an economic power, which could
compete with, and potentially harm, US trade interests (see also Chapter 14).
Americans also wanted Europeans to pay their way and contribute more to
their own defence. The 'Atlantic Community' became most concrete in the
economic sphere, leading to substantial tariff reductions between the two
economies in the GATT Kennedy Round.

In the political realm, no firm plans emerged that could have given content and shape to an 'Atlantic Community'. In defence, the Kennedy administration proposed a multilateral force (MLF) within NATO which promised to associate European countries with nuclear weapons. However, the proposals were never uniformly welcomed by the Europeans and caused more rift among NATO allies than they created unity. De Gaulle's rejection of British membership in January 1963 and ultimately Kennedy's assassination on 22 November of that year ended the transatlantic grand design. Crucially, de Gaulle caused a crisis in NATO when in 1966 he decided to withdraw from its integrated military structure. Overall Kennedy's grand design did not bring Europeans and Americans closer together politically or militarily.

# 2. Crises, 1963–6

The origins of the Community crises of the 1960s are complex and multifaceted. Generally, member states by 1963 were more invested in the EEC and were also becoming more concerned about the costs of certain policy areas such as the CAP or, alternatively, the cost of not having them. Crucial questions about membership and the institutional make-up as well as the balance of power in the Community were also at the heart of these controversies (Ludlow 2006).

## The question of Britain's membership

Life outside the EEC was never going to be comfortable for the UK. Compared to the EEC, which encompassed the larger economic powers of Europe, EFTA was only ever a second-best option for the UK. In 1962 the UK's exports into the EEC were worth £762m while the goods it exported into EFTA countries only amounted to £519m (Kaiser 1996: 108). An internal re-evaluation of the country's economic and political interests led the British government under Prime Minister Harold Macmillan to apply for EEC membership in August 1961. This was not an easy decision as it came with the growing realization that Britain was not a great power anymore. Membership would allow Britain to partly regain its great power role as a leading member of the EEC. Domestic economic considerations such as balance of payments issues and GDP growth rates lagging behind that of EEC countries also made the idea of membership more attractive. While membership promised economic advantages, some of the early decisions of the Six, notably the CAP, were difficult to accept for the British government. Denmark, Ireland and Norway, the UK's closest trading partners in EFTA, also applied for EEC membership. Accession negotiations with Britain got off to a difficult start. Macmillan had set the bar high from the outset, insisting on long-term access to food imports from the Commonwealth, exceptions from the CAP and long transition periods and a special deal for the other EFTA members. De Gaulle did not trust Macmillan, and his trust was undermined further after it emerged that in December 1962 Macmillan had agreed to purchase US Polaris missiles for British submarines. For de Gaulle this was proof that British membership would have given the United States direct influence in the Community through Britain. Indeed, he later said: '[the EEC] would appear as a colossal Atlantic community under American dependence and direction' (de Gaulle 1963). On 14 January 1963, at a press conference, de Gaulle unilaterally announced the end of the accession negotiations. The five other member states, especially the governments of Belgium and the Netherlands, were furious. They had always advocated for British membership and were looking forward to British influence in the EEC, also to balance France's dominating role. Only German Chancellor Adenauer (but not his cabinet) sided with de Gaulle (Chapter 16).

De Gaulle's veto was a major setback for the Community, and it brought into the open diverging views about the EEC's future direction. No doubt, UK membership would have threatened French leadership in Europe. It would have changed the EEC in a way that would not have corresponded to de Gaulle's idea of Europe as a third force between the Soviet Union and the United States. Last but not least, he feared that once inside the British would work to change the CAP, a policy that was so important to France.

## The empty chair crisis, 1965/66

After the British accession crisis, the Community soon went back to business as usual. Another milestone in the CAP was completed when the Council of Ministers agreed to common prices for cereals on 15 December 1964. However, the next deadline was already looming: on 30 June 1965 the provisional financial arrangement for the CAP was due to expire. This time, the Commission took a gamble and tried to tie the CAP financial arrangement to further institutional developments that would strengthen the European Parliament and the Commission. Hallstein felt that France's interest in the CAP and its financing was so great that de Gaulle would be prepared to accept the deal. The Commission's proposal consisted of three elements: firstly, proposals for the financing of the CAP; secondly, the creation of independent revenue for the Community (also known as 'own resources'); and thirdly, proposals for gradually extending the powers of the European Parliament in budgetary matters to increase its democratic control in the Community. The Commission also proposed to speed up the completion of the customs union and the Common Market for agricultural products and to achieve these by 1 July 1967. At this point, therefore, the common external tariff for industrial and agricultural imports would be in place. The revenue from these customs duties and levies, the Commission argued, should be made available to the Community as its own resources.

Before that, the CAP was financed through ad hoc budgets and member states paid direct contributions to the EEC budget. Under the new proposal, the Commission and the European Parliament would gain a regular source of income, and they would be able, together with the Council of Ministers, to decide how this money was going to be spent.

Although it was daring, there was logic behind the Commission's proposals of tying them together in one package. It would advance European integration in a way that agreed with the Commission, and it would strengthen the democratic accountability of the Community by giving more powers to the European Parliament to scrutinize the budget. Member states were set to gain as well; while France was particularly interested in the CAP financial arrangement, the other member states were very supportive of the idea of strengthening the European Parliament. But Hallstein's bargain did not pay off. Instead, it triggered the most severe crisis the Community had hitherto experienced. Negotiations in the Council of Ministers started on 28 June. When no agreement was reached, shortly after midnight on 1 July, the meeting's chair, France's foreign minister Couve de Murville, ended the meeting. While the breakdown of negotiations in the Council was nothing unusual and France's partners expected negotiations to resume shortly, the extent of the crisis became clear in the next few days when the French government withdrew its permanent representative from Brussels, leaving an 'empty chair' for more than six months (Ludlow 2006; Palayret and Wallace 2006). De Gaulle then escalated the crisis. He did so because, firstly, he was opposed to strengthening the EP and the Commission. The empty chair crisis was thus an emergency break to prevent undesired institutional developments. Secondly, the breakdown of negotiations was for him an opportunity to seek what he thought was the best possible outcome for France – the financing of the CAP without agreeing to the other measures. Thirdly, the EEC Treaty had foreseen for the Council to take more decisions by majority voting from January 1966. There was thus a real danger that majority voting could put France in a minority and impose decisions on her that she did not agree with.

De Gaulle was convinced that by threatening to break up the Common Market, he would be able to impose his will on the other five member states. His maximalist demand was a revision of the treaty to curtail the role of the Commission and remove references to majority voting. However, his tactics only worked to a limited extent. Firstly, de Gaulle faced internal criticism over his handling of the issue, particularly from France's agricultural lobby keen to see the CAP completed. He also had to stand for re-election in the presidential elections in December 1965 in which he did not gain an outright majority. Secondly, the other five member states called de Gaulle's bluff and were convinced that it was against France's interests to leave the EEC. After the difficult presidential elections, the French government was prepared to return to the negotiation table.

The foreign ministers of the Six met twice in January 1966 in Luxembourg to find an agreement. The final compromise reached at these negotiations was far from the maximalist demands of the French government and included provisions that the Commission work more closely with the Council of Ministers and inform the Council before publishing important proposals. As to the veto in the Council, the solution was an agreement to disagree. The foreign ministers agreed that if 'very important interests of one or more partners are at stake', no decision would be taken by majority and negotiations would continue until a solution was found (Council of Ministers 1966). While France then declared that no decision should be taken in such a case, the five were not drawn into agreeing to this.

As these agreements did not fundamentally change the Community, why is this so-called Luxembourg Compromise important? Firstly, the crisis amounted to a power struggle between the different institutions of the Community, in particular the Council of Ministers and the Commission. While disagreeing with France's tactics, the other member states also disliked the idea of a strong Commission, and Hallstein had little backing among the five. The crisis confirmed that the member states would continue to play the most important role in the EEC. Secondly, the crisis was, at its core, about national sovereignty of individual member states. Had the EEC moved to more majority decision making in the Council of Ministers, as the treaty decreed should happen from 1966, the national sovereignty of democratically elected governments would have been undermined. The Luxembourg Compromise made sure that a member state's 'vital national interests' were respected. Again, this was important not only for France but also for other member states like Germany that had started to worry about the effects of majority voting. A third reading of the Luxembourg Compromise is that in January 1966 the six member states, including France, took a conscious decision to preserve the EEC as it was, even the institutional arrangements. It simply had too many advantages.

# 3. Recovery to relaunch, 1966–8

In the first half of 1966 the EEC was back in business. In a series of meetings the Council decided to complete the customs union and the common market for agricultural products by 1 July 1968, eighteen months ahead of schedule. The crisis had delayed, but not thwarted, these decisions. However, de Gaulle's second veto to UK membership in November 1967 confirmed that any progress in terms of membership as well as further development of the EEC would be possible only after he had left office (Daddow 2016). This occurred sooner than some would have expected. France was deeply affected by the student protests of May 1968. The protests also targeted de Gaulle and his leadership style. After he lost a referendum on a government reform that he had proposed, de Gaulle resigned in April 1969. This opened the path to British as well as Irish and Danish membership. The Community also embarked on an ambitious programme to complete outstanding issues such as a permanent mechanism for financing the CAP and developing initiatives and new policy areas such as economic and monetary union.

Within ten years the Community had created the customs union, the CAP and a common external tariff. No doubt the timetable provided in the treaty for completing the customs union within twelve years helped to focus minds. In contrast, many other policy areas mentioned in the EEC Treaty were not developed. The crises of the 1960s touched on core issues of European integration and how it should develop. What should the balance be between the institutions? Was the Commission a government in the making, as Hallstein liked to believe, or was its role more modest as that of a mediator and facilitator? While most governments supported the expansion of the EP, few relished the idea of a strong Commission telling them what to do. The crises also presented European governments with a choice: sticking with the EEC or abandoning it for something else. And all of them, even France, agreed that, in the words of Commissioner Marjolin (1986: 357), 'the EEC represented a framework they could no longer dispense with, in which their economic activity could expand and without which they would simply be reduced to their status of small or medium nation in a world dominated by the Great Powers'. Arguably, the Luxembourg Compromise even facilitated British accession to the Community, reassuring the British government that the member states remained in charge.

# Five key questions

1. Why did the Six opt for the EEC (and a Common Market) and not a free trade area?
2. Why did President de Gaulle oppose British membership in the EEC?
3. What were the causes of the crises of the EEC in the 1960s?
4. Why were these crises ultimately resolved rather than leading to a break-up of the EEC?
5. How would you characterize the relationship between the United States and the EEC?

# Ten key readings

Coppolaro, L. (2016), *The Making of a World Trading Power: The European Economic Community (EEC) in the GATT Kennedy Round*, London: Routledge.

Deighton, D., and A. Milward, eds (1999), *Widening, Deepening and Acceleration: The European Economic Community 1957–1963*, Baden-Baden: Nomos.

Dumoulin, M., ed. (2007), *The European Commission, 1958–72: History and Memories*, Luxembourg: Office for Official Publications of the European Communities.

Kaiser, W. (1999), *Using Europe, Abusing the Europeans: Britain and European Integration, 1945–63*, Basingstoke: Palgrave.

Kaiser, W., B. Leucht and M. Rasmussen, eds (2009), *The History of the European Union: Origins of a Trans- and Supranational Polity 1950–72*, London: Routledge.

Loth, W., ed. (2001), *Crises and Compromises: The European Project 1963–1969*, Baden-Baden: Nomos.

Ludlow, N. P. (2006), *The European Community and the Crises of the 1960s: Negotiating the Gaullist Challenge*, London: Routledge.

Seidel, K. (2010a), *The Process of Politics in Europe: The Rise of European Elites and Supranational Institutions*, London: I. B. Tauris.

Varsori, A., ed. (2006), *Inside the European Community: Actors and Policies in the European Integration 1957–1972*, Baden-Baden: Nomos.

Warlouzet, L. (2011), 'De Gaulle as a Father of Europe: The Unpredictability of the FTA's Failure and the EEC's Success (1956–58)', *Contemporary European History*, 20(4): 419–34.

# 3

# From the Hague Summit to the Maastricht Treaty: Creating the European Union (EU), 1969–92

## *Laurent Warlouzet*

## Introduction

How did the small 'Common Market' of the Six become an ambitious semi-federal European Union (EU) between 1969 and 1992? In 1969, when the heads of state and government met at the Hague Summit, the six countries of the European Economic Community (EEC) had barely recovered from six years of regular crisis triggered by the French President Charles de Gaulle, which has been described as the 'Gaullist challenge' (Ludlow 2006). Thirteen years later, the twelve-strong EU was committed to creating a federal monetary union and was considering its enlargement to most of the continent.

The path was open to the synecdoche of 'Europe' – that is, the EU now corresponding also to the continent of Europe (a synecdoche being a figure of speech in which a part refers to the whole). This chapter will evaluate to what extent this development was a response to external shocks, such as the economic crisis or the end of the Cold War, and to internal actors, such as national governments, transnational networks and supranational activists.

# 1. The Hague triptych, 1969

The period began with auspicious omens as new leaders more inclined towards European integration than their predecessors came to power in 1969–70. French President Georges Pompidou, elected in 1969, replaced the abrasive Charles de Gaulle. A Gaullist himself, Pompidou was more accommodating in style and less hostile to Britain than his predecessor. He was ready to accept the enlargement. In Germany, the new chancellor, Willy Brandt, who also came to power in 1969, was willing to develop European integration towards new fields, such as social and monetary policies, and wielded more authority than his predecessor Kurt Georg Kiesinger. Last but not least, outside the EEC, in Britain, Edward Heath, one of the most Europhile prime ministers ever, took the helm of the government in 1970.

Pompidou, Brandt and other EEC leaders gathered at the Hague, Netherlands, on 1–2 December 1969. In their final declaration they created the triptych 'completion, deepening and enlargement'. 'Completion' was a French request for ensuring the long-term viability of the common agricultural policy (CAP) and hence of the European budget (Chapter 2). 'Deepening' referred to the necessity to widen the EEC's scope in technological policy, social policy and research (with the aim of setting up a 'European university', which eventually became the European University Institute), above all, 'with a view to the creation of an economic and monetary union' (Final Communiqué 1969, point 8). Enlargement, or 'widening', referred to admitting new member states to the EEC, in particular Britain, whose membership de Gaulle had vetoed twice in the 1960s. Tellingly, the European leaders implemented this agenda through a series of high-level summits, including heads of state and government, as well as the president of the European Commission: first in Paris on 19–21 October 1972, and then in Copenhagen on 14–15 December 1973, this time with nine countries, including the three new member states.

With regard to the 'completion' agenda, the implementation was swift: the 1970 Budgetary Treaty created the so-called own resources. Instead of relying only on national contributions, the EEC was allowed to fund itself by collecting customs duties (and import levies on agricultural products) and by receiving a small percentage of national revenues from value-added tax (VAT). The European Parliament (EP) gained the power to amend the annual budget but only within certain narrow limits. Paradoxically, by insisting on the 'completion' agenda in order to secure the CAP, the French government accepted the delegation of some powers that were vehemently refused by de Gaulle during the 1965–6 empty chair crisis. Once the CAP was ring-fenced, the enlargement negotiations could start. They went on from 1970 to 1972. The UK accepted the EEC as it stood, without any renegotiations of either the Treaty of Rome or past decisions. Instead, all new member states had to accept what was from then on called the *acquis*

*Communautaire* – encompassing all the treaties, secondary legislation and case law passed since 1958. After a lengthy debate in the House of Commons in October 1971, which dealt with all topics, including thorny issues such as the CAP (Ludlow 2015), a majority of the British members of Parliament accepted to join the EEC.

Britain was not alone in joining. Ireland followed its powerful neighbour, to which it was closely linked economically. Denmark, whose two main trade partners, Germany and the UK, already either belonged to the EEC or were due to join, also chose to join. Lastly, Norway was also accepted as an EEC member; but a referendum held in that country in September 1972 resulted in a majority of 'No' votes. The recent discovery of the massive oil reserves in the North Sea convinced the Norwegians that they could manage on their own.

The 'deepening' part of the agenda was multifaceted, since it concerned monetary, social and foreign policies. Regarding in particular foreign policy, 'European political cooperation' emerged in 1970 as a non-binding commitment by EEC member states to consult one another in such matters. While the move was modest, it signalled a willingness by European leaders to tackle non-economic issues. In the same vein, on 14 December 1973, during the Copenhagen Summit, a declaration on 'the European identity' was adopted. It defined 'Europeanness' in rather vague terms and insisted on liberal and democratic values. Although transatlantic relations were strained following the reassessment by US President Richard Nixon's administration of its economic foreign policy objectives, an Atlantic dimension was present in the document via the assertion of a close relationship with the United States. An incipient attempt at defining a specific European way of life was inserted with references to 'social justice' and to 'the increasing convergence of attitudes to life'. The Community's purposes were peace and 'to ensure the survival of the civilization which they have in common'.

Regarding social policy, the 1972 Paris summit ended on a statement aiming at a 'co-ordinated policy for employment and vocational training, at improving working conditions and conditions of life, at closely involving workers in the progress of firms, [and] at facilitating on the basis of the situation in the different countries the conclusion of collective agreements at European level' (Statement 1972). European leaders envisaged a targeted social policy focused on working conditions and opportunities, in line with the conception of the EEC's being first and foremost a 'Common Market' and not a comprehensive welfare state (Chapters 8 and 12). In addition, a 'regional policy' aimed at helping the poorest areas of the Community, particularly those resulting from the preponderance of agriculture and from industrial change'. The statement referred to the Italian South (the Mezzogiorno) and Ireland on the one hand, and the British rust-belt areas on the other, Britain being the first country to experience the crisis of traditional manufacturing on a large scale. Heath had lobbied hard to get this policy, notably to offset the negative financial impact of the CAP: what London would relinquish to the CAP, it would expect to recover from regional policy (Chapters 9 and 17; George 1994).

The most ambitious part of the 'deepening' agenda was undoubtedly monetary policy. It was widely believed that a close coordination of national monetary policies was indispensable to keep the Common Market afloat (see Chapter 10). Without stable exchange rates, for example, a member state could offset the removal of customs duties by a unilateral currency devaluation to render its products cheaper and thus more competitive. More generally, some feared a return to the currency wars of the 1930s and to protectionism. The problem was particularly acute for the CAP, which was predicated on a system of common prices. Any devaluation and revaluation of a currency seriously undermined the unity of the Community market. When the French franc was devalued in 1969, following its weakening after the events of May 1968, a complex series of measures known as 'monetary compensatory amounts' was devised. They amounted to extra taxes on weak-currency products and additional aids on hard-currency ones. More generally, pro-European thinkers such as Jean Monnet, Robert Marjolin and the Belgian economist Robert Triffin had devised projects of European monetary integration designed to increase intra-European solidarity in case of monetary disruptions since the early 1960s. Monnet had persuaded Willy Brandt to support this endeavour.

At the 1969 Hague Summit, the heads of state and government commissioned a report on Economic and Monetary Union to Pierre Werner, the prime minister of Luxembourg and a former banker (Chapter 10). On 8 October 1970, he released the ambitious 'Werner Report', which outlined a three-stage process to create a fully fledged Economic and Monetary Union by 1980. Less than a year after the release of the report, US President Nixon severed the link between the dollar and gold on 15 August 1971. This created havoc in the International Monetary System, precipitating a progressive move towards floating currency rates.

In this adversarial environment, all European countries had an incentive to better coordinate their monetary policies with those of their neighbours, even if the plan to move to a common currency remained purely theoretical, as no country was ready to surrender its sovereignty in this issue. Europeans disagreed over how to act. The debate pitted so-called 'economists' and 'monetarists', to borrow the vocabulary of that time (the term 'monetarists', however, is not to be confused with monetarism advocated by Milton Friedman and his followers), against each other. The 'economists', and in particular the German negotiators, requested a convergence of economic policies towards stability-based policies before accepting any solidarity with weak-currency countries (notably, to assist them with central bank intervention in case of monetary crisis). By contrast, the 'monetarists', the countries with weak currencies, such as France and Italy, requested an automatic solidarity in case of crisis without constraining measures in terms of economic convergence.

Eventually, in March 1972, the Europeans decided to create the 'snake', a non-binding political commitment to limit EEC fluctuations to 4.5 per cent. The European currencies' rate of exchange moved as a snake within the 'tunnel' (which had been created by international agreement in late 1971 and included non-European currencies, permitting initially a wider fluctuation margin of 9 per cent). The October 1972 Paris Summit confirmed the snake arrangement and heralded ambitious measures in social and regional policy, as well as in 'industrial, scientific and technological policy'. However, the subsequent oil shock seriously disrupted the implementation of the ambitious triptych agreed upon at the 1969 Hague Summit.

# 2. The crisis of the 1970s

The 1973 oil shock nearly quadrupled the price of oil (OPEC prices). Combined with the second oil shock, in 1979, prices grew tenfold. Higher prices of the major source of energy (and of raw materials for certain chemicals) hampered growth in Europe, fuelled inflation and increased unemployment. It also manifested the assertion of the 'South', the developing countries that had proudly proclaimed in 1974 their wish for a 'New International Economic Order' more favourable to them at the United Nations. In 1973 the famous Trilateral Report on 'the crisis of democracy' listed the shortcomings of the major Western powers and notably of many EEC countries. As a matter of fact, political violence cast a shadow over Germany, Italy, the UK and, outside the EEC, Spain, which faced a troubled transition to democracy.

In addition to these external challenges, the EEC also had to cope with an internal trial: the threat of Britain's departure from the Community it had just joined. In 1974 Heath lost the election. Labour leader Harold Wilson returned to power and requested a renegotiation of the enlargement terms, mostly for internal party-political reasons. Brussels granted a few concessions to London in March 1975 – in particular, the promise to take into account Britain's link with the Commonwealth and to correct the budgetary mechanism. A referendum held shortly thereafter gave a comfortable lead for the 'Yes' vote, at 67 per cent; but it signalled that UK membership would be difficult right from the start. Later, all British prime ministers insisted on getting a reduction to their contribution to the EEC budget. When Thatcher came to power in 1979, she took over this pledge with a much more confrontational stance, hectoring her colleagues by announcing, 'I want my money back', at the Dublin European Council of November 1979 (Chapter 17).

This long-standing quarrel became known as the BBQ, or 'British Budgetary Question' – or even the 'Bloody British Question'. On the one hand, the British case was relatively straightforward: since Britain imported many agricultural products from outside the EEC, it had to pay heavy import duties into the EEC budget. Conversely, as a relatively small producer of agricultural goods, it received few subsidies. Since the CAP represented a vast chunk of the EEC budget, Britain was considered the largest net contributor to the budget. Internal British documents underlined how unfair the situation was, especially compared to other countries such as the Netherlands, which was a net beneficiary of the Community budget, whereas it was much richer than the UK in terms of per capita GDP (Warlouzet 2018a).

On the other hand, the British case was impossible to defend, as it altered the principle of European solidarity. From the Commission's point of view, it was pointless for member states to think of themselves as net contributors or benefactors, since the Community brought intangible benefits such as extra opportunities of trade and travel, lower prices and so on – not to mention more peaceful relationships. In addition, the sums in question were relatively negligible, as the EEC budget represented less than 1 per cent of member states' GDP.

# 3. Economic deepening in the 1970s

This gloomy context notwithstanding, the EEC managed to pursue its economic integration both domestically and on the global stage. Like in the 1960s, the European Commission again represented the Community, in close cooperation with the member states, at the General Agreement on Tariffs and Trade (GATT) negotiations. The Tokyo Round (1973–9) led to a further round of reductions of customs duties (by one-third on average) (Coppolaro 2016). Most of all, it manifested its participants' refusal to embark on the protectionist path chosen after the previous world economic crisis, in 1929 – one which haunted many leaders who still referred to it even in the 1970s (Warlouzet 2018a).

The association policy with former colonies was also affected by the 'deepening' and 'enlargement' agendas. The 1975 Lomé Convention replaced the previous Yaoundé Convention. Following enlargement, former British colonies joined the French, Belgian and Dutch territories already concerned by the Yaoundé Convention. Lomé associated forty-six African, Caribbean and Pacific Group of States (ACP) with the EEC. Following some of the New International Economic Order's requests, it gave trade preferences to ACP countries without full reciprocity (i.e. the EEC market was more open than the ACP's) and established a system known as STABEX to stabilize export earnings from the South (Migani 2014a). It propped up the export prices of some raw materials, since many of the poorest ACP countries relied on a few exports of this type for their revenues. Aid was granted to development projects through the European Development Fund.

Beyond those areas of traditional EEC activity, Brussels managed to make forays into new areas. In social policy, the Commission passed a few directives on working conditions. The social policy section of the 1972 declaration of the Paris Summit of the heads of state and government further resulted in the development of an EEC consumer policy (Chapter 11). More often than not, decisions in Brussels occurred after a mobilization from civil society (Chapter 12). In gender equality, activist lawyers such as the Belgian Éliane Vogel-Polsky actively promoted a wider interpretation of Article 119 of the Treaty of Rome on 'equal remuneration for equal work' for men and women. The article was largely left unimplemented during the first decade of the EEC. By defending Gabrielle Defrenne – a Belgian flight attendant dismissed at the age of forty by the Belgian airline Sabena, like all its female flight attendants, while men could continue until the age of fifty-five – Vogel-Polsky obtained a favourable ruling from the Court of Justice of the European Union (CJEU), the so-called *Defrenne* II case, in 1976 (Case 43–75).

In environmental policy too, European regulations often followed the mobilization of activists (Chapter 11). This was the case for the 1979 bird directives on the protection of birds, which were considered a European issue since they moved across borders. The mobilization of Northern European and Italian associations created a momentum that allowed the directive to be adopted in 1979 (Meyer 2010b). Its scope was considerably enlarged in 1992 with the Habitat directive.

Lastly, the European Monetary System (EMS) was set up in 1979 (Chapter 10). At its core, the mechanism was the same as the snake: both of them were intergovernmental agreements targeting monetary stability vis-à-vis other European currencies, except for the British pound (Mourlon-Druol 2012a). It was the first time that London received an exception – the first in what would become a long list – but it did not stir a major controversy at the time. Compared to the snake, the EMS encompassed a 'European Currency Unit', known as the Ecu, which was also the name of a medieval French coin, that served as a common point of reference. But the system was as unbalanced as the snake, since weak currencies were still pressured to converge towards the stability-oriented policies of the strong currencies if they wanted to get financial assistance from the latter. Politically, the agreement on the EMS stemmed from a Franco-German convergence that originated in the new stability-oriented economic policy of French Prime Minister Raymond Barre, who was appointed in 1976. The excellent relationship between the two leaders Helmut Schmidt in Bonn and French President Valéry Giscard d'Estaing in Paris was not enough to dispel the economic mistrust – especially since Schmidt was relatively drawn towards the Anglo-Saxon world (Haeussler 2019) – until Barre took office. The second oil shock did not put into question their cooperation (Chapter 16).

# 4. Adapting the institutional framework

With the return to democracy in Greece, Portugal and Spain in 1974–5, enlargement policy focused on the South. The Nine became Ten in 1981, when Greece joined. Greek enlargement was mainly a political issue: it was actively defended by French President Giscard d'Estaing for cultural and political reasons. Greece was considered the cradle of Western democracy, and its binding to the West was important at a time when East–West relations deteriorated and entered what was sometimes called a 'second Cold War' (Karamouzi 2014).

In the meantime, the EEC's institutions kept the same balance between intergovernmentalism and supranationalism that had characterized the 1960s. Member states remained firmly in control, and even more so after the foundation of the European Council. After a proposal by French President Giscard d'Estaing at the Paris Summit of 9–10 December 1974, the Nine decided to regularly convene the national heads of state and government and representatives of the European Commission to set the broad priorities of European affairs. To some extent, this proposal, which had been inspired by, among others, Monnet, was a Europeanization of the Gaullist Fouchet Plan of the 1960s (Chapter 2). Tellingly, Giscard d'Estaing proposed at the same time to institutionalize regular meetings of Western leaders, a project which materialized in the Group of Six (G6, later G7) in 1975 (Mourlon-Druol and Romero 2014). Overall, the creation of both the European Council and the G7 symbolized the determination of Western countries to work together to fight the crisis and to avoid a relapse into nationalism and protectionism, as had happened in the 1930s.

Regarding foreign policy, the European political cooperation that emerged in 1970 was nothing more than a forum to avoid misunderstandings rather than to form a common position. On almost every issue – such as the 1973 oil shock, the 1974 war in Cyprus and the sanctions against South Africa's apartheid regime – the Nine disagreed. They coordinated themselves effectively during the Helsinki Conference on Security and Cooperation in Europe (1973–5), which was a diplomatic success for the Community (Romano 2009); but they were not able to form a common front over the Afghanistan War and the boycott of the 1980 Moscow Olympics.

At the same time, the supranational character of the European Communities became more entrenched. This was visible thanks to the 'integration-through-law' dynamic (see Chapter 6) – that is, the fact that the Court of Justice supported a teleological interpretation of European law, transforming it into a federal device. After a first string of landmark cases in the 1960s, the momentum continued in the 1970s, most importantly with *Cassis de Dijon* in 1979, which limited the member states' ability to restrict trade within the Community (Alter and Meunier 1994; Albors-Llorens, Barnard and Leucht 2021). *Cassis de Dijon* shaped the concept of 'mutual recognition' but allowed states to restrict the acceptance of foreign goods for reasons linked to 'the effectiveness of fiscal supervision, the protection of public health, the fairness of commercial transactions, and the defence of the consumer' (Case 120–78). As a consequence, the harmonization of national legislations was often still a necessary precondition for liberalizing trade in the EEC, and as the Council of Ministers has used unanimity in its decisions rather than using majority vote, this was a slow process. However, this newfound judicial activism met with some resistance among national governments. In Paris in 1979, French diplomats considered reforming the court to curb its power before renouncing the idea (Warlouzet 2018a).

That very same year, a breakthrough occurred for European democracy: the first direct election of the members of the EP. This reform had already been mentioned as a possibility in the 1957 Treaty of Rome. At the 1974 Paris Summit, European leaders decided to implement it. The Act of 20 September 1976 enshrined it in law. The first election was held on 7–10 June 1979. The 62 per cent participation rate was decent, but the Europeanization of the public space was still in its infancy: political parties and candidates still campaigned mainly on national issues, and the EP's powers were limited (Chapter 7). Nevertheless, this move was symbolically very significant, not least because the first elected president of the Parliament, Simone Veil, was both a figure of Franco-German reconciliation and a feminist (Figure 3.1). A former deportee to Auschwitz, she was the minister in charge of enacting the first French abortion law, at the request of President Giscard d'Estaing, and overcame fierce internal opposition to do so.

# 5. The 'relaunch of Europe', 1984–6

The 'relaunch of Europe' designates the three years from 1984 to 1986 during which ancient bones of contention were solved and major institutional and economic reforms were launched. Tellingly, this expression was also used by member states' leaders at the time, including the British (Warlouzet 2018a). The three major and interlinked bones of contention were the British budgetary question, the CAP and Spanish enlargement. The British requested a rebate on their contribution. A convenient means to achieve this end would have been to cut CAP expenditures, but countries that depended on it – such as France and the Netherlands, as well as Germany, whose minister of agriculture had always lobbied for higher farm prices – reneged. In addition, Paris delayed Spanish enlargement over fears of harsh competition for Southern French agricultural goods.

Eventually, thanks to the strong bonds forged between two new leaders, the French President François Mitterrand and the German Chancellor Helmut Kohl, a breakthrough occurred at the 1984 Fontainebleau Summit. The British got a near-permanent rebate and a slight curb of CAP expenditures (through milk quotas). Lastly, Mitterrand accepted the

FIGURE 3.1 *Simone Veil, first president of the directly elected European Parliament, 5 September 1979. Photographer: Jean-Louis Debaize. Courtesy of European Communities, 1979.*

unavoidable, the Spanish enlargement, as it was politically impossible to deny EEC membership to a country that had undergone a difficult but successful transition to democracy since 1975. This paved the way for the enlargement to Spain and Portugal in 1986.

Once those hurdles were cleared, the 'relaunch' materialized via a new common project: the internal market. The objective was to remove internal borders by creating a vast European market aimed at unleashing growth. The model was the United States, whose growth surpassed that of the EEC in the early 1980s. While this project was defended by various groups of actors (Chapter 8), it necessitated a major institutional reform by national governments: namely, the adoption of the procedure of qualified majority voting at the Council of Ministers. Otherwise, the harmonization of many national laws on trade with products necessitating border checks (e.g. due to differing technical standards) would be slow and cumbersome.

Jacques Delors, the new president of the European Commission from 1985 onwards, placed this bargain at the core of his presidency (Figure 3.2). Much like a head of government, he unveiled his Commission's programme by delivering his first speech before the EP on 14 January 1985. He insisted on the urgent task of setting up a genuine internal market by removing all border controls by 31 December 1992, thus inventing the catchy '1992' slogan. In this speech and during his presidency, Delors constantly linked the neoclassical vision of the market with notions of social, regional and industrial policies (Warlouzet 2018a).

Institutional change gathered momentum. Several reforms had been devised before, such as the increased use of qualified majority and a strengthening of European political cooperation, notably in the 1975 Tindemans report (written by the Belgian Prime Minister Leo Tindemans) and in the 1981 Genscher-Colombo initiative (released by the German and Italian Foreign Affairs Ministers, Hans-Dietrich Genscher and Emilio Colombo, respectively). The EP had also already mobilized and produced, under the chairmanship of the Italian federalist activist Altiero Spinelli, a draft 'Treaty establishing a European Union' on 14 February 1984 that encompassed many supranational reforms, notably by empowering the Parliament (Chapter 13).

National leaders were more cautious. At the 1984 Fontainebleau Summit, they decided to create two committees: one in charge of delivering proposals on institutional reforms (the Dooge Committee, named after its chairman, the Irish former Foreign Affairs minister James Dooge) and the other on promoting the Community to its citizens, notably by easing freedom of movement (the Adonnino Committee, named after Pietro Adonnino, an Italian member of the EP). The Adonnino Committee, as well as the impetus of the Commission and of certain states, gave rise to the 1987 Erasmus programme, which facilitated student mobility. The 1985 Schengen agreement on the removal of border controls for people was also a major landmark even though it was only an intergovernmental treaty among

FIGURE 3.2 *Jacques Delors giving his inaugural speech as European Commission president at the European Parliament in Strasbourg, January 1985. European Parliament Multimedia Center. Courtesy of European Union, 2022.*

five governments – France, Germany and the Benelux countries – and necessitated subsequent legislation, notably to improve police cooperation and convergence on visa policy. The 1990 Schengen Convention was eventually implemented in 1995 and integrated into EU treaties in the 1997 Amsterdam Treaty.

The main proposal of the Dooge Committee was to convene an intergovernmental conference (IGC) to negotiate a new treaty. The three staunchest defenders of intergovernmentalism, the British, Danish and Greek governments, adamantly refused such a move. Eventually, at the June 1985 Milan Council, the Italian chairman, Prime Minister Bettino Craxi, and Italian Foreign Minister Giulio Andreotti, wielded an unusual tool, a recourse to majority voting, whereas unanimity had always ruled within the European Council. The majority voted in favour of the IGC. Then, after relatively swift negotiations, a new treaty was signed in 1986, the Single European Act. Its major component was the internal market programme, with the objective to be completed by 31 December 1992. To achieve this, qualified majority voting and enhanced powers for the EP (through a procedure known as 'cooperation') were enforced for all legislation directly related to the internal market programme. The 1966 Luxembourg compromise came to an end (Chapter 2). This extension of majority voting explicitly excluded social and fiscal affairs, which remained wedded to the intergovernmental realm governed by unanimity. This rule also prevailed in fields newly incorporated into the EEC institutional system, such as environmental and regional policies and European political cooperation.

At the same time, the European Commission strove to extend its reach to the average European citizen (Calligaro 2013). Delors chose symbols for the European Community, sometimes by borrowing some already devised by the Council of Europe, such as the European flag (blue with twelve yellow stars). Brussels also fostered the European capital of culture scheme, which was launched in 1983 by the Greek minister of culture, the actress and opponent to the Greek dictatorship Melina Mercouri, with Athens being the first recipient in 1985. Taking all those decisions together, combined with the 1987 Erasmus programme and the removal of border control foreseen in 1993, it seemed as if European integration was focusing on European citizens much more directly than before.

# 6. Momentum towards a monetary and political union, 1987–92

The '1992' slogan, launched by Delors in 1985 and encapsulated in the 1986 Single Act, materialized as planned: on 31 December 1992, borders were open and goods circulated freely within the Union. The Single Market was born. This outcome was built on a steady pace of harmonization of national norms, with more than three hundred pieces of European legislation being adopted between 1987 and 1992 (Chapter 8), which created a political momentum for further European integration.

Monetary integration was next in line. A growing number of Europeans considered that cooperation through the EMS was insufficient and that a fully fledged merger of currencies was necessary for a variety of reasons (Chapter 10). From a technical point of view, the European Commission explained that the creation of a common currency would smoothen the functioning of the internal market and save billions of Ecus in transaction costs. From a financial point of view, weak-currency governments, notably in Paris and in Rome, lamented their lack of monetary autonomy, since they were forced to follow the German Central Bank's monetary policy; otherwise, their currency would decrease in value and their cost of borrowing would increase. Merging with the mighty deutschmark was seen as indispensable to lowering interest rates, and thereby to facilitating the funding of states, companies and citizens, a prerequisite for economic revival. Lastly, from a political point of view, European monetary union was considered the new frontier, the ultimate reaction of an Old Europe now facing the challenges of globalization. Those political arguments were necessary to overcome the reluctance of hard-currency countries, especially West Germany, who did not want to pair with their seemingly uncompetitive Southern neighbours.

This growing consensus was also the result of a convergence towards stability-oriented policies, since Keynesian stimuli that were deemed efficient in the 1950s and 1960s seemed to generate only more inflation, without reducing unemployment following the oil shocks. The 1976 British and the 1977 Italian financial crises and the 1983 barely averted French financial crisis forced weak-currency governments to find other ways to restore growth and reduce unemployment (Warlouzet 2018a). Hence, whereas the rise of neoliberal ideas, starting in the UK with the premiership of Margaret Thatcher (1979–90), also played a role in this move, it was not the only force. For French and Italian left-wing rulers, the path towards monetary union was also the path to recovery, less unemployment and sustainable support of the welfare state.

The collapse of the Soviet Bloc further increased the pressure to deepen European integration. In June 1989 in Poland, the first free elections since the outbreak of the Cold War were organized in the Soviet Bloc. The first democratic government led by Tadeusz Mazowiecki was sworn in in August. The democratic momentum soon reached all Central and Eastern European countries, including Germany with the Fall of the Berlin Wall on 9 November 1989. Chancellor Kohl reacted quickly by proposing, on 28 November 1989, his 'Ten-Point Plan' towards a quick reunification led by West Germany. Bonn had to react quickly since millions of East German emigrants were moving to West Germany, and since it feared that the Soviet policy could change. Eventually, German reunification was secured on 3 October 1990, de facto enlarging the EEC to the former East Germany once its Länder were incorporated into the German Federal Republic. In 1991, the Soviet Union collapsed, and new countries became independent. Some of them, such as the Baltic Republics, were eager to join Western organizations.

The end of the Cold War and the prospect of a unified Germany at the heart of Europe gave rise to the question of the organization of the European continent and of the possible extension of the EEC to the East. In the short term, the Community was vindicated by the G7 decision, taken in 1989, to put it in charge of coordinating Western financial aid to Poland and Hungary (the 'PHARE' scheme) and then to other ex-Soviet countries. Quickly thereafter, and as early as his Bruges speech delivered on 17 October 1989, Delors supported German reunification. By contrast, during the December 1989 Strasbourg Council, which was held just after the announcement of Kohl's Ten-Point Plan, all European leaders, with the exception of the leaders of Spain and Ireland (i.e. the two countries that did not take part in the Second World War), expressed a form of coldness towards the quick pace of German reunification (Ludlow 2017). Mitterrand was weary but quickly rekindled the Franco-German bond, in contrast with the persistent hostility manifested by Thatcher.

Later on, Mitterrand tried to defuse what he perceived as a possible 'dilution' of the European Community, which could be transformed into a mere free-trade area if all former Communist countries were to join (Bozo 2009). In 1990, the French president aired an ambiguous project of European confederation stretching from the Atlantic to Moscow that was destined to forestall this predicament. It was resolutely rejected by former Communist countries eager to join the Community instead of a second-league organization.

The role of the Fall of the Berlin Wall in the conclusion of the European Monetary Union is disputed. Many scholars have argued that the consensus on this idea predated the dramatic events of 1989 (Dyson and Featherstone 1999; James 2012). The decisive move was made during the Hannover Summit of 27–28 June 1988, when Kohl, reassured by the adoption of the directive on the free movement of capital that he had long requested, accepted to commission a report on the European Economic and Monetary Union. The committee was composed of central bankers and chaired by Delors himself, who personally oversaw the monetary field within the Commission. The subsequent Delors report was of tremendous importance as it was endorsed by the EU leaders at the 26 and 27 June 1989 Madrid Council. It envisaged a fully fledged federal monetary union backed by an independent Central Bank.

The Fall of the Berlin Wall was important to overcome the mighty resistance to monetary union that persisted in West Germany. Internally, Kohl became more popular than before, and, externally, he faced the wariness of the other European member states towards a possible renaissance of a mighty Germany, once the Cold War was over. He responded by accepting the opening of intergovernmental negotiations on monetary union and on political union at the 1989 Strasbourg Council.

# 7. The Maastricht Treaty, 1992

Both negotiations eventually led to the Maastricht Treaty, concluded on 7 February 1992. It set up a three-stage plan to create a fully fledged European Monetary Union by 1999. The monetary part was entirely federal, because a common currency (later named 'euro') was to be created and managed by an independent central bank, while the economic wing remained intergovernmental. Governments remained completely in charge of their economic policies, even if they had to abide by the so-called convergence criteria to join the Union. Even though it was mentioned in the Delors report, banking supervision was ignored and the common budget was not increased – two missing points that were to play a huge role in the eurozone crisis in 2010–15 (Chapter 10).

On the whole, the arrangements followed the German model as it was considered the most successful in Europe: the central bank would be fully independent and mostly geared towards low inflation (although Article 105 of the Maastricht Treaty defining the European Central Bank mandate also referred to 'the objectives of the Communities as laid down in article 2'); the 'convergence criteria' enshrined the predominance of stability-oriented policies; and, finally, the social and industrial parts of the treaty remained modest (Warlouzet 2019a).

The other major innovations of the Maastricht Treaty concerned the political union: a 'European Union' inhabited by 'European citizens' was created. European citizenship brought concrete benefits such as diplomatic protection outside the EU, the right to vote at local and European elections and enhanced freedom of movement, work and residence. The EU replaced the EEC and shelved the 'economic' adjectives. It encompassed three pillars: the first was devoted to economic policies in a wider sense, including monetary union, while the other two dealt with justice and home affairs and the Common Foreign and Security Policy (CFSP). Hence, almost all core competences of the member states were affected by the EU. In addition, the principle of subsidiarity was upheld. A committee of regions was set up. Even though it was a purely advisory body, this shows the growing importance of local authorities at the national level, as well as at the European level, through the co-management of European cohesion funds.

The decision-making process became slightly more Europeanized, as the EP gained co-decision power on certain issues. It meant that for a growing number of pieces of legislation, the Commission proposed a draft text to both the Council of Ministers and the EP. The Parliament was also entrusted with a formal vote on the nomination of the president of the Commission. As a result, a better coordination between the EP election and the inception of the Commission was organized (Chapters 5 and 7).

However, the Maastricht Treaty was a far cry from a move towards a federal union. It created a complex three-pillar structure, of which only the first one – the economic pillar – was managed by a mixture of intergovernmental and supranational procedures. The other two pillars, justice and home affairs and the CFSP, remained fully intergovernmental, with a decision-making process based on unanimity in the Council of Ministers. In addition, Britain opted out of EMU and did not sign the social chapter annexed to the treaty.

Europe and the world entered a new era. With the collapse of the Soviet Union, which was officially dissolved on 26 December 1991, the United States became the indisputable superpower, as the 1991 Gulf War against

Iraq demonstrated. At roughly the same time, in November 1992, the Blair House compromise between the EU and the United States paved the way for the completion of the GATT Round, which deepened trade liberalization, this time even for agriculture.

However, the ebullient mood of Maastricht quickly faded. Less than two months after its signature, on 31 March 1991, war broke out in Yugoslavia, without any coordination among European states or any influence on the ground. This blatant failure added to the already gloomy economic mood, since the Western world was affected by an economic depression, and to a growing Euroscepticism, visible in the contested Danish and French referenda on the Maastricht Treaty.

# Conclusion

Between 1973 and 1992, the small 'Common Market' was transformed into a larger 'European Union' that most European countries – in particular, those just freed from dictatorship – wanted to join. This process did not happen spontaneously. It occurred because of the convergence of many European actors towards the idea that the Community represented a strategic element in solving the deep and multifaceted economic and political crisis of the 1970s. The United States was no longer an unconditional ally but rather had become a fierce competitor within the Atlantic Alliance; new challengers such as Japan came to the fore, forcing France, West Germany, the UK and other European member states to converge and to accept the renewal of the Commission's leadership under Delors. This situation explains the persistence of the interlinkage between deepening and enlargement – in terms of both the economic and the institutional developments of the Community – agreed upon at the Hague in 1969. This does not mean that the road forward was uncontested, since crises were manifold, both externally and internally (in particular, due to Britain); but it does show that the Community's structure proved flexible and resilient enough to reinvent itself within the same framework defined in 1957.

# Five key questions

1.  Why did European leaders agree to the 'triptych' of completion, deepening and enlargement in 1969?

2.  Were internal factors, such as individual personalities, or external factors, such as the general economic situation, more important in shaping European integration in the 1970s and 1980s?

3.  What are the links between deepening and enlargement of the EEC/EU?

4.  How can we account for the acceleration of European integration since the mid-1980s?

5.  What was the 'relaunch' of Europe, and is the expression appropriate?

# Ten key readings

*Note*: For the entire period, the basic in-depth studies in political science are: Moravcsik (1998) for the grand bargains, and Dyson and Featherstone (1999) for EMU. Verdun (2002a) provides an overview of the enormous literature on EMU. In history, archival-based accounts with a broad perspective exists for the entire 1973–86 period (Warlouzet 2018a) and for the history of EMU (James 2012).

Drake, H. (2000), *Jacques Delors: Perspectives on a European Leader*, London: Routledge.

Dyson, K., and K. Featherstone (1999), *The Road to Maastricht: Negotiating Economic and Monetary Union*, Oxford: Oxford University Press.

Grin, G. (2003), *The Battle of the Single European Market: Achievements and Economic Thought, 1985–2000*, London: Paul Kegan.

Jabko, N. (2006), *Playing the Market: A Political Strategy for Uniting Europe, 1985–2005*, Ithaca, NY: Cornell University Press.

James, H. (2012), *Making the European Monetary Union: The Role of the Committee of Central Bank Governors and the Origins of the European Central Bank*, Cambridge, MA: Harvard University Press.

Ludlow, N. P. (2015), 'Safeguarding British Identity or Betraying It? The Role of British "Tradition" in the Parliamentary Great Debate on EC Membership, October 1971', *Journal of Common Market Studies*, 53 (1): 18–34.

Moravcsik, A. (1998), *The Choice for Europe: Social Purpose and State Power from Messina to Maastricht*, Ithaca, NY: Cornell University Press.

Mourlon-Druol, E., and F. Romero (eds) (2014), *International Summitry and Global Governance: The Rise of the G7 and the European Council, 1974–1991*, London: Routledge.

Verdun, A. (2002a), 'Why EMU Happened: A Survey of Theoretical Explanations', in P. Crowley (ed.), *Before and Beyond EMU: Historical Lessons and Future Prospects*, 71–98, London: Routledge.

Warlouzet, L. (2018a), *Governing Europe in a Globalizing World: Neoliberalism and Its Alternatives Following the 1973 Oil Crisis*, London: Routledge.

# 4

# Enlargement, treaty reform and crises, 1993–2021

## *Magdalena Frennhoff Larsén*

## Introduction

The end of the Cold War had a significant impact on the development and integration of the European Union (EU) for many years. It opened up the possibility of new countries joining the Union. With the disappearance of bloc divisions between East and West, the three neutral countries of Austria, Finland and Sweden joined the EU in 1995. For these countries, membership of a deeply integrated Western organization had been considered incompatible with their neutrality stance during the Cold War. The collapse of Communism and the dissolution of the Soviet Union also made it possible for the ten newly independent Central and Eastern European Countries (CEECs) to seek EU membership and eventually join the Union in 2004–7, together with Cyprus and Malta.

The change in East–West relations allowed the EU to rethink its international role, a process that had started in the 1970s and became enshrined in the Maastricht Treaty in 1992 with the formal introduction of a Common Foreign and Security Policy (CFSP). This became ever more urgent with the Yugoslav wars raging on the doorstep of the EU during the 1990s. The war exposed the limited capacity and capabilities provided by the CFSP.

Both enlargement and these international ambitions necessitated additional treaty reform. After the Maastricht Treaty there were three new treaties: the Amsterdam (1997), Nice (2001) and Lisbon (2007) Treaties. They all advanced the integration process in different ways. However, while there was strong support for further integration among European leaders, the ratification process of these treaties, including the failure to ratify a Constitutional Treaty in 2005, signalled increasing levels of scepticism towards continued integration among the citizens across the EU.

This Euroscepticism increased further with both the eurozone crisis, triggered by the financial crisis starting in the United States in 2008, and the so-called migration crisis, which followed from the unprecedented numbers of people fleeing to the EU from war-torn Syria, Afghanistan, Iraq and North Africa in 2014–16. Euroscepticism culminated with the people in the UK voting to leave the EU in 2016.

This overview chapter, which covers the period from 1993 to 2021, first explains the widening and deepening of the EU through enlargement and treaty reform. It then explores how the EU responded to the eurozone and migration crises, which both exposed widely diverging views among member states and increasing levels of Euroscepticism. The chapter concludes with a brief discussion of the UK's exit from the EU, or Brexit, which for the first time in the EU's history led to a reduction in the number of member states.

# 1. EU enlargement: From 12 to 28

## EFTA enlargement

The collapse of the Soviet Union and the disappearance of bloc divisions opened up the prospect for the neutral countries of Austria, Finland and Sweden to join the Union. With the Soviet threat disappearing, their neutrality commitments were no longer considered incompatible with EU membership. While these countries had been militarily neutral, they had gradually aligned economically with the West during the Cold War. Austria and Sweden were part of the seven countries that established the European Free Trade Association (EFTA) in 1959–60, and Finland became a full member in 1986. As a result, the accession of these three countries is often referred to as the 'EFTA enlargement'.

By 1992 all three countries had applied for EU membership, and the negotiations that followed were quick and uncontroversial. The countries were small in terms of population and, would not significantly change the existing balance of power within the EU. They had well-functioning market economies and strong democratic political systems. And they would all be net contributors to the EU budget. There was consequently considerable support for accession among the existing twelve members. The three applicants, on their part, had strong economic motivations to join the EU, especially after the establishment of the Single Market.

In 1994 the membership terms were agreed. Following ratification by the existing twelve member states and national referenda in the three acceding countries (share of vote in favour of joining: Austria, 67 per cent; Finland,

57 per cent; Sweden, 52 per cent), they joined the EU in January 1995. Given their already close alignment with the EU, the three countries quickly adapted to their new roles as member states. Norway had also applied and negotiated its membership terms, but Norwegians again rejected membership in a referendum with 52 per cent voting against it.

## Enlargement to the East, and Cyprus and Malta

Following the dissolution of the Soviet Union in 1991, the ten CEECs – Bulgaria, the Czech Republic, Estonia, Hungary, Latvia, Lithuania, Poland, Romania, Slovakia and Slovenia – expressed a desire to reintegrate into Europe and initiated far-reaching economic and political reforms, with an eye on potentially joining the EU (Ther 2016). The EU supported these reforms by providing extensive funding and concluding association agreements with individual CEECs between 1991 and 1996. These agreements provided for close trade and political cooperation.

At the early stages of these association negotiations, the EU, which at the time was very much focused on the EFTA enlargement process and preparations for Economic and Monetary Union (EMU), did not envisage actual EU membership for the CEECs in the near future. The CEECs had just come out of decades of Communist rule and needed to significantly transform their political, economic and social systems if they were to join the EU. However, as it became increasingly clear that the CEECs were likely to apply for membership, EU leaders started expressing support for the idea. At the European Council meeting in Copenhagen in June 1993 the EU leaders agreed 'that the associated countries in Central and Eastern Europe that so desire shall become members of the European Union' (European Council 1993). The leaders also agreed on explicit criteria for joining. These accession criteria, referred to as the Copenhagen criteria, set out the political, economic and administrative conditions of admission (Box 4.1).

### BOX 4.1 THE COPENHAGEN CRITERIA

Before candidate countries can join the EU, they need to meet the following accession criteria adopted at the European Council meeting in Copenhagen in 1993

Stability of institutions guaranteeing democracy, the rule of law, human rights and respect for and protection of minorities

A functioning market economy and the capacity to cope with competition and market forces within the Union

> Administrative and institutional capacity to effectively implement the
> full body of common rights and obligations that are binding on all EU
> member states
> The Union's capacity to absorb new members, while maintaining the
> momentum of European integration, is also an important consideration.
>                                                      (European Council 1993)

While the only criterion set out in the Rome Treaty of 1957 had been the
requirement for applicants to be *European* (which had led to the rejection of
Morocco's application in 1987), later treaties made reference to the need to
respect the rule of law and human rights, as well as conforming to an open
market economy. However, with the likelihood of up to ten CEECs joining
the EU, existing members felt it important to strengthen the accession criteria
to ensure convergence between their own and new members' political and
economic systems to safeguard the functioning and future development of
the Union (Nugent 2017).

The sudden emergence of a firm commitment to Eastern enlargement
by the EU has been described as somewhat of a puzzle (Schimmelfennig
2001). Even if several member states, including Denmark, Sweden and the
UK, were strongly pro-enlargement, others expressed caution. After all,
the CEECs were to become structural net recipients, with their budgetary
contributions being much smaller than the funds they would receive
back through the EU's structural and agricultural policies. This would
disproportionately affect existing net recipients, including Greece, Ireland,
Portugal and Spain. In addition, for some member states, in particular
France, there were worries about a potential geopolitical shift from the
West to the centre of Europe. Yet, despite these concerns, member states
committed to Eastern enlargement. One explanation for this is that political
and normative, rather than economic, motivations came to prevail (see also
Chapter 14).

The EU is founded on the norms of European unity and the desire to
overcome past divisions of Europe. It is committed to European peace,
stability and welfare, as well as a pan-European liberal order. Both the
applicants and the member states in favour of enlargement frequently
referred to these norms during the early 1990s. They stressed the political
and moral obligation of the EU to welcome the applicants, as it was an
opportunity to create a complete Europe (Chapter 15). For example, the
British Prime Minister Margaret Thatcher proclaimed that 'we can't say
in one breath that they [the CEECs] are part of Europe and in the next
our European Community Club is so exclusive that we won't admit them'
(Schimmelfennig 2001, 71). Given such rhetoric, it became difficult for
those member states advocating a delay to the accession process to raise

reservations, as it would contradict the very foundations on which the EU was built.

For the applicants, there were strong economic, political and security motivations for seeking EU membership. Economically, they would benefit from the Single Market as well as from the EU's increasing number of preferential trade agreements with third countries. They would also gain from further foreign direct investment and from being net recipients of EU funds. Politically, accession would help strengthen their relatively young democratic systems. It would also allow them to influence EU decisions – many of which would affect them irrespective of whether they were members or not – and to shape EU relations with the rest of the world. Security-wise, membership would offer soft security protection, particularly against the potential revival of Russian power.

The ten CEECs applied for membership between 1994 and 1996, and between 1998 and 2000 accession negotiations started with all of them, as well as with Cyprus and Malta. While the latter two are not CEECs, but rather see themselves as Western European countries, they became part of the Eastern enlargement round. In April 2003 the enlargement negotiations were concluded, and accession treaties were signed with Cyprus, Malta and all CEECs, apart from Bulgaria and Romania. By September 2003, existing member states had ratified the treaties, and referenda had been held in all ten countries apart from Cyprus, which only required parliamentary ratification (share of vote in favour of joining: Czech Republic, 77 per cent; Estonia, 67 per cent; Hungary, 84 per cent; Latvia, 68 per cent; Lithuania, 91 per cent; Malta, 54 per cent; Poland, 78 per cent; Slovakia, 94 per cent; Slovenia, 90 per cent). This cleared the way for ten new countries joining the EU in May 2004 – the largest single expansion of the EU.

Bulgaria and Romania, which had not progressed as quickly as the other CEECs on meeting the Copenhagen criteria, were given slightly longer time to make the necessary political and administrative changes. But in April 2005 they signed their accession treaties, which were ratified in their respective parliaments, and in January 2007 they joined the EU, thus concluding the Eastern enlargement process.

Eastern enlargement, which is seen as one of the most important developments in EU history, had a significant impact on the EU (for a full overview of the role of the Eastern Europe, see Chapter 15). It represented a final end to Cold War divisions and to the EU being a purely 'Western' league (McCormick 2020, 107). It increased the EU population by 105 million (20 per cent), but the GDP by only 5 per cent, which initially meant a significant change in terms of distribution of EU funding. It also increased the levels of intra-EU labour mobility, with many citizens moving from the CEECs to work in the EU-15. Institutionally, such a substantial increase in member states and population triggered reforms to the decision-making and composition of the institutions (see section titled 'Treaty reform' in this chapter). In terms of the EU's external engagement, this enlargement round shifted the EU's boundaries eastward, necessitating clearer policies on how to engage with its neighbourhood. However, there were signs of a renewed commitment to enlargement when European leaders identified Ukraine and Moldova as candidates, and Georgia as a potential candidate, in the summer of 2022.

## Western Balkan and Turkish enlargement

At the time of the Eastern enlargement, Turkey had already been a formal candidate to join the EU since 1999, and six Western Balkan countries – Albania, Bosnia and Herzegovina, Croatia, the then former Yugoslav Republic of Macedonia (now North Macedonia), Serbia and Montenegro – had been given potential candidate status at a European Council summit in Thessaloniki in 2003. This reflected the EU's continuous commitment to enlargement. After all, it had been hailed as the EU's most successful policy, given the way in which it had helped reform society in countries wanting to become members. However, since the Eastern enlargement only Croatia has joined the EU in July 2013, after a referendum in which 67 per cent voted in favour. The accession process has started with all the other countries, apart from Kosovo and Bosnia and Herzegovina, which remain potential candidates. Yet, it is clear that this enlargement round faces greater obstacles than previous ones.

The Western Balkan region is more unstable, and compliance with the political criteria is made harder by the history of ethnic conflict, and greater levels of political polarization, corruption and organized crime. In terms of the economic criteria, many Balkan countries still need to fully transform into functioning market economies. Member states reluctant to move forward with this enlargement point to limited progress made in the applicant countries but also to the increasing levels of 'enlargement fatigue' in existing member states after the Eastern enlargement (Juncos and Pérez-Solórzano Borragán 2016).

In the case of Turkey, which opened accession negotiations with the EU in 2005, the process has been particularly difficult. While it made progress on meeting the economic aspect of the Copenhagen criteria, there have been concerns about the political developments in areas of rule of law, human rights and protection of minorities. In addition, the un-resolved Cyprus issue, which became an EU problem with the accession of Cyprus, is complicating the negotiations. And after the attempted coup in Turkey in 2016, and the subsequent drift to further authoritarianism, the EU Turkey accession process became de facto frozen. As things stand, the strong commitment to enlargement that emerged around the Eastern enlargement has been replaced by greater hesitation.

# 2. Treaty reform: From Amsterdam to Lisbon

## The Amsterdam and Nice Treaties, 1996–2003

Treaty reform is a slow and complex process, taking place through intergovernmental conferences (IGCs), where representatives of the governments of all member states meet to discuss and agree treaty change by consensus. Once the IGC has reached agreement, the treaty needs to be approved by national parliaments and in some cases also by national referenda. In other words, no treaty reform can take place unless all member states agree to it.

When it became clear that the CEECs were to join the EU, an IGC was launched in March 1996 to discuss how to prepare for enlargement. The conference led to the adoption of the Amsterdam Treaty at the European Council summit of June 1997 during the Dutch presidency. Substantively, the treaty introduced a new employment chapter and improved social provisions, as well as increased cooperation in the area of justice and home affairs, including on matters such as asylum and immigration. Institutionally, the use of qualified majority voting in the Council was extended somewhat to facilitate decision-making with a larger number of member states. The role of the European Parliament (EP) was also strengthened to increase democratic scrutiny. Through a streamlined co-decision procedure, it was put on an equal footing with the Council in many policy areas, and it was given greater involvement in the approval of the president of the European Commission. To prevent the EP from becoming too big once new member states joined, the treaty also set a ceiling at 700 members of the EP (MEPs). With 626 MEPs at the time, this meant future enlargements would inevitably lead to a reduction in the number of MEPs of existing member states.

To strengthen the EU's international role following its failures in the Yugoslav war (1991–5 mainly), the treaty introduced a new post of high representative for the CFSP to support the Council in its foreign policy work. It also provided for closer relations with the Western European Union – an association for coordination of European security and defence matters – which would provide the EU with access to crisis management capabilities for engagement in the so-called Petersberg tasks of 'humanitarian and recue tasks, peacekeeping tasks and tasks of combat forces in crisis management, including peacemaking' (Article J.7.2). These changes reflected ways of trying to strengthen the CFSP and develop a more independent foreign and security policy, separate from that of the United States. The end of the Cold War had opened up the possibility to think strategically about the EU's international role, but also the necessity to do so, as witnessed by the violent break-up of Yugoslavia.

These achievements were however relatively modest, and the main institutional issues around the weighting of the votes in the Council, further

extension of qualified majority voting and the size of the Commission were
left unresolved. Given the uncontroversial nature of the treaty, the ratification
process in the fifteen member states proceeded without significant problems,
and the treaty entered into force in May 1999.

By this time, however, accession negotiations with some CEECs as well
as Cyprus had already started, and the urgency to tackle the unresolved
institutional 'left-overs' from the Amsterdam Treaty increased (Nugent
2017, 88). Consequently, another IGC was launched in February 2000, and
concluded in December of the same year, with the adoption of the Nice
Treaty during the French presidency.

The Nice Treaty changed the way votes were weighted in the Council
under qualified majority voting to more closely reflect member states' share
of the EU population. This was to ensure that the more populous member
states would not lose too much of their vote share with enlargement, which
would bring in several new small countries. However, despite this change,
smaller states still remained over-represented in terms of their population
size, while Germany, the biggest member state, remained significantly under-
represented. The use of qualified majority voting was also extended to a
number of new policy areas. In terms of the size of the Commission, the
treaty established that it should only include one national of each member
state, meaning the five biggest member states – France, Germany, Italy, Spain
and the UK – would no longer appoint two commissioners each from 2005.
It also stipulated that once the number of member states reached twenty-
seven, a decision should be taken on the future size of the Commission.
The number of commissioners should then be less than the number of
member states, and a rotation system would have to be established. While
the Amsterdam Treaty had capped the number of MEPs at 700, the Nice
Treaty revised this to 732 as member states became wary of reducing their
national representations as enlargement loomed.

As for the EUs international role, the treaty introduced a European
Security and Defence Policy (ESDP) to support EU foreign policy. Some
member states, including France and Germany, had pushed for greater EU
involvement in defence already during the IGC of Amsterdam, but this had
been blocked by the UK, which for decades had opposed any direct military
role for the EU and had prioritized the North Atlantic Treaty Organization
(NATO) (Howorth 2017). However, following the election of a new, more
pro-European British government in 1997, there was a 'sea-change' in the
UK position on EU defence (Rutten 2001, 8). In December 1998 the British
Prime Minister Tony Blair met with his French counterpart, President
Jacques Chirac, at an Anglo-French summit in St Malo, where they agreed
that 'the Union must have the capacity for autonomous action, backed up by
any credible military forces, the means to decide to use them and a readiness
to do so' (Joint Declaration on European Defence 1998). This agreement
between the two main military powers of the EU paved the way for the IGC
at Nice to include defence policy in the treaty, making it possible for the EU

to generate its own instruments to engage in the Petersberg tasks to respond to international crises. The Kosovo war of 1998–9 had made it clear that the changes made to foreign policy in the Amsterdam Treaty were insufficient, as once again, the EU was left as a bystander in a conflict on its doorstep (Bailes and Messervy-Whiting 2011).

Given the narrow focus of the Nice Treaty, member states were expected to ratify it without problems. However, in Ireland – the only member state to hold a referendum on the treaty – 54 per cent of voters rejected it. This came as a shock to the Irish government, although it had done little to promote or explain the treaty (McCormick 2020). One of the issues that had caused concern was the compatibility of Irish neutrality with the ESDP. To placate these worries, the European Council in June 2002 confirmed in a binding declaration that the treaty 'does not impose any binding mutual defence commitments. Nor does the development of the Union's capacity to conduct humanitarian and crisis management tasks involve the establishment of a European army' (European Council 2002). With these reassurances, and a better-organized government information campaign, the Irish approved the treaty with 63 per cent voting in favour of it in a second referendum in October 2002 (McCormick 2020).

The Nice Treaty, which entered into force in February 2003, was a precondition for expanding the Union. Consequently, the Irish ratification cleared the hurdle for Eastern enlargement. However, there was still a sense among many EU leaders that the treaty did not go far enough to move the integration process forward and ensure the EU would be able to function effectively as a much larger and more heterogeneous union. Consequently, it had been agreed in Nice that another IGC would be convened to discuss the development of a possible constitution for the EU. To prepare the ground for this, a Convention on the Future of Europe was established to discuss how to make the EU institutions more open and closer to the citizens, how to organize politics and decision-making in an enlarged Union, and the EUs role in a globalized world (European Council 2001).

# The Constitutional and Lisbon Treaties, 2002–9

The Convention on the Future of Europe brought together 105 representatives from governments and national parliaments of the EU member states and the candidate states, as well as the European Commission and the EP, under the chairmanship of former French President Valéry Giscard D'Estaing. From February 2002, the representatives met on a regular basis and also held consultations with civil society organization. The aim was to involve a broad set of voices in the discussion about the future direction of the EU. Yet, while the Convention strived for transparency by publishing its papers and opening up its plenaries to the public, it attracted limited media and public attention and was seen as a largely elite-driven project.

The result of the Convention was a 'Draft Treaty Establishing a Constitution for Europe' finalized in July 2003. The draft provided the basis for an IGC tasked with agreeing on a Constitutional Treaty. The final Constitutional Treaty adopted by the EU leaders in June 2004 would replace all existing EU treaties with one single constitutional document, which was meant to be simpler and more accessible than the cumbersome treaties it would have replaced (see also Chapter 13). While most of the text came from the existing treaties, there were a number of new elements. Qualified majority voting would be extended to more policy areas, although unanimity would be retained for sensitive areas, such as taxation, enlargement and treaty revision. It would also be changed to one of double majority, consisting of at least 55 per cent of the member states, comprising at least 65 per cent of the population of the Union. This would address the concerns of bigger countries, in particular Germany, which had so far been under-represented in relation to its population. Institutionally, the powers of the EP would be further extended, the size of the Commission would be limited and two new posts would be introduced: a president of the European Council and a Union minister for foreign affairs. As for constitutional elements, the Charter of Fundamental Rights would be legally binding on member states, and there were references in the preamble of the treaty to EU symbols, including the flag, anthem ('Ode to Joy' from Beethoven's Ninth Symphony) and motto ('United in Diversity').

The ratification process of the Constitutional Treaty started with the Lithuanian Parliament ratifying it in November 2004, and continued with positive votes in ten other member states, including referenda in Spain and Luxembourg, where 77 and 57 per cent, respectively, voted in favour. However, in late spring of 2005 the citizens of France and the Netherlands, which had both committed to holding referenda, rejected it (share of vote opposing the treaty: France, 55 per cent; the Netherlands, 67 per cent). The ratification process was eventually abandoned since any treaty requires the unanimous support of all member states. The French and Dutch rejections threw the EU into a deep crisis. For the first time in its history, two of its founding members had blocked the integration process. It was clear that a growing gap between political leaders and voters was emerging, and this constitutional crisis was a sign of rising Euroscepticism across many parts of the EU (Dinan, Nugent and Paterson 2017).

After a period of reflection, in which there was limited appetite to re-engage in a constitutional debate, Germany took the initiative and during its presidency of the first half of 2007, initiated a discussion on how to proceed. Given the wide range of reasons behind the 'no' votes in France and the Netherlands, with some of them contradictory and others relating to domestic rather than EU-level issues, it was difficult to interpret what the votes meant in terms of citizens' views on the actual treaty. It was also assumed that the sentiments expressed by the 'no' votes in France and the Netherlands were not necessarily shared across the EU (Church and Phinnemore 2016). After all, citizens in Spain and Luxembourg had already voted in favour of the Constitutional Treaty. Another IGC was launched to identify and address the concerns expressed specifically about the Constitutional Treaty and to negotiate a conventional amending treaty, rather than a new constitutional treaty. The work of the IGC took place during the Portuguese presidency and resulted in the Lisbon Treaty, which was signed in December 2007.

While the Lisbon Treaty dropped the word 'constitution' and references to symbols, such as the EU flag, anthem and motto, it incorporated most of the institutional content of the Constitutional Treaty but was far less accessible. The double voting majority system in the Council was adopted and extended to new policy areas. The Charter of Fundamental Rights became legally binding, although Poland and the UK secured a protocol limiting its application in their respective countries. The powers of the EP were increased, the size of the Commission reduced and the new post of president of the European Council was established.

As for the minister for foreign affairs, the title was changed to high representative of the Union for foreign affairs and security policy, but the role and responsibilities remained the same as those set out in the Constitutional Treaty. By making this person both the vice president of the Commission and the chair of the Foreign Affairs Council, it was hoped the coherence and effectiveness of the EU's external engagement would increase. A new European External Action Service was established to support the high representative. The need for greater collective action in international affairs had become more pressing with the rise of emerging powers, as well as the challenges facing the EU in its neighbourhood to the East, especially Russia.

During 2008, the Lisbon Treaty underwent parliamentary ratification in twenty-six out of the twenty-seven member states. Only Ireland held a referendum on the treaty, and 53 per cent of voters opposed it. In addition to the lack of information about the treaty, some of the reasons for the 'no' vote were concerns about the reduced size of the Commission, which could lead to Ireland losing 'its' commissioner, and the threat to Irish neutrality as well as its ban on abortion. So yet again, the Irish government had to secure guarantees from the other member states. It was agreed that the number of commissioners would continue to be equal to the number of member states and that Ireland's neutrality and abortion ban would not be affected by the treaty (Church and Phinnemore 2016). Following these guarantees, Ireland held a second referendum, in which 67 per cent voted in favour of ratification. Once all member states had ratified the treaty, it entered into force in December 2009.

The Lisbon Treaty concluded a continuous, albeit far from smooth, reform process since the Amsterdam Treaty. The process reflected a deepening of EU integration to make the Union able to function effectively with an increasing number of member states. The changes brought into effect by the Lisbon Treaty were seen to have achieved 'a stable constitutional equilibrium', making the EU able to enlarge and reform without additional treaty reform (Moravcsik 2007). The ratification difficulties, which had exposed increasing levels of Euroscepticism, had also led to a sense of 'reform fatigue', making EU leaders reluctant to engage in another treaty reform process (McCormick 2020). In addition, there were a number of other looming crises that would require much of their attention over the next few years.

# 3. From crisis to crisis

## The eurozone crisis, 2008–15

The ratification process of the Lisbon Treaty coincided with the beginning of the global financial crisis in 2007–9. The crisis started in the United States but quickly spread to the rest of the world. In Europe a combination of a growth, banking and sovereign debt problem led to the eurozone crisis (see Chapter 10 and Tooze 2018). The crisis, which peaked in 2010–12 but lasted for many years, was the most serious financial and economic crisis in Europe since the Second World War, and it was perceived as 'existentially threatening' to the EU, given the importance attached to the EMU in the integration process (Dyson 2017, 65).

The establishment of the EMU and the subsequent introduction of the single currency, the euro, in 1999 had proceeded relatively smoothly. The euro became an important and tangible symbol of EU integration and was seen as one the EU's main policy achievements (Dinan, Nugent and Paterson 2017). Granted, there had been some scepticism towards the project, particularly in the UK, Denmark and Sweden, which decided not to adopt the euro. Germans were reluctant to give up the deutschmark, which was seen as closely linked to the German 'economic miracle' after the Second World War, but in the end, they saw it as a way of reconfirming their commitment to the EU following German reunification after the end of the Cold War. Once the euro coins and notes were in full circulation from 2002, there was generally strong support for the euro across the EU (McCormick 2020).

However, the eurozone crisis brought out the underlying structural weaknesses of the EMU, as set out in the Maastricht Treaty. On the one hand, it had established strong integration of monetary policies, with the creation of the European Central Bank (ECB), a single monetary policy and a single currency. On the other hand, the integration of economic policies remained limited, with member states maintaining significant control over their fiscal policies. In addition, the convergence criteria for joining the euro had not been followed by all member states, and many had developed significant budget deficits. Economic structures and policies thus diverged widely between the eurozone countries. These divergences meant that the crisis affected countries in different ways, and a cleavage between 'core' and 'periphery' countries emerged.

The core countries, with Germany at the centre, were impacted less dramatically by the crisis, whereas the periphery countries, in particular Greece, Ireland, Portugal, Spain (the so-called GIPS countries) as well as Cyprus and Italy, went through severe financial and economic turmoil (Laffan 2017). During the lead-up to the crisis, the periphery countries, mostly situated in Southern Europe, had accumulated a significant amount of public debt by borrowing extensively from the core countries in the North. Once the crisis hit, it became clear that they would no longer be able to repay their debts. Given the 'incomplete governance architecture' of the EMU (Jones, Kelemen and Meunier 2016, 1011) and the lack of economic integration, there were no clear processes to follow or a mechanism that would automatically transfer money from central funds to countries in need. Instead, member states had to decide how to deal with the crisis.

In the years that followed, frequent emergency meetings of the European Council were held. Here, Germany, as the biggest member state with the strongest economy, under the leadership of Chancellor Angela Merkel (Box 4.2 and Figure 4.1), came to play a decisive role (Bulmer and Paterson 2017). There was a clear divide between Chancellor Merkel, supported by

FIGURE 4.1 *High-level meeting between (left to right) Jean-Claude Juncker, Commission president; Xi Jinping, president of the People's Republic of China; Emmanuel Macron, president of France; and Angela Merkel, German chancellor, Paris, 26 March 2019. Courtesy of European Union, 2019.*

# BOX 4.2  ANGELA MERKEL

One of the most influential political leaders during these thirty years was the German Chancellor Angela Merkel. Growing up in East Germany, she witnessed the construction of the Berlin Wall in 1961, as well as its fall in 1989, at the age of thirty-five. She studied physics and earned a PhD in quantum physics before entering politics. In 1990 she joined the Christian Democratic Union (CDU), and in the first post-reunification election of that year, she won a seat in the Bundestag, the German federal parliament. She was elected head of the CDU in 2000, and in 2005 she became Germany's first female and youngest person to be elected chancellor.

During the following fifteen years, she came to be seen as a 'de facto leader of the European Union' (Vick and Schuster 2015). She was committed to the EU integration process and played a key role in its decision-making and development. As a leader, she has been described as calm and pragmatic, wanting to have all the facts before making a decision. She preferred thorough analysis to rash decision-making and was prone to compromise and consensus building – key skills in German and EU politics. While Merkel was willing to change direction because of new information, she had a few core principles she would not trade away.

Throughout the eurozone crisis she was determined to save the euro, which she saw as central to the future of the EU itself. In her own words: 'If the euro fails, then Europe fails' (Merkel 2011). She drew from her own experience of economic collapse in East Germany following the fall of the Berlin Wall and stressed the need for financial support for the indebted Southern eurozone members, in particular Greece. However, she made it clear that such support was dependent on the debtor countries reforming and putting their public finances in order. She became known as the taskmaster of austerity, an approach ardently opposed by those it was imposed upon. Yet, the commitment to austerity prevailed.

A defining moment of her leadership was in 2015, when she opened Germany's borders to people fleeing war and instability in Syria and elsewhere, convinced that it was the right thing to do morally and legally. Although it was seen as an unpopular move by many, both in Germany and elsewhere in the EU, it was a principle she was not willing to give up on. At the European Council meeting of October 2015, she responded to a proposal by Hungary's President Victor Orbán to erect fences and introduce border controls within the Schengen area by referring to her experience from East Germany: 'I have lived a long time behind a fence, it is not something I wish to do again' (Qvortrup 2017). To many, she personified the new, open and tolerant Germany, which distanced itself from its past.

other leaders of core countries, and the leaders of the periphery countries on how to solve the crisis. The core countries saw the necessity of making funds available to save the euro and avoid scenarios such as 'Grexit', where Greece would have to leave the euro, which would have severe effects on all eurozone countries. However, they pushed for strict austerity policies to be followed as a way of reducing public debt. Many of the periphery countries, on the other hand, argued that such policies would hamper economic growth further.

Member states eventually agreed on a number of extensive bailouts and financial instruments, such as a permanent rescue fund. However, these instruments were accompanied by measures introducing tighter economic and fiscal controls to ensure governments operated within balanced budgets.

These new measures, together with the establishment of a banking union and a strengthened role for the ECB, reflected a significant move towards further financial and economic integration, which in the end supported the EU's recovery from the crisis. As has often been the case in the history of the EU, a crisis highlighted weaknesses in previously agreed policies or structures, and member states responded by pursuing further integration. However, the cleavage between the Northern core and the Southern periphery came to have a significant and lasting impact, not least politically.

This was seen in election results across EU member states, as well as in the EP elections of 2014, where Eurosceptic parties on both the radical left and the radical right increased their vote share. In the Northern European creditor countries, radical right parties (including France's National Front, Alternative for Germany and the Dutch Freedom Party) performed well on a platform of hostility towards the European project and further integration. A narrative emerged, which blamed the irresponsible Southern debtor countries or the EU's inefficiency for the crisis. In the Southern debtor countries, it was instead the radical left parties (including Greece's Syriza and Spain's Podemos) that did well, pushing an anti-austerity agenda. They did not oppose the European project as such but expressed criticism towards the stringent conditions associated with the bail-out programmes. They wanted an EU which reflected more solidarity between member states (Hobolt 2015).

# The migration crisis, 2014–17

Just as the eurozone crisis started to wane, another exogenous shock hit the EU. In 2014 there was a sharp rise in the number of people fleeing from war and instability in Syria, Iraq, Afghanistan and North Africa. Many of them, in particular those who escaped from the civil war in Syria, ended up in Jordan, Lebanon and Turkey, but there came a point when these countries could no longer accommodate everybody, and Europe was the next place of refuge. The so-called migrant crisis that subsequently developed was a result of widely diverging positions within the EU on how to respond to the situation, and a lack of solidarity between member states, as well as towards the migrants. The border-free Schengen area, which symbolizes one of the founding principles of European integration – that of free movement – was threatened, as member states introduced temporary border restrictions and controls between internal Schengen borders.

The large number of crossings into the EU exposed the flaws of the EU's migration and common asylum policies. The Schengen area had abolished internal border controls between the member states and established a common external border. However, responsibility for policing this external border and processing asylum requests remained with the individual member states. The EU's 'Dublin system' stipulated that unless there were specific criteria, such as family unity, asylum applications must be processed by the first member state to which asylum seekers arrive. This put immense pressure on frontline countries, in particular Greece and Italy, which were already hard hit by the eurozone crisis. From July 2015 to May 2016 alone, 1 million people applied for asylum (Buonanno 2017, 102). Without an EU-wide system in place to support these countries, they were eventually unable to conduct their asylum procedures and allowed migrants to move onto other Schengen countries.

Just as in the eurozone crisis, the positions between member states on how to respond to this situation diverged. Some member states advocated for an open approach. As it became clear that the EU would be a destination for people fleeing war for years to come, Swedish Prime Minister Fredrik Reinfeldt pleaded for people to 'open their hearts' and welcome the refugees (Milne 2014). In a similar spirit, German Chancellor Angela Merkel announced that her country was open to refugees, declaring that 'we will manage' (Delcker 2015). However, this approach was met by fierce opposition from other member states, not least the CEECs, and in particular Hungary and Slovenia, which became transit countries. The frontline countries, on their part, lamented the lack of EU support and solidarity from other member states.

In response to the crisis, the Commission presented a relocation proposal, obliging all Schengen members to accept a proportionate number of migrants from Italy and Greece. The destination and frontline countries supported the proposal, but it was opposed by the CEECs, which saw it as a costly scheme infringing on their sovereignty (Nugent 2017). As a result, it was never fully implemented. Instead, the EU reached a temporary agreement with Turkey in 2016. In exchange for Turkey imposing stricter border controls, and taking back Syrian migrants who reached the EU illegally, the EU agreed to provide financial assistance and re-energize Turkey's accession negotiations. This agreement contributed to a decline in the number of migrants reaching the EU from Turkey.

Although steps were taken, such as increasing the size and funding of Frontex – the EU's Boarder and Coast Guard Agency – this crisis did not lead to further integration, as had been the case in the eurozone crisis. Instead, many member states moved away from the EU's core principle of free movement by temporarily suspending the Schengen regime and erecting fences and introducing border controls. This crisis also highlighted, once again, the volatility of the EU's neighbourhood and the need for the EU to play a more effective role internationally. Closer cooperation with countries in the Southern and Eastern neighbourhood around migration was indeed identified as one of the priorities of the EU's security strategy drawn up by its high representative Federica Mogherini in 2016.

Like the eurozone crisis, the migration crisis generated a rise in Euroscepticism, particularly on the political right. Right-wing Eurosceptic parties performed well both nationally (in particular in Italy in 2018) and in the EP elections of 2019. These parties mobilized around an anti-immigration agenda – an agenda that also contributed to the result of the UK referendum in 2016 (Hobolt 2016).

# Brexit, 2016–21

In June 2016 another crisis hit the EU when the UK voted to leave the EU by 52 to 48 per cent in a referendum. Although the UK had been described as a somewhat 'awkward partner' (George 1994), with its many opt-outs from EU policies (including the EMU, Schengen and Charter of Fundamental Rights) and its high levels of Euroscepticism, the result came as a shock to the EU. It was a significant setback that one of its biggest and most powerful member states would leave the Union. Despite its 'awkwardness', the UK had played a key role in the integration and development of the EU, not least in the establishment of the Single Market and through its strong support for enlargement (Chapter 17). It had also been an influential member state in EU trade, development and climate change policies. And through its diplomatic clout, military capabilities and permanent seat at the United Nations Security Council, it had contributed to the EU's global ambitions.

Yet, despite the shock and regret of the referendum result, the EU started preparing for the Brexit process. One of the innovations of the failed Constitutional Treaty, which was pasted into the Lisbon Treaty, was Article 50, which for the first time set out the process to be followed in case a member state chose to leave the EU. There was consequently a legal basis for the Brexit process. The EU-27 and the UK had to negotiate a withdrawal agreement, setting out the terms of the UK's exit. The main aim was to minimize the disruption caused by Brexit and reach agreement on citizens' rights, the UK's financial commitments and how to avoid a hard border on the island of Ireland, which would become an external border of the EU when the UK left. After more than two years of negotiations, and a number of failed ratification attempts on the UK side, an agreement was eventually reached and ratified, and the UK left the EU on 31 January 2020 after forty-seven years of membership. For the first time in its history, the EU saw a reduction in the number of member states.

Although the UK was no longer an EU member, the Withdrawal Agreement provided for a transition period during which it would remain part of the Single Market and customs union, while the two parties negotiated an agreement on their future relationship. As a result, there was another year of negotiations, leading to the EU–UK Trade and Cooperation Agreement, which was signed in December 2020 and entered into force on 1 January 2021.

After the constitutional, eurozone and migration crises, Brexit clearly added further uncertainty to the EU's future. Yet, it also differed from previous crises. Rather than leading to widely divergent positions between the member states, Brexit generated unprecedented levels of unity among the EU-27. For them, it was a question of minimizing the negative effects resulting from Brexit and maintaining the integrity of the Single Market (Frennhoff Larsén and Khorana 2020). In addition, while Brexit itself reflected increasing Euroscepticism, the levels of support for the EU actually increased during the course of the Brexit negotiations. The process proved more difficult and complex than expected, and it highlighted some of the benefits of EU membership. Consequently, the initial expectations that Brexit might trigger other member states to leave the Union did not materialize. Instead, polls indicated growing levels of support for the EU among its citizens (Eurobarometer 2019). And although Eurosceptic right-wing parties performed well in the EP elections of 2019, many of them had toned down their principled opposition to EU membership (the UK's Brexit Party being a clear exception). In addition, there were surprise victories for many pro-integrationist parties (Treib 2020).

However, Euroscepticism has far from disappeared, and the long-term consequences of Brexit are still unknown. The Brexit vote certainly served as a wake-up call for the EU and intensified the discussion about the nature and future direction of EU cooperation.

Just as the UK was leaving the EU, the Union was faced with yet another crisis. When the global Covid-19 pandemic emerged, member states initially responded by adopting national measure with little EU coordination. However, over time a more coordinated response emerged, particularly on the development and distribution of the vaccines. Whether this crisis will lead to more unity among the member states and further integration in the area of health policy remains to be seen. Covid-19 will also test the EU's commitment to playing a more influential role internationally by ensuring equitable access to vaccines across the globe. As of now, there is a long way to go.

# Five key questions

1. Why did the EU expand so considerably following the end of the Cold War?
2. What effects did enlargement have on the EU?
3. Why did EU treaty reform become necessary in the 1990s and early 2020s?
4. Why was Euroscepticism on the rise in many EU member states?
5. What factors prevented the EU from devising an effective and united response to the eurozone and migration crises?

# Ten key readings

Börzel, T., A. Dimitrova and F. Schimmelfennig (2018), *European Union Enlargement and Integration Capacity*, London: Routledge.

Bressanelli, E., and N. Chelotti (eds) (2021), 'What Brexit Means for Europe: EU Institutions and Actors after the British Referendum', *Politics and Governance*, 9 (1) [special issue on Brexit].

Craig, P. (2013), *The Lisbon Treaty: Law, Politics, and Treaty Reform*, Oxford: Oxford University Press.

Dinan, D., N. Nugent and W. E. Paterson (eds) (2017), *The European Union in Crisis*, London: Palgrave.

Kaiser, W., and J. Elvert (2005), *European Union Enlargement: A Comparative History*, London: Routledge.

Laursen, F. (ed.) (2008), *The Rise and Fall of the EU's Constitutional Treaty*, Nijhoff: Brill.

Marelli, E., and M. Signorelli (2017), *Europe and the Euro: Integration, Crisis and Policies*, London: Palgrave Macmillan.

McCormick, J. (2020), *European Union Politics*, London: Macmillan International.

Ther, P. (2016), *Europe since 1989: A History*, Princeton, NJ: Princeton University Press.

Vassilou, G. (2007), *The Accession Story: The EU from 15 to 25 Countries*, Oxford: Oxford University Press.

# PART II

# Institutions and Policies

## Institutions

# Introduction: EU institutions and the development of a trans- and supranational European community

## *Katja Seidel*

This section explores three of the European Union's (EU) core institutions – the European Commission, the Court of Justice and the European Parliament (EP) – analysing their role and evolution in EU history. The Council of Ministers and the European Council will not be discussed in a separate chapter. Rather, both institutions are referred to in most chapters in this volume (see especially Chapter 2 for the Council of Ministers and Chapter 3 for the European Council).

The Council of Ministers has existed since 1957. It is the main decision-making organ of the EU, a role that more recently it has come to share with the EP. In the Council of Ministers elected government ministers of the member states meet and take policy decisions on proposals from the European Commission resulting in EU regulations, directives and decisions.

The European Council had not been conceived of by the drafters of the Treaty of Rome in 1957 and was only formally written into the Maastricht Treaty (1992) (Chapters 3 and 10). Since its creation in December 1974 the European Council has assumed a leadership role in the Union. The European Council consists of the heads of state and government of the member states who meet regularly to take decisions on important issues and to agree on the overall political direction of the Union.

The Council of Ministers and the European Council can be described as the 'intergovernmental institutions' of the EU, representing the elected governments of member states. However, when member states resort to qualified majority voting (as has increasingly been the practice since 1987), the Council is in itself transformed into a supranational institution.

In contrast, the three institutions discussed in this section are often referred to as the 'supranational' institutions of the EU as they are nominally independent from the member states and are meant to have the interests of the EU at heart. An analysis of their emergence and development, as well as the decisions and events that have shaped them, will contribute to a better understanding of the EU and how it works. These institutions fulfilled a key function in the development of a transnational and supranational Union that in many respects differs from other international organizations.

It is however important to bear in mind that no single Community institution exists or works in isolation. Each institution plays a different role in the EU and is part of a European political system that has evolved over the past seven decades. Community institutions as well as the member states are components of what political scientists have termed 'multilevel governance' in the EU (Hooghe and Marks 2001). There are other, less important, institutions that are part of this multilevel governance. For example, the Treaty of Rome also provided for an Economic and Social Committee where representatives of employers, trade unions and other interest groups meet to discuss and comment on Community legislation – without having the power of changing it. Other examples include the European Court of Auditors, created in 1977 to oversee the finances and budget of the Union, and the European Anti-Fraud Office (OLAF), created in 1999 to investigate fraud and corruption in EU institutions and the member states linked to EU funds.

# 5

# The European Commission: A government in the making?

## Katja Seidel

## Introduction

When sceptics of European integration refer to 'Europe' or 'Brussels', they usually have the European Commission in mind, which they regard as a faceless and unwieldy bureaucracy that has nothing better to do than impose nonsensical rules on bent bananas on hapless European citizens. It has been difficult for this institution to debunk such myths, not least because national governments and media often blame the Commission for unpopular policies and decisions even if these were taken by the Council of Ministers, the elected government representatives of the member states. The Commission is a unique organization. It resembles a secretariat of an international organization (IO), but it is in fact closer to a national government administration. Some have wanted it to become the executive in a European government, but it lacks the executive powers and the democratic legitimacy of a national government. The best scholars have come up with is to call the Commission a 'hybrid' organization to do justice to its many roles and functions (Nugent and Rhinard 2015).

The Commission, together with the European Parliament (EP) and the Court of Justice of the European Union (CJEU), is considered to be one of the 'supranational' institutions of the European Union (EU), acting independently of member states, whose interests are represented in the Council of Ministers and, since 1974, the European Council.

In recent years, particularly since the Maastricht Treaty (1992) when the European Economic Community (EEC) became the EU, the legitimacy of the Commission has been questioned. The Commission's considerable gain in competences since the 1990s, as well as the increased scrutiny of the EU in the member states, has given rise to a widespread discourse of the 'democratic deficit' of the EU with the Commission as an unelected bureaucracy at the centre. The Commission's legitimacy was initially thought to come from sources other than those linked to democratically sanctioned *input* legitimacy such as elections. Efficiency, expertise and high-quality proposals were among the sources of the Commission's legitimacy, referred to as *output* legitimacy (Schmidt 2013). The diverse national, linguistic and professional background of Commission staff, the European civil servants, was also considered an asset and a source of legitimacy. Their profound knowledge of the Union's member states, societies, cultures and economies has certainly been helpful for relevant policy formulation within the Commission (Seidel 2010a). But at the same time the Commission has not been able or willing to remain an unpolitical actor. Time and again it has aspired to a role of political leadership in the Community, and it has had to address the issue of its perceived lack of legitimacy and accountability, though with little success.

The Commission's role as an independent 'supranational' administration has been at the centre of many of the EU's crises. The Union's institutional developments, including the question how much power the Commission should have (and, linked to this, how much power member states should abandon), has been discussed controversially since the 1960s. Politicians such as French President Charles de Gaulle in the 1960s or British Prime Minister Margaret Thatcher in the 1980s resented what they felt was too much influence for an unelected administrative body encroaching on the sovereignty of member states. This can be linked to the continued tensions in European integration between preferences for intergovernmental and supranational integration, between member state control over the process of European integration and strong and independent Community institutions.

The tensions between democratic legitimacy and bureaucratic expertise as well as between supranational and intergovernmental visions for European integration provide the backdrop for this chapter. The first part of the chapter outlines the structure and internal functioning of the Commission. Proceeding chronologically, the focus will then be on three periods of the Commission's history. For ease, these periods are named after the Commission presidents of the time, even though the focus will not (only) be on the presidents: the Hallstein Commission (1958–67), the Jenkins Commission (1976–80) and the Delors Commission (1984–94). Each of these periods presented the Commission with opportunities and constraints, some of them internal, others external. The final part of the chapter addresses the Commission's development since the millennium.

# 1. How the Commission functions

## The formal and informal powers of the Commission

The core principle of the EU, distinguishing it from many other IOs, is that members delegate a portion of their sovereignty to independent agencies such as the Commission, the EP and the CJEU. The Treaty on European Union (TEU) outlines the formal powers of the Commission (Box 5.1).

## BOX 5.1 TREATY ON EUROPEAN UNION. TITLE III: PROVISIONS ON THE INSTITUTIONS – ARTICLE 17

1. The Commission shall promote the general interest of the Union and take appropriate initiatives to that end. It shall ensure the application of the Treaties, and of measures adopted by the institutions pursuant to them. It shall oversee the application of Union law under the control of the Court of Justice of the European Union. It shall execute the budget and manage programmes. It shall exercise coordinating, executive and management functions, as laid down in the Treaties. With the exception of the common foreign and security policy, and other cases provided for in the Treaties, it shall ensure the Union's external representation. It shall initiate the Union's annual and multiannual programming with a view to achieving interinstitutional agreements.
2. Union legislative acts may only be adopted on the basis of a Commission proposal, except where the Treaties provide otherwise. Other acts shall be adopted on the basis of a Commission proposal where the Treaties so provide.

In the EU the Commission has the *right of initiative*. This means that the Council of Ministers can only decide on a matter if it has a proposal from the Commission before it. The Council can only amend a Commission proposal if it decides so unanimously (but it can reject or accept it outright). As *guardian of the treaty*, the Commission has to act impartially. It oversees implementation of Community rules and legislation. It can decide that an infringement of the treaty or Community legislation has taken place and take action, for example, by sending a letter to a member state or a business, asking it to explain and remedy the matter. In case of further non-compliance, the Commission can forward the matter to the court. In the special case of competition policy, the Commission can investigate agreements between businesses and even impose fines and penalties on businesses contravening competition rules. Such and other powers have been delegated to the Commission either through the treaties or decisions of the member states. The powers the Commission holds in various policy areas differ; they depend on the policy area and member states' willingness to abandon sovereignty.

Finally, the Commission is *in charge of external relations*, particularly commercial negotiations – at the General Agreement on Tariffs and Trade (GATT), later the World Trade Organization (WTO) – and more recently also the Brexit negotiations. During such negotiations the Commission follows a brief it has been given by the member states. It is also in charge of association agreements and of representing the Community in enlargement negotiations (see Chapter 14). The Treaty of Lisbon (2007) created a new office, the EU's high representative of the Union for foreign affairs and security policy. The high representative is one of the Commission's vice presidents and chairs the Foreign Affairs Council, thus providing a unique link between the Commission and the Council of Ministers in a policy area where member states are keen to maintain their sovereignty and freedom of action, but where close collaboration among them is often deemed desirable.

In addition to the powers conferred upon it by the treaty, the Commission has acquired a number of *informal powers*. As the treaty requires the Commission to act independently of national interests and representing the European interest, its role is to discern the common European interest and to promote it through its initiatives and proposals. In the literature the Commission is often referred to as an 'honest broker' as its role in Council negotiations, intergovernmental conferences on treaty reform and enlargement negotiations is to bring about agreement.

## The college of commissioners

The term 'Commission' refers to the institution itself and to the small group of people leading the Commission, also called the college of commissioners. The commissioners provide the institution with political leadership. Each commissioner is in charge of one or several policy areas. Between 1958 and 1973 the Commission had nine commissioners – two for the large member states and one each for the smaller member states. In 1973, when the UK, Denmark and Ireland joined the Community, the number of commissioners was increased to thirteen; the UK nominated two commissioners, Ireland and Denmark nominated one each. With each enlargement, the number of commissioners increased. Now each of the twenty-seven member states has one commissioner.

In 2001 a system of rotating commissioners was envisaged, with two-thirds of member states being represented in the Commission at any one time from 2014 onwards (TEU Article 17.5). In fact, this change was never implemented as member states feel, rightly or wrongly, that 'their' commissioner represents their interests within the Commission, even though commissioners are meant to be impartial. In fact, the treaty (TEU Article 17.3) enshrines the independence of commissioners and asks member states to respect their independence. Commissioners are nominated for a term lasting five years.

As the commissioners are nominated by elected national governments, the Commission can be argued to have democratic legitimacy, albeit an indirect one. While it is still up to the member states to nominate the president of the Commission, since 1993, the EP has played a more important role in the nomination and the scrutiny of the president and commissioners. Member states nominate their preferred members of the Commission in consultation with the designated commission president. Each candidate for the Commission has to undergo a hearing in the EP, which can reject individual candidates. It did so, for example, in 2019 with the candidates from France, Hungary and Romania. The college of commissioners as a whole also needs to be voted in by the EP.

The role of the commission president, previously seen as a *primus inter pares* (a first among equals), has been enhanced in recent years – both formally through treaty changes and informally. Nowadays the commission president, rather than member state governments, allocates portfolios to the other commissioners and nominates the vice presidents, except for the high representative of the Union for foreign affairs and security policy, who is selected by the European Council and automatically becomes a vice president (TEU Article 17.6). The president can ask a commissioner to resign. The president also proposes a political programme upon investiture. However, there are limits to what has been called the 'presidentialization' of the Commission (Nugent and Rhinard 2015); decisions are still taken collectively by the college of commissioners, in the Commission's weekly meetings. The commissioners seek to reach consensus in their decisions, but they can and do resort to a vote (one vote per commissioner, including the president) if disagreements persist.

## The directorates-general and the services

Between 1958 and 2021 the Commission's administration grew from around one thousand to just over thirty-two thousand civil servants (Seidel 2010a; European Commission 2021). As the EU's competences expanded over time to include new policy areas, the number of directorates-general (DGs) and services also multiplied, from eleven in 1958 to forty-five in 2021. Staff working at the Commission forms part of a European civil service. The key principle of the European civil service is its independence from the member states, though national interests and influence from member states do penetrate the Commission. Competitive entrance exams take place regularly across the Union to create a pool of applicants to recruit from.

An additional criterion for recruitment is the national origin of candidates, as the Commission endeavours to ensure that no member state is unduly over- or under-represented in its services. This obviously contradicts the idea of an independent civil service, but it is arguably necessary to increase the legitimacy of the Commission as it ensures member states feel represented by the Commission and its staff. Like the commissioners, European civil servants bring different viewpoints to the Commission; they come from different cultures and have different linguistic backgrounds. In Brussels they work in a multinational environment. While commissioners change every few years, European civil servants represent continuity, many spending their entire careers in the Commission and often developing strong pro-European attitudes and convictions.

## 2. From honeymoon to crisis: The Hallstein Commission, 1958–67

The Commission's administration had to be created from scratch when the EEC Treaty entered into force on 1 January 1958. The first president of the EEC Commission, Walter Hallstein (1958–67), had an ambitious vision for the Commission and its role in the Community. Hallstein, a German law professor, former secretary of state in the German Foreign Ministry and an ardent European federalist, conceived of the Commission as the future government of a United States of Europe. The administrative decisions when setting up the institution in the late 1950s and early 1960s were therefore at the same time practical and highly political. Hallstein wanted the Commission to be a strong, independent and permanent organization. He therefore modelled the DGs to resemble national ministries. Like ministers in national governments, each commissioner was put in charge of one or more policy areas managed by DGs (Seidel 2010).

The commissioners in the Hallstein Commission were on the whole a talented group of men (there were no female commissioners until 1989). Many of them had been former ministers in their home countries. All were convinced Europeans, though they differed in their views on how far integration should go and how powerful an institution such as the Commission should be. It is therefore important to acknowledge that the Commission is not a monolithic block. Each commissioner came to Brussels with his specific national, cultural and political background.

Most commissioners are politicians; in the 1960s most were either Christian Democrats, like Hallstein, or Social Democrats/Socialists, like the

French Commissioner Robert Marjolin. While each commissioner was in charge of a policy area such as agriculture, proposals that the Commission wanted to submit to the Council of Ministers for decision needed to be approved in the weekly meetings of the commissioners (Figure 5.1). Here proposals were discussed in frank exchanges, and if no unanimous decision was possible, the commissioners voted on a proposal. For instance, the German Commissioner Hans von der Groeben was rather sceptical about the common agricultural policy (CAP) that Dutch Commissioner Sicco Mansholt and his staff designed as he regarded the policy as too protectionist. Commissioners' different approaches to economic policy is another theme that runs through the history of the Commission. In the Hallstein Commission, von der Groeben preferred a liberal economic policy where competition rules provided the framework for behaviour of businesses in

FIGURE 5.1 *The last meeting of the Hallstein Commission, 1967. Hallstein sits furthest to the right. Courtesy of European Communities, 1967.*

the Common Market, while Marjolin felt that an EEC-wide programme of economic planning was the way forward (Seidel 2016; Warlouzet 2019a). These views largely reflected those of the German and French governments at the time.

Hallstein's vision of a United States of Europe with strong supranational institutions clashed with French President de Gaulle's vision of an intergovernmental Europe of nation states and limited influence of supranational institutions. In 1965 Hallstein took a gamble which propelled the Community into a crisis and demonstrated the limits of supranational integration. In the spring of 1965, the Commission proposed a regulation to ensure the financing of the CAP, controversially combining this with the establishment of the Community's own income from customs tariffs as well as a new procedure for adopting the Community budget which would strengthen the budgetary powers of the EP. The Commission's quest to strengthen the EP was motivated by the wish to increase its own accountability and legitimacy.

Hallstein thought that the strong interest the French had in the CAP would override de Gaulle's reluctance to strengthen Community institutions. Not all members of the Commission agreed with Hallstein's move. Marjolin doubted that the French government would agree to the proposed trade off given de Gaulle's hostility towards supranational integration. He felt Hallstein was going too far, but he was outvoted in the Commission. Marjolin was right; instead of agreeing to the deal, the French government interrupted the negotiations and decided to boycott the Community for six months, a period known as the empty chair crisis (Chapter 2).

In spite of the crisis, the balance sheet of the Hallstein Commission is overall quite impressive. In its first decade, the Commission played a vital role in implementing the Treaty of Rome, accelerating the timetable for creating the customs union by eighteen months as well as designing the CAP and common competition rules (Chapters 2, 8 and 9). The Commission also assumed an important role in external trade negotiations, for example, in the GATT (Chapter 14).

However, given the vast scope of the EEC Treaty, the Commission did not succeed in establishing other policies provided for in the treaty, for instance, a common transport policy or a common economic policy, as in these areas member state interests were diverging too far to find common solutions. The successes of the Hallstein Commission were due to a favourable context of a general pro-integration attitude in the member states, good general economic conditions and a competent Commission with on the whole a talented and enthusiastic staff. Relations became more frayed in the mid-1960s. It was then that member state differences over individual policies, but also over larger questions such as the future development of Community institutions, came to the fore. This limited the role the Commission was able to play in the integration process. Thus the Commission's efficiency not only depends on the efficiency of its services, its expertise, the quality of its proposals and its leadership but also on external circumstances such as member states' interests and willingness to cooperate.

# 3. The Commission in the 1970s

During the 1970s the Commission grappled with two sets of problems. The first related to its own organizational structure: in 1967 the High Authority of the European Coal and Steel Community and the Commissions of the EEC and the European Atomic Energy Community (Euratom) were merged to form a single Commission. (Euratom was founded alongside the EEC in 1957; it also had a Commission consisting of five members.) The first enlargement in 1973 added to these organizational problems as the Commission needed to accommodate staff from three new member states, the UK, Denmark and Ireland, who brought with them new languages and administrative cultures. The second set of problems related to the more challenging political and economic context of the 1970s, reducing the appetite of EEC member states for supranational integration and a strong Commission. The oil crisis of 1973 curbed economic growth and led to unemployment and high inflation rates in the member states.

For most of the 1970s, the Commission had weaker presidents who did not have the political clout or strength to assert themselves in such challenging times. This was also due to the reluctance of the member states to appoint another strong president like Hallstein. Hallstein's immediate successor was the Belgian Jean Rey (1967–70). Rey was a veteran of European integration and had been a member of the Hallstein Commission since 1958. But his time in office was too short for him to make his mark. His successor, the Italian Franco Maria Malfatti (1970–2), only stayed in the Commission for a short time, preferring to return to Italian domestic politics where he became a mere member of parliament in Rome. The Dutchman Sicco Mansholt (1972–3) took over from Malfatti as a caretaker until the new Commission under the Frenchman François-Xavier Ortoli (1973–6) took office. Ortoli had been a high-flying civil servant in the French administration. At the age of thirty-two he had been the youngest director-general in the Commission in 1958–61 before returning to Paris to take charge of the administration coordinating French European policy, the Secrétariat Général du Comité Interministériel (SGCI), and later becoming a minister under Presidents Charles de Gaulle and Georges Pompidou. In 1973 he returned to Brussels as Commission president. Ortoli was highly experienced and convinced of the benefits of European integration, but he was not someone who would confront the member states preferring a more conciliatory style than Hallstein. The Ortoli Commission now included thirteen members as commissioners from the new member states, Denmark, Ireland and the UK, joined.

While the 1970s certainly presented the Commission with a difficult economic context, historians now consider the 1970s in fact as a period in which many new European integration initiatives and policies were initiated (Chapter 3). While in many areas the Hallstein Commission was guided by firm timetables in the EEC Treaty, for example, when setting up the customs union and the CAP, by the 1970s these policies were largely completed. In the 1970s new policy initiatives emerged; some of these were policies contained in the treaty that had not been a priority in the 1960s but obtained more urgency in the 1970s due to external economic circumstances such as regional policy or monetary cooperation. The Commission also started developing policy areas that were not explicitly mentioned in the EEC Treaty. Environmental policy is such an example. Here the Commission worked closely with other EEC institutions such as the EP. It also responded to wider concerns in society about the environment (Chapter 11).

In 1976 Roy Jenkins succeeded Ortoli as Commission president. Jenkins is regarded as another strong Commission president. He was a prominent UK Labour party politician and an ardent supporter of UK membership in the EEC. His nomination was widely supported, including by France and Germany. Jenkins identified monetary stability as the focus of his presidency. He launched the idea of creating a European Monetary System (EMS) in late 1977 and focused in particular on persuading the leaders of the large member states, France, Germany and the UK, of his plan (Ludlow 2016). Rather symptomatically for the tendencies towards intergovernmentalism and the limited influence of the Commission of the period it was German Chancellor Helmut Schmidt and French President Valéry Giscard d'Estaing who made sure that the EMS saw the light of day in March 1979 (Mourlon-Druol 2012a). At the same time, Jenkins successfully fought for a place for the Commission president at the table of the G7, a forum of the seven largest industrial nations created in the mid-1970s. The 1970s appeared to be a difficult period for the Commission and the EEC as a whole, with challenging external conditions and less willingness by the member states to embrace far-reaching integration initiatives. However, this narrative of a weak Commission and lack of progress in European integration in the 1970s is too limited. Commission staff remained committed to European integration and advanced policy proposals in old and new policy areas. New flagship policies such as the EMS emerged alongside budding new areas such as environmental and regional policies. During this period the Commission worked closely with the EP and the CJEU who often took the role of agenda-setters, prompting the Commission to develop proposals.

# 4. A new dawn? The Delors Commission, 1985–95

During the last two decades of the twentieth century the European integration process picked up speed. No doubt some of the developments were a continuation of the work the Commission had undertaken during the 1970s. However, member states also became generally more favourable to advances in European integration, particularly market integration (Warlouzet 2018a).

In January 1985, Jacques Delors, a French Socialist politician, former member of the EP and former minister of the economy and finance, took over the helm of the Commission. He remained in post for ten years (1985–95). Delors's candidacy for the Commission was widely supported by European leaders, including British Prime Minister Margaret Thatcher. Seen as a moderate Socialist who embraced market economy, Delors was thought to be a good choice for the Commission leadership.

Once in office, the Delors Commission identified the completion of the Single Market as its first objective. The Commission felt that a well-defined project to remove barriers to the movement of goods and, to a lesser degree, services, capital and people was bound to be popular with member-state governments keen to kick-start their economies at the end of a long period of recession. Economic policies of the neoliberal kind had taken hold in some member states, particularly the UK (Chapter 3). This ideology was shared by some commissioners, in particular, Peter Sutherland from Ireland and British Commissioners Leon Brittan and Lord Arthur Cockfield.

It was Cockfield who was in charge of the internal market portfolio and who, with his DG, drafted the Commission's White Paper *Completing the Internal Market* in 1985 (European Commission 1985). Member states agreed to the programme and to an intergovernmental conference (IGC) to negotiate a new treaty, the Single European Act, concluded in 1986. The more propitious economic and political context of the mid-1980s certainly helped the Delors Commission to realize an ambitious project and win support for it in the member states – not only governments but also businesses.

While the Single Market programme had the full backing of Thatcher, Delors also stood for ideologies and policies she did not agree with. Delors convinced the Commission and European leaders, though not Thatcher, that the realization of the Single Market required institutional reform, most importantly qualified majority voting in the Council of Ministers, to speed up decision-making. Delors was also convinced that a European single market needed to be counterbalanced by social and cohesion policies to balance out the negative effects economic integration and free competition could have. This went against Thatcher and general neoliberal beliefs in the self-regulation of the market. However, following the enlargement with three poorer Southern European countries, Greece (1981) and Spain and Portugal (1986), the gap between richer and poorer countries and regions in the EEC had widened even further. In 1988 the 'Delors I package' was adopted, which increased the EEC budget and doubled the money going into structural funds such as the European Regional Development Fund.

Delors's next aim was full Economic and Monetary Union (EMU). In 1988 the European Council agreed to pursue EMU. It set up a committee of central bankers, which Delors chaired. The Delors Committee duly drew up

FIGURE 5.2 *Meeting of the European Council, June 1986. Margaret Thatcher is flanked by Jacques Delors on the left and German Chancellor Helmut Kohl on the right. Courtesy of European Communities, 1986.*

the 'Delors Report' to realize EMU in three stages (Chapter 10). The report was adopted by heads of state and government, but as EMU required far-reaching measures and even the founding of new institutions (a European Central Bank, for example), it needed to be incorporated into the treaties. Just at this moment, the Berlin Wall came down. The fall of Communism in Eastern Europe and the Soviet Union in 1989–91 and the prospects and uncertainties this brought acted as an accelerator for EMU and further European integration.

While Delors can take some of the credit for the Maastricht Treaty, signed in 1992, and committing member states to EMU, national leaders such as German Chancellor Helmut Kohl and French President François Mitterrand played a crucial role as they understood that, for historical reasons, a united Germany needed to be embedded into a strong and united Europe (Chapter 16). Due to the high stakes and the loss of national sovereignty EMU would entail, in the IGC leading to the Maastricht Treaty Delors played a much less prominent role than in the previous IGC. In the end he was disappointed with the outcome. Delors had dreamed of full economic and political union and EU-wide social policy, but the fragmented structure of the EU as it was created through the Maastricht Treaty exposed the limits of this dream.

The considerable increase in new policies and competencies for the Commission since 1992 led to the institution becoming overstretched.

The Commission came under attack for how it handled its executive responsibilities. Firstly, this affected the output legitimacy of the Commission. Secondly, politicians and European citizens became increasingly wary of losing more sovereignty to the EU. The lack of input legitimacy of the Commission, that is, democratic legitimacy, became a common theme. From then on, institutional reform in the EU tended to focus on increasing the powers of the EP and not of the Commission, while the Commission underwent a period of administrative reform with the aim of turning it into a modern twenty-first-century public administration (Kassim et al. 2013).

# 5. A period of crisis and reform

A serious overhaul of the Commission's administrative structures did not occur until the late 1990s. Commission President Jacques Santer (1995–9) from Luxembourg initiated a reform process including more sound financial management. As the competences of the EU had increased exponentially since the Single European Act and the Maastricht Treaty, so had the size and complexity of the EU budget and the Commission's responsibilities in the administration and oversight of spending programmes.

It is ironic that the Santer Commission's term was cut short by a scandal of mismanagement and corruption that forced the entire Commission to resign before its term ended. Many issues were due to mismanagement in the member states, but allegations were directed against one commissioner in particular, the French politician Edith Cresson, who had given dubious work and research contracts to her friends and even her dentist. The case was hugely damaging for the Commission and fuelled ideas of the Brussels 'gravy train'. The issues also resulted in a power struggle between the EP and the Commission. The EP appointed a Committee of Independent Experts to investigate the Commission and threatened to hold a vote of confidence in the Commission. The results of the report were damaging, outlining weaknesses in the Commission's organization and in particular its financial management. Faced with the threat of losing a vote of confidence in the EP, the Santer Commission resigned collectively on 15 March 1999.

Santer's successor, Romano Prodi (1999–2004), a former Italian prime minister, had a strong mandate for far-reaching reform. Tackling both financial management and administrative reform, Prodi appointed a British Labour politician, Neil Kinnock, as vice president and commissioner for administrative reform. Kinnock stated that 'while Europe and the union have altered hugely over four decades ... the Commission as an organization didn't keep pace' (cited in Wille 2013, 48). Kinnock's *Reforming the Commission: A White Paper* (European Commission 2000) announced the aim of instilling a 'culture based on service' in the Commission, founded on the principles of responsibility, accountability, efficiency and transparency, and less on pro-European credentials as in the early years.

While the reforms were due to modernize the Commission and increase its efficiency, they were also aimed at making the organization more responsible and accountable to European citizens. One simple but effective measure to demystify the Commission was the renaming of its DGs, using abbreviations rather than numbers, for example, DG VI became DG Agri[culture]. To increase the accountability of each service, the Commission required each DG to produce an annual activity report, including full information on expenditure authorized by the DG and its staff. DGs now assumed full financial responsibility for spending and the correct use of budgetary resources. Finally, the Commission put a new auditing system in place with the enhanced Internal Audit Service.

Did the reform result in a better Commission? As some observers perceived it, the reforms seem to have introduced more bureaucracy into the Commission due to the checks and balances that were created. This might have weakened the Commission's power of initiative with staff having to spend more time managing and applying procedures (Dujardin et al. 2019; Kassim et al. 2013). In addition, some researchers found that the reforms affected the morale of Commission staff who felt the Commission had been turned into just another IO or business (Georgakakis 2017).

## 6. The Commission since the millennium

In the past twenty years, the problem of the perceived democratic deficit of the Commission (and the EU as a whole) has not gone away. The actions of the Commission since the millennium have therefore focused on further enhancing the transparency and accountability of the Commission. In this vein, Commission Presidents Santer (1995–9), Prodi (1999–2004), the Portuguese José Manuel Barroso (2004–14) and the Luxembourger Jean-Claude Juncker (2014–19) vowed to make 'fewer but better legislation' to counter the idea of the Commission as a power-grabbing, unaccountable technocracy. Another way of gaining democratic legitimacy for the Commission has been to call for the strengthening of the EP. Indeed, the EP has increased its role as a co-legislator in the EU since the Maastricht Treaty. It has also gained more control over the Commission and the nomination of its college of commissioners (Chapter 7). While certainly these procedures have increased the scrutiny, accountability and control of the EP over the Commission, this was not necessarily to the advantage of the Commission whose image in the wider population of the EU has arguably not improved much.

In May 2014 for the first time the large party groups in the EU entered the European elections with 'lead candidates', the so-called *Spitzenkandidaten*. The candidate whose party came out on top in the elections would consequently become Commission president (although TEU Article 17.7 only specifies that the European Council needs to take the outcome of the European elections into account when proposing who should head the Commission). This change was thought to enhance the political accountability of the Commission and address the democratic deficit of the EU. However, if rigorously applied, this system would have weakened the European Council, previously in charge of nominating the Commission president. In fact, this system was only applied once, in 2014, when Juncker, the *Spitzenkandidat* of the European People's Party (EPP), the strongest group in the EP, became Commission president. As the EP elections in May 2019 show, there is no automaticity between the election result and the appointment of the *Spitzenkandidat* as Commission president (Box 5.2).

The most recent Commissions, the Barroso and Juncker Commissions, were challenged by two events: enlargement with ten Southern and Eastern European countries in 2004 and 2007 which transformed the EU as a whole and the Commission in particular. For example, the number of commissioners in the Commission rose to twenty-eight in 2013 which made the Commission much more difficult to lead. The second issue was to manage the economic and financial crisis, which hit the EU from 2008. The financial crisis has become a watershed for the EU and has exacerbated centrifugal tendencies and divisions in the Union, not only regarding the management of the crisis but also revealing divisions about 'the institutional architecture of the European polity and, more importantly, about the future of the EU' (Ellinas and Suleiman 2012, 3).

The Juncker Commission continued on the path of the Barroso Commission trying to play a restrained and useful role, though Juncker, an old hand in EU politics, has arguably been more assertive than Barroso. First, Juncker restructured the Commission to better manage a college of twenty-eight commissioners by delegating presidential powers to the vice presidents who were put in charge of steering and coordinating groups of commissioners in related policy areas. Regarding policy, Juncker's first aim was to boost growth and investment within the EU to contribute to economic recovery after the financial crisis. As part of the 'Juncker Plan', he proposed to set up a European Fund for Strategic Investment (EFSI), endowed with 315 billion euros. The EFSI is run by the European Investment Bank and has been extended to run until December 2020.

Free trade agreements that had long been in the making were concluded, for example, with Canada (2016), Japan (2019) and the Mercosur countries of South America (2019). The Juncker Commission was challenged by unanticipated events, among them the so-called migrant crisis of 2015 and the vote of the UK to leave the EU in June 2016 (Chapter 4). The second half of Juncker's term in office was thus dominated by preparing for Brexit and negotiating a withdrawal agreement with the UK government. The Commission played an important role in these negotiations and, as guardian of the treaties, made sure that the core principles of the EU were upheld. Shortly after the German Ursula von der Leyen took over from Juncker in late 2019 (Box 5.2), the Covid-19 pandemic broke out and challenged the Commission to coordinate national responses to the crisis and devise EU-wide solutions, most notably in the acquisition and distribution of vaccines. This was not always successful, particularly in the first few months of the vaccine roll-out. In the end, the Commission-centred approach ensured that all countries – no matter how rich they were and whether they produced vaccine themselves – had the same supply. It should also be noted though that public health policy is an area where the EU does not have many powers.

## BOX 5.2 URSULA VON DER LEYEN, COMMISSION PRESIDENT, 2019–24

In July 2019 the European Council selected Ursula von der Leyen to succeed Jean-Claude Juncker. For the first time the European Commission has a female president. Many deplored that the backroom deal that got her the nomination undermined democracy in the EU as von der Leyen had not been a *Spitzenkandidat* at the European elections. However, she has a background that qualifies her for the role. She had been a government minister in Germany since 2005, serving as minister for family and youth, social affairs and labour and minister for defence. She belongs to the EPP party group which came out top in the 2019 European elections, is fluent in French and English and was even born in Brussels, as her father worked in the EEC Commission in the 1950s and 1960s. Von der Leyen emerged as a compromise candidate as neither of the two *Spitzenkandidaten*, Frans Timmermans from the Alliance of Socialists & Democrats and Manfred Weber from the EPP, was acceptable to all of the member states. Weber was seen as lacking international experience and he had never held a government position in Germany, his country of origin. Von der Leyen's nomination shows that EU leaders do not feel bound by the *Spitzenkandidat* procedure, wanting to maintain control over who leads the Commission.

# Conclusion

The Commission has evolved from being a relatively small organisation trying to find its role to 'one of the most powerful bureaucracies in the world enjoying more autonomy than most national and international administrations' (Ellinas and Suleiman 2012, 206). During the past twenty-five years, many observers have diagnosed a decline of the Commission in the face of an assertive EP and European Council. Yet, the Commission remains at the centre of EU policymaking, administration and implementation. Studying the evolution of the Commission over sixty years has brought to the fore some of the core issues about this organization and its place in EU governance. The first is the ongoing conflict between supranational and intergovernmental modes of governance. Rather than becoming more supranational or more intergovernmental, the EU embodies a dynamic relationship between supranationalism and intergovernmentalism. The Commission's role as a supranational bureaucracy has allowed it to play the role of the impartial broker and mediator and guardian of the treaty, but it has also made it vulnerable to criticism of lacking legitimacy and accountability.

The second issue is leadership. The effectiveness and influence of the Commission depends on leadership, most importantly of its president. The Commission has had three strong presidents: Hallstein, Delors and Jenkins. The small country of Luxembourg has so far provided three Commission presidents with Gaston Thorn, Jacques Santer and Jean-Claude Juncker. This may seem surprising, but it demonstrates that small states can punch above their weight in the political system of the EU. A president from this small member state, where almost every citizen is fluent in French and German, is also usually seen as a mediator between large member states. Yet, being effective as a president is not enough; the third issue is context and timing. The Commission's projects must also be relevant and desirable for the member states. With twenty-seven member states, it might become more difficult for the Commission to identify a shared interest among member states and desirable areas for action. The final issue this chapter has highlighted is that of the Commission as a diverse organization, composed of commissioners and European civil servants from all member states. While this has often led to tensions and conflicts over policies and what the right solution to a given problem is, it also means that the Commission includes many different viewpoints. It could even be argued that ultimately the Commission is a mirror image of member-state societies.

# Five key questions

1.   What are the different roles of the Commission?
2.   What challenges has the Commission faced since the Maastricht Treaty?
3.   What factors determine whether a Commission is perceived as successful or not?
4.   Does the president of the Commission resemble more the prime minister of a nation state or the secretary general of an international organization such as the United Nations?
5.   To what extent does the Commission suffer from a democratic deficit?

# Ten key readings

Bussière, E., et al. (eds) (2014), *The European Commission 1973–1986: History and Memories*, Luxembourg: Office for Official Publications of the European Communities.

Dujardin, V., et al. (eds) (2019), *The European Commission 1986–2000: History and Memories*, Luxembourg: Office for Official Publications of the European Communities.

Dumoulin, M. (ed.) (2007), *History of the European Commission 1958–1972*, Luxembourg: Office for Official Publications of the European Communities.

Edwards, G. (ed.) (2006), *The European Commission*, 3rd ed., London: John Harper.

Ellinas, A., and E. Suleiman (2012), *The European Commission and Bureaucratic Autonomy: Europe's Custodians*, Cambridge: Cambridge University Press.

Georgakakis, D. (2017), *European Civil Service in (Times of) Crisis: A Political Sociology of the Changing Power of the Eurocrats*, Basingstoke: Palgrave.

Kassim, H., et al. (eds) (2013), *The European Commission of the Twenty-First Century*, Oxford: Oxford University Press.

Ludlow, N. P. (2016), *Roy Jenkins and the European Commission Presidency, 1976–1980: At the Heart of Europe*, Basingstoke: Palgrave Macmillan.

Nugent, N., and M. Rhinard (2015), *The European Commission*, 2nd ed., London: Palgrave Macmillan.

Seidel, K. (2010a), *The Process of Politics in Europe: The Rise of European Elites and Supranational Institutions*, London: I. B. Tauris.

# 6

# The Court of Justice of the European Union and Integration Through Law

## *Bill Davies*

## Introduction

One of the most intriguing enigmas of European integration history is found in the role of the European Union's (EU) judiciary. Former Commission President Walter Hallstein once remarked, 'Previous attempts to unify Europe depended on force or conquest ... The majesty of the law is to achieve what centuries of "blood and iron" could not' (1972, 30). Law, the product of reasoned debate and compromise and instrument of equal regulation and treatment, would be the means through which peace and unity could be achieved in Europe. A court would achieve through enlightened deliberation that which centuries of violence and bloodshed could not. While the political institutions of the EU have grappled, sometimes in vain, with recalcitrant member-state governments and charismatic nationalist leaders and even eventually struggled to win legitimacy with the European people, the Court of Justice of the European Union (CJEU) seems to have emerged as the one unquestionably authoritative supranational institution.

The CJEU's case law, or *jurisprudence constant* to capture the Court's own phrasing, has established the direct effect of the EU treaties (in some cases its legislation also) and, on those occasions where member-state and EU law find themselves in conflict, the primacy of EU law as well. This combination created a 'new legal order' of a type unseen before in legal history – a binding supranational legal system. Moreover, the CJEU's decisions have built out a human rights jurisprudence for the EU, and as the competencies of the Union have evolved, the CJEU's authority is felt ever more closely in the daily lives of the EU's citizens. All in all, the CJEU's activism is said to have transformed the international treaties of the EU into a working constitution in all but name, with binding treaty obligations and the CJEU itself acting as the Union's ultimate constitutional arbiter (Weiler 1999). Whilst ostensibly a political process, Europe has been integrated through law, a reality captured in Hallstein's famous comment in the opening paragraph of this chapter. This finding is, in essence, the heart of the scholarly agenda known as Integration Through Law (ITL). This title originates in the field-defining work of Cappelletti, Seccombe and Weiler (1986b), whose collective efforts in comparing the federal experiences of the United States and the EU became the launching pad for generations of students and scholars of EU law.

Given the importance of the CJEU for European integration and the opacity of the CJEU's decision-making process, in which the CJEU issues opinions as a single college and deliberations are not published, various explanations from across a range of scholarly disciplines have been developed seeking to explain the CJEU's success. Legal scholars allude to the 'benign neglect' enjoyed by the CJEU as an institution in its early years during which its foundational case law could be built (Stein 1981), the inevitable logic of treaty law, in which inducing ever closer union between the member states was written into the CJEU's very own DNA, as well as the cold determinacy of legal reasoning: What other decisions could a court have possibly reached given the facts in the cases before it? Alternatively, political science theories have drawn from the different time frames of judicial and political actors (Alter 2001), principal-agent dynamics in which the court (the 'agent') expanded its powers beyond the parameters established by member states (the 'principals') (Pollack 2003), the empowerment of lower courts and other legal actors (Garrett 1995), as well as the unspoken self-interests of the member-state governments, who reap the benefits of deeper integration forged by the CJEU's rulings but struggle to sell legal concessions to political opponents and reluctant electorates (Moravcsik 1998). Finally, sociologists have pointed to the development of new transnational networks of legal elites working in the blurred lines of national and supranational governance, forging a new realm of power for themselves and their allies (Vauchez 2010).

It has only been during the past decade or so that historians have finally started to find and analyse the original sources that explain what really happened in and around the CJEU. This 'new history' of EU law (Davies and Rasmussen 2014) reveals a historical reality more complicated and indeterminant than imagined by ITL scholarship. It describes conflicting patterns of resistance and support, neglect and interest across time and geography by a broad variety of actors. It has highlighted both those actors with a grand design for Europe's legal future and those who have opposed this either intentionally or inadvertently. This new history has focused on both contextually and critically readdressing the theoretical assumptions of the ITL canon (Davies and Nicola 2017). This chapter will provide a detailed outline of the findings of the new history within this broader scholarly context and point to areas yet to be answered by historical research. In doing so, it reveals the core dynamic at the heart of scholarship surrounding the CJEU, namely that the scholarship places the Court both at the heart *and* at the periphery of its focus. This means being sure the CJEU as a judicial institution working within the broader framework of European integration is the main focus of inquiry. But at the same time, the arguments around the Court – supporters and detractors of its jurisprudence, different epistemic communities studying the institution – are just as much a subject of inquiry as the Court itself.

# 1. The Court, its competencies and identity

The CJEU is the highest judicial authority within the EU. Sitting as part of a complex network of member-state courts and tribunals large and small, the CJEU is responsible for the observance of law and the interpretation and application of the treaties. It is one of the original institutions of the integration project, created as part of the European Coal and Steel Community (ECSC) by the Treaty of Paris in 1952. The CJEU's composition and competencies have expanded together with the Union itself and are detailed in Articles 251–81 of the Treaty on the Functioning of the European Union (TFEU).[1] The CJEU has three main judicial functions: it reviews the legality of the acts of the institutions of the EU; it ensures that the member states comply with their treaty obligations; and, most importantly for understanding the *historical* significance of the CJEU, it interprets EU law at the request of the national courts and tribunals through a Preliminary Ruling Procedure (Art. 267 TFEU). The CJEU consists of two separate courts: the European Court of Justice (ECJ) (since 1952), the EU's highest court; and the General Court (since 1988), composed of two judges per member state and acting as court of first instance for direct actions brought by member states and individuals, with some exceptions.

At first glance, a comparison between the US Supreme Court and the CJEU – both highest courts in complex federal polities – would seem worthwhile. While the two panels do indeed address some common issues, the CJEU is a unique institution in its own right. Several qualities and characteristics make the Court standalone, beyond easy comparison with any other court in the world. Based in Luxembourg and working in French, the CJEU's highest gremium, the ECJ, is home, post-Brexit, to twenty-seven judges, one from each of the member states. Judges are appointed for six-year terms, based on selection from the member-state governments and approval

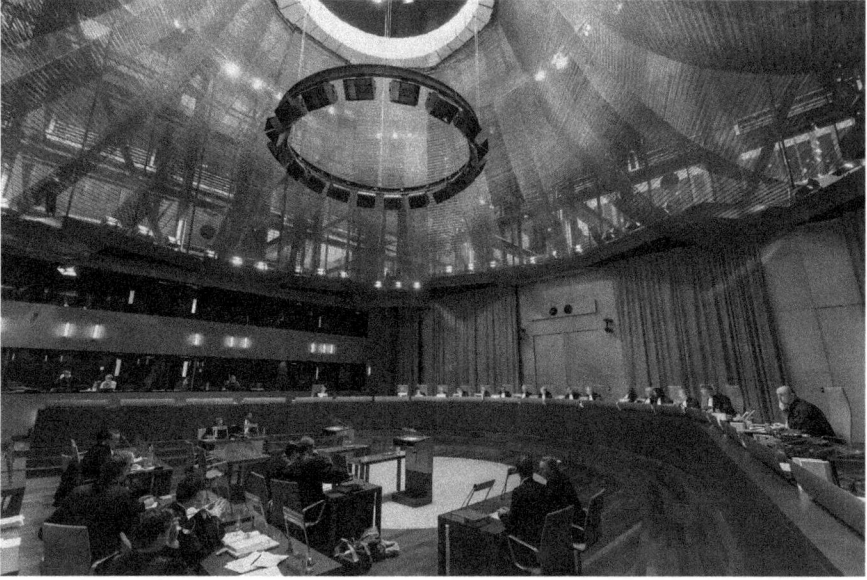

FIGURE 6.1 *A hearing of the Court of Justice Grand Chamber. Courtesy of Court of Justice of the European Union.*

through a judicial selection panel (Art. 255 TFEU). The Court adjudicates in panels ('chambers') of three, five or (rarely) fifteen members (Figure 6.1).

The Court issues opinions with a single voice, neither detailing judicial voting nor publicizing deliberations in the case. This is a result partially of the short-term limit of the judges (compared with lifetime appointments on the Supreme Court) and the delicate nature of the (re)appointment process and its dependence on selection by national authorities. The secrecy affords some levels of independence against national scrutiny and has also shielded EU judges from the kinds of public-political cross-examination placed on their US counterparts. This works both in the present and in the past, with deliberative documents emanating from the Court's archives being censored for current-day scholars. The Court's functioning is assisted by eleven advocate generals, whose role it is to participate in cases and to formulate non-binding opinions for the Court to consider prior to formal judgement. Behind the scenes, the Court is aided by a formidable bureaucracy led by the Court's registrar. Of particular importance in this machinery are the 'lawyer-linguists' who are necessary due to the multilingual nature of EU law and the specialized nature of the Court's institutional competencies.

However, beyond the idiosyncrasies within the institution itself, what really makes the CJEU unique is the network of interlocuters that engage in the EU legal system and enable the Court's decision-making. Far and away, the majority of the CJEU's roughly sixteen hundred annual cases are issued in response to questions from member-state judges dealing with issues they perceive to be within the jurisdiction of the CJEU. To ensure the uniform application of EU law across an entity with half-a-billion citizens and multiple official languages, the treaties have included from the start a mechanism that allows member-state courts to stay a proceeding before it and to request a 'preliminary ruling' on any case in which EU law could be involved. The CJEU has broadly interpreted what constitutes a court or tribunal in the EU, effectively extending its hand out to a huge network of judicial actors, large and small. It has been in response to Preliminary Ruling questions from lower national courts (as opposed to high courts and other courts of last instance) that the CJEU has been able to build out its constitutional interpretation of the treaties. In this vein, the most significant examples of the Court's jurisprudence have been in response to Preliminary Ruling requests from a Dutch tariff commission (Case 26–62 *Van Gend en Loos v. Nederlandse Administratie der Belastingen*) and a Milanese justice of the peace (Case 6–64 *Costa v E.N.E.L.*). This cooperative dialogue between judicial panels has allowed European 'Integration Through Law' to proceed to some degree insulated from the pressures of political compromise and created a capability for national enforcement of EU law that does not exist at the supranational level.

# 2. The 'Constitutional Revolution' of Integration Through Law

At the heart of the ITL claims that the CJEU successfully constitutionalized the EU treaties are two foundational cases. The first of these resulted from a Preliminary Ruling request from the Netherlands in 1962. In this case, Case 26–62 *Van Gend en Loos v. Nederlandse Administratie der Belastingen* (hereon: *Van Gend*), the CJEU was able to rule that under certain conditions – clarity and unconditionality – EU law was 'directly effective' – granting rights and obligations for legal subjects within member states that were enforceable by national courts. Drawing on the general 'scheme and spirit' of the Treaty of Rome, the CJEU found grounds to consider EU law an entirely 'new legal order', different from the norms of international law, which, generally speaking, applies to governments only. The Court wrote in its decision:

> The conclusion to be drawn ... is that the Community constitutes a new legal order in international law, for the benefit of which the states have limited their sovereign rights, albeit within limited fields, and the subjects of which comprise not only Member States but also their nationals. Independently of the legislation of Member States, *Community law*,

therefore *not only imposes obligations on individuals but is also intended to confer upon them rights which become part of their legal heritage.* These rights arise not only when they are expressly granted by the Treaty, but also by reason of obligations which the Treaty imposes in a clearly defined way upon individuals as well as upon the Member States and the institutions of the Community. (Emphases added)

In stating this, the CJEU empowered businesses of all kinds and even individuals to seek use of the Preliminary Ruling mechanism in national courts to enforce their newly granted rights under the EU treaties. Through *Van Gend* and the Preliminary Ruling mechanism, EU law became an integral part of national legal systems.

The inevitable question to arise from this was: if EU law and national law both imposed duties and rights on citizens, what was to happen in cases of conflict? The CJEU answered this by establishing the doctrine of legal primacy in the Case 6–64 *Costa v. E.N.E.L.* (hereon: *Costa*) in 1964. Reinforcing the 'originality' of EU law as a distinct and new legal order, the Court stated:

By contrast with ordinary international treaties, the Community treaty has created its own legal system which, on the entry into force of the treaty, became an integral part of the legal systems of the member states and which their courts are bound to apply. By creating a Community of unlimited duration, having its own institutions, its own personality, its own legal capacity and capacity of representation on the international plane and, more particularly, real powers stemming from a limitation of sovereignty or a transfer of powers from the states to the community, the member states have limited their sovereign rights and have thus created a body of law which binds both their nationals and themselves ... The law stemming from the treaty, an independent source of law, could not because of its special and original nature, be overridden by domestic legal provisions, however framed, without being deprived of its character as community law and without the legal basis of the community itself being called into question.

If the *Van Gend* decision integrated the Rome Treaties into member-state legal systems, then *Costa* granted EU law precedence in cases of conflict between the two. According to the logic of the CJEU, the treaties had explicitly created a special community, which pooled national competencies in institutions to carry out a specific purpose on behalf of the member states. How could such a community carry out its clearly stated purpose without having such powers? Such decisions are inherent in the very ontology of the EU.

Subsequent decisions of the CJEU further extended and deepened these doctrines (Table 6.1), extending primacy to apply not only to national

**Table 6.1** *Timeline of key legal developments in the European Union, 1952–93. Shaded rows refer to the Integration Through Law debate*

| | |
|---|---|
| 18 April 1951 | The Treaty of Paris ratified between France, Italy, West Germany and the three Benelux countries (Belgium, Luxembourg and the Netherlands), establishing the ECSC |
| 1952 | The European Court of Justice is established through the Treaty of Paris |
| 1952–54 | Creation and failure of the European Defence Community and European Political Community |
| 21 December 1954 | First hearing at the European Court of Justice: Case 1–54 *France v. High Authority* of the ECSC |
| 25 March 1957 | The Treaty of Rome (or EEC Treaty) signed to bring about the creation of the European Economic Community (EEC), the best known of the European Communities, as well as and the European Atomic Energy Community (Euratom) |
| 12–14 October 1961 | Establishment of the International Federation of European Law (FIDE), an academic association designed to promote the study of EU law |
| 22 January 1963 | French veto of British entry to the European Communities |
| 5 February 1963 | Judgement of *Van Gend*, establishing the doctrine of direct effect, creating enforceable rights and obligations from European law enforceable by national courts |
| 15 July 1964 | Judgement of *Costa*, establishing the doctrine of the primacy of European law over national law |
| July 1965–January 1966 | Empty Chair Crisis and French boycott of the Communities. Resolved through the Luxembourg Compromise, preserving national veto in the European legislative process |
| 27 November 1967 | Second French veto of British entry |

(continued)

**Table 6.1** *(continued)*

| | |
|---|---|
| 17 December 1970 | Judgement of *Internationale Handelsgesellschaft*, reinforcing the primacy of European law even against national constitutional law and confirming the existence of human rights in European law inspired by the traditions within the member states |
| 31 March 1971 | Judgement of *ERTA*, creating the doctrine of implied powers allowing European regulation beyond explicit competence from the treaties |
| 1 January 1973 | Accession of Britain, Denmark, Ireland |
| 18 December 1973 | Judgement of *Frontini* (Italian Constitutional Court), establishing limits on the supremacy of European law in Italy, particularly in regard to fundamental principles of constitutional law |
| 29 May 1974 | Judgement of *Solange I* (German Constitutional Court), withholding the right of the German Constitutional Court to rule on the constitutionality of European law for as long as the European Communities lacked an equivalent fundamental rights catalogue approved by a democratically elected body |
| 4 December 1974 | Judgement of *Van Duyn*, expanding the doctrine of direct effect |
| 20 February 1979 | Judgement of *Cassis de Dijon*, establishing mutual recognition of trade standards and further prohibiting restrictions on European trade |
| 7–10 June 1979 | First direct elections of the European Parliament held |
| 13 December 1979 | Judgement of *Hauer*, in which the CJEU cited both the European Convention of Human Rights and national rights traditions as its own human right standard |
| 1 January 1981 | Accession of Greece |
| January 1981 | Publication of Eric Stein's 'Lawyers, Judges, and the Making of a Transnational Constitution' in the *American Journal of International Law* |
| December 1985 | Publication of the Book 1 of Cappelletti, Seccombe and Weiler's (1986b) *Integration Through Law* project |
| 1 January 1986 | Accession of Spain and Portugal |

**Table 6.1** *(continued)*

| | |
|---|---|
| 17 and 28 February 1986 | Single European Act signed |
| 23 April 1986 | Judgement of *Les Verts*, in which the Court of Justice first refers to the treaties as its 'constitutional charter' |
| 1 June 1986 | Publication of Hjalte Rasmussen's *On Law and Policy in the European Court of Justice*, one of the prominent critiques of perceived activism by the CJEU and a scholarly counterweight to the ITL school |
| 22 October 1986 | Judgement of *Solange II* (German Constitutional Court), lifting the German court's review of the constitutionality of European law domestically, given the direct elections to the European Parliament and the improvements in CJEU's rights jurisprudence (see *Hauer* above) |
| 24 October 1988 | Court of First Instance instituted |
| 10 November 1989 | Fall of the Berlin Wall |
| 1 November 1993 | Maastricht Treaty on European Union becomes law |

legislation but also to constitutional law (Case 11–70 *Internationale Handelsgesellschaft*), establishing a notion of pre-emptive power (Case 22–70 *ERTA*) and extending direct effect, with some conditions, to secondary EU legislation (Case 41–74 *Van Duyn*), beyond the treaties and the explicitly provisioned direct effectively EU regulations (Art. 288 TFEU). Seen in totality, the CJEU's actions represent a massive erosion of national sovereign competencies, over and above those explicitly conceded in the foundational treaties of European integration. How could the Court achieve these in-roads into powers that member-state governments would typically only surrender very reluctantly? Which forces allied with the CJEU to sell its vision of a European legal system, and in contrast who resisted it and why?

# 3. Explaining the CJEU's success

This legal revolution was brought to widespread scholarly attention in the late 1970s by the work of Eric Stein, an international law professor and European Jewish emigree working at the University of Michigan Law School. Claiming that the revolution had occurred without much fanfare with the CJEU 'tucked away in the fairyland Duchy of Luxembourg and blessed … with benign neglect by the powers that be and the mass media', Stein (1981, 1) argued that the revolution was a sea change in Europe's history and the CJEU's interpretation of the treaties should be defended and protected by the legal community. Taking up the gauntlet a few years later, Mauro Cappelletti, professor of law at the European University Institute (EUI) and Stanford University, began a substantial research project entitled 'Integration Through Law: Europe and the American Federal Experience' (Cappelletti, Seccombe and Weiler 1986b). Cappelletti was joined by Monica Seccombe and Joseph Weiler, both fellow scholars at the EUI, in a comparative analysis of the EU and US legal systems. Ultimately, the project concluded, with Stein, that the CJEU had indeed fashioned a constitutional system, quasi-federal in nature, akin to both the United States and other explicitly federal entities. The Court had achieved what the politicians could not – functioning European federalism in all but name, with the potential for further integration in the future.

Joseph Weiler, Cappelletti's junior companion on the ITL project, continued his analysis of the EU legal system into the 1990s and became the champion of the ITL idea. In a series of writings, which served as a source of inspiration for a whole generation of subsequent scholars, Weiler highlighted the notion that perhaps the member-state governments had turned a blind eye to the revolution emanating out of the Grand Duchy because at around the same time in the mid-1960s, the governments had gained a veto in the legislative Council of Ministers via the Luxembourg Compromise (Weiler 1999). The spaces in which the CJEU had made escape from treaty obligations impossible were compensated by the fact that the member states now had seized firm control of the EU's legislative process by requiring unanimity in the adoption process. But as such, subsequent developments in European integration, especially the Single European Act of 1986, which reintroduced qualified majority voting and ended the need for unanimity in the Council, might fracture the equilibrium achieved in the mid-1960s by emphasizing the strength of legal obligations imposed on member states, who may not have wished to have supported the legal obligation in the first place. In effect, Weiler went beyond the original ITL project by emphasizing that the legal revolution was not just legal but essentially political in nature too.

Weiler's work evolved in an entirely different landscape in European integration history, with the formal creation of the 'Union', citizenship and a common currency through the Maastricht Treaty in 1993, as well as the problematic, vitriolic ratification of the treaty in many of the member states. The 'pillar system' of the Maastricht agreement had locked the CJEU out of foreign and security policy and justice and home affairs, both of which stayed firmly in the competency grasp of the member states. It certainly seemed that Weiler's prediction of the end of the passive acceptance of the CJEU's revolution was coming to an end.

Galvanized by the insights of Weiler on the inherently political nature of the legal revolution, international relations (IR) scholars and political scientists began to construct theoretical vehicles to explain not *if* EU law had been constitutionalized but *how* it had come to be so. Different schools emerged to resolve this quandary. Realists co-opted the rational-choice model approximated the intergovernmental theory in IR scholarship by emphasizing the delegated nature of the CJEU's authority, which merely carried out a specialist role that the member states do not wish to undertake themselves (Garrett 1995; Moravcsik 1998). The CJEU's agenda consisted of extending 'the ambit of European law and [its] authority to interpret it', while at the same time winning the 'acquiescence' of member states' governments for its declarations (Garrett 1995, 173). The Court would not afford provoking the member states into collective responses which might circumscribe the Court's authority. As such, the CJEU was an inherently political animal, conscious not only of the formal legal logic of the case before it but also of the interests and potential reactions of the broader forces at work. In a similar vein, theorists employed models of delegation and agency to demonstrate the potential overreach of the CJEU in its constitutionalization agenda, resulting in claims of a 'democratic deficit', which might cause the principals (member states) to tighten controls over their agent (CJEU) (Pollack 2003).

In contrast, theorists of the Functionalist school emphasized the dynamics of integration beyond the control of the member states and diminished the possibility that any one government within the EU had a monolithic set of interests on which they chose to act. Rather, the success of the CJEU could be explained through its mobilization of subnational actors, such as lower national courts, and transnational, pro-EU legal elites, who had a vested self-interest in the development of a burgeoning EU legal practice. Interaction between the CJEU and these groups occurred through the ever-increasing number of Preliminary Ruling requests. Scholars such as Mattli and Slaughter (1995) cited the exponential growth in Preliminary Rulings as proof of not just how the system worked efficiently, but also how the momentum of successful Preliminary Rulings promoted its ever-wider use by lower national courts. Such self-sustaining 'spillover' of successful tactics is typical of Functionalist accounts of European integration and suggested, by extension, that the legal revolution would continue even in the face of member-state reluctance because any 'backlash' would necessitate highly coordinated, and therefore unlikely, national resistance.

More cautiously, Karen Alter's (2001) account of the establishment of the primacy doctrine in the early 2000s highlighted the fact that the legal revolution had *not* taken place without resistance. In fact, the judiciaries of France and Germany, the two largest member states, had indeed reacted to the CJEU's decisions and had pushed back against what was perceived to be overreach by the Luxembourg court. Alter's ground-breaking work was based heavily on empirical research, including interviews with key actors in the early years – now out of office and more able to speak freely to scholars. This more contextualized approach to EU law became a source of inspiration for historians, who had been socialized into the legal and political science scholarship explaining the CJEU's success but who wanted to test the theoretical assumptions against the sources that might emerge from national and European archives.

# 4. The Court in context: A new history of EU law

In the early 2000s, historical studies of the CJEU's jurisprudence as well as the subsequent academic, political and public debates of those decisions, based on the utilization of archival source materials and employing historical methodologies, began to appear. It soon became apparent that a wealth of archival materials existed in a variety of national archives (different actors dealt with EU law in different member states), European archives (particularly those of the European Commission and its Legal Service) and even private archives of key participants in the Court's key decisions. Such breadth in source material possibilities was particularly necessary in the writing of EU legal history due in part to the fact that much of the CJEU's success rested on its need for its decisions to be received by the wider academic, political and public audience, but also more pragmatically that the CJEU could not open its own archive until safeguard measures were implemented to protect the sacrosanct nature of judicial deliberations that may have been included in any archival deposits. The CJEU decided it was ready to open its archive in 2014. By this time, initial historical scholarship had begun to mine the rich lodes of information that were found in other archives around that of the Court's. Archival materials employed by historians of EU law included the classic documents of legal history generally, including judicial decisions, case materials (where available), treaty negotiation documents and writings by judges and lawyers. They also extended beyond to incorporate private archival materials, such as letters, diaries and oral histories, academic texts and speeches, bureaucratic archives of national agencies and, in some cases, newspaper and other media sources. In most cases, historical research has been limited in temporal scope by archival provisions to end at the year thirty years prior to the present one.

The first published histories of the Court's decision-making hinted at the fact that the perceived success of the CJEU in integrating Europe through law and in constitutionalizing the treaties may have been overstated. These historical accounts demonstrated clearly that Stein's 'benign neglect' had never really existed and that the member states and the national judiciaries had contested the CJEU's decisions from the onset. In fact, histories of the very earliest phase of EU legal history demonstrated that even before the legal revolution of the mid-1960s, contestation about the future nature of EU law was occurring in all the member states (Boerger 2012; Davies 2015). This contestation eventually morphed into judicial resistance by national judiciaries, in which the 'constitutional paradigm' espoused by the CJEU, and a wider alliance of actors, remained an aspiration that was never fully accepted without condition by the member-state judiciaries. What made the whole environment so complex and interesting is the fact that national resistance occurred in different forms, according to different national legal cultures, on different issues and at different times. Different national contexts and legal traditions have resulted in varying conditions being placed on the acceptance of the constitutional paradigm. With such a disparate, patchwork reception, it is problematic to argue that the treaties had been morphed uniformly into a federal constitution. Instead, the rather fragile equilibrium achieved between the CJEU and a variety of national actors on which it depends for enforcement and referrals has been described as a 'constitutional practice', rather than a full-blown constitution in which power and authority is clearly delineated (Davies and Rasmussen 2014) member states' resistance to the CJEU's constitutional aspirations was not blowing into the wind. The CJEU's authority rests a great deal on the acceptance of its decisions by national actors. It must listen when agents on which it depends are reluctant to cooperate. Resistance culminated in real changes to the nature of European governance. As such, the member-state judiciaries and legal communities were equal co-authors of the supranational constitutional system, even when, in some cases, their resistance was opposed by their own national governments.

Nowhere is this clearer than in the case of Germany (Davies 2012). In this example, German judicial resistance, particularly by the German Constitutional Court, resulted in significant backlash against the constitutional aspirations of the CJEU. The particular legal-cultural context in this case was defining on the nature and ultimate success of the resistance. Germany had emerged from the Second World War morally bankrupt, divided and in search of a new 'home' for itself in the Cold War era. It found this particularly in its staunch political and economic support for European integration, and, as such, West Germany was very willing to pool sovereign competencies in the name of European unity. At the same time, part of Germany's post-war reinvention also involved its strict adherence to the rule of law, commitment to democracy and inviolable human rights provisions of its domestic constitution. The constitutionalization of EU law created a conundrum for the German legal community that proves difficult to resolve even today, namely how to honour the commitment to European integration whilst at the same time ensuring the integrity of the domestic constitutional order in the face of EU law that the CJEU claimed overruled it.

This issue came to a head in the mid-1970s, after the CJEU has issued its *Internationale Handelsgesellschaft* ruling at the request of a lower German court. In its Preliminary Ruling, the CJEU motioned that EU legal provisions had primacy even over national constitutional law. The case involved a German firm, and, ultimately, the case was referred to the German Constitutional Court. In its own ruling in the case, the German Constitutional Court withheld the right to adjudicate on the constitutionality of EU law in Germany as long as (German: *Solange*) EU law did not have democratic and rights safeguards equivalent to those found in the German constitution. This requirement of having sufficient 'structural congruence' between national and European polities for a legitimate transfer of competencies to take place was just the next stage in an argument in the German legal academy about EU law that had been raging since the negotiation of the original treaties in the 1950s (Davies 2015).

What really stands out about the German resistance, however, was just how much impact it had. As a staunchly pro-European member state, and equally so the richest and most populous, German resistance to the constitutionalization paradigm truly mattered. Moreover, the pressure was multiplied by the fact that the Italian Constitutional Court had made a very similar ruling to its German counterpart a short time before (*Frontini v Minister delle Finanze* [1974] 2 CMLR 372 [Italian Constitutional Court]). Despite public outcry within the European Parliament and other institutions, behind the scenes, negotiations were taking place to find ways to acquiesce to the German court's admonition. Eventually, a compromise was reached that saw the supranational institutions publicly commit themselves to adhere to the European Convention on Human Rights (ECHR), and the CJEU itself followed suit by citing the ECHR in a number of cases in the late 1970s. With the inception of direct elections to the European Parliament in 1979, the German Constitutional Court felt sufficiently reassured in the democratic and rights improvements within the EU that it modified its 'Solange' demands at the next opportunity ('*Solange* II', 1986). However, the uneasy relationship between the German Constitutional Court and CJEU continues to this day as the two courts continue to find ways to exert their own authority in ways acceptable to the other.

Other historical studies have revealed that resistance to the CJEU in other member states has been different in nature, but just as fierce. In France, for instance, two competing elite groups sought to influence the European project in entirely different directions, with their accomplishments determined as much by their success in domestic politics as by any other factor. In fact, the success of Gaullist forces within France largely shaped the French reception of EU law, leading to a hostile reaction by the Conseil d'Etat and the ultimate passing of the 'Aurillac Amendment', which limited the impact of EU law in France until the mid-1980s (Bernier 2012). Equally, in the case of Denmark, an uneasy stability with the constitutionalization of EU law was achieved by political and administrative control of the Preliminary Ruling mechanism to such a degree that requests were vetted prior to being sent to Luxembourg by a special administrative committee set up by the Danish government (Pedersen 2016). This, it was hoped, would help to shield the

Danish socio-economic model from the full effects of EU legislation and prevent the kind of coalition between the CJEU and lower national courts from emerging that the Functionalists describe.

While much effort has been placed on documenting historical resistance to the constitutionalization process, equally the forces in favour of constitutionalization have also been studied. Here much attention has fallen not on the CJEU itself but rather on the actors who prompted, enabled and defended the CJEU in its constitutional ambitions. The key player in this advocacy has been the Legal Service of the European Commission. Present in all cases before the CJEU in the formative years of integration, the Legal Service has a particularly prominent position in the development of the constitutional paradigm. Its early director general, Michel Gaudet, has been cited in many studies as the driving force in the entire movement, featuring not only in the negotiation of the Treaties of Rome as a legal adviser but also pushing a seemingly reticent CJEU to adopt pro-federalist positions in cases as early as the 1950s (Rasmussen 2014). In addition, Gaudet and the Legal Service supported financially and intellectually the development of a European legal community, including the Fédération Internationale pour le Droit Européen (FIDE), an academic association which sought to evangelize and educate national legal elites on the authority of the EU legal order (Rasmussen 2012).

The CJEU itself has been the subject of some scrutiny, although for reasons mentioned above, direct research into the court can be difficult. Historians have instead focused on the biographies and writings of judges prior to and after their time on the Court (Fritz 2020). In some exceedingly rare cases, it has been possible to make educated guesses about the nature of deliberations, individual authorship of certain rulings and even voting patterns. For instance, it has been documented that the *Van Gend* decision was achieved with a very narrow 4–3 vote, with the introduction of two new judges the year before proving vital in emboldening a Court that Michel Gaudet had failed to convince in the years prior (Rasmussen 2014). Another example of indirect historical insights into the internal workings of the Court was the attribution of the aforementioned *Internationale Handelsgesellschaft* ruling to Judge Pierre Pescatore through tracking of wording in extra-judicial writings and the ruling itself (Davies and Nicola 2017). However, due to the nature of the Court's deliberations and its need for secrecy, the Court remains much of a black box to historical scholarship. The recent opening of Court archives promises to make a shift in this reality.

The picture of the CJEU itself, like the reaction of member-states judiciaries, is both varied and multifaceted. It is possible already to see clearly demarcated historical 'terms' in the functioning and outlook of the Court. For instance, we can see that despite the already well-formed ideas of the Commission's Legal Service, the CJEU refused – despite opportunity – to endorse a constitutional reading of the treaties throughout the 1950s. We might speculate either that it did not feel institutionally secure enough to do so or perhaps that a majority of the judges felt unconvinced by the logic of the constitutional argument. We see however a shift around 1962, with the selection of Judges Robert Lecourt and Alberto Trabucchi to the Court. Within a year, the constitutional revolution was begun. The deepening of the CJEU's constitutional jurisprudence, such as the development of a human rights jurisprudence, occurred predominately in the decade between 1967 and 1976, a time when the Court was presided over by – again – Robert Lecourt and was also home to the eminently influential and charismatic Judge Pierre Pescatore (Fritz 2020). We might now recognize this as the 'Lecourt Court', analogous to the way in which legal historians of the United States refer to the Marshall or Warren Courts. This shift, we might speculate, was a result of the Court's (perhaps erroneous) perception that its initial constitutional decisions of the early 1960s had been well received – German and Italian court reactions to the constitutional decisions did not arrive until the mid-1970s. The shift in the Court's focus might also be tied to broader changes in European politics and society at the time as the intergenerational turmoil of the late 1960s brought issues of democracy, human rights, environmentalism and inclusion to the forefront. The year 1968 was both the year of mass student protest across many European capitals and the United Nations' International Year of Human Rights. We might again speculate that the judges in this atmosphere felt galvanized to develop the EU's human rights catalogue and democratic credentials, both of which were perceived to be insufficient at the time.

Pierre Pescatore warrants a particular mention in any history of EU law, being both present at the birth of the Treaty of Rome as a Luxemburgish negotiator and serving as a member of the Court for nearly two decades between 1967 and 1985 (see Figure 6.2). It was at his particular urging, enabled by the support of Robert Lecourt, the Court's president for much of the period, that the CJEU continued to build on the legal revolution begun in the mid-1960s. Pescatore was the Judge Rapporteur (the judge appointed to marshal the arguments of the parties and, crucially, to author the first draft of the judgement which the remaining judges use as their basis for deliberation) in key constitutional cases, such as the aforementioned *ERTA* and *Internationale Handelsgesellschaft*, as well as most of the prominent cases detailing the CJEU's stance on human rights protections during the 1970s. Not content with his judicial role, Pescatore also actively participated in the legal academy, attending academic conferences, delivering speeches and writing for a multitude of venues in a number of European languages. It is not an entirely unreasonable claim to suggest that Pescatore enjoyed the single most influence of any individual on the development of EU law in its history.

In recent years, attention of historical contextual research has shifted slightly away from the grand contest between constitutionalization and resistance to focus more deeply on the forces at play within individual rulings (Davies and Nicola 2017). Most notably, much scholarly attention

FIGURE 6.2 *Pierre Pescatore (1919–2010). A prolific academic and prominent political figure from Luxembourg, Pescatore was involved in the negotiations of the founding treaties in the 1950s and was appointed judge at the court in 1967. His judicial tenure lasted until 1985, in which time Pescatore's intellect and personality shaped a generation of EU jurisprudence. Courtesy of European Communities, 1975.*

has been given to the seminal *Cassis de Dijon* ruling (Case 120–78 *Rewe-Zentral AG v. Bundesmonopolverwaltung für Branntwein*), which paved the way for the mutual recognition of standards across member states (see, for instance, the collective efforts in Albors-Llorens, Barnard and Leucht 2021). Such studies of individual decisions serve as windows into the particular legal, cultural and political forces at work within an EU legal case at any one moment. They also demonstrate that despite the narrative aesthetic of a battle between opposing armies over the nature of EU law, EU law – like any legal system – is often at the mercy of radically indeterminant influences that produce sometimes unpredictable outcomes. Who might have guessed, for instance, that the Preliminary Ruling request in the *Francovich* ruling (the foundation of EU law on state liability) only reached Luxembourg because the postman in Strasbourg (home of the entirely separate European Court of Human Rights) knew where to correctly redirect it (Davies and Nicola 2017)? Or that the Chinese immigrant involved in the *Chen* decision, vilified by the Irish and British press as an economic migrant, was in fact a wealthy Chinese millionaire seeking to escape the constraints of China's one-child policy (Davies and Nicola 2017)? Such insights not only add colour and life to the study of what might be a rather formal and dry subject but also show that reliance on grand narratives in historical retelling can come at the cost of losing the finer details involved.

Much research remains to be done both into the individual cases before the Court and into those broader forces shaping the success and failure of the Court's interpretation. Of particular interest now is the rough decade starting in 1986 with the Single European Act and ending with the introduction of the Maastricht Treaty. This is when European integration was given new impetus, the initial constitutional rulings of the CJEU were seemingly accepted (see the German case) and the reintroduction of qualified majority voting occurred. How this impacted the Court and the member states it interacted with is especially crucial in understanding the development of EU law in the post-Maastricht era. Equally, more work remains to be done on the very earliest years of the CJEU and how it found its own voice as an entirely new judicial institution. Finally, the history of EU law needs to be contextualized into the broader legal history of the twentieth century. The CJEU was by no small measure the only new court in this time period, and placing the development of EU law – clearly a conspicuous and unique phenomena – within a broader framework of Cold War relations, international judicialization and other socio-economic pressures is crucial for a holistic understanding of this story. This wider contextualization of the CJEU's evolution is a point most clearly articulated recently by Karen Alter (2021).

# Conclusion

The CJEU has been a key motor driving European integration by locking in the legal obligations imposed by the European institutions and enabling European citizens to use rights granted by EU law. Distanced from the political machinery in Brussels and Strasbourg, the Luxembourg panel has sought to play the role of a neutral umpire, adjudicating only the law and the strengths and weaknesses of the arguments bought before it. However, the CJEU is a product and servant of the treaties and their pursuit for ever closer, ever deeper union. Trying to serve as a dispassionate panel of adjudication whilst being bound by the foundational logic of integration places the Court in a fascinating ontological tension, making it worthy of our historical study and continued observation. Adding in the extra tensions caused by the need for cooperation from national judiciaries and legal elites places the CJEU at the heart of the question of what it means to be a supranational institution.

The Court's success in the past will create new problems for it in the future. As more and more citizens feel the impact of EU legislation in their daily lives, the Court's decisions will resonate ever more deeply with the public. Public and political review of the Court, its judges and its decision-making processes will increase, eventually even perhaps becoming akin to the scrutiny given to the US Supreme Court. The Court's gain in power featured prominently in the arguments of those opposed to continued membership of the EU during the UK's 2016 Brexit referendum. The judicial appointment process may become more politicized, questions will arise about the demographic representativeness of the Court and almost certainly the Court will be asked to review its rather opaque voting mechanisms. As a key driver of integration, the Court will also likely step more into the crosshairs of those who are resistant to integration, as was the case during the Brexit referendum debates, and those who wish to relocate competencies back to the member-state level, particularly those constitutional or supreme courts who feel their raison d'être having been usurped by the rise of the Luxembourg institution.

# Five key questions

1.  Why did legal mechanisms become such a prominent feature of European integration?
2.  What factors gave the Court the ability to become a key motor of integration?
3.  To what extent can it be argued that the ITL scholarship assumed a key role in this process?
4.  Has the Court's success in driving integration, even in the face of political or popular reticence, strengthened the Union?
5.  As EU law reaches ever more deeply into the lives of European citizens, what challenges will the Court begin to face?

# Note

1  To reflect its focus on the legal development of the EU, this chapter – exceptionally – refers to articles from the most recent version of the treaty, which is in line with conventions in legal scholarship.

# Ten key readings

Alter, K. (2001), *Establishing the Supremacy of European Law: The Making of an International Rule of Law in Europe*, Oxford: Oxford University Press.

Boerger, A. (2012), 'Negotiating the Foundations of European Law, 1950–1957: The Legal History of the Treaties of Paris and Rome', *Contemporary European History*, 21 (3): 339–56.

Cappelletti, M., M. Seccombe and J. H. H. Weiler (1986b), *Integration through Law: Europe and the American Federal Experience*, Berlin: W. de Gruyter.

Davies, B. (2012), *Resisting the European Court of Justice: West Germany's Confrontation with European Law 1949–1979*, Cambridge: Cambridge University Press.

Davies, B., and F. Nicola (eds) (2017), *EU Law Stories: Contextual and Critical Histories of European Jurisprudence*, Cambridge: Cambridge University Press.

Rasmussen, H. (1986), *On Law and Policy in the European Court of Justice: A Comparative Study of Judicial Policymaking*, Leiden: Brill Nijhoff.

Rasmussen, M. (2014), 'Revolutionizing European Law: A History of the Van Gend en Loos Judgment', *International Journal of Constitutional Law*, 12: 136–63.

Stein, E. (1981), 'Lawyers, Judges and the Making of a Transnational Constitution', *American Journal of International Law*, 75: 1–27.

Vauchez, A. (2010), 'The Transnational Politics of Judicialization: *Van Gend en Loos* and the Making of EU Polity', *European Law Journal*, 16 (1): 1–28.

Weiler, J. H. H. (1999), *The Constitution of Europe – 'Do the New Clothes Have an Emperor?' and Other Essays on European Integration*, Cambridge: Cambridge University Press.

# Cases referenced

## Court of Justice of the European Union decisions

Case 26–62 NV *Algemene Transport- en Expeditie Onderneming van Gend & Loos v. Netherlands Inland Revenue Administration*. ('*Van Gend*')

Case 6–64 *Flaminio Costa v. E.N.E.L.* ('*Costa*')

Case 11–70 *Internationale Handelsgesellschaft mbH v Einfuhr- und Vorratsstelle für Getreide und Futtermittel*. ('*Internationale*')

Case 22–70 *Commission of the European Communities v. Council of the European Communities*. ('*ERTA*')

Case 41–74 *Yvonne van Duyn v. Home Office*. ECLI identifier ('*Van Duyn*')

Case 120–78 *Rewe-Zentral AG v. Bundesmonopolverwaltung für Branntwein*. ('*Cassis de Dijon*')

Case 44–79 *Liselotte Hauer v Land Rheinland-Pfalz* ('*Hauer*')

Case 294–83 *Parti écologiste 'Les Verts' v. European Parliament*. ('*Les Verts*')

## National Court decisions

*Frontini v. Minister delle Finanze* [1974] 2 CMLR 372 (Italian Constitutional Court). ('*Frontini*')

2 BvL 52/71 – *Solange I*, 29 May 1974 – BVerfGE 37, 271 (German Constitutional Court). ('*Solange I*').

2 BvR 197/83 – *Solange II*, 22 October 1986 – BVerfGE 73, 339 (German Constitutional Court). ('*Solange II*').

# 7

# The European Parliament: Empowering the talking shop

## *Christian Salm*

## Introduction

The Common Assembly of the European Coal and Steel Community (ECSC), the forerunner of the European Parliament (EP), held its first plenary session on 10 September 1952. As delegates from the ECSC founding member states' national parliaments, seventy-eight parliamentarians met in the building of the Council of Europe in Strasbourg. France, Germany and Italy sent eighteen parliamentarians each, Belgium and the Netherlands sent ten each and Luxembourg sent four. From an historical perspective, it is remarkable that this plenary session took place at all. Seen as the founding act of today's European Union (EU), the Schuman Plan announced by French Foreign Minister Robert Schuman in May 1950 proposing European cooperation in the form of the ECSC did not mention a *supranational* parliamentary representation at the European level (Chapter 1).

The idea of a common assembly entered the negotiations on the 1951 Paris Treaty, establishing the ECSC, only at a late stage. Jean Monnet, advisor to the French government at the time and guiding light of the Schuman Declaration, had designed the High Authority, today's European Commission, as the ECSC's executive branch in the form of a small, completely independent and highly powerful body. In particular following the Benelux countries' demand on the creation of various bodies controlling the High Authority, further entities were added to the institutional set-up. Among them was the Common Assembly.

Compared with national parliamentary assemblies, as the key normative point of reference (Rittberger 2009), the formal powers of the Common Assembly were very limited and restricted to purely advisory and controlling functions. Instead of a powerful assembly marking a European federation, the ECSC member states' governments had only agreed to establish the Common Assembly as a virtually powerless institution when negotiating the Paris Treaty. The Common Assembly's limited formal power was symbolized by the need to borrow for its meetings the building of the Council of Europe, founded in 1949. The 1957 Treaties of Rome, establishing the European Economic Community (EEC) and the European Atomic Energy Community (Euratom), did not change this situation although the Common Assembly was to also represent the two newly added communities. The EEC Treaty only added a very general right to censure the European Commission, the equivalent of the High Authority in the new EEC, and the right to participate in legislative and budgetary matters through the weak consultation procedure to the Common Assembly's policymaking portfolio. In other words, its formal power remained very restricted – leading to the designation of the Common Assembly and also of its successor, the EP, as a talking shop.

The EP could mitigate this public and academic perception of its parliamentary role only after a long time. In fact, it was only after the growing politicization of the EP's work as a result of the 1992 Maastricht Treaty and the transformation of the European Community into the EU that the EP was perceived as an important policymaker. Today there is no doubt that as a key forum for transnational cooperation at the European level, the EP is a crucial player in EU politics and policymaking, and thus European integration. Moreover, with 705 parliamentarians, called Members of the European Parliament (MEPs), from 27 member states and representing about 450 million citizens, the EP is the world's largest multinational parliament. Its development from a talking shop to an important policymaker can be told in five time periods, as this chapter will do.

# 1. Building a real supranational parliament, 1952–7

The 1951 Paris Treaty did not include specific details on how the Common Assembly of the ECSC was to be established. At the first plenary session in September 1952, the members' seats were thus just allocated in alphabetical order. Hence, some members found themselves sitting beside a neighbour with different political preferences. For instance, the Belgian socialist Fernand Dehousse, with a strong federalist agenda for Europe, sat next to the French Gaullist Michel Debré. Cooperation and coordination between members sharing political ideologies was therefore rather cumbersome (Guerrieri 2015). Furthermore, as delegates from the member states' national parliaments, the members had a dual mandate, one each in their national parliament and in the Common Assembly.

In the new Assembly, informal contacts and networks developed quickly and organically between members from different countries who belonged to parties of the same political persuasion (van Ouedenhove 1962). The importance of these informal contacts and networks, with political connotations for the ECSC Common Assembly's decision-making processes, were already apparent when on the second day of the first plenary session in September 1952, the members had to elect the first president of the Assembly. As Jacob Krumrey (2018a) has described it, the Belgian Socialist Paul-Henri Spaak was a surprise candidate for the role in comparison to the candidacy of two Christian Democrats, François de Menthon of France and Heinrich von Brentano of Germany. Against all odds, however, Spaak won the election as he could muster the votes of all the French-speaking members from Belgium, France and Luxembourg, and of all the Socialist members, including the German Social Democrats.

Besides electing its governing body, comprised of the president, five vice presidents and the college of quaestors assigned to oversee administrative and financial matters, another first task of the Common Assembly was to define its rules of procedure. A committee (on rules of procedures and budget) was set up to deal with the Assembly's rules of procedures and to look into matters such as the number, composition and competences of the committees to be formed. The Common Assembly had a high degree of autonomy with regard to its rules of procedure and was able to decide on its internal affairs without the consent of the ECSC Council of Ministers (Mittag 2001).

In fact, the Common Assembly made plentiful use of the possibility of self-organization. As a first major step, the members decided to establish seven committees. These were the Committee on the Common Market; the Committee on Investments, Finance and the Development of Production; the Committee on Social Affairs; the Committee on Political Affairs and External Relations of the Community; the Committee on Transport; the Committee on the Accounts and Administration of the Community and the Common Assembly; and the Committee on the Common Assembly's Rules of Procedure, Petitions and Immunities.

The members' second major decision on the Assembly's organization was the institutionalization of political groups, even though this was not provided for in the ECSC Treaty. Already Spaak's election as the Common Assembly's first president contributed greatly to triggering a debate as to whether political groups should be created. At the second plenary session, in January 1953, the ideological division within the Assembly was openly recognized. In this plenary session, a debate took place on whether the appointment of members to committees should attempt to be representative of both the member states and the various political traditions. A broad consensus on the issue emerged from that session, exemplifying the members' view of the

Common Assembly's political nature and the role of political groups within it. For example, the Belgian Christian Democrat Paul Struye underlined the paradox of the Assembly introducing a first provision making national delegations the lead decision-making entity (as was the case in the Council of Europe's Parliamentary Assembly), especially as the ECSC Common Assembly would be an Assembly with much greater supranational spirit than the Council of Europe. In fact, the members' opposition to nationalism was crucial for the creation of political groups. They considered political groups to provide a way to overcome national representation, to push towards transnational representation and to develop the ECSC Common Assembly as a real supranational institution.

As a consequence, at its plenary session in June 1953, and thus only a couple of months after its inauguration, the Common Assembly unanimously decided to insert the creation of political groups into its rules of procedure. Three political groups were officially authorized: the Christian Democratic Group, the Socialist Group and the Group of Liberals. All three political groups are still represented in today's EP, albeit under different names.

By forming political groups, the ECSC Common Assembly was operating in a different manner compared to all other international assemblies of the time. Political scientists Simon Hix and Amie Kreppel (2003) have two explanations as to why the ECSC Common Assembly took this decision. They mention first that the newly developed European institutions in the early 1950s were shaped by the existing domestic political practices of the six founding member states. The Common Assembly's members were appointed by their national assemblies and thus were established parliamentary politicians. When faced with organizing themselves in a new European-level assembly, they naturally decided to create ideologically based political groups. The second explanation from Hix and Kreppel is grounded in the assumption that national political parties sharing an ideology and similar persuasions had a greater incentive to organize transnationally in the new ECSC Common Assembly because, unlike the other international institutions of the time, it had more significant powers. Because of these powers, the new Assembly at European level formed an important midpoint between a national parliament and the classical type of international assemblies with much less power.

Despite lacking legislative and budgetary rights, the Common Assembly underlined with its organizational set-up that it did not consider itself a mere international conference, but rather an assembly with traditional parliamentary structures, tasks and rules. Especially the establishment of transnational political groups contributed in a significant way to the politicization of the Common Assembly in the years from 1952 to 1957. From a strictly legal perspective, the only real parliamentary power the Common Assembly had was to enforce the dismissal of the members of the High Authority. However, it was able to secure political authority for itself that went beyond that originally intended as will be shown in the next section.

# 2. Relaunching the Parliament, 1957–69

The texts of international treaties do not normally reveal anything about the history of how they came about. The 1957 Treaties of Rome, aimed to revitalize the European integration process, are no exception to this rule. Without having initiative and (co-)decision rights, the Common Assembly was not directly involved in the deliberations and negotiations leading to the treaties establishing the EEC and Euratom.

Nevertheless, the Common Assembly's members attempted to influence the shaping of treaty content and sought to push the negotiations forward. To that end, in May 1955, the Common Assembly formed a special working group with tasks such as informing the Assembly on matters relating to the extension of the Community's special competences and the further general integration of the common market. The working group shadowed the work of both the Committee of National Experts preparing the technical details of the treaty and the Intergovernmental Conference of Foreign Ministers negotiating the final treaties. In addition, the Common Assembly issued a range of reports and resolutions to push forward and influence the deliberations and negotiations at decisive phases leading to the Rome Treaties. For instance, shortly before the publication of the important report by the Committee of National Experts, the Common Assembly adopted a resolution at the end of March 1956 addressing the governments of the ECSC member states. The resolution demanded the rapid conclusion of a treaty to establish a general common market in the form of a customs and economic union, including not only goods, services and capital but also the free movement of workers (Chapter 1).

The discussions on the formation of a new economic community inevitably led to an intense reflection on the Common Assembly's own role within the emerging revised institutional set-up at European level. The Common Assembly clearly aimed to overcome its largely subsidiary and consultative role and to achieve firm formal involvement in the Community's legislative processes. The most outstanding initiative was the interim report produced by French Socialist rapporteur Gilles Gozard, who presented his report during a plenary session in June 1956, at a time when the technical deliberations for the EEC Treaty were well advanced. As a direct response to the proposals formulated by the Committee of National Experts, the report contained an institution-by-institution analysis. Among the proposals formulated in the report were demands concerning the role of the Common Assembly. They included: gradually making the Council of Ministers accountable to the Common Assembly; giving the Common Assembly the power to discuss the budget chapter by chapter and to amend it; and giving the Common Assembly the power to confirm appointments of members of the European Commission in the new EEC.

In contrast, as the decisive phase in the Intergovernmental Conference negotiations on the final treaties began, the Common Assembly saw a strong parliamentary element within the institutional architecture of the EEC and Euratom watered down. Plans to combine all three communities (ECSC, EEC and Euratom) and to create *one* parliament based on the ECSC Common Assembly had been stopped because of the French parliament's veto of a strong supranational design for Euratom. As an alternative, the Intergovernmental Conference decided to form a new assembly only for the two new communities (EEC and Euratom). This did not come about, however. The then Common Assembly president, the German member Hans Furler, presented an idea for the establishment of one parliament for all three communities at the conference of the six foreign ministers taking place at Val Duchesse, Brussels, on 4 February 1957. Furler's idea was to develop a formula to abolish the Common Assembly at the very moment when the new assembly was constituted, with the latter fully incorporating the competences exercised by the ECSC Common Assembly, along with the additional competences included in the new treaties. In fact, when the bodies established by the Rome Treaties were formed, a single assembly was constituted at the first plenary session of the new common assembly in March 1958, to be called European Parliamentary Assembly (EPA) from then on.

Moreover, various long-standing demands concerning the Assembly's rights and powers were met by the Rome Treaties. This is especially true of three far-reaching treaty provisions: first, Article 144 of the EEC Treaty (Euratom Treaty, Article 114) introduced the generalized right for the Assembly to censure the European Commission (previously restricted, by Article 24 of the ECSC Treaty, to the context of the debate on the annual general report); second, numerous articles in both treaties introduced, through the consultation procedure, the formal right to parliamentary involvement in the legislative process; and third, Article 203 of the EEC Treaty (Euratom Treaty, Article 178) introduced parliamentary (consultative) involvement in the budgetary procedure (Westlake 1994). All in all, however, the new Assembly's formal powers remained very limited.

Apart from that, the new EPA grew in size. The number of members increased from 78 to 142. The practice of the dual mandate was maintained. It was then perceived as a means of linking the Assembly to the member states' national parliaments. At the first plenary session in March 1958, Robert Schuman was elected president by acclamation. The number of committees also grew. The former seven committees were joined by six others (Committee on Commercial Policy and Economic Cooperation with Third Countries; Committee on Agriculture; Committee on the Association of the Overseas Countries and Territories; Committee on Energy Policy; Committee on Scientific and Technical Research; and Committee on Safety and Hygiene at Work and Health Protection). Moreover, the EPA decided to stop the practice of seating members in alphabetical order. From now on, members belonging to the same political group sat together in the plenary. This helped to facilitate the political groups' parliamentary work further, but also highlighted the political nature of the Assembly as a supranational institution. Finally, the number of political groups also grew. In 1965, the French Gaullists split from the Liberal Group and formed the European Democratic Union Group.

The members kept pushing for strengthening the Assembly's standing in the newly emerging governance system at the European level. Words mattered in this context. By adopting the title 'European Parliament' in March 1962, it claimed a larger role for itself, even if the new name was not officially recognized by the other institutions (Patel and Salm 2021b). In addition, the members were strongly determined to make the Rome Treaties' constitutional obligation of direct elections come true. They argued that democratizing the EEC by holding EP direct elections would eliminate the existing participatory deficit and increase the stake and interest of European citizens in EEC policy- and decision-making. Therefore, in May 1960, the EPA voted on a draft convention on direct elections, prepared by the Belgian Socialist Fernand Dehousse. However, it was only in December 1969, at the summit meeting in the Hague, that the heads of state and government of the EEC declared themselves in favour of direct elections.

# 3. Professionalizing the Parliament's work, 1969–79

The 1969 declaration of the EEC heads of state and government in favour of direct elections provided a new impetus for the EP's political groups to extend and strengthen their organizational structures. The political scientist David Marquand (1978) anticipated a much greater role for the political groups in view of the increased politicization of EEC politics in the wake of first direct elections. This was symbolized by the creation of new political groups at the margins of the EP's political spectrum. In 1973, the European Conservative Group and the Communist and Allies Group were formed. In addition, the Community's 1973 enlargement with the arrival of new group members from the UK, Denmark and Ireland required changes in the groups' organizational structures and working procedures. As a result, the groups' secretariats mushroomed. Furthermore, over the course of the 1970s, the political groups' professionalization increased through the establishment of various units and working parties on specific political topics to support its members' parliamentary work.

As a further result of the declaration of the EEC heads of state and government, the extra-parliamentary dimension of the political groups started to professionalize. In fact, the EP's political groups pushed for the foundation of political parties at the European level to define and permanently defend their policies in EEC politics. The political groups' national member parties reacted by founding new European party associations based on previous more loose and informal cooperation forms. As the first, the Socialist and Socialist Democratic parties founded the Confederation of Socialist Parties in the Community in April 1974. In March 1976, the liberal parties followed by founding the Federation of Liberal and Democratic Parties in Europe, renamed one year later as European Liberals and Democrats. Likewise, the Christian Democratic parties pushed forward the formalization of their transnational cooperation by founding the European People's Party (EPP) in April 1976. However, the parties' extra-parliamentary formal cooperation was rather weak at that time and depended on financial and organizational support from the EP's political groups.

Crucially, in the course of the 1970s, the EP gained in formal power due to competency expansion in budgetary issues. First, in 1970, the Treaty on Own Resources introduced the EP's right to have the last word on non-compulsory Community expenditure. Second, in 1975, the Budgetary Powers Treaty gave the EP the right to reject the EEC budget in total. Both budgetary decisions substantially increased the EP's say and put it suddenly on an even level with the Council of Ministers after having been deprived of any budgetary powers at all before. According to Mechthild Roos (2021a, 2021b), the EPs newly gained say in budgetary issues allowed it to be formally involved in many more policymaking processes than had previously been the case. At a symbolical level, this power increase was represented by the EP gaining its own debating chamber, the hemicycle for the plenary sessions, in use from 1973 on in the EP's Schuman Building in Luxembourg.

In the 1970s, the EP also fine-tuned its informal policymaking means. It especially developed strong roles as a discursive power and an agenda-setter. In terms of discursive power, it contributed more and more to shaping policymaking discourses between the Council of Ministers, the Commission and the member states. It did so, for example, by constantly sending messages about its political missions such as speaking for the European people and defending democracy. This helped to strengthen its discursive power vis-à-vis the other institutions. In terms of agenda-setting, the EP expanded its initiatives with the emergence of new policy fields at the European level such as social, environmental or foreign policy coordination in the 1970s. It often aimed for setting issues on the EEC's agenda that were far from its official remit. For example, the EP attempted to shape the EEC's agenda in the field of human rights (Gfeller 2014), a policy field that especially got attention in the second half of the 1970s.

In the course of the 1970s, the EEC was increasingly confronted with discussions on its democratic deficit. The EEC's democratic deficit was acutely demonstrated by the fact that the EP was still not legitimized by direct elections. Following the pressure of the EP and others, including the Commission, the

FIGURE 7.1 *Simone Veil chairing the first plenary session of the European Parliament elected by direct universal suffrage in July 1979. Courtesy of European Communities, 1979.*

Council of Ministers finally issued the Electoral Act proposing the elections of MEPs by direct election. Held for the first time in June 1979, direct elections thus took place about nineteen years after the EP had first submitted a proposal for direct elections. A milestone in the EP's history was reached when 180 million European citizens were called to vote for the MEPs (for examples of election posters, see Figures 7.2 and 7.1). High-ranking politicians, such as the former German Chancellor Willy Brandt and the former French Minister of Health Simone Veil, stood for elections.

The turnout in the first direct elections was around 63 per cent. The practice of the dual mandate was discouraged with the first elections (and officially abolished in 2009), while the number of MEPs grew to 410. Based on the election result, seven political groups were constituted at the EP's opening session in July 1979. In addition to the six existing political groups, the Group for the Technical Coordination and Defence of Independent Groups and Members was established. The MEPs voted for Simone Veil to become the EP's president, the first female politician in this office (Figure 7.1). A Jewish survivor of the Nazi concentration camps, Veil's election can be seen as a symbolic stand against the nationalism that was one of the causes of the First and Second World Wars.

While it has been often argued that the first elections were a decisive turning point in the EP's history (e.g. Brunn 2004), the latest research has shown that this was less the case (Patel and Salm 2021a). Although the

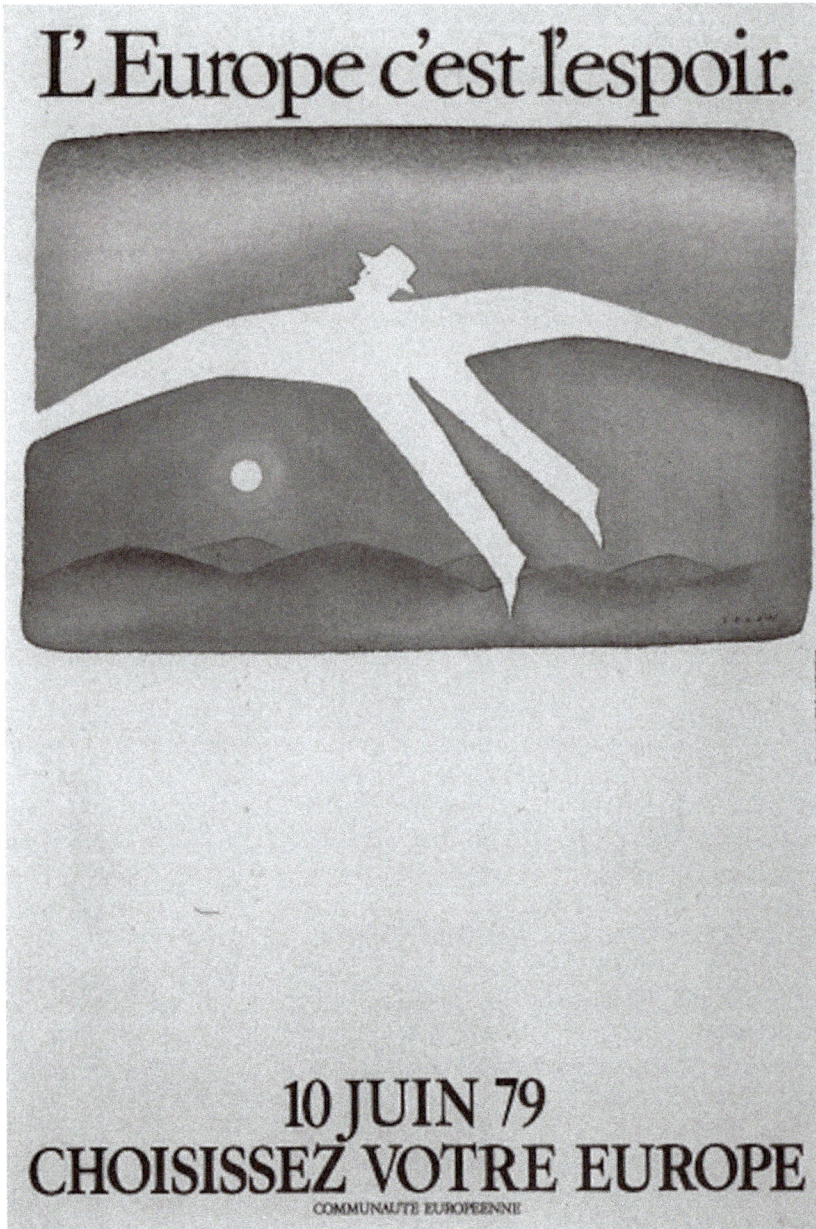

FIGURE 7.2  *Election poster, France, 1979. Courtesy of Jean-Michel Folon [illustration], European Communities, 1979.*

FIGURE 7.3 *Election poster, UK, 1979. Courtesy of Kathleen Ramboer [illustration], European Communities, 1979.*

EP increased its assertiveness vis-à-vis the other institutions by boosting its legitimacy through direct elections, by 1979 it had already developed crucial means such as discursive power and agenda-setting for impacting EEC policy- and decision-making. In addition, with the two budgetary treaties of 1970 and 1975, the EP had already gained in formal power within the Community's governance system.

# 4. Working out the Parliament's powers, 1979–92

The first legislative period of the directly elected EP from 1979 to 1984 (elections take place every five years) started with a big bang. In December 1979, the EP risked stormy relations with the Commission and the Council and rejected the EEC budget for 1980 by a large majority for the first time in its history. Combining its right to reject the EEC budget in total and its legitimacy as the only directly elected EEC institution, the EP underlined with the rejection of the budget its newly gained formal power. It demanded an increase of non-compulsory expenditure. At the same time, it criticized the excessive expenditure on the EEC's common agricultural policy. The Council and the Commission did not really react to the EP's budget criticism and made little attempt to meet the EP's demands. As a consequence, it took six months to sort out the issues and to adopt the 1980 budget. However, it was by far not the budget the EP had fought for. Nevertheless, the EP continued its strategy and rejected a supplementary budget in 1982 and again the entire EEC budget in 1984. By doing so, the EP cemented its central role in the field of budget policy (Wassenberg and Schirmann 2019).

Besides budgetary matters, the EP worked for realizing EEC institutional reform in the 1980s. By using its limited powers to extract procedural concessions from the Commission and the Council, the EP attempted to change institutional rules and practices for achieving its vision of a Community with greater efficiency and much more democratic decision-making structures (Kaiser 2021). Altiero Spinelli, a former Italian commissioner and MEP since 1979, was a driving force for institutional reform (Chapter 13). As an arch federalist, he pushed for a constitution for Europe and supported plans for an almost federal EU. Accordingly, when becoming EP rapporteur for a draft on a treaty establishing the EU, he suggested a completely new treaty with several new EEC competences instead of implementing piecemeal institutional reform within the scope of the Rome Treaties. Organized by Spinelli, the EP adopted by a large majority the Draft Treaty on European Union (DTEU), also known as the Spinelli draft, in a plenary session in February 1984. However, the DTEU was never ratified and did not trigger any major institutional reform. Nevertheless, it included ideas and concepts for institutionalizing the EEC that were incorporated into later institutional reform, such as the Single European Act (SEA) of 1986 and the Maastricht Treaty of 1992.

As the Community's first major treaty revision, the SEA entailed some crucial amendments for the EP. Above all, it extended the EP's formal power by introducing the cooperation procedure. Applied to important areas such as the legislative harmonization of the Single Market, specific research programmes, regional funds decisions and some social policy matters, it allowed the EP to impede by two readings the adoption of proposed legislation by the Council. Although somewhat moderate, the EP thus finally gained formal influence in EEC law-making. Furthermore, the SEA made the EP's formal consent obligatory for accessions of new states to the EEC as well as for association agreements with third countries. Moreover, as the first official document referring to 'the European Parliament', the other EEC institutions now officially recognized that title.

The EP's strengthened role in the course of the 1980s was also marked when Commission President Jacques Delors, just after taking office, presented his political agenda to the EP plenary in January 1985. This was something previous Commission presidents had not done. Having been an MEP himself from 1979 to 1981, Delors understood the EP's importance from the start, both as a platform for preparing and explaining his policy initiatives and as an ally to tackle any resistance from recalcitrant member states. As a consequence, the Commission became more open and sensitive to the EP's demands. Conversely, the EP continued to defend the Commission as the EEC's legislative powerhouse.

The EP's formal power expansion by the cooperation procedure and the increase in its assertiveness as the only directly legitimized EEC institution, however, stood in stark contrast to the turnouts of the European elections in 1984 and 1989. While in 1984 the turnout, at 61 per cent, was close to the turnout in the first election, it fell further in the 1989 election, to 59 per cent. The public interest of 1979, when some big names such as Veil and Brandt had campaigned for an EP seat, could not be repeated. The 1984 and 1989 elections did not change in the representation of the different political groups in the EP. As in 1979, the Socialist Group formed the biggest group, closely followed by the group of the EPP. With ten political groups for the parliamentary term starting in 1989, it was the largest number of political groups ever to be simultaneously represented in the EP, stretching across the political spectrum from far left to far right.

As after the 1979 elections the number of MEPs increased and was to increase further in the 1984 and 1989 elections; the EP's hemicycle in the Schuman Building in Luxembourg became too small, and plenary meetings were again more often held in Strasbourg. At the same time, the EP shifted more and more parliamentary activities, such as committee meetings, to Brussels. In 1992, the decision of the member-state governments to lay down where the EU institutions are officially seated had important consequences for the EP's working practices. Its official seat and venue for most plenary sessions became Strasbourg. Committee meetings were to take place in Brussels. The official place of the EP's Secretariat became Luxembourg. This decision by member-state governments thus officially established the EP's travelling circus with hundreds of MEPs and staff members commuting monthly between Brussels and Strasbourg to this day.

# 5. Getting on equal footing with the Council, 1992–2014

Often described as the greatest milestone in European integration, the 1992 Maastricht Treaty involved the most significant extension of the EP's formal powers in its history. A new legislative procedure, known as the co-decision procedure, put the EP on nearly equal footing with the Council of Ministers in terms of law-making in some fields. Basically, an upgrade of the cooperation procedure of the SEA, the co-decision procedure requires that both the EP and the Council have a deciding vote in the legislative process and may amend legislative proposals. The main changes included the EP's right for a third reading and to refer a legislative proposal to a conciliation committee composed of members of the Council and the EP in case the Council did not accept its amendments. Policy areas subject to the co-decision procedure included the EU's internal market, customs union, competition and structural policy, trade and consumer protection.

With the extension of the EP's legislative authority, the Maastricht Treaty was a reaction to concerns about a widening democratic deficit as a result of the SEA. Although the SEA had extended the EP's formal power with the cooperation procedure, it always lagged behind the transfer of competence to the European level, thus enhancing the gap between decision-makers in Brussels and EU citizens directly represented by the EP. Therefore, the co-decision procedure aimed at increasing the new EU's democratic legitimacy in law- and decision-making. Seeing itself as the representative of the EU people and thus providing democratic legitimacy to the EU more than the other EU institutions, the EP did not wait long to make full use of its new formal decision-making instrument (Dinan 2014).

Nevertheless, informal means of decision- and policymaking remained important for the EP and its political groups to have an impact in the EU's complex governance system. As one result thereof, the political groups' extra-parliamentary dimension in the form of transnational party cooperation began to transform into real European political parties in 1992 with the Maastricht Treaty establishing the framework. For example, the Confederation of Socialist Parties converted into the Party of European Socialists. Together, the European political parties and the EP's political groups are the hub to define European policies and to put these on the EU's agenda. Naturally, European political parties also campaign in EP direct elections. Since 2004, European political parties are funded by the EP.

The political groups themselves grew in size in the course of the period 1992 and 2014. This time with the consent of the EP, the EU enlargement rounds of 1995, 2005, 2007 and 2013 constantly increased the number of both the political groups' MEPs and staff members (Chapter 4). After the 2014 election, for example, the two biggest groups, the EPP and the Socialist Group, calling itself Progressive Alliance of Socialists and Democrats (S&D) since 2009, had 221 and 181 MEPs, respectively. Clearly, the biggest political groups have the highest number of different nationalities of members. They are heterogeneous entities. Thus, the various national delegations within the political groups make the EP a far more complex political institution than national parliaments.

Despite the European political parties and their national member parties campaigning, the trend of continuously falling election turnouts from the 1980s continued in the 1990s, the 2000s and 2010s. Therefore, even though the 1992 Maastricht Treaty had turned the EP into a co-legislator, the issue of democratic legitimacy due to the persistent lack of public enthusiasm for the EP remained highly salient. In order to make citizens feel they have a say in EU politics, the EP's formal powers were further increased in the 1990s and 2000s. For example, the 1997 Amsterdam Treaty broadened the scope of legislation adopted by the co-decision procedure. It also gave the EP the power to approve the appointment of the Commission president. Other candidates for the Commission needed to undergo interviews by the relevant EP committees. This made the Commission more politically accountable vis-à-vis the EP as witnessed with the resignation of the Santer Commission in 1999 (Chapter 5).

The 2007 Lisbon Treaty further strengthened the EP's budgetary, legislative and supervisory powers and extended the co-decision procedure to important policy areas such as immigration and asylum policy. In addition, the EP again acquired even more influence in the appointment of the Commission and its president by permanently recognizing the EP's vote of confidence and the EP's right to remove the Commission from office by a two-thirds majority of votes cast and by a majority of MEPs.

Furthermore, the Lisbon Treaty established an explicit link between European elections and the Commission president. As a consequence, the 2014 European election introduced the *Spitzenkandidaten* process, an approach whereby European political parties nominate their lead candidate ahead of European elections, and the largest EP political group after the election is considered to have a mandate to provide the Commission president (Chapter 5). Despite this political and institutional development, the turnout fell to a historical low in 2014 with an EU average of 42 per cent. It was only in the 2019 elections that the turnout, at 51 per cent, increased for the first time since the first direct election in 1979. More than 50 per cent of EU citizens eligible to take part in the elections went to the polls, making it the largest transnational election ever held. According to the Lisbon Treaty, the EU citizens elected 751 MEPs. However, the EU withdrawal of the UK (Brexit), to which the EP gave its consent when approving the Brexit deal in January 2021, reduced the number of MEPs to 705. After a long time of permanent increase, it was the first time in the EP's history that the number of MEPs decreased.

# Conclusion

The EP matters in today's EU governance system and did so since the beginning of the European integration process in the early 1950s. As is the case with national parliaments, among the EP's main functions are the duty to check and challenge the work of the executive, to make and change laws and to debate political issues of the day. Nevertheless, the EP is a very special creature (Patel and Salm 2021b) and not only due to it being a supranational parliament. Compared to the main functions most national parliaments fulfil in liberal democracies, it still lags behind in terms of formal powers. The EP still has no formal right to initiate legislation, which is still the prerogative of the Commission and to a limited but increasing extent also of the Council of Ministers and the European Council.

In the course of its long history, the EP always looked for ways to compensate for its formal weakness. Therefore, informal ways of policymaking were crucial for the EP. It was most dynamic and effective in its roles as discursive power and agenda setter. In addition, after the first European elections in 1979, the EP argued that as the only directly elected representative of the people it would be logically entitled to have a decisive say in EEC, and later EU, policy- and decision-making processes. In fact, this argument helped a lot to increase the EP's assertiveness despite constantly falling election turnouts until 2019. The EP has always been the key institution to tackle the EU's sensitive issue of democratic legitimacy for European integration. With its MEPs representing the EU citizens' political will at the European level, it contributes to close the gap between EU policy- and decision-makers and EU citizens, identified (e.g. Habermas 2011) as the EU's democratic deficit.

From today's point of view, the EP's constant extension of formal powers leading to joint legislative authority with the Council appears logical. Looking back to the EP's founding years in the form of the then ECSC Common Assembly with its purely advisory and controlling functions, however, it has taken the most remarkable development of all EU institutions. The cooperation procedure introduced with SEA and the co-decision procedure implemented with the Maastricht Treaty were milestones in this development. They were, inter alia, aimed to turn the EP into the incarnation of the EU's democratic legitimacy. In the EP's self-perception, it always was.

# Five key questions

1. How did the ECSC Common Assembly underpin that it understood itself as a supranational parliamentary representation?
2. What kind of policymaking means did the EP develop to compensate for its lack of formal power, and how did it make us of them?
3. Why was it so difficult to extend the EP's formal power?
4. How can we explain concerns about the EU's democratic legitimacy despite the EP's co-legislating role?
5. What were the main developments in the history of the EEC/EU towards increasing the EPs power and influence?

# Ten key readings

Corbett, R., F. Jacobs and M. Shackleton (2021), *The European Parliament*, 9th ed., London: John Harper.

Héritier, A., K. L. Meissner, C. Moury and M. G. Schoeller (2019), *European Parliament Ascendant: Parliamentary Strategies of Self-Empowerment in the EU*, Basingstoke: Palgrave Macmillan.

Kreppel, A. (2002), *The European Parliament and Supranational Party System: A Study in Institutional Development*, Cambridge: Cambridge University Press.

Mény, Y. (2009), *Building Parliament: 50 years of European Parliament History, 1958–2008*, Luxembourg: Office for Official Publications of the European Communities.

Patel, K. K., and C. Salm (eds) (2021), Special Issue on the European Parliament, *Journal of European Integration History*, 27 (1).

Priestly, J. (2008), *Six Battles That Shaped Europe's Parliament*, London: John Harper.

Rittberger, B. (2005), *Building Europe's Parliament: Democratic Representation beyond the Nation State*, Oxford: Oxford University Press.

Roos, M. (2021a), *The Parliamentary Roots of European Social Policy: Turning Talk into Power*, Basingstoke: Palgrave Macmillan.

Soldwisch, I. (2021), *Das Europäische Parlament 1979–2004: Inszenierung, Selbst(er)findung und politisches Handeln der Abgeordneten*, Stuttgart: Kohlhammer Verlag.

Tulli, U. (2017), *Un Parlamento per l'Europa. Il Parlamento europeo e la battaglia per la sua elezione (1948–1979)*, Milan: Mondadori.

# Policies

# 8

# The construction of a single market: Liberalization and its regulation

## *Laurent Warlouzet*

## Introduction

This chapter will explore the economic developments of the European Union (EU) and its forerunners from 1948 onwards, by focusing on the establishment of a unified European market. The key question this chapter will address is: why did European integration place the economy, and in particular the market, at its core? It will argue that the European economic integration process has been multifaceted as it encompasses three main dimensions, namely a market-oriented, a socially oriented and a neomercantilist dimension (Warlouzet 2018a and 2022); these three dimensions will be introduced in the first section of the chapter. The first dimension was prevalent with the establishment of a unified European market between the Marshall Plan and 1992 (Sections 2 and 3), reinforced by an ambitious and contested agenda of liberalization (Section 4), including competition and trade policies (Sections 5 and 6). By contrast, the setting up of an industrial policy was largely a failure (Section 7). However, a regional policy emerged and represented an embryonic social dimension (Section 8).

# 1. The three economic Europes

All economic policies are characterized by a mix of three features: (1) a market-oriented dynamic that focuses on removing obstacles to free trade in order to unleash growth; (2) a socially oriented approach that aims at protecting the weakest from the detrimental effects of the market; and (3) a neomercantilist thrust that nurtures national companies by shielding them from free market dynamics (Figure 8.1) (Warlouzet 2018a, 2022). The second category includes social and environmental policies, while the third usually refers to industrial policy.

All of these three orientations can be pushed to their extremes. In the market-oriented orientation, one can drift into neoliberalism when the aim is to destroy the welfare state. Socialism is the extreme form of a socially oriented approach; and outright protectionism combined with autarky is

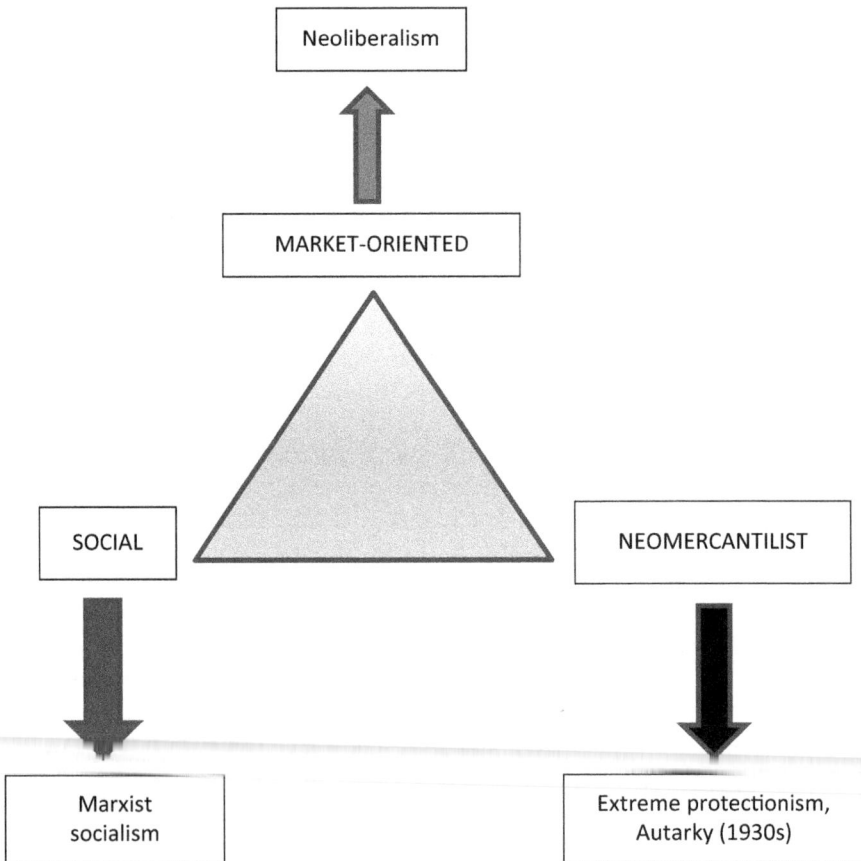

FIGURE 8.1 *The three types of economic policy.*

the ultimate form of neomercantilism. All three of these approaches can be combined: in most Western European countries, the post-war boom was marked by an association between socially oriented and neomercantilist features. Neoliberal ideas rose in the 1980s at their expense. However, from 2017 to 2021, US President Donald Trump embodied a peculiar combination of neoliberalism and neomercantilism.

Even though social and even neomercantilist features are visible, European integration has been mostly driven by a market-oriented streak since its origins.

# 2. From the Marshall Plan to the Common Market, 1948–1970s

The idea of building Europe around the market did not come out of the blue. It emerged in the interwar period as a tool to promote a lasting peace on the continent after the devastation brought by the First World War, to rekindle economic growth and to overcome the new boundaries emerging in Europe after the dissolution of the German, Russian and Austrian-Hungarian Empires. Work on trade liberalization took place within the framework of the League of Nations in the 1920s, without much success. After the Wall Street Crash of 1929 triggered a deep economic crisis, most countries chose protectionism instead of international cooperation. The most radical version of this orientation took the form of autarky promoted by the totalitarian regimes.

After the war, the 1930s served as a cautionary tale for the Western elites who enjoyed the support of the majority of their population. After 1945, they adopted what John Ruggie (1982) later described as 'embedded liberalism', which united both the commitment to international free trade in order to defuse protectionist tendencies that could fuel nationalism and the building of a strong national welfare state to alleviate poverty, in order to integrate all social classes in a prosperous society.

In 1948, under strong pressure from the US government, the Marshall Plan led to the creation of the first European organization, the Organization for European Economic Cooperation (OEEC). This organization oversaw both the dispensation of US grants to its members and a gradual opening of European markets. The OEEC imposed the progressive removal of quotas (a set quantity of imports of a given good for one year), but customs duties, also known as 'tariffs' (a tax imposed on imports, regardless of their quantity), remained. In case of economic or monetary troubles, a safeguard clause could be applied to erect temporary protectionist barriers. In 1950, the European Payments Union (EPU) was created to facilitate intra-European monetary transactions, which were hampered by the lack of fully convertible currencies such as the US dollar. Building on an initial endowment by the

United States, and thanks to the multilateralization of trade balances, the EPU facilitated intra-European payments (Chapter 1).

In 1951, the European Coal and Steel Community (ECSC) aimed at creating a common market for coal and steel. Its High Authority, a predecessor of the European Commission, was set up to ensure that fair rules prevailed for every economic actor. As a result, the ECSC lifted quotas, but also tariffs and other barriers, such as cartels, mergers and different price scales. For the French steel industry in particular, it was important to get access to German coal at the same price as their German competitors; otherwise, competition would be skewed. In other words, a regulated market, albeit only for coal and steel, was shaped.

In 1957, the same logic was applied to the development of the 'Common Market', a widely used alternative name for the European Economic Community (EEC). The EEC applied the ECSC blueprint to all sectors of the economy except agriculture, which was concerned with specific provisions (Chapter 9), and a few other strategic industries. The European Commission exercised its prerogatives over a wider set of sectors than the ECSC High Authority but with less detailed power to regulate industries.

The Common Market was set up swiftly, and more quickly than expected. The Treaty of Rome foresaw a transition period ranging from twelve to fifteen years after it had entered into force on 1 January 1958, which translated into the opening of a custom-free zone between 1 January 1970 and 1 January 1973. Instead, the pace of trade liberalization was accelerated twice, in 1960 and 1962; and the Common Market was opened on 1 July 1968, eighteen months ahead of schedule (Chapter 2). All internal quotas and customs duties disappeared at that date. But many barriers to trade remained, since customs officials had to control the compliance of goods with non-tariff barriers, such as national standards and taxes.

Logically, the Commission then planned to embark on a further stage of deeper market integration via the removal of non-tariff barriers, such as technical standards. On 5 March 1968, the Commission released its 'General program for elimination of technical barriers to trade due to disparities in national legislation' (doc. COM [68] 138), which encompassed the adoption of hundreds of directives harmonizing legislation and reciprocal recognition of national controls. The document proposed several methods, ranging from total harmonization at the European level, to a minimalistic harmonization limited to security norms defined by an international standardization board.

However, each technical barrier had to be eliminated following the procedure of Article 100 EEC, which required unanimity in the Council. In other words, all six, soon to be nine, member states had to agree unanimously on every single piece of legislation. Since every national norm expressed a delicate balance between market-oriented, neomercantilist and social (in particular, health and security) concerns, it was a daunting task. The enlargement, which brought countries with different legal traditions into the EEC – especially the UK's and Ireland's common law – as well as the renewal of protectionist tendencies linked to the economic crisis of the 1970s, mired this agenda in quicksand.

# 3. Opening up the 'Internal Market', 1986–92

The breakthrough came only with the 1986 Single Act, which launched the Internal Market programme. It replaced unanimity in the Council of Ministers with qualified majority voting for all proposals related to this endeavour. This watershed originated in three dynamics.

First, it was a long-standing project of the supranational institutions, as the 1968 Commission's memorandum demonstrated. In 1979, the Court's *Cassis de Dijon* ruling revived the issue somewhat (Chapter 6). It limited the scope of national non-tariff barriers that were considered disproportionate. *Cassis de Dijon* promoted the principle of mutual recognition, which had already been sketched out before, but left many exemptions (Albors-Llorens, Barnard and Leucht 2021). Ground eight of the *Cassis de Dijon* decision (Case 120–78) listed four areas in which national legislation could still prevail: 'the effectiveness of fiscal supervision, the protection of public health, the fairness of commercial transactions, and the defence of the consumer'.

Because those were broad exemptions, the Commission considered the *Cassis de Dijon* ruling helpful but not revolutionary (Warlouzet 2018a). When the German expert Karl-Heinz Narjes (a convinced European who had written his doctoral thesis on customs unions), the commissioner for the internal market, wanted to promote its draft legislations aimed at removing non-tariff barriers between 1980 and 1984, his proposals became stuck in the Council, as the rule of unanimity prevented any progress. Narjes was successful in promoting a new agenda of creating a genuine 'internal market' in terms of communication, but not in terms of decisions actually taken.

Therefore, it took a second decisive factor to bring about the reform: the convergence of member states (Warlouzet 2018a). In 1984, unemployment reached 10 per cent in the UK, France and Belgium, whereas the United States had recovered more quickly from the second oil shock after 1982 (the US unemployment rate fell to 7 per cent in 1984). The 'American challenge' (see below) remained prevalent and was even supplemented by a 'Japanese challenge', since a new formidable competitor in all high-value-added sectors had emerged in Eastern Asia since the 1970s.

In France, President François Mitterrand, a Socialist, had chosen a national recovery plan in 1981 by unleashing a large economic stimulus programme. It led to more inflation and yawning deficits, which put France on the brink of requesting International Monetary Fund (IMF) lending in 1983. Moreover, the protectionist policy dubbed as 'reconquest of the internal market' ended in ridicule. In 1982, in order to thwart the imports of Japanese tape recorders and to protect the French producer, the Minister of Industry Laurent Fabius invented an original non-trade barrier: the obligation for all Japanese tape recorders to undergo customs procedure in Poitiers, a town in central France, far from the harbours where the goods had arrived, and far from the main urban areas where they were to be sold. This blatant protectionist measure triggered strong criticism from France's trade partners, including those within the EEC, as it could possibly herald a protectionist chain reaction and was inefficient. In 1983, the French Socialists chose another tactic: to flag up what they considered to be protectionism on the part of their European partners. Mitterrand pointed out that all countries were protectionist, and not just France, if non-tariff barriers such as the German beer law were taken into account. The French president was referring to the so-called German purity law dating back to the sixteenth century, which stated that only three ingredients should be used for beer production: water, barley and hops. As a result, beers using other ingredients such as spices or additives, dubbed in Germany as 'chemical beers', were banned from the German market. In 1983–4, French officials explored ways to remove technical barriers through bilateral Franco-German talks, but these soon floundered. In the end, the only viable solution seemed to be the European one.

This concern about a perceived German technical protectionism was shared on the other side of the Channel. There, neoliberal Margaret Thatcher supported the Internal Market agenda as a second-best option since her project of worldwide negotiations to free trade had stalled in the early 1980s. In Germany too, support for the Internal Market stemmed from a commitment to promote free trade. However, the German government was concerned about the downgrading of standards that could result from a European harmonization (hence a fear of 'chemical beers' if the standards were relaxed). More generally, for most member states, the Internal Market became consensual, even if it was usually only a second best.

Third, transnational networks mobilized around this idea in the 1980s. A growing number of Members of the European Parliament (MEPs) supported the agenda of completion of the Internal Market for the same reasons as member states and supranational institutions. They formed a transpartisan grouping to promote this idea known as the 'Kangaroo' group, named after the marsupial's ability to jump across barriers (Warlouzet 2020). The Kangaroo group was animated by a group of MEPs from various backgrounds, including mainly Basil de Ferranti, a British Conservative (and a businessman involved in the Ferranti telecommunication firm); Karl von Wogau, a German Christian Democrat; Dieter Rogalla, a German Social Democrat; Eline Boot, a Dutch Christian Democrat; and Christiane Scrivener, a French Liberal (who went on to become European Commissioner for taxation and customs union from 1989 to 1995). The Kangaroo group held meetings and sometimes organized high-profile events. Rogalla, a former customs official himself, organized a 'cycling for Europe' tour to promote the removal of internal borders (Figure 8.2).

FIGURE 8.2 *Dieter Rogalla, a member of the European Parliament, on his bicycle, promoting a 'Europe without borders', June 1987. Courtesy of European Parliament, 1987.*

Lastly, business organizations such as the UNICE, the federation of national business associations, and the European Round Table of Industrialists (ERT), an association of big multinationals set up in 1983, were also in favour of this agenda of removing non-tariff barriers, with some of the ERT members also advocating neomercantilist measures such as a European preference for the public procurement of certain products (van Apeldoorn 2003).

When Delors took the helm of the European Commission, he pledged to 'eliminate all frontiers within Europe by 1992' in the opening speech of his presidency, delivered before the European Parliament (EP) on 14 January 1985. He used canny metaphors to disparage the Community as a 'feudal State where barriers, customs posts, formalities and red tape proliferate'. He linked the removal of borders with a broader political agenda, nothing less than 'the birth of effective citizenship' (through freedom of movements of people) and 'the renaissance of democracy'. He unveiled an ambitious programme linking the completion of the Internal Market and the promotion of social, regional and industrial policy, that is, a balance between the three types of economic policies (Warlouzet 2018a, 192–3; Delors 1985).

The market-oriented part of this programme was then spelled out in a white paper supervised by Arthur Cockfield, a former minister under Thatcher and the commissioner who had succeeded Narjes. Released on 14 June 1985, it listed around three hundred directives that needed to be adopted to remove non-tariff barriers and hence all border controls. A treaty change was necessary to impose qualified majority voting, the only solution to overcome the threat of one state vetoing important measures. The Milan Council held in June 1985 paved the way for intergovernmental negotiations on a new treaty, the Single Act, which was eventually signed in February 1986. It imposed the use of qualified majority voting for all legislation related to the completion of the Internal Market, except in fiscal and social affairs. Article 18 stated that the harmonization of laws concerning health, safety, environment and consumer protection should be accomplished in order to ensure a 'high level of protection'.

The Internal Market as a borderless space was opened as planned on 31 December 1992. Between 1987, the year when the Single Act entered into force, and 1992, a flurry of European legislation was adopted in many different areas, from toy safety to car emissions. Building on the *Cassis de Dijon* case, the Commission promoted the so-called New Approach, which shied away from total harmonization, opting instead for the definition only of the essential health and safety requirements and the delegation of rulemaking to private standardizing bodies through a contractual relationship (Egan 2001).

For each regulation, the tensions between market-oriented, social and neomercantilist concerns were obvious. Regarding car emissions, for example, environmental concerns called for lower emissions of lead and nitrogen oxide, not only to protect health but also to limit acid rain. On the other hand, the neomercantilist concerns of the carmaker Peugeot motivated its CEO, Jacques Calvet, to lobby actively against the directive. But the tide moved against him, both within member states and within the European Commission, where the Italian environmentalist Carlo Ripa di Meana took up the issue in 1989 and secured the adoption of the directive imposing lead-free engines (Warlouzet 2021). In the end, European pressure forced France to adopt a tighter legislation than it had envisaged. Progress was slow, but since the 1990s the EU has gradually become a global leader in promoting greener legislation (Kelemen and Vogel 2010) (Chapter 11).

In the meantime, the Commission ensured the intellectual promotion of its flagship programme by commissioning the Cecchini Report, named after Paolo Cecchini, an Italian economist and former Commission official. Released in 1988, it estimated the total potential economic gain of the

1992 programme at roughly 200 billion European currency unit (Ecu) in 1988 prices, or 5 per cent of GDP. The whole programme was derided by some British and US newspapers in the late 1980s as 'fortress Europe'. Indeed, a draft banking directive containing relatively restrictive measures was imagined but never implemented. Like in the 1960s, when the British derided the 'wall' of the Common Market, even though the British tariffs were actually higher than those of the EEC (Warlouzet 2018a, 79), this accusation of protectionism was largely unfounded, except in the area of agriculture.

# 4. A contested agenda of liberalization

After 1992, the opening of physical borders did not end the effort to deepen the unity of the Internal Market. A rolling agenda of liberalization was put in place. It focused first on ensuring that the decisions voted in Brussels were implemented by national governments (through the transposition of directives in national law) and by certification bodies (Grin 2003). Second, it enlarged the freedom of movements to other areas, notably in the service sector, which represented more than 70 per cent of EU jobs.

Here, the dynamic became contested, especially with the draft directive on the liberalization of services proposed in 2004 by the Dutch Commissioner for the Internal Market Frits Bolkestein (Crespy 2016). A zealous neoliberal, Bolkestein promoted a deep liberalization of the service sector by promoting the country-of-origin principle, according to which the social standards of the country of origin should prevail over those of the host country in certain cases, for certain provisions and for specific sectors. Hence, a fear of a deluge of 'Polish plumbers' cast a shadow over several countries in Western Europe, representing a rare occurrence of a genuinely pan-European public issue, with complaints about the 'polnischer Klempner' in Germany and the 'plombier polonais' in France. This draft text embodied the 'social dumping' that was denounced by Delors in his (aforementioned) January 1985 speech, also referred to as a 'race to the bottom'. Eventually, after much Europe-wide protest, the Bolkestein directive was watered down before its adoption in 2006.

More generally, the liberalization of the service sector is politically sensitive as it touches areas such as health, education or the legal system, which lie at the core of each national identity. In other areas, such as the liberalization of air transport, telecommunications, postal services and energy, which the Commission had advanced since the late 1980s (see below), the resistance came for neomercantilist reasons, that is, to protect the existing companies against new competitors, as well as for social reasons. For example, the national postal and telecommunications monopolies performed certain social tasks, such as providing basic phone and postal services at the same price for remote areas as for densely populated ones.

Here too, a backlash of the defenders of a more social Europe, organized around left-wing parties, trade unions and representatives of former national monopolies, lobbied Brussels since the 1990s. They obtained the legal recognition of 'Service of General Interest' in the 2007 Lisbon Treaty (Crespy 2016). It curtailed the neoliberal dynamic by recognizing instances in which companies could be subsidized for social purposes.

# 5. The rise of competition policy

Liberalization also occurred through European competition policy. Known as 'antitrust' in the United States, competition policy designates the surveillance of market actors by public authorities and aims at ensuring a fair and free competition. It targets some cartels (an association between independent companies) and mergers (a conflation of companies into one single unit). Agreements between companies and mergers are not forbidden per se but are if they unduly restrict market forces by artificially increasing prices and hence benefits.

The development of a competition policy at the European level began in 1951 with the ECSC (Leucht 2010). It was an important innovation, not only because it was a genuine supranational policy – the High Authority was in charge of its implementation alone, with only the judicial control of the Court – but also because very few European countries had provisions in this area in those years. This initiative stemmed from Americanization on the one hand (i.e. the willingness of Americans to export their model and of Europeans to emulate it), and the reform of Germany on the other. Cartelization was associated with the National Socialist period, and Americans were keen to break it by implementing their model of antitrust. In addition, since the French wanted to get cheap German coal for their steel mills, it was useful to entrust a supranational referee to ensure that the same rules applied for both German and French steel plants.

Another functional argument played into the debate: since the ECSC was predicated on the setting up of a common market in coal and steel, it was important to ensure that when public obstacles to trade such as quotas or customs duties were removed, they were not replaced by private obstacles to trade, such as cartels. If steelmaking companies chose to revive the well-known 1926 International Steel Cartel, then the opening of markets would be pointless, even if, in the 1920s, this cartel had been associated by its founder Emile Mayrisch with a willingness to promote European cooperation (Chapter 1).

However, even if the ECSC High Authority received strong prerogatives, it implemented them cautiously, mediating between competing national interests rather than imposing a fully fledged supranational approach (Warlouzet and Witschke 2012).

This ECSC precedent influenced the debate of the Treaty of Rome, and hence the EU's current competition policy, which is still largely based on the articles devised in 1957. The ECSC experience ensured that relatively important powers were granted to the European Commission in this area, albeit slightly less so than for the High Authority, as there was no merger control at first.

In the meantime, a new pro-competition constituency had taken over the European Commission, namely Germans influenced by ordoliberal thinking, led by Hans von der Groeben, one of the main negotiators of the Rome Treaty, who became the first commissioner for competition (Seidel 2010a). For the ordoliberals, the construction of a stable liberal democracy was linked to the setting up of independent authorities ensuring the implementation of free market rules, hence the creation in 1957 of an independent central bank, the Bundesbank, as well as the German cartel authority, which was the most powerful authority of this kind in Europe. Von der Groeben and his team (notably his Chief of Staff Ernst Albrecht, the father of the current Commission President Ursula von der Leyen) managed to pass an ambitious cartel regulation in 1962 (Warlouzet 2016). It entrusted the Commission with a monopoly of information (all agreements had to be notified to it) and of decision (it decided alone, without any votes from the Council).

However, this newfound activism in competition policy proved short-lived. The Commission was unable to implement the cartel regulation swiftly because it became bogged down with tens of thousands of notifications. It took only a handful of decisions. All in all, during the 1960s and the 1970s, European and most national competition policies remained quite weak.

The change came in the 1980s. Dynamic commissioners influenced by the US legal experience, such as the Irishman Peter Sutherland (1985–9), and by British neoliberal reforms, such as the British Commissioner Leon Brittan (1989–93), a former minister of Thatcher, provided a new impetus (Warlouzet 2018a). The European Internal Market programme provided a further ideological boost, even if the Single European Act left the legal framework completely untouched in this area. Sutherland and Brittan targeted more aggressively restrictions of competition by national authorities, and not only by private companies. They implemented a stern state aid control policy: Brussels now requested state aid to be repaid by the company, and financial assistance to be strictly limited to what a private investor would have done. From 1988 onwards, they also liberalized sectors previously shielded from competition such as telecommunications, which was traditionally dominated by national monopolies, and air transports, which was managed by oligopolies of national companies. Both sectors also underwent huge technological disruption, with a decreasing cost of communication, and a wave of deregulation coming from the United States (Thatcher 2007). Crucially, Sutherland and Brittan's initiatives ensured that the liberalization path, which European countries might have gone down anyway, was coupled with a Europeanization dynamic.

Later on, in the 1990s, the Commission strived to widen the scope of liberalization to other sectors such as postal services, where it was successful, and rail transport and energy, where it remained modest due to the huge cost of infrastructure and the strategic factors at play in energy.

Geopolitics also played a role when the Commission targeted the US giant of high tech, starting with IBM in 1984 (even if a settlement was eventually concluded). Mario Monti (commissioner for competition policy from 1999 to 2004) fined Microsoft for abuse of dominant position in the 2000s. Despite considerable political pressure from Washington Monti blocked the merger between two US firms, GE and Honeywell, on competition grounds, even though the merger had been authorized in the United States itself.

Ten years later, the Danish Margaret Vestager (commissioner since 2014) increased the profile of EU competition policy by fining Google, Amazon and Apple for abuse of dominant position and illegal state aids. But her creative interpretation of EU rules was sanctioned by the Court: in 2020, the Tribunal of First Instance rejected her record-breaking 2016 decision against Apple, ordering it to repay 13 billion euros of fiscal aid granted by the Irish government. More generally, the European courts had rejected the Commission's decision many times, forcing the institution to reform itself in the early 2000s by strengthening its economic expertise (Gerber 2007; Warlouzet 2019b).

All in all, the neomercantilist tendency of EU competition policy appears limited. Longitudinal studies conducted over hundreds of EU competition cases show that there is no particular anti-US bias (Billows, Kohl and Tarissan 2021; Bradford, Jackson and Zytnick 2017). If a bias could be found, it was against former national monopolies (such as the companies who dominated the national market in telecommunications, energy or air transport).

# 6. Managing globalization

On the world stage, the Union has played a major role in managing globalization (Chapter 14), which shows how it projects its dual dynamic of liberalization and regulation (in a social and/or in a neomercantilist way). The EEC created a custom union, that is, a zone without internal customs duties and with a common external tariff, and hence a common trade policy. As early as 1964, the European Commission was entrusted with representing the Six at the General Agreement on Tariffs and Trade (GATT) 'Kennedy Round', the first major international negotiations to liberalize trade (Chapter 14; Coppolaro 2013). The Commission acted in close cooperation with the six member states, including Gaullist France, even during the empty chair crisis (July 1965–January 1966) (Chapter 2). The advantages of the leverage a common front of the Six had in the negotiations were not lost in Paris. The Kennedy Round ended in 1967 with a 35 per cent reduction in tariffs for industrial goods on average. The same outcome – roughly a one-third reduction – was achieved by the next grand bargain, the 1973–9 GATT Tokyo Round (Coppolaro 2016).

In the 1970s, in the face of growing competition from new exporters of goods, such as Japan and other Asian countries, the EEC also negotiated neomercantilist measures aimed at protecting its firms from unrestricted competition. The move began in textile with the Multi Fibre Arrangement on textiles and garments, signed in 1974 and renewed regularly. Later on, European countries (and the United States) negotiated the so-called voluntary export restraints with Japan, first on a national basis and then through the Commission. For example, imports of Japanese cars were subjected to quotas until the 1990s (Ballor 2022).

In the meantime, the Community had developed a specific trade relationship with some of its member states' former colonies (Chapter 14). Following a French request, the Yaoundé Convention was set up in 1963 to formalize the association of some of the former French and Belgian African colonies with the EEC, through trade relations and with dedicated development aid. The scheme was later extended to some former British colonies with the 1975 Lomé Convention, concluded with forty-six so-called ACP (Africa-Caribbean-Pacific) countries (Migani 2014b) (Figure 8.3). To some extent, this scheme was a response to the call for fairer world trade relations from the poorer countries of the South, known as the 1974 'New International Economic Order' programme (Garavini 2012). The Lomé Convention included inverted trade preferences (the EEC market was more open to ACP products than the reverse), development aid and the STABEX, a scheme designed to stabilize ACP export earnings. The ACP's revenues

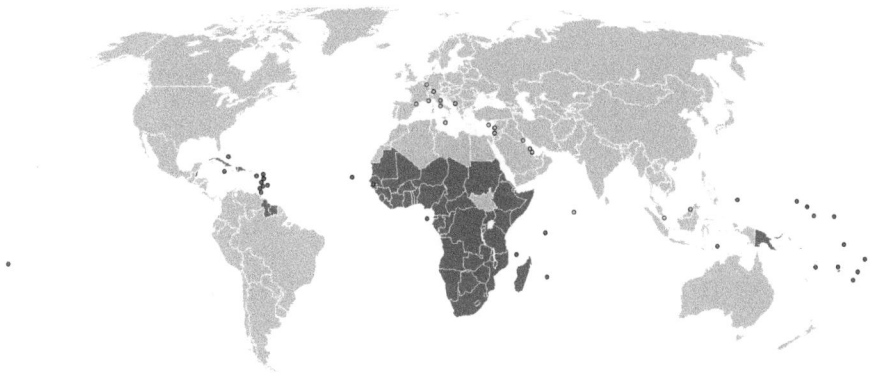

FIGURE 8.3 *Map of the Lomé associated countries (African, Caribbean and Pacific Group of States). https://en.wikipedia.org/wiki/ACP–EU_development_coop eration#/media/File:African,_Caribbean_and_Pacific_Group_of_States_member_ nations_map.svg.*

were often dependent on the exports of a few commodities whose prices fluctuated a lot. When it fell below a certain point, the STABEX provided extra assistance.

The pace of liberalization intensified in the 1980s. The Commission negotiated the GATT Uruguay Round (1986–94), which also concerned agricultural goods for the first time. Its conclusion coincided with the end of the neomercantilist agreements of the 1970s such as the Multi Fibre Agreement and the Japanese voluntary export restraints. At the same time, the GATT was replaced by the more ambitious Word Trade Organization (WTO), with a more elaborate mechanism to deal with trade dispute. The Commission played a major role in it, not least of which was to mediate the recurrent trade disputes with the United States, notably on steel and on Airbus. In addition, when US President Ronald Reagan imposed harsh sanctions on European companies involved in the construction of a Soviet gas pipeline in 1982, the Commission coordinated the European response and obtained a lifting of sanctions a few months later.

With the stalemate of the WTO Doha Round launched in 2001, the EU has shifted its focus towards bilateral trade agreements, such as the Comprehensive Economic and Trade Agreement (CETA) signed in 2016 between the EU and Canada. However, those treaties are more difficult to conclude because they concern not only customs duties, which have already been rather low since the end of the Uruguay Round, but also non-tariff barriers, such as those concerning health, consumer protection and protected geographical indications (for cheese, for example). While the EU has certainly become a norm exporter in many areas (Bradford 2020), the discussions become harder as they encroach on culturally sensitive issues, for example, the European bans on genetically modified organisms and 'chlorinated chickens', that is, chemically cleansed chickens, which are common in North America. Since national parliaments must ratify those so-called mixed agreements, the CETA ratification was stalled at some point by the regional Parliament of Wallonia in 2016. Under insistence from its leader Paul Magnette (who happens to be an academic specialized in EU affairs), the Walloon Parliament obtained a non-binding declaration interpreting the CETA with a slightly more social and neomercantilist tip (Magnette 2005 and 2017).

# 7. The absence of European industrial policy

In 1967, the French journalist Jean-Jacques Servan-Schreiber released the 'American Challenge', which became an international bestseller after it was translated into English in 1968 (Servan-Schreiber 1968). It warned Europe against the domination of American multinationals, notably in high technology. It is often overlooked that this book was also a wake-up call for the development of a supranational industrial policy to counter this

'American challenge'. As a matter of fact, the book was co-written by a European Commission civil servant, Michel Albert, who did not sign it.

From a functional point of view, the case for developing an EEC-wide industrial policy was obvious. Concerning high technology, it would have enabled Europe to share the tremendous costs of development while at the same time providing a larger market for these new products. For traditional manufacturing, a better coordination of national policies of assistance, which were widespread in all countries, would have prevented a subsidy race and fostered rationalization.

However, member states with strong national industrial policies, such as France, found it difficult to Europeanize it without losing control. Conversely, in West Germany, the sheer notion of 'industrial policy' did not exist as such officially, as it smacked of Soviet-style socialism.

Even when a consensus existed on the necessity to have a European-wide industrial approach, disputes erupted over the fair return principle: each state wanted to get a share of jobs corresponding to its share of funding the project, but this usually contradicted the necessity of centralizing the industrial process in a few places. Servan-Schreiber and Albert proposed to overcome this problem by multiplying European industrial cooperation, in order to offset a loss in one programme by a gain in another. A few years later, the federalist Commissioner for Industrial Affairs Altiero Spinelli (1973–7) took over the idea, but member states refused it. At the same time, the variety of national responses to the oil shocks shattered any hopes at building a European energy policy. This field was already marked by the blatant failure of Euratom, the European community set up in 1957 to foster research and cooperation in the atomic energy sector, for lack of interest among member-states.

The debate was rekindled in 1980 in steel (Mény and Wright 1987; Warlouzet 2018a). In 1979, the second oil shock wreaked havoc in European steelmaking with dwindling orders all over the Community. The influential Belgian Commissioner for Industrial Affairs Etienne Davignon (1977–85) proposed to create a Community system of quotas and of state aid control to avoid a race to subsidies. In 1980 the Council accepted this solution, which some officials dubbed a 'cartel managed by the Commission'. It was implemented for a few years but remained exceptional, as member states refused to extend it to other sectors in crisis, despite Davignon's requests to implement it in shipbuilding or in synthetic fibres.

The only EEC industrial initiatives that emerged were confined to Research and Development. In 1984 the Community adopted the European Strategic Program in Information Technology (ESPRIT). Later on, from 1985 to 1995, Delors strove to foster various schemes of industrial policies, especially in high technology when he chaired the Commission, but they mostly failed.

The rise of neoliberal ideas in the 1980s rendered the ideological context more adversarial. According to their promoters, notably Thatcher, industrial policy was an inefficient burden on business and prone to regulatory capture (i.e. the state favoured those with whom it had cosy ties, not those who were the most efficient). The conflict between the neomercantilists and the neoliberals also occurred within the Commission. In 1991, the French-Italian manufacturer of regional aircraft ATR planned to buy its Canadian competitor De Havilland. Delors supported the operation; but Commissioner for Competition Leon Brittan, a former minister of Thatcher, banned the merger, arguing that the resulting company would have been too dominant. Brittan mustered a majority against Delors within the college of commissioners in favour of his decision to ban the operation. In the end, Delors chose to abstain.

The only successful industrial projects were intergovernmental ventures devised outside the European Community, such as Airbus and Ariane. Airbus originated in a 1967 association between British, French and German companies. In 1969, the British left the consortium after quarrels with the French over industrial leadership. They came back in 1978, when the first Airbus A300 met with some commercial success, with a first breakthrough on the US market. Profits came in the early 1990s, after decades of subsidies that were deemed necessary (even by some US economists such as Paul Krugman) to overcome the huge barriers of entry into this market (Warlouzet 2018a, 122). The role of the Commission has been negligible, except to defend the company at the WTO against a US accusation of unfair subsidies. As of today, only four countries (the original three plus Spain) have been involved; otherwise, the division of the production process would have been too difficult.

In the same fashion, Ariane, an intergovernmental venture that originated in the European Space Agency (ESA) founded in 1975, became an international commercial success in the late 1980s. The Commission has lately played a more important role in this venture through the programme of the global navigation satellite system Galileo, launched in 2003 as a joint ESA-EU initiative.

In the end, it was these intergovernmental ventures that took up the 'American Challenge' via a European neomercantilist approach, while the Internal Market provided a free market framework.

# 8. Correcting regional imbalances

Market integration in Europe was associated with a redistribution element right from the start. When the OEEC was set up in 1948, it was designed both to distribute the US Marshall Plan aid, and to progressively open up the European markets mired in protectionism. After the end of the Marshall Plan, redistribution was left to national governments, which steadily beefed up their welfare states (Milward 1984, Milward et al. 1992).

The situation changed only when Britain joined the EEC in 1973. During the enlargement negotiations, British Prime Minister Edward Heath requested a European scheme to assist the poorest regions, namely those affected by the decline in traditional manufacturing (coal mines, textile, shipbuilding and steelmaking). London received strong support from the poorest countries, that is, Italy (whose Southern region, *Mezzogiorno*, was much poorer than its affluent North) and Ireland.

This endeavour materialized with the creation of the European Regional Development Fund (ERDF) in 1975, a rather modest redistributive scheme in terms of funding and of devolution of powers to the Commission, especially because the new British Labour government was much less enthusiastic about the EEC than Heath (George 1994). Regional policy was based on co-funding with national authorities.

In 1986, the Southern enlargement to Portugal and Spain combined with the Internal Market rekindled the debate. For leaders of the poorest countries, notably Spanish Prime Minister Felipe Gonzalez, and for Delors, it was indispensable to complete the 1986 Internal Market programme with a revived regional policy. Rebranded 'cohesion policy', and largely reoriented towards the poorest EEC member states (Greece, Ireland, Portugal and Spain), its funding was doubled by the 1988 'Delors Package', which also capped common agricultural policy (CAP) expenditures. As a result, from 1985 to 1993, the share of regional policy went from 12 per cent to 32 per cent of the EU budget, while the share of the CAP decreased from 68 per cent to 53 per cent (Allen 2010). The German Chancellor Kohl, as the head of the largest net contributor, played a major role in this compromise.

The perspective of the Eastern enlargement delivered a further boost. As early as 1989, the Commission launched the PHARE programme, to help first Poland and Hungary (the acronym stood for 'Poland and Hungary Assistance for the Restructuring of the Economy'), and then all countries of the ex-Soviet bloc. The aid was not only financial but also structural, as a market economy had to be built from scratch. Many different assistance programmes were set up beyond PHARE, amounting to what Philipp Ther (2016) labelled a belated 'Marshall Plan' in the 2000s, with on average 1,000 euros per Polish citizen, for example – roughly the same amount as foreign direct investments. Much like the original Marshall Plan, it was not a windfall of unconditional aid, but rather strategic subsidies aimed at easing the transition to a market economy integrated into the EU (Chapter 15).

This is the result of the limited size of the EU budget, which represents slightly more than 1 per cent of EU GDP. By contrast, the US federal budget amounts to 25 per cent of US GPD, and the total amount of public expenditures of EU member states in the EU amounted to 46.6 per cent of GDP in 2019 (i.e. before the Covid-19 crisis). Calls to increase the EEC/ EU budget to 2 or 3 per cent of GDP are ancient, dating back to the 1977 MacDougall report, and were taken up by Delors.

London's stern opposition has always prevented such a move, but many actors have hidden behind the uncompromising Brits. After Brexit, the so-called Frugal Group made up of Austria, Denmark, the Netherlands and Sweden (joined by Finland) played a pivotal role in the 2020 negotiations over the budget, and over the pandemic stimulus plan, to curtail the Commission's spending plans. They were already part of the coalition that obtained the first reduction of the EU budget in relative terms (as a share of GDP) in 2013, along with the UK and Germany at the time. In 2020, Chancellor Angela Merkel abandoned her austerity stance in this issue, probably because the shock of the pandemic was massive and global, irrespective of local economic choices.

Has EU integration, and in particular cohesion policy and the Internal Market, reduced inequalities among EU countries? The answer is a resounding yes for Ireland, which benefited from a windfall of cohesion funds and from the adhesion to a large Internal Market in which the command of the English language and Ireland's low-tax policy have helped to attract foreign investments. Southern Europe also quickly caught up with the average, likewise thanks to the cohesion funds and to integration in the Internal Market, but only up to the 2010 euro crisis. The harsh austerity linked to belated aid packages reversed the convergence process. Former ex-Communists have weathered the crisis better, despite brutal austerity packages in some places such as Latvia, and have pursued their slow convergence with the West (Chapter 15).

# Conclusion: Regulated market integration

European integration has led to regulated market integration. As harmonizing national industrial and welfare state policy was impossible, the market became the main medium for building Europe. Negative integration (i.e. the removal of obstacles) prevailed over positive integration (the creation of common tools) for not only functional reasons but also political ones: Social-Democrat and neomercantilist constituencies have been less interested in European integration than the pro-market centre and centre-right during the first decades. Since the 1980s, this market-oriented dynamic has been affected by a neoliberal streak (Slobodian 2018), first in competition policy and then in the monetary field (see Chapter 10 on European and Monetary Union).

However, the European market-driven integration has encompassed many socially oriented features, notably for social and environmental legislations, which are sometimes more progressive than at the national level, and for regional policy (now cohesion policy). Those elements were designed to flank the Internal Market rather than to create a fully fledged European welfare state (Warlouzet 2023). The neomercantilist dimension has been largely absent at the European level, except for attempts at mitigating free trade in the 1970s and for the Airbus and Ariane ventures. But those successful ventures were set up outside the EEC/EU framework.

# Five key questions

1.  Why was European economic integration mainly driven by market forces? Why was the setting up of a unified internal market so central?

2.  To what extent a European welfare state has been set up ?

3.  To what extent did competition policy prevail over industrial policy in European integration history?

4.  Did European integration lead to more convergence or to more divergence in terms of wealth among European countries?

5.  Was European economic integration influenced by German ordoliberalism, French dirigisme or Thatcherite neoliberalism?

# Ten key readings

Albors-Llorens, A., C. Barnard and B. Leucht (eds) (2021), *Cassis de Dijon: 40 Years On*, London: Hart.

Coppolaro, L. (2013), *The Making of a World Trading Power: The European Economic Community (EEC) in the GATT Kennedy Round Negotiations (1963–1967)*, Burlington: Ashgate.

Egan, M. (2001), *Constructing a European Market*, Oxford: Oxford University Press.

Garavini, G. (2012), *After Empires: European Integration, Decolonization, and the Challenge from the Global South, 1957–1986*, Oxford: Oxford University Press.

Migani, G. (2014), 'Development Aid: Historic Priorities and New Dynamics', in E. Bussière et al. (eds), *The European Commission, 1973–1986: Histories and Memories of an Institution*, 393–411, Luxembourg: Publications Office of the European Union.

Milward, A., with the assistance of G. Brennan and F. Romero (1992), *The European Rescue of the Nation-State*, London: Routledge.

Moravcsik, A. (1998), *The Choice for Europe: Social Purpose and State Power from Messina to Maastricht*, Ithaca, NY: Cornell University Press.

Warlouzet, L. (2016), 'The Centralization of EU Competition Policy: Historical Institutionalist Dynamics from Cartel Monitoring to Merger Control (1956–91)', *Journal of Common Market Studies*, 54 (3): 725–41.

Warlouzet, L. (2019), 'The EEC/EU as an Evolving Compromise between French Dirigism and German Ordoliberalism (1957–1995)', *Journal of Common Market Studies*, 57 (1): 77–93.

Warlouzet, L. (2023), 'A Flanking European Welfare State: The European Community's Social Dimension from Brandt to Delors (1969–1993)', *Contemporary European History*, online, to be published in print.

# 9

# Milk lakes and butter mountains: The common agricultural policy

## *Katja Seidel*

## Introduction

Opinions on the common agricultural policy (CAP) are strongly divided; some see in the CAP a successful example of a common European policy that fulfilled its purpose set out in the Treaty of Rome establishing the European Economic Community (EEC) in 1957, namely of protecting the income of farmers whilst ensuring the supply of consumers with agricultural products (Article 39). At a political level, the founders of the EEC considered the establishment of a CAP as a great success for European integration. The CAP was indeed to an extent a successful policy as it helped to manage the structural changes the agricultural sector had been undergoing since the middle of the twentieth century, namely the reduction in the number of farms and farm workers, many of whom moved into other sectors of the economy. The CAP helped to address the income gap between farming and other sectors of the economy and to manage the modernization of the sector through technological and scientific advances. Later on, the CAP slowly adapted to further challenges such as environmental problems created by large-scale farming and the use of pesticides and fertilizers, public health crises such as the BSE scandal in the 1990s or the more recent demands of consumers for food security and, even more recently, organically grown food.

For others, however, the CAP represents 'the worst agricultural policy' (Federico 2009), a trade distorting, bureaucratic nightmare of red tape and wasted resources; a policy that at its worst led to expensive accumulation of agricultural surpluses, the 'wine lakes' and 'butter mountains'. The original CAP principle of subsidizing farmers' incomes through relatively high commodity prices not only contributed to agricultural surpluses but also had environmental consequences as it favoured intensive farming. It also meant that consumers paid the price for European farm subsidies through their food bills.

While certainly not all was well with the CAP, as one of the first truly supranational policies set up by the EEC, the CAP is an important policy that until recently received the largest slice of the European Union's (EU) budget. This chapter will explain why the EEC set up a CAP in the 1960s at all, and why it took the shape that it did. It then discusses the problems of the CAP and challenges it posed both in terms of the EEC budget and in the EEC's external relations with its trading partners and developing countries. These challenges led to a reform process that started in the middle of the 1980s and is still ongoing, something the final part of the chapter will explore.

# 1. Subsidizing agriculture in Europe: The logic of continuity

The CAP can be placed in the tradition of protectionist agricultural policies that existed in continental Europe long before the policy was conceived of. The CAP therefore reflected national agricultural policies in the member states as they existed before the founding of the EEC. Due to this 'path dependence', it would have been surprising had EEC member states set up a very liberal agricultural policy, one that exposed European agriculture to market forces and international competition, without providing any protection to its farmers.

According to Knudsen (2009a), one of the keys for understanding the CAP lies in its nature as a welfare policy. After the Second World War creating a welfare state was the goal of European governments. Even though others have demonstrated that the CAP had limited success as a welfare policy as the wealth distribution through the CAP was too unequal and favoured richer farmers in Northern Europe, the intention of policymakers was certainly to financially support farmers (Spoerer 2015). In the 1950s farming was still an important, if declining, economic activity in most EEC member states. Memories of post-war food shortages were still fresh and partly explain the support given to agriculture in continental Europe. Developing the agricultural sector and expanding production were also seen as vital means to avoid dependence on expensive imports and improve a country's external trade balance. Crucially, moreover, many politicians held romantic ideas of the 'family farm' forming the backbone of Western society (Knudsen 2009a).

Most EEC founding member states had thus enacted legislation in the 1950s, protecting the farming sector through various means such as price and market support, structural and investment aids and even investments into agricultural research. Policymakers responded to what they thought were the special characteristics, and challenges, of the agricultural sector: price fluctuations on the market affecting farm incomes and a variable environment with conditions that farmers could not control, such as the weather, geography and soil conditions. As farm incomes did not increase as quickly as incomes in other economic sectors, some national agricultural laws also enshrined the idea that farm incomes should develop similarly to non-farm incomes.

These national laws protecting *one* single sector of the economy were unique in post-1945 Western Europe. No other sector was as well supported as agriculture, which in part owed to the influence of agricultural lobby organizations and their excellent links to ruling parties, for example, the Christian Democrats (CDU/CSU) in West Germany. The 'farm vote' was seen as important, particularly for centre-right parties, and farmers were seen as important allies against the rise of Communism, especially in the early Cold War. In Germany 90 per cent of farmers were organized in the Deutscher Bauernverband. Following the formation of the EEC, farmers' lobbies organized transnationally in the Committee of Professional Agricultural Organizations (COPA), formed effective links with the European Commission, while continuing to lobby their national governments.

# Creating the foundations for the CAP

The preparation of what would become the EEC Treaty started in 1955 in the so-called Spaak Committee, led by Belgian Foreign Minister Paul-Henri Spaak. The discussions on agriculture built on the lessons learned from the failed initiative at setting up a 'Green Pool' in the framework of the Organization for European Economic Cooperation (OEEC), initially the European arm of the Marshall Plan administration, between 1950 and 1954 (Griffiths and Girvin 1995; Thiemeyer 2009). Unlike in the Green Pool negotiations, in the Spaak Committee, agriculture was presented as part of a wider integration initiative, a common market for industrial products and integration in the field of nuclear energy. And while the Spaak report was careful to avoid becoming bogged down in detailed proposals on agriculture, it affirmed the special characteristics of the agricultural sector and recognized that in many countries, this had resulted in protective legislation for the sector.

Due to the complexity of the issue the articles on agriculture in the EEC Treaty, signed in March 1957, presented a set of options regarding a future CAP. The options ranged from agreeing to common competition rules and coordinating national market organizations to a complete integration of individual products in a European market organization (Article 40.2). Patel called the treaty articles 'a projection screen for diverging viewpoints and hopes' (2009b, 143). However, from the beginning, Sicco Mansholt, the Dutch commissioner for agriculture in the EEC Commission, pushed for the closest possible integration in the form of a CAP through common market organizations for the different agricultural products.

## BOX 9.1 THE OBJECTIVES OF THE FUTURE CAP, SPELLED OUT IN ARTICLE 39(1), EEC TREATY, WERE:

(a) to increase agricultural productivity by promoting technical progress and by ensuring the rational development of agricultural production and the optimum utilization of the factors of production, in particular labour; (b) thus to ensure a fair standard of living for the agricultural community, in particular by increasing the individual earnings of persons engaged in agriculture; (c) to stabilize markets; (d) to assure the availability of supplies; (e) to ensure that supplies reach consumers at reasonable prices.

Treaty article 39(1) lists the partly contradictory aims of the CAP (Box 9.1). Increasing the productivity in farming in order to secure food supplies (a and d) (and to increase agricultural exports to improve the trade balance) had been a widespread aim of post-war agricultural policies. To stabilize markets (c) was to address the volatility of agricultural production and trade. A fair standard of living and increased earnings reflected national agricultural policy aims of securing farm incomes which were lagging behind wage increases in other sectors of the economy. The final aim, providing consumers with products at reasonable prices (e) was not necessarily compatible with the other aims, particularly that of increasing the income of farmers.

The treaty decreed that the policy should be up and running by the end of the transition period, that is, 31 December 1969, at the same time the customs union was to be established. Progress in the two areas was thus linked – a link the French and Dutch governments and the Commission as the drivers of the agricultural integration process in the 1960s used to their advantage.

## Developing the CAP

In July 1958, the Commission convened a conference of agricultural ministers and civil servants as well as agricultural lobbies of the member states in the Italian spa town of Stresa. There was disagreement among participants over how protectionist the new policy should be. Mansholt advocated a modernization of the agricultural sector to increase its productivity and competitiveness. This would allow for lower levels of protectionism but was opposed by those emphasizing the special characteristics of the agricultural sector. It is not surprising therefore that the Stresa Resolution did not map out a clear path towards the CAP.

But participants agreed on two basic premises that reconciled both the protectionists and the modernizers: firstly, agriculture was defined as a sector with special characteristics and participants 'unanimously declared [their] intention to safeguard this family character' of farming. Secondly, to improve the productivity of the family farm, agricultural structures needed to be modernized to allow those working in farming to maintain or achieve an income comparable to that in other sectors of the economy. This should make possible a price policy, which would avoid agricultural surpluses and leave room for competition (Communauté européenne 1958).

As it emerged in the 1960s, the CAP neglected the aspect of modernizing farming structures and instead emphasized the support of farmers' incomes through agricultural prices. The latter was certainly the politically less controversial policy path, but one that had severe consequences. On 30 June 1960, the Commission presented its proposals for a CAP. The document contained proposals for a managed internal market for agricultural products protected from excessive third-country competition through variable levies (tariffs) imposed on imports at the EEC's borders. Price support was intended to stabilize the agricultural market and guarantee a reasonable income to farmers. Member states agreed with this proposal as it corresponded to their own preferences for sheltering their domestic agriculture from external competition and allowed the continued use of price policy as income policy.

In December 1960 the Council of Ministers decided to create common market organizations and a variable levy system as the CAP's central mechanism. In January 1962 the Council decided on the adoption of a common price level for agricultural products and created the European Agricultural Guidance and Guarantee Fund (EAGGF) through which the CAP would be financed. In late 1962, in a marathon session the Council of Ministers decided on a range of commodity regimes, the common market organizations. Finally, in December 1964, the ministers adopted the last building bloc of the closely integrated agricultural market: the common price level for the main types of cereals. On 1 July 1967, the common market for cereals, pig meat, eggs and poultry meat came into effect (see Table 9.1 for a chronology of the CAP).

This timeline conceals the fact that these decisions were highly controversial at the time and could only be achieved through extensive bargaining in the Council of Ministers (Knudsen 2009a; Ludlow 2006; Patel 2009a). This multiparty bargaining would become characteristic for decision-making in the CAP. So-called package deals, presented by the Commission, should ensure that each agricultural minister could save face and bring home a 'victory' from the negotiations. The Council was particularly tempted to

**Table 9.1** *CAP timeline, 1958–2021*

| | |
|---|---|
| July 1958 | Stresa Conference |
| June 1960 | Commission proposal for the CAP |
| December 1960 | Council of Ministers adopts central features of the CAP: common market organizations and a variable levy system |
| January 1962 | Council of Minister agrees on common price level for agricultural products and European Agricultural Guidance and Guarantee Fund (EAGGF) |
| December 1962 | Council of Ministers adopts common market organizations |
| December 1964 | Council of Ministers adopts the common cereals price |
| July 1965–January 1966 | Empty Chair crisis – a conflict between France and her partners over the financing of the CAP and other issues (Chapter 2) |
| July 1967 | Common market organizations for cereals, pig meat, eggs and poultry meat come into effect |
| 1968 | Launch of the Mansholt Plan 'Agriculture 1980' to reform the CAP |
| 1970 | Council of Ministers agrees on the financing of the CAP through own resources |
| June 1984 | European Council adopts milk quotas to curb milk production |
| May 1992 | European Council agrees on MacSharry reform |
| March 1999 | Agenda 2000 reform adopted by the European Council |
| June 2003 | Council of Ministers adopts Commissioner Fischler's 'mid-term review' reform |
| 2009 | 'Health-Check' of the CAP |
| 2013 | CAP reform |
| 2021 | EU adopts another CAP reform, focused more on sustainability |

increase commodity prices, seen as directly linked to farmers' incomes. As other stakeholders such as finance ministers or consumers were not involved in CAP decision-making, the budgetary consequences of the decisions taken were deemed secondary. Ultimately, this type of decision-making contributed to the CAP becoming an extremely complex, opaque and expensive policy.

The final piece in the CAP edifice was the decision on the financing of the CAP enshrined in the Council's decision on the Community's own resources, taken in April 1970. Before then, the Community had been financed through contributions made by member states, but the Budget Treaty introduced Community own resources (provided for in Article 201, EEC Treaty) (Knudsen 2009b). Income from agricultural levies and customs tariffs on imports from third countries would no longer flow into national coffers but the Community budget. While this was hailed as a great step towards European integration, it meant that countries that traditionally imported more – foodstuffs or industrial goods – from third countries would proportionately pay more into the Community budget. This model of 'financial solidarity' 'created a structural imbalance in the distribution of gains and losses from the whole Community enterprise' (Knudsen 2009a, 288). This arrangement disadvantaged Germany and, following accession in 1973, also the UK but benefited large agricultural exporters such as France and the Netherlands. By 1972 the CAP claimed two-thirds of the budget, 2,094 million Units of Account (UoA) of a total expenditure of 3,074 UoA (Tracy 1989, 272). The increasing burden of the CAP on the budget would ultimately make CAP reform unavoidable.

# 2. Problems of the CAP

Since the 1960s the CAP has rested on three principles that have remained largely unchanged: a *single market* – undistorted trade throughout the Community; *Community preference* – domestically produced food has preference over that produced outside of the Community; and *financial solidarity* – the Community bears the costs of the CAP. However, there were problems from the beginning that called into question the three principles. In the CAP's history, three areas have turned out to be particularly problematic and highlighted the wastefulness of the CAP, the first of which is the issue of overproduction and the creation of 'food mountains'. The second problem is that of the monetary compensatory amounts, which undermined the single agricultural market, and the final one is that of fraud. This section discusses all three issues in turn.

The problem of overproduction is not unique to the EEC. Throughout the Western world productivity in agriculture increased through technological advancements and innovation in the development of pesticides and fertilizers. However, policy decisions on the CAP's design and mechanisms contributed to exacerbating the problem. Generally, the CAP incentivized production through setting high commodity prices for products such as

EWG – GIPFEL

„OBEN VOM BUTTERBERG HABEN WIR EINE HERRLICHE AUSSICHT AUF DEN ZUCKERKOGEL, DAS GETREIDEMASSIV UND GANZ IN WEITER FERNE AUF ENGLAND "

FIGURE 9.1 *Cartoon EEC summit, 1969. Georges Pompidou to Willy Brandt: 'From the summit of the butter mountain, we have a splendid view of the sugar mountain and the cereal range, and in the far distance we can just make out Great Britain.' Courtesy of H. E. Köhler Wilhelm-Bush-Gesellschaft e.V.*

cereals and milk. As a result, many products produced in the EEC were not internationally competitive as world market prices were usually lower than prices within the Common Market. EEC production could thus only be exported if the Community artificially reduced the price of cereals upon export and paid the farmer the difference between the lower world market price and the higher Community price (export subsidies).

As the CAP guaranteed that farmers could sell their produce at a certain price, they were neither concerned with the surpluses nor penalized for producing too much. As a consequence, agricultural surpluses plagued the Community in the 1970s and 1980s (Figure 9.1). Problem sectors were dairy, cereals, beef, wine as well as fruit and vegetables. Surplus produce was sold into intervention storage. The Community then tried to sell off this produce, either on the world market or through trade deals, for example, controversially with the Soviet Union. Creative solutions had to be found such as distilling wine as higher percentage alcohol to be used in the chemicals industry. In addition to the costs of overproduction, the images of food mountains and rotting fruit and vegetables tainted the image of the CAP in the eyes of consumers, not to mention the moral issue of destroying food when in other parts of the world people went hungry. Since the CAP reforms of the 1990s, the situation has improved. CAP support has been shifted from the principle of guaranteed prices as income support to direct income payments, thus disincentivizing overproduction.

The second issue tainting the image of the CAP was the monetary system for agriculture lasting from 1969 to 1999. This system became synonymous with the CAP's lack of transparency and extreme complexity, and it seriously undermined one of the core principles of the CAP: that of the single agricultural market. The origins of the agrimonetary system, or 'green money', lie in the difficult international economic environment and the breakdown of the international monetary system in the late 1960s and early 1970s. Agricultural prices in the EEC were calculated in Units of Account, which initially corresponded to the value of the US dollar and in relation to which all member-state currencies were set. When France devalued the franc and Germany revalued the deutschmark in 1969, this fixed relationship was disrupted and the unity of the agricultural market came under threat. The consequence of currency fluctuations was that in France agricultural products would have become cheaper, in Germany dearer. The Community came up with what it called monetary compensatory amounts (MCAs) to balance out these differences. In practice, export levies were imposed at the French border to increase the price of French produce which would otherwise have had a competitive advantage as it was cheaper than German produce. For German products an export subsidy was paid at the border to lower prices.

What was meant to be a temporary measure became a permanent feature of the CAP when in the early 1970s the Bretton Woods system of fixed exchange rates with a dollar pegged to the price of gold broke down and currencies started fluctuating. All member states had MCAs and the levels of MCAs became part of the annual agricultural price negotiations in the Council of Ministers. They rendered the CAP system even more complex, opaque and expensive. It is estimated that by 1977 MCAs added 12 per cent to the costs of the CAP (Knudsen 2014). Grant argues that member states were reluctant to get rid of the system as it allowed them to pursue 'national agricultural and food policies while remaining within the common market' (1997, 85). It took until 1999, and the introduction of the euro, for 'green money' to become a thing of the past, at least for those member states who have adopted the euro.

The third problem is that of fraud. Undoubtedly, the lack of transparency and the complexity of the CAP have given rise to fraud. It is estimated that by the mid-1990s 10 per cent of the EU budget were wasted through fraud (Grant 1997). Fraud in the CAP has been difficult to detect and to prosecute, not least as the Commission is dependent on member states to report fraud cases. However, the Commission undertakes its own investigations and has implemented an Anti-Fraud Strategy in the early 2000s (which is not limited to the CAP). The EU's anti-fraud office, OLAF, founded in 1999, is also monitoring agricultural and rural policy and detected, for example, the involvement of organized crime in defrauding Agricultural Funds (European Union 2018). The financial impact of reported fraud for the period 2013–17 was 1.83 per cent of the EU payments made to member states through the agricultural and other structural funds (European Union 2018).

The inequality in the payments received by farmers has also come to the fore since the introduction of the direct farm payments in the 1990s. This made it easier to confirm that a few very large farms and landowners still receive the bulk of CAP payments (see farmsubsidy.org). In view of the social, cohesion and welfare objectives of the EU, such revelations made it more difficult to justify the payments to rich farmers who are not dependent on such subsidies. However, member states, particularly those with more efficient farmers, have resisted attempts to modulate farm payments and pay less to richer farmers or landowners. Within the EU the CAP funds are also unequally distributed with only 25 per cent of direct payments going to the Central and Eastern European member states, still among the poorest in the EU.

# 3. Towards CAP reform

Attempts to reform the CAP were as old as the policy itself. Serious CAP reform was only tackled in the early 1990s, however. Not only was CAP reform politically controversial, but for many in the Community the policy was for a long time seen as an achievement and an important building block of European integration. Agricultural ministers, who were in charge of decision-making in the CAP, were not accountable for financial implications of their decisions. Ultimately though, CAP reform became inevitable and was primarily driven by the spiralling budgetary costs of the CAP and secondarily by outside pressures, including the multilateral negotiations in the framework of the General Agreement on Tariffs and Trade (GATT) from the 1980s and Eastern enlargement in the early 2000s.

The first of four major attempts to reform the CAP came from the Commission itself. Commissioner Mansholt (Box 9.2 and Figure 9.2) became concerned that high commodity prices and agricultural surpluses increased the costs of the CAP. At the same time, the CAP had not significantly improved farm incomes, particularly those of smaller farms. Mansholt took this as an opportunity to return to his initial goals of modernization and structural adaptation of European agriculture (Seidel 2010b). In 1968, the Commission drew up a memorandum, entitled 'Agriculture 1980', also known as the 'Mansholt Plan'. Mansholt predicted that by 1980 five million of the then ten million farmers would have given up farming, leaving fewer people to farm larger entities. Farming more efficiently, this would allow a lowering of agricultural prices. His proposals were geared towards facilitating these developments. Firstly, Mansholt proposed to incentivize farmers who wanted to leave the farming sector to work elsewhere, offering training and education and financial incentives. Secondly, he envisaged measures to help those who wanted to buy more land and increase the size of their farms to create more viable and efficient agricultural enterprises. Grants and training should become available to those farmers. The reaction to the Mansholt Plan was mixed, but farmers' unions were unanimous in rejecting the plan. Farm ministers were thus opposed to adopting such a controversial proposal. However, the plan led to the first three structural policy directives, adopted in 1972, which provided aid for the modernization of farms, the cessation of farming as well as vocational training. These were not Community programmes, however. It was up to the member states to propose such programmes which would be co-financed by the Community.

## BOX 9.2 SICCO MANSHOLT

Sicco Mansholt (1908–1995) was a Dutch politician and farmer. During the 1930s he briefly worked on a tea plantation in Java, then a Dutch colony. He then returned to the Netherlands to run his own farm. A member of the Dutch Socialist party (PvdA), he became minister for agriculture in 1945, remaining in the post until 1958 when he joined the European Commission as its vice president in charge of agriculture. By then, Mansholt was already a key figure in post-war European integration in the agricultural field, playing a leading role in the failed 'Green Pool' negotiations in the early 1950s before realizing his aim of a Europe-wide agricultural market within the EEC – the CAP. In 1972 Mansholt briefly became Commission president. In the early 1970s Mansholt became increasingly concerned about environmental issues and became heavily influenced by the Club of Rome Study *The Limits to Growth* (1972) as well as the German environmentalist Petra Kelly. Concerned about the limits of natural resources, he advocated negative or at least zero economic growth.

The experience of the Mansholt Plan put the Commission off large-scale reform. In the 1970s and 1980s the costs of the policy spiralled but were met with only timid initiatives towards its improvement (Grant 1997). Price and market support incentivizing farmers to produce more in order to improve their income thus remained largely unchanged – with the

FIGURE 9.2 *Sicco Mansholt on his sailing boat. Courtesy of European Communities, 1964.*

exception of the introduction of milk quotas in 1984 – until the launch of the second major reform attempt, the MacSharry reform of 1992. Named after the Irish Agricultural Commissioner Ray MacSharry, the reform introduced direct income payments to farmers while at the same time considerably lowering the market prices for cereals and beef which were the problem sectors at the time. Farmers were fully compensated for income losses experienced by the price cuts. The effects of the reform were to make cereals and beef more competitive on the world market and comply with GATT rules (see below). The MacSharry reform crucially achieved a paradigm change and set the CAP on a new path towards a diversification of the support instruments.

After 1992, further CAP reform was seen as necessary for budgetary and international trade considerations. From the 1990s the CAP was also increasingly viewed through a broader societal lens no longer exclusively focusing on farmers but highlighting the environment and consumers (Chapter 11). These societal concerns were linked and gained much publicity in the BSE, or 'mad cow disease' scandal. Against this backdrop, a third round of reforms began in 1999, when the European Council agreed to a reform that became part of the so-called Agenda 2000 reform package of the EU. With this reform, the EU created a 'two-pillar' CAP. The first pillar comprised the old market support instruments whereas rural development became the second pillar of the CAP. Commissioner Franz Fischler's initial aim had been to limit farm support to 300,000 euros per farm, but this was vetoed by farmers running large farms, particularly in Britain and France. However, only in 2003, in the context of Eastern enlargement and discussions about the applicability of the CAP (and the costs for this) to the new member states could Fischler realize some of his more ambitious objectives. The modestly called 'mid-term review' reform introduced the Single Farm Payment (SFP) in view of achieving a complete decoupling of support from production. This has drawn criticism as farmers actually do not need to produce anything to receive the SFP as long as they adhere to certain environmental, food safety, animal welfare and occupational safety standards. Generally, recent CAP reforms have given member states more opportunity to adapt CAP measures to regional and national needs and priorities, a trend that has continued with the CAP's most recent 2021 reform.

Fourth, further attempts at reform were initiated in 2008 with the 'health check' of the CAP, focusing on the policy's financial aspects, and completed with the wider 2013 reform. This reform was the result of a broad and lengthy consultation process attempting to get the public and stakeholders involved in the debate on the CAP (European Commission 2010). The public's demand for a fairer and 'greener' CAP were however not entirely met, as the Council of Ministers and the European Parliament, for the first time involved in major CAP reform through the co-decision procedure, again sided with farm interests and limited the reach of the reform, in particular in terms of environmental aims. In the first pillar (direct payments and market management) through which the bulk of the CAP budget is spent, only 30 per cent of direct payments are linked to farmers observing practices that are beneficial for the environment and the climate. Some therefore say the reform did not go much beyond a change of discourse to include terms such as 'greening', 'ecosystem services' and 'public good' (Fouilleux and Ansaloni 2016, 316). However, the reform included climate action as one of the new general objectives for the CAP. This referred to both a greener agricultural sector, for example, reducing agricultural emissions, but also shielding farmers from the effects of climate change. The Commission's plans for a post-2020 CAP, launched on 1 June 2018, aim (yet again) for a greener, more environmentally friendly agricultural policy supporting the general climate change and sustainability goals the EU has set for itself. The reform, adopted in December 2021, is also meant to simplify the CAP which many complain is still too complex and thus subject to fraud.

# 4. CAP in the world: Trade and development

The CAP has an impact on relations of the EEC/EU with the rest of the world. Developing and developed countries have criticized the Community for subsidizing its farm sector and having gained a competitive advantage unfairly while using trade barriers such as the variable levies to limit imports. There is agreement among researchers that protectionist agricultural policies such as the CAP distorted the world market (Raikes 1988). While in other sectors the EEC/EU advocates trade liberalization, in agriculture this has not been the case. There can be little doubt that these underlying conflicts between trade liberalization and agricultural protectionism have shaped and at times even obstructed the external relations of the EEC (Seidel 2019).

The first time the CAP became an issue in international trading relations was within the GATT. These global trade talks about the reduction of barriers to trade were for a long time dominated by the United States and the EEC as the world's largest trading blocs. While the United States put pressure on the EEC to modify the CAP and open up its markets for US exports, the CAP survived the first three GATT rounds in the 1960s and 1970s largely unchanged (Seidel 2020a). This is because in the late 1940s the United States itself had insisted on special rules for agriculture in the GATT agreement. In the Dillon and Kennedy Rounds in the 1960s, the EEC refused to compromise on a policy that was still under construction (Coppolaro 2013). Another reason for American acquiescence to the EEC's refusal to limit the CAP's protectionism was the US administration's general support for European integration which overrode their trade interests, as well as the fact that they subsidized their own farmers (Josling and Tangermann 2015).

The GATT Uruguay Round (1986–94) put more pressure on the EEC/EU to liberalize access to its agricultural market and dismantle export subsidies which gave Community farmers a competitive advantage on the world market. Mid-sized agricultural exporting nations such as Australia and Argentina had formed the 'Cairns Group' of fair trading nations. This group led the attack on the CAP together with the United States. The GATT round almost collapsed at the Brussels Ministerial Meeting in December 1990 due to lack of progress in agriculture. This was unacceptable to EEC member states interested in a success of the round and the boost trade liberalization in industrial goods and services would give to their domestic economy.

This moment provided the Commission with a golden opportunity for CAP reform. Shortly after the failure of the ministerial meeting, the Commission launched its reform proposal that it had been working on for the past couple of months. The MacSharry reform was agreed in record time in May 1992. International pressure therefore provided the key incentive for the EU to finally reform the CAP. It was then possible in turn to conclude the GATT round and sign the Agreement on Agriculture in 1994. As part of the Uruguay Round agreement, the EU agreed to transform agricultural levies into tariffs and lower them on average by a third as well as lowering export subsidies. The start of the next round, the World Trade Organization (WTO, the successor of GATT) Doha round in 2001, led to further CAP reforms in 1999 and 2002, making sure the CAP payments conformed with WTO rules.

The CAP affected not only trade between industrialized nations but also developing countries. The policy's protectionism affected developing countries in different ways and to different degrees, however. One group of developing countries that was somewhat shielded from competition on world markets was the group of African, Caribbean and Pacific countries (ACP). These are the former colonies of EEC member states, which benefited from preferential access to the EEC market for some of their agricultural products. Since 1975, the EEC put in place a preferential trading arrangement with the ACP countries in the Lomé Conventions. Under Lomé, ACP exports enjoyed free access to the common market, and this included agricultural commodities such as sugar, but the reverse did not apply. It was only a small amount of imports the EEC had to accept, though, and the bulk of the products were often without much competition from European producers, for example, tropical products (Seidel 2019). In 2000 the Cotonou Agreement was signed between the EU and 79 ACP countries. Between 2018 and 2022 the EU and the ACP states negotiated a new agreement to replace the Cotonou Agreement.

# Conclusion

The CAP was the EEC's first common policy, and it was seen as a great success for European integration. Indeed, the CAP realized some of the aims of the EEC Treaty by increasing productivity, stabilizing markets and securing supplies for consumers. The support system of the CAP was in the tradition of previous national protectionist agricultural policies and thus enjoyed considerable political legitimacy. For the first three decades, the CAP's core mechanisms and institutions were very difficult to modify. It was only when the policy entered a period of permanent crisis in the 1980s that reform became possible and a reality in the face of external pressure in the form of the GATT negotiations.

At the same time the view of agriculture as a special sector that needs protection has prevailed in the EU. While, compared to the 1960s, the current CAP has changed almost beyond recognition, one important continuity of the policy has been the aim to pay subsidies to farming. However, the justification for doing so has clearly changed from a more narrowly defined support of farming families to a broader narrative of the important role of agriculture in rural and also urban society, in maintaining the landscape and even in protecting the environment. Since the 1990s, the slogan of the 'multifunctionality of agriculture' has entered policymakers' vocabulary, more recently supplanted by the idea of the countryside as a 'common good', as a means to justify the continued support the EU is giving to the farm sector.

# Five key questions

1.  How can we explain the centrality of the CAP in the EEC Treaty and in the early years of the EEC's existence?

2.  What motives did member states have to protect their farming sectors?

3.  Why was it so difficult to reform the CAP, in particular before the 1990s?

4.  What does the CAP tell us about the links between the development of a core EU policy and the EU's relations with the wider world?

5.  In which ways has the CAP responded to shifting societal concerns, from those of the farming sector to those of consumers and environmentalists?

# Ten key readings

Garzon, I. (2006), *Reforming the Common Agricultural Policy: History of a Paradigm Change*, Basingstoke: Palgrave Macmillan.

Grant, W. (1997), *The Common Agricultural Policy*, Basingstoke: Palgrave Macmillan.

Josling, T., and S. Tangermann (2015), *Transatlantic Food and Agricultural Trade Policy: 50 Years of Conflict and Convergence*, Cheltenham: Edward Elgar.

Knudsen, A. L. (2009a), *Farmers on Welfare: The Making of Europe's Common Agricultural Policy*, Ithaca, NY: Cornell University Press.

Ludlow, N. P. (2005), 'The Making of the CAP: Towards a Historical Analysis of the EU's First Major Policy', *Contemporary European History*, 14 (3): 347–71.

Ludlow, N. P. (2006), *The European Community and the Crises of the 1960s: Negotiating the Gaullist Challenge*, London: Routledge.

Patel, K. K. (ed.) (2009a), *Fertile Ground for Europe? The History of European Integration and the Common Agricultural Policy since 1945*, Baden-Baden: Nomos.

Seidel, K. (2019), 'The External Dimensions of the Common Agricultural Policy', in U. Krotz, K. K. Patel and F. Romero (eds), *Europe's Cold War Relations: The EC towards a Global Role*, 165–84, London: Bloomsbury.

Seidel, K. (2020a), 'The Challenges of Enlargement and GATT Trade Negotiations: Explaining the Resilience of the European Community's Common Agricultural Policy in the 1970s', *International History Review*, 42 (2): 352–70.

Tracy, M. (1989), *Government and Agriculture in Western Europe 1880–1988*, New York: Harvester/Wheatsheaf.

# 10

# Economic and Monetary Union: From 1957 to the euro crisis

## *Alexis Drach*

## Introduction

The euro crisis that started in November 2009 has triggered much debate over the extent to which the eurozone was viable.[1] While the wider public mostly heard about indebted countries, and of the risk of default, most specialists stressed that the crisis revealed structural weaknesses of the eurozone (Claeys 2017). The whole architecture of the Economic and Monetary Union (EMU) has since come under intense scrutiny. But what does 'economic and monetary union' mean exactly, and why was it created?

Independent states willingly surrendering their currency, and adopting a common one is a rather rare event, because monetary policy forms an important part of sovereignty. Although monetary measures seem very technical, they are very much embedded in the political, economic and social context of the time. Monetary policies have close links with credit policies, budgetary policies, employment policies, banking supervision and regulation, and international relations. In addition, member states of the European Economic Community (EEC) and European Union (EU) have always been tempted to preserve their individual national interests, in particular in times of crisis.

While some scholars have emphasized the role of the 'founding fathers' of the euro in the creation of EMU (such as Robert Marjolin, Pierre Werner,

Jacques Delors or Tommaso Padoa-Schioppa, to name but a few), others have underlined the importance of other actors, such as experts, national and European civil servants or central bankers (James 2012). 'Economic and monetary union' encompasses all the policies that EU policymakers enacted to make the adoption of a single currency (the euro) possible and to support its functioning. The 'E' in EMU, that is, the economic dimension of monetary union, is often forgotten in accounts of European monetary integration. It refers to areas that European policymakers considered fundamental for the proper functioning of a single currency area. It includes the coordination of member states' budgets, financial transfers within the eurozone and the coordination of national banking regulatory and supervisory systems. Monetary affairs closely intertwine with other economic affairs, and the proper functioning of a single currency area implies a high degree of economic coordination and integration.

This question, however, is not new, and there have long been discussions over the economic prerequisites of a possible EMU in the European Economic Community (EEC). This chapter will show that monetary issues *and related economic* questions have come a long way in the history of European integration and have been through many crises and disputes (Mourlon-Druol 2020b). Member states have, in particular, disagreed on key economic and monetary policy choices.

The chapter will explore the various reasons why European policymakers adopted an economic and monetary union and how it evolved since its adoption. It will first analyse the early projects for monetary union in the 1960s and 1970s, then examine the road to the Maastricht Treaty which marked the adoption of EMU and finally address the eurozone crisis and its consequences.

# 1. Early projects

The Treaty of Rome establishing the EEC in 1957 did not mention the possible creation of a fully fledged economic and monetary union. However, it laid the foundations for future progress in the area by calling for a high degree of economic coordination and progressive liberalization of capital flows (Articles 103–9). It also set up a Monetary Committee whose task was to monitor and coordinate member states' monetary and financial policies (Bakker 1996). Monetary policy, in particular exchange rates, was seen as a matter of common concern to ensure the smooth running of the common market. In the meantime, the European Payment Union (EPU) set up after the Marshall Plan disappeared (Chapter 1).

Important European actors such as Jean Monnet (at the helm of the Action Committee for the United States of Europe), Robert Marjolin (a Frenchman who became the first commissioner for economic and monetary affairs in 1958) and Robert Triffin (a Belgian economist who worked with the latter two) had plans for monetary union in the EEC since 1958 (Seidel

2016; Warlouzet 2018a). In the 1960s, even though agricultural policy and customs tariffs dominated the integration agenda, European policymakers already discussed the need for increasing monetary cooperation in the EEC. Monetary affairs efforts were primarily geared towards ensuring the proper functioning of the Common Market and the common agricultural policy (CAP): an excessive variation in exchange rates could hamper intra-EEC trade and thereby hinder the objective of the common market (Chapters 2 and 8). In the 1950s and 1960s, the international monetary order was governed by the Bretton Woods system, established in 1944, whereby currencies were pegged to the dollar with fixed exchange rates. The system worked relatively well until the late 1960s, sheltering European currency relations from instability. Therefore, the need for further monetary integration was limited.

Article 67 of the EEC Treaty decreed the liberalization of capital flows. In the early years of the EEC, most countries exerted control on capital flows, primarily for monetary reasons, in the sense that these controls existed for fighting inflation or protecting the currency against speculative attacks, but also to limit tax losses. However, not all countries agreed on the desirability and usefulness of these controls: in particular, the West German government opposed them because it considered that the absence of controls was better for fighting inflation and saw the freedom of capital movements as a healthy constraint on economic policy. The liberalization of capital flows rapidly progressed in the early 1960s, with two directives in 1960 and 1962, but came to a halt later in the decade. Countries disagreed on the question, and France, in particular, opposed the removal of controls, arguing that it did not want to go further before a clear plan for a European capital market was devised. In 1966, the Segré report, submitted by an expert group chaired by a Commission official, Claudio Segré, provided a roadmap for future reflection on financial and monetary integration in Europe.

The end of the decade, however, was not favourable to the liberalization of capital movements. First, several countries had monetary difficulties, which did not encourage them to liberalize capital movements further. Second, the development of the Eurodollar market (dollars exchanged outside the United States) and the related increase in short-term capital movements raised several challenges. This market escaped EEC governance, as it was mainly hosted in London, and it could have destabilizing effects on monetary policies. Altogether, these difficulties brought plans for further liberalization of capital movements to an end.

The summit meeting of the EEC's heads of state and government at the Hague in December 1969 was a landmark in the history of monetary cooperation in the EEC (Chapter 3). The customs union planned by the Treaty of Rome had been completed ahead of time, the CAP had been established and member states agreed that the EEC needed a new impetus comparable to that of the late 1950s. The departure of French President Charles de Gaulle also helped unlock French reservations about the progress of European integration. At the Hague summit, member states agreed to accept three new members, the UK, Ireland and Denmark, as well as moving forward with EMU. EEC member states charged a group chaired by the Luxembourg Prime Minister Pierre Werner to study how an EMU could be attained. In 1970, the group submitted a report known as the Werner Report: it provided a roadmap for attaining EMU by 1980 in three stages.

However, the 1970s brought major changes to the international monetary and economic system. The Eurodollar market was growing fast and was seen to fuel speculation and monetary instability. In August 1971, US President Richard Nixon gave a famous speech on TV, stating that because of monetary instability, of the need to fight inflation and of speculators making a profit on instability, the United States would suspend the convertibility of the dollar into gold: foreign governments would no longer be able to exchange their dollars for gold. The end of the convertibility of the dollar was a serious challenge for the Bretton Woods system. Western countries had lived under fixed exchange rates since the war, and the perspective of a floating exchange rate system, even though several economists advocated it, was worrisome to many policymakers. Despite the fact that the US decision was initially temporary, the Bretton System was falling apart. After failed attempts to coordinate with the United States for maintaining fixed exchange rates, European governments tried to coordinate their monetary policies between themselves. The international monetary upheavals of the 1970s pushed the Europeans to search for a European monetary identity.

The first attempt of EEC countries to respond to these monetary challenges was the establishment of the European monetary 'snake'. The snake was the nickname given to an exchange rate system narrowing the fluctuation margins between European currencies to 2.25 per cent by intervening in the currency market. It was part of the measures contained in the Werner Plan. Initially, the snake was connected to another agreement, made between the so-called Group of Ten (G10) countries in December 1971, at the Smithsonian Institution, to limit fluctuations of their currencies vis-à-vis the dollar to 4.5 per cent. However, after the final act of the collapse of the Bretton Woods system in 1973, the EEC countries decided to let their currencies float but to maintain the 2.25 per cent (the snake) limit on their fluctuations. The snake faced considerable difficulties because of the period's monetary instability; the burden of adjustment fell on weaker currency countries (France, Italy and the UK). EEC member states also had diverging economic policy orientations (expansionary or disciplinary policies). As a result, the UK, France and Italy quickly left the system, and the snake essentially became a deutschmark zone. The upheavals of the early 1970s show the interconnectedness of European and global monetary affairs, in particular the link between European monetary affairs and the dollar.

A more successful initiative than the snake was the European Monetary System (McNamara 1998; Mourlon-Druol 2012a). With the economic crisis following the 1973 oil shock and the failure of the snake in the mid-1970s, European policy leaders became alarmed at the risk of a dislocation

Young people demonstrate in support of a European currency in front of the Berlaymont, 5 December 1977.

FIGURE 10.1 *Young people demonstrate in support of a European currency in front of the European Commission headquarters (the Berlaymont), 5 December 1977. Courtesy of European Communities, 1977.*

of Europe. Moreover, high inflation and rising unemployment following the 1973 oil crisis were a major concern. For some observers, a European monetary response was necessary (Figure 10.1).

In late 1977, Roy Jenkins, the president of the European Commission, delivered a speech in Florence where he called for a European monetary union. Shortly after, in 1978, French President Valéry Giscard-d'Estaing and German Chancellor Helmut Schmidt pushed for negotiating a new system, which entered into force in 1979: the European Monetary System (EMS). The European Council, a new EEC institution created in 1974 in which the heads of state meet, had also been an important player in the construction of this new system (Chapter 3). The EMS was in many aspects similar to the snake. However, it added three new elements: a divergence indicator, credit mechanisms and a European currency unit (Ecu), a currency basket, in which all participating EEC currencies entered with different weightings.

As it was the strongest currency, the deutschmark tended in practice to be at the centre of the system.

# 2. Economists versus monetarists: Macroeconomic coordination and convergence

A long-standing debate about monetary union in the EEC revolved around macroeconomic coordination and convergence, and in particular opposed 'monetarists' and 'economists'. Monetarists, in this context, had nothing to do with Milton Friedman's monetarism, that is, the control of money supply in the economy. In the EEC context, monetarists were those considering that monetary union would induce economic convergence. Economists, on the contrary, believed that economic convergence was a prerequisite for monetary union. Therefore, the economists' view was sometimes nicknamed the 'coronation' theory, as monetary union would be the final step of a lengthy process of economic convergence. Even though lines were not rigid in this matter, the French and Italian governments were often portrayed as economists, whereas the German and the Dutch governments were often portrayed as monetarists. For monetarists, economic convergence was important but would never materialize unless a constraint, such as monetary union, would exert enough pressure on governments. For economists, a monetary union without sufficient economic convergence would be unstable. Compared to the slow-moving 'coronation' approach, the monetarists' approach has also been referred to as the 'Nike approach': 'Just do it' (Mourlon-Druol 2012a, 17). It is possible to trace these debates from the 1960s until today.

Like other areas of EMU, macroeconomic coordination is an integral part of EMU and has been considered so from at least the 1960s. It primarily concerns the coordination of EEC/EU member states' budgets, but also economic policy guidelines, for instance, labour market reform. Macroeconomic coordination affects exchange rates fluctuations, which can themselves affect trade. However, it has always been a heated subject because it pertains to member states' sovereignty. The two first commissioners for economic and financial affairs, Marjolin (1958–67) and Raymond Barre (1967–73), two Frenchmen, stressed the need to better synchronize European economic policymaking. Their economic thinking was influenced by the French tradition of economic planning, which the German tradition of ordoliberalism opposed (Seidel 2016; Warlouzet 2019a). In the 1960s, various committees were created to foster the coordination of macroeconomic policies: a short-term economic policy committee in 1960, a budgetary policy committee and a medium-term economic policy committee in 1964. In 1974 these committees were merged into the Economic Policy Committee. These committees offered useful forums to exchange ideas and national practices, but the concrete results of this coordination were limited at best.

Finally, like other policy areas central to EMU, financial transfers in the EEC/EU have a long history (Chapters 8 and 12). The EEC Treaty already foresaw the creation of a European Social Fund and a European Investment Bank. The European Coal and Steel Community also had redistributive schemes for workers and regions affected by the crisis of these sectors in the 1960s. Some observers also considered the CAP, established in 1962, as a form of 'social policy'. The European Social Fund, the first 'structural fund', aimed at improving social cohesion and focused on the retraining of workers in all sectors except agriculture. The European Investment Bank borrowed funds on financial markets and lent them to projects that supported the EEC's objectives. Thus, several EEC programmes long had a redistributive logic, implying transfers from richer to poorer areas. However, the amounts involved were minimal.

The question of financial transfers became more important in the 1970s, when the economic crisis hit EEC countries. On the insistence of the UK and Ireland joining the Community, and with the strong support of Italy, the European Regional Development Fund was created in 1975. During the EMS negotiations in 1978, there was also much debate over the extent to which richer member states could support the participation of weaker currency countries by financial transfers. The UK, Italy and Ireland, in particular, argued that their participation in the EMS would be difficult without such support. Even though these discussions did not lead to a notable political outcome, they were revealing of the relations between monetary integration and financial transfers.

Three major reports addressed this issue in the second half of the 1970s: the Marjolin Report and the Tindemans Report in 1975, and the MacDougall Report in 1977. Belgian Prime Minister Leo Tindemans called for greater economic integration in support of monetary integration. Marjolin advocated a massive increase in the EEC budget. A last report by a group chaired by Donald MacDougall, requested by the Commission, enquired further into the role of public finances in European integration. It also advocated an increase in the EEC budget to support a monetary union (Dyson and Quaglia 2010). The budget of the EEC was indeed very limited compared to that of federal states in a monetary union: it was about 0.7 per cent of the EEC's GDP, whereas other federations had a federal budget of about 20–25 per cent of their GDP. These discussions show that financial transfers in support of monetary integration were also discussed well before the creation of the euro.

# 3. The 1980s, Maastricht and the start of the euro

The 1980s witnessed a new dynamism in the European integration process, including a relaunch of plans for a future EMU. The 1985 White Paper of the

Commission proposed about three hundred directives aiming to complete the single European market by 1992 (Chapters 3 and 8). Its focus was really on the EEC internal market, but some actors, in particular Jacques Delors, the president of the European Commission (1985–95), and the Italian economist Tommaso Padoa-Schioppa, a former Commission official who drafted an important report on this topic in 1988, considered that the establishment of an EMU was a necessary further step for completing the Single Market. Without an EMU, exchange rate variability could form a non-tariff barrier to intra-EEC trade.

An integrated financial sector was also conceived as a necessary condition for a well-functioning EMU. However, creating an integrated banking and financial market proved difficult. The Commission devised early plans for a common market in banking in the mid-1960s and slowly constructed this common market through so-called banking directives, particularly the first banking coordination directive of 1977 and, most importantly, the second banking directive of 1989 (Drach 2020). These directives were supposed to ensure banks' freedom to establish and provide services within the Community. The Council of Ministers adopted similar directives for the insurance and securities industry. In negotiating these directives, governments disagreed about what degree of openness was desirable towards non-EEC countries. While the UK fiercely opposed anything that could resemble a 'fortress Europe', other countries, in particular France, wanted to impose reciprocity conditions for entering the EEC market in order to have leverage over non-EEC countries. Eventually, the directives adopted a liberal approach, with no strict reciprocity conditions. However, European banks stayed very rooted in their national markets. When involved in international activities, banks were more interested in global than in European affairs. Furthermore, national banking authorities were not ready to lose control over their banking systems.

The Commission's single market project included many directives in the financial sector. In particular, a directive on full liberalization of capital movements in the EEC was enacted in 1988 (Drach 2021). European policymakers considered this directive as a necessary step before establishing an EMU. Other directives in securities, banking and insurance aimed at establishing a single financial market. However, the single financial market was never fully realized.

The functioning of the internal market could also be disturbed by the free movement of capital. Padoa-Schioppa put forward the idea of the 'inconsistent quartet', meaning that one could not have at the same time free trade, free capital movements, fixed or managed exchange rates and monetary policy autonomy. In that perspective, the single market, therefore, necessitated a monetary union. In the meantime, EEC finance ministers and central bank governors were looking for ways to strengthen the EMS. In 1987, the EEC central bank governors, meeting in Basel, issued a report on 8 September, and the EEC finance ministers endorsed it on 12 September, during a meeting in Nyborg, in Denmark. What became the 'Basel-Nyborg agreement' aimed at strengthening the EMS. It reinforced the surveillance of policy inconsistencies among EMS countries and introduced intra-marginal interventions, whose aim was to help prevent currencies from reaching their limit and to fight speculation.

In June 1988, the European Council asked Commission President Delors to chair a committee that would study how a monetary union could be achieved in the EEC. The 'Committee for the Study of Economic and Monetary Union', better known as the Delors Committee, was primarily composed of central banks governors; this was a major difference from the Werner Committee, which included the presidents of the EEC committees relevant to economic and monetary cooperation and integration, known for being favourable to EMU (Mourlon-Druol 2020a). Delors considered that one of the reasons why the Werner plan had failed was that central bankers had not been involved at the time of its conception. Central bank governors were considered to be less favourable to the progress of EEC monetary integration, particularly the governor of the Bank of England, Robert Leigh-Pemberton, and the president of the Bundesbank, Karl-Otto Pöhl. The fact that they sat on the Committee in their personal capacity and not as representatives of their institution and that their work was confidential and based on mutual trust helped the discussion. The group also included a few other experts, such as the Belgian Alexandre Lamfalussy, the general manager of the Bank for International Settlements.

In April 1989, the group submitted a report proposing the creation of an EMU in three stages (cf. chapters in Dyson and Maes 2016). It was, to some extent, quite similar to the 1970 Werner Report. However, it was deliberately vague regarding the timetable for stages two and three. Delors thought that a too rigid timetable had prevented the Werner plan from being implemented. A second difference was that the Delors Report insisted less on the economic dimension of EMU than the Werner Report. Indeed, the Werner Report had also contained ambitious plans for the coordination of economic policy in the EEC. The first stage of the Delors Report required the reinforcement of economic and monetary cooperation and the completion of the single market. That stage did not necessitate a new treaty, but such a treaty would be needed for the second stage, which focused on introducing a new European system of central banks. The third and last stage involved the irrevocable fixing of parities and the transfer of monetary authority to an EEC institution. The members of the Delors Committee unanimously endorsed the report. Most central bank governors did not expect that anything significant would come out of it, however. But it proved very influential on the 1992 Maastricht Treaty and is now seen as having been the first roadmap to the euro (Dyson and Featherstone 1999).

The EEC heads of government endorsed the Delors Report, and a political process towards EMU began, completing the internal market plan already on the way and supported by many business circles. The fall of the Berlin Wall, in November 1989, and the prospect of German reunification accelerated the process, as the French and German leaders were convinced that a reunified

Germany needed to be integrated into a strong European framework. The programme of the Commission for the creation of a Single Market by 1992 was also triggering much enthusiasm in business circles (Chapter 3). Even in the City of London, which was initially sceptical about the advantages of European integration, there was optimism. In July 1988, at a meeting of City actors chaired by the Bank of England on the subject of the creation of the single market by 1992, Jeremy Morse, head of Lloyds Bank and of the British Bankers' Association, declared that 'it was difficult not to be excited by the sense of movement' (Drach 2020, 791). As the establishment of EMU necessitated a new treaty, and as a new treaty necessitated an intergovernmental conference (IGC), the Strasbourg European Council of December 1989 called for an IGC, despite the opposition of the UK.

The IGC started in December 1990 and led to the Maastricht Treaty, signed on 7 February 1992. The Maastricht Treaty largely incorporated the Delors Report of April 1989. Four criteria were established to join the euro: price stability, government finances, exchange rate stability and convergence of interest rates. The government finances criteria became the most famous one and required that deficits not exceed 3 per cent of GDP and public debt 60 per cent of GDP. The Maastricht Treaty devised three stages, like the Delors Report had suggested, to establish EMU. Stage 1 was to run from 1 July 1990 to 31 December 1993, stage 2 from 1 January 1994 to December 1998 and stage 3 from January 1999. Economic convergence, central bank independence and fiscal discipline were the central pillars of EMU.

The process towards EMU was disturbed by a severe monetary crisis in 1992–3. Just a few months after the Treaty of Maastricht was signed, several of the currencies composing the EMS went through heavy speculative attacks, which forced some of them to leave its Exchange Rate Mechanism. As the agreement to move forward towards EMU had just been made, the crisis was a major threat to the whole project, but also an occasion for some countries, in particular France, to show their commitment to it. Furthermore, it revealed the rising importance of global financial markets, as it appeared as a battle between states and markets.

On 2 June 1992, the Danish voters rejected, by a slight majority, the Maastricht Treaty (Chapter 18). That is usually considered as the start of the crisis, as it generated doubt about the future of EMU. The day after, the French President François Mitterrand declared that a referendum on the Maastricht Treaty would be held in France, too. If polls were initially giving a large majority to a 'yes', they quickly became much more uncertain, which spread doubt on the soundness of the EMU project among financial markets and, thereby, on the EMU. In addition, the economic consequences of German reunification impacted other EEC countries: in order to fight inflationary pressures, the Bundesbank was setting high interest rates, which threatened the Exchange Rate Mechanism of the EMS. Lastly, European economies were going through a recession at that time. In this context, private financial actors could bet that some currencies were overvalued and could be forced to leave the EMS and devalue if they exerted enough pressure, triggering massive currency speculations.

These speculations first hit the British pound sterling and the Italian lira. When the pound had joined the EMS in 1990, many observers thought it was overvalued. In September 1992, several financial institutions massively sold their pounds in the hope of forcing the UK to devalue and then make a profit on the difference. In particular, the Quantum Fund of George Soros played a leading role in the pressure to devalue the sterling, selling one billion pounds on 15 September 1992 alone and eventually forcing the British currency to leave the EMS on 16 September, a day that became known as 'Black Wednesday'. On 14 September, the Italian government had already devalued by 7 per cent. On 17 September, both the Italian lira and the pound sterling left the EMS. Speculation then turned to the Spanish peseta and the Finnish markka, both forced to devalue too. On 20 September, the approval of the Maastricht Treaty by a referendum in France was much tighter than expected: speculation turned to the French franc, and on 22 September, the Bank of France used in a few hours its entire foreign currency reserves to purchase francs and defend its currency. The cooperation with the German Bundesbank was critical, as it supported the purchase of francs by the Bank of France by unlimited deutschmark credits. The Banque de France and Bundesbank issued a joint statement on 23 September. Eventually, speculation receded. However, it boomed again in late November 1992, against the French franc, the Spanish peseta and the Portuguese escudo. In February 1993, speculation hit the French franc again, in the context of upcoming legislative elections, as well as the Irish pound. After a final and exceptional speculation wave in July 1993 against all EMS currencies except the deutschmark, the EMS governors and finance ministers, meeting in the Monetary Committee of the EEC, decided to widen the EMS margins from 2.25 to 15 per cent: the speculation ended once and for all. The cooperation between central banks had proved critical in this crisis resolution, but also the political pressure on the Bundesbank to help the French franc. The fact that France had not devalued the franc was interpreted as a commitment towards EMU.

Two major possible weaknesses of EMU were already widely discussed by central bankers at the time of the Delors Report and have attracted much attention since then: the coordination of member states' budgets (often called 'fiscal discipline') and banking regulation and supervision. The first issue dominated the 1990s. Germany was a strong supporter of fiscal discipline and of a strict interpretation of the 3 per cent deficit rule of the Treaty of Maastricht when assessing which country qualified for the euro. However, while being above the Maastricht limits, some countries could not reasonably be excluded from EMU: Belgium had a debt of 130 per cent of GDP in 1997 but was host to many European institutions and was in a monetary union with Luxembourg, whose credit was excellent. Italy's debt was high (120 per cent of GDP), but lower than that of Belgium, so it could not be excluded if Belgium was accepted. In the mid-1990s, the German Finance Minister Theo Waigel proposed a Stability Pact that would implement the Maastricht rules on debt and deficit. Under French pressure to take economic growth into consideration, the Stability Pact became a Stability and Growth Pact (SGP). However, in 2003, both France and Germany infringed the SGP and pushed for its suspension, arguing that there was a risk of recession. In 2005, the European Council revised the SGP, softening the disciplinary procedure in case of infringement. The fact that the two biggest countries of the eurozone had violated the SGP outraged several other member countries. The question of financial regulation and supervision, however, proved more urgent in the wake of the Global Financial Crisis.

In 1998, the European Commission and the European Monetary Institute, which had been created as part of stage two of EMU as a transitional institution before the European Central Bank (ECB) was established, submitted their convergence reports examining which country could join EMU (Box 10.1). Eleven countries met the criteria: Austria, Belgium, Finland, France, Germany, Ireland, Italy, Luxembourg, the Netherlands, Portugal and Spain. In 1999, parities between exchange rates were irrevocably fixed, and the euro came into force on an immaterial basis. Coins and banknotes were introduced in 2002. Eleven countries adopted the euro. Greece joined them in 2001, and others did so too from 2007 onwards (Table 10.1). During its first years of existence, the euro worked reasonably well. However, things would turn much more difficult after the Global Financial Crisis hit.

# 4. The euro crisis

In 2007–8, the outbreak of the Global Financial Crisis devastated the financial systems and economies of many countries in the world. Although many American observers anticipated a US-China crisis, the actual crisis had a profound North Atlantic character, and revealed the deep financial ties between the North American and the European financial systems (Tooze 2018). The US domestic consumer market had been in part funded by European credits. While the crisis weakened large European banks, European governments' debt also increased in the wake of stimulus packages enacted to fight the social and economic effects of the crisis.

In October 2009, the newly elected Greek government announced that the country's public deficit would be much higher than the figures notified to Brussels. In November, it announced a 12.7 per cent deficit, instead of the official 5.7 per cent. This declaration is often considered as the start of the eurozone crisis. One month later, rating agencies downgraded Greece's sovereign credit rating, and Greece and other European countries entered into a debt crisis threatening the whole euro architecture. Doubts about

## BOX 10.1  TIMELINE OF ECONOMIC AND MONETARY UNION

1944 Bretton Woods agreement of stable exchange rates

1950 European Payments Union

1957 Treaty of Rome

1960s EEC Monetary Committee, first directives on liberalization of capital flows

1969 The Hague summit: EMU becomes official EEC policy

1970 Werner Report: EMU by 1980

1979 European Monetary System

April 1989 Delors Report

1992 Treaty of Maastricht

1990–1993 First Stage of EMU

1994 Creation of European Monetary Institute

1994–1998 Second Stage of EMU

1999 Third Stage: launch of euro currency and European Central Bank

2002 Introduction of euro coins and bank notes

debt sustainability soon hit Portugal, Spain, Italy and Ireland, and a series of bailout negotiations tore Europe apart.

Beyond the Greek episode, the European debt crisis exposed the structural weaknesses of EMU. In particular, some observers stressed the lack of financial transfers (the so-called fiscal transfers) and of common supervisory and regulatory mechanisms in the eurozone, while others underlined that the ECB was excessively focused on monetary stability. In addition, the crisis revealed the profound economic divergence of Southern and Northern

**Table 10.1** *Enlargement of the Eurozone*

| Year | Country |
| --- | --- |
| 1999 | Austria, Belgium, Finland, France, Germany, Ireland, Italy, Luxembourg, Netherlands, Portugal, Spain |
| 2001 | Greece |
| 2007 | Slovenia |
| 2008 | Malta, Cyprus |
| 2009 | Slovakia |
| 2011 | Estonia |
| 2014 | Latvia |
| 2015 | Lithuania |
| 2023 (scheduled) | Croatia |

European countries. Lastly, the crisis was not only an economic one: it was also a deep political and social crisis, with European national media taking sides for or against indebted countries. From 2009 to 2012, the Greek GDP shrank by 25 per cent and unemployment rocketed.

The crisis also revealed to the general public the intertwining of financial, monetary and fiscal issues. During the years preceding the crisis, there had been a massive flow of capital from Northern to Southern Europe. Because there was a monetary union, borrowers from Southern Europe were able to borrow at lower interest rates than they would otherwise have been able to, which, according to some observers, incited them to become overindebted. With the Global Financial Crisis, the capital flows within Europe diminished, and the growth performances of Southern European countries looked much grimmer than before. That cast doubts on the ability of states to repay their debts.

In addition, Northern European banks had lent to Southern European states, and in general European banks had lent to their own states: that created a bank-state 'doom-loop', whereby banks were exposed to states, and states depended on banks, in addition to being the banks' regulators and potential lenders of last resort. As the financial and sovereign crisis deepened in Europe, financial fragmentation increased: banks were retreating within their national markets to reduce their exposure to risky indebted states, sometimes under the guidance of banking supervisors who urged them to withdraw from these areas. If financial flows had widely circulated within the eurozone before the crisis, banking structures had, in fact, remained profoundly national, at least in Western Europe. The withdrawal of banks from Southern European markets aggravated the crisis and reduced the access of Southern European countries to funding. In October 2010, French President Nicolas Sarkozy and the German Chancellor Angela Merkel agreed to involve private lenders in the crisis resolution. However, this increased private lenders' anxiety, as financial actors now considered that a risk of default was a plausible possibility, whereas they previously considered that was impossible (James 2016).

The crisis triggered considerable debate about the architecture of the euro area and the role of the ECB. While the ECB could not act as a lender of last resort, contrary to other central banks in the world, ECB President Jean-Claude Trichet did launch a broad series of operations from 2010 onwards. The Securities Market Programme (SMP), started in 2010, enabled it to buy sovereign bonds on secondary markets. The Long-Term Refinancing Operations, started in 2011, was meant to support bank lending and bank liquidity. The Outright Monetary Transactions (OMT), launched in 2012, was similar to the Securities Market Programme, which aimed to buy sovereign bonds on secondary markets, but this time had no ex-ante quantitative limits. Lastly, in 2015, the ECB launched the Public Sector Purchase Programme (PSPP), officially marking its adoption of quantitative easing through a regular purchase of sovereign bonds and securities to support economic growth. This programme ended progressively in 2018.

The use of rhetoric and persuasion of financial markets of the credibility of the euro also played a major role in the handling of the crisis: on 26 July 2012, Mario Draghi, the new president of the ECB who had replaced Trichet in late 2011 (see Figure 10.2), pronounced his famous phrase at the Global Investment Conference: 'The ECB is ready to do whatever it takes to preserve the euro. And believe me, it will be enough.' The speech had an important effect in reassuring markets. Eventually, the euro survived the crisis, and Greece stayed in the eurozone, warding off fears of a 'Grexit' that had spread at the peak of the crisis.

The reaction to the euro crisis came together with a new, or reinforced, political economy for the eurozone. That included austerity measures, the enactment of a series of actions aiming at strengthening the Single Market (Single Market Act I and Single Market II, in 2011 and 2012, respectively), a new financial assistance framework for the eurozone and a new framework for the eurozone's economic governance. Several observers consider that austerity measures aggravated the crisis rather than helped solve it (Sandbu 2015). Public debt being a central issue of the Euro crisis, reducing it through limiting public spending seemed the easiest way out. However, it also contributed to reducing people's income and consumption and to increasing poverty.

Critics also condemned the excessive austerity measures imposed on Greece, their limited impact on Greece's indebtedness or the fact the ECB's quantitative easing measures tended to favour the wealthiest part of the

FIGURE 10.2 Handover of the presidency of the ECB, represented by a bell, between Jean-Claude Trichet, on the left, and Mario Draghi, 2011. Courtesy of European Union, 2011.

population who held financial assets. Austerity measures were compensated by the Growth Pact of 2012, a stimulus package aiming to stimulate the EU economic growth, but which was mainly based on already existing mechanisms and funds. The new financial assistance framework was created in the wake of the Greek sovereign debt crisis: in June 2010, the eurozone member states created the European Financial Stability Facility, a temporary rescue mechanism issuing bonds on the capital markets and lending them to countries facing difficulties. In 2012, the European Stability Mechanism (ESM) was introduced as a permanent mechanism. Lastly, the eurozone's economic governance was reformed in the wake of the euro crisis. The Stability and Growth Pact, introduced in 1997 and reformed in 2005, was further reformed with two series of regulations in 2010 and 2011: the 'Six Pack', comprising six measures improving macroeconomic surveillance, and the 'Two Pack', comprising two regulations on the frequency of the monitoring. In addition, the European Semester was introduced in 2010. It aimed at helping member states coordinate their economic and social policies through a dialogue between the Commission and member states during the elaboration of national budgets. In 2012, the Treaty on Stability, Coordination, and Governance was signed: it aimed at limiting deficits, improving macroeconomic coordination and strengthening correction mechanisms.

One of the most important political outcomes of the euro crisis for the eurozone was the development of the European banking union, from 2012 on. The rationale of banking union was to move banking regulation and supervision from the national to the supranational level, giving particular supervisory powers to the ECB. Banking union is composed of two pillars, the Single Supervisory Mechanism (SSM) and the Single Resolution Mechanism (SRM), and is based on the Single Rulebook. The SSM means that it is now the ECB, and not national supervisory organizations, which is in charge of supervising large banks in the eurozone, that is, the daily control of their activities to prevent excessive risk-taking. The ECB took on this role in November 2014. The SRM is a scheme designed to handle the failure of a bank (with possible multiple entities all over the eurozone and beyond) in the eurozone through a common resolution authority, the Single Resolution Board. The SSM and SRM are based on the regulations established on the Single Rulebook, which sets the rules, such as capital requirements, governing the financial sector in the entire EU (and not in the eurozone only). A proposal for setting up a European scheme for deposit insurance, which would form a third pillar to the European banking union, is still under discussion but faces considerable political obstacles. The banking union is therefore not considered as complete.

The measures enacted to establish banking union in the eurozone were not new ideas: coordinating banking regulation and improving banking supervision have long been discussed in the EEC. From the mid-1960s on, much work has been done in these two areas. However, the exercise proved long and arduous: differences in regulatory and supervisory systems were too large for them to be completely harmonized. For a long time, a middle way was preferred: that of cooperation between national supervisory and regulatory systems. Eventually, the Euro crisis provided the political impetus for a major change in the area. Though apparently mostly technical, the banking union was a major political and institutional change, as it moved banking supervision to the supranational level. However, most observers consider that EMU is not complete, and the political economy of the eurozone is still a hotly debated topic.

# Conclusion

The history of EMU shows that some of the weaknesses of the euro's architecture that became apparent at the time of the euro crisis had already been widely discussed before. The other takeaway point is that EMU cannot be understood in isolation, but is and has always been closely linked to national and international economic policies, trends and events. Furthermore, this chapter underlines the importance of the 'E' in EMU (Mourlon-Druol 2020b): the story of EMU is not only about monetary cooperation and integration but also about the *economic* conditions for making EMU work. Macroeconomic coordination, financial regulation and supervision and financial transfers have long been discussed in the EEC/EU. EMU has also been considered as a major step for the completion of the Single Market. In addition, even though the need for a reinforced monetary integration in the EEC emerged from the global monetary upheavals of the late 1960s/early 1970s, monetary cooperation and integration were already discussed before. Therefore, the history of EMU is economic, monetary and political at the same time.

EMU entails several advantages and disadvantages, which partly explains its complex historical path (Verdun 2002b). On the one hand, it eliminates exchange-rate risk, strengthens the single market, facilitates cross-border financial transactions, makes travelling easier for consumers and reinforces the EU as an international actor. On the other hand, it entails a loss of national sovereignty, removes exchange rate flexibility that could absorb asymmetric shocks, exacerbates the need for greater cohesion and convergence and raises democratic concerns, in particular concerning the control of the ECB.

Whether it was the incomplete architecture of EMU or the economic policies taken by member states that caused the severity of the euro crisis remains the subject of much debate. However, the entanglement of economic and monetary affairs with critical political and social stakes is undeniable. Despite its technicalities, EMU affairs have a long and multifaceted history, with no simple path leading to ever closer integration, but with crises, disputes and reversals. The fact that the EMU survived the euro crisis not only showed its centrality to the European economy and the European project, but also the many issues still to be resolved for its completion. The fact that the EMU project is closely linked to the EU project as a whole certainly plays a role in eurozone member states' commitment to it.

# Five key questions

1. Was the creation of a monetary union the logical outcome of the creation of a unified market?
2. Why and how was the euro created?
3. What are the advantages and disadvantages of forming an Economic and Monetary Union in the European Union?
4. What were the weaknesses of EMU that observers stressed in 1992? And did observers during the Euro crisis flag up similar issues?
5. What does the 'E' in EMU refer to, and why does it matter?

# Note

1 This chapter builds on a project, titled 'The Making of a Lopsided Union: Economic Integration in the European Economic Community, 1957–1992' (EURECON), that has received funding from the European Research Council (ERC) under the European Union's Horizon 2020 research and innovation programme (Grant agreement no. 716849).

# Ten key readings

Dyson, K., and K. Featherstone (1999), *The Road to Maastricht: Negotiating Economic and Monetary Union*, Oxford: Oxford University Press.
Dyson, K., and I. Maes (eds) (2016), *Architects of the Euro: Intellectuals in the Making of European Monetary Union*, Oxford: Oxford University Press.
James, H. (2012), *Making the European Monetary Union*, Cambridge, MA: Harvard University Press.
James, H. (2016), 'The History of Economic and Monetary Union', in H. Badinger and V. Nitsch (eds), *Routledge Handbook of the Economics of European Integration*, 22–37, Abingdon: Routledge.
McNamara, K. R. (1998), *The Currency of Ideas: Monetary Politics in the European Union*, Ithaca, NY: Cornell University Press.
Mourlon-Druol, E. (2012), *A Europe Made of Money*, Ithaca, NY: Cornell University Press.
Sandbu, M. (2015), *Europe's Orphan: The Future of the Euro and the Politics of Debt*, Princeton, NJ: Princeton University Press.

Tooze, A. (2018), *Crashed: How a Decade of Financial Crises Changed the World*, London: Allen Lane.

Verdun, A. (ed.) (2002b), *The Euro: European Integration Theory and Economic and Monetary Union*, Boulder, CO: Rowman and Littlefield.

Warlouzet, L. (2018a), *Governing Europe in a Globalizing World: Neoliberalism and Its Alternatives Following the 1973 Oil Crisis*, London: Routledge.

# 11

# A citizens' Europe? Consumer and environmental policies

## Brigitte Leucht and Jan-Henrik Meyer

## Introduction

When Ursula von der Leyen, the new, and first female, president of the European Commission, took office in late 2019, she programmatically placed her presidency under the heading of the so-called European Green Deal. She promised to put economic and ecological issues on equal footing and to address forcefully the ever more pressing problem of climate change. However, the Commission's Communication on the Green Deal did not only promise to work towards transforming Europe's 'economy and society' and 'to put it on a more sustainable path' but it also aimed to turn the European Union (EU) into 'a global leader on climate and environmental measures' and on 'consumer protection, and workers' rights' (European Commission 2019, 2).

It is by no means coincidental that the Commission is presenting environmental, social and consumer issues as being part and parcel of the same thing. Such reasoning goes back to the origins of these policies. When consumer policy and environmental policies were first introduced in the early 1970s into what was then primarily a growth-oriented economic community, they were intended to strengthen the then European Economic Community's (EEC) appeal to its citizens, at a time when the EEC was heavily criticized for their butter mountains (Chapter 9), their bureaucracy, and – by leftists – for being an agent of corporate power. In the face of such criticism, the Commissioner for Industry Altiero Spinelli, an Italian socialist and long-time European federalist, advocated a new focus on policies directly benefitting citizens (Chapter 13). Such policies, he argued on 1 July

1971 with a view to the environment, would help the Community find a new 'vocation' (Spinelli 1991, 180).

However, the original Treaty of Rome did not provide a legal base for the new policy concerns emerging only in the late 1960s, such as environment and consumer protection. Thus, Spinelli skilfully subsumed them under social policy, for which the EEC had some limited competence. In line with the treaty, environmental policy was defined as a social policy aiming at the 'improvement of living and working conditions' (mentioned in Article 117 of the Rome Treaty) and the 'quality of life' (Spinelli 1972), a new buzzword across media and international organizations (IOs) in the early 1970s. When the heads of state and government of the enlarged Community met at the Paris summit in October 1972 and gave their go-ahead to the introduction of both environmental and consumer policies, consumer protection featured within the section on social policy, while environmental policy was mentioned under a separate headline, in two short sentences (Box 11.1).

## BOX 11.1 PARIS SUMMIT DECLARATION, 19–20 OCTOBER 1972

Social Policy
6. The Heads of State and Government emphasized that vigorous action in the social sphere is to them just as important as achieving Economic and Monetary Union. They consider it absolutely necessary to secure an increasing share by both sides of industry in the Community's economic and social decisions. They ask the Institutions after consulting both sides of industry to draw up an action programme before 1 January 1974 ...
The programme must implement a coordinated policy for employment and vocational training, to improve working and living conditions, secure the collaboration of workers in the function of undertakings, facilitate according to the conditions in each country the conclusion of collective European agreements in appropriate areas and strengthen and coordinate action for protecting the consumer ...

The Environment
8. The Heads of State and Government stressed the value of a Community environment policy. They are therefore requesting the Community Institutions to draw up an action programme with a precise schedule before 31 July 1973.
    Source: 'The First Summit Conference of the Enlarged Community, including Declaration, Paris, 19–20 October 1972', *Bulletin of the European Communities* 10/1972, pp. 19–20.

This chapter argues that environmental and consumer policies, as two of the most important new policies of the 1970s, have more in common than their origins at the summit of Paris of 1972 and their initial lack of a proper legal base. The chapter will present the role of both policies as part of the history of European integration, pointing to similarities and differences. It will start out by explaining both policies' key objectives and instruments and relevant actors, before exploring the origins and development of both policies, problems and solutions. For a conclusion we will compare both policies, with a view to their (perceived) success or failure and the reasons accounting for them.

# 1. Key issues and actors

Both environmental and consumer policies were intended to address problems so far overlooked in the development of the European Communities. European economic integration had contributed to the spectacular economic growth and technological development of the post-war period, which, as many citizens increasingly noted, came at a price. By the late 1960s, river and water pollution, air pollution, waste piling up and the uncontrolled presence of actually and potentially toxic chemicals on farms, in households and consumer goods threatened to undermine the benefits of economic prosperity for citizens. At the same time, corporate power and a lack of relevant rules to the contrary allowed companies to rig consumer markets in their favour, despite the existence of a competition policy. Many complex consumer goods or pre-packaged foods did not come with sufficient information, which limited actual and informed consumer choice. In the worst of cases this threatened human health and well-being, as in the case of cosmetics or food additives. Since the late 1960s, such issues were increasingly and controversially discussed. Pollution and health scandals helped putting such issues on the public and subsequently also on the political agenda – at national but also at the EEC level (Meyer 2020). Environmental and consumer policies were intended to prevent or limit such problematic developments.

## Actors

Environmental and consumer policies did not only emerge at the same time but they also were administered and promoted at the European level by the same actors within the European institutions. With the go-ahead of both policies, in 1973 the European Commission established a Service for the Environment and Consumer Protection (SEPC). In 1981, the SEPC was turned into a separate directorate-general (DG) for the Environment, Consumer Protection and Nuclear Safety, after the accession of Greece, with a new Greek director general. Initially, the SEPC only had very few officials – some lawyers and economists, but mainly engineers and natural scientists, who informally cooperated across the two fields (Meyer 2019; Van de Velde 2014). Someone who spent most of his career in the SEPC and DG environment was the German lawyer Ludwig Krämer (Meyer forthcoming); and see Box 11.2 and Figure 11.1).

## BOX 11.2  BIOGRAPHY OF LUDWIG KRÄMER

| | |
|---|---|
| 1939 | Born in Stettin, Pomerania (today Szczecin, Poland); family fled to Kiel, West Germany, at the end of the Second World War |
| 1957 | Participation in a youth exchange programme, sponsored by the Council of Europe, which served as a first introduction to 'Europe' and European institutions and sowed the seeds for an interest in the construction of Europe and learning languages |
| Until 1968 | Study and practical training in law in Kiel, Munich and Paris |
| 1969 | Judge at the Kiel District Court (*Landgericht*) |
| 1972 | Joined DG Competition's special consumer department (see Section 3 in this chapter) |
| 1973 | Moved with Consumer Unit to the new Service for the Environment and Consumer Protection |
| 1980 | Collaborated on compilation of the first comparative study of the state of consumer law in the nine member states of the Community (Micklitz 2015; Reich and Micklitz 1980) |
| 1984 | Moved from the consumer protection to the environment part of DG Environment, Consumer Protection and Nuclear Safety, where he built up the Legal Unit, seeking to improve the implementation of European environmental law by taking member states to court |
| 1985 | PhD in Law University of Hamburg on European Consumer Policy (Krämer 1985) |
| 1991 | Removed by Commission administration from Legal Unit to Waste Unit |

| 1995 | Given 'Twelve Star Award' by the European Environmental Bureau, the oldest European environmental NGOs, in recognition of work to ensure implementation of EU environmental law |
| 2001 | Shifted by Commission administration to Unit on Environmental Governance |
| 2004 | Retired from Commission, continued publishing extensively, on environmental law |

FIGURE 11.1 *Ludwig Krämer. Photograph courtesy of Ludwig Krämer.*

The European Parliament (EP) remained unelected until 1979 and powerless in terms of legislation. However, with a view to environmental and consumer policies it was an important agenda-setter, an ally of both the SEPC and the environmental groups. It constituted an important forum and proxy European public sphere for raising and debating new policy priorities, connecting with European societies (Chapter 7). With the introduction of the new policies, the EP adjusted its committee structure. The Committee on Public Health and Social Affairs, within which the first calls for EEC environmental policy had emerged, was replaced by the Committee on Public Health and the Environment, and from 1976 on the Environment, Public Health and Consumer Protection (Meyer 2021).

The development of both policies was influenced right from the start by European-level interest groups and civil society. The first European-level institution including consumer representatives was the European Economic and Social Committee, an advisory body composed of different interest groups. This body had existed already since 1958. However, the accession of the UK and Denmark to the EEC in 1973 greatly strengthened consumer organizations within it, as both new member states had well-developed consumer protection regimes (Van de Grift 2018). The establishment of the European Consumer Organization (BEUC) in 1962 in Brussels predated the creation of the separate policy by a decade (Van Zon, Schimmel and Grift forthcoming). A similar umbrella organization, the European Environmental Bureau (EEB), representing national and subnational environmental groups from European EEC member and non-member countries, set up shop in Brussels in 1974, to give the environment(alists) a voice with regard to the – (rightly) anticipated – growing importance of the European institutions for the new policy field. National member organizations provided much of the expertise regarding specific policy projects, and the EEB met and cooperated in particular with the SEPC on a regular basis (Meyer 2013). By the late 1980s, with the arrival of Greenpeace, WWF, Friends of the Earth and others, the virtual monopoly in Brussels of the EEB was replaced by what is today the G10 of environmental groups in Europe (Van de Grift, Rodenburg and Wieman 2020).

# 2. Origins and development of environmental policy

The Paris Council 1972 marks the official go-ahead of both environmental and consumer protection policies, as declared by the heads of state and government. However, by that time, preparations for such policies were long underway.

The ambitions for an environmental policy at Community level were part of a larger, international development: the rise of the environment as a political concept and thus as a new field for public policy, and of environmentalism as an idea and a movement. All of this happened within a few years around 1970. The environment encompassed previously separate problems of pollution control, mostly administered locally, and resource and nature conservation, concerns that nature protection groups and IOs had dealt with since around 1900 (Meyer 2017b). There was a sense of urgency in the concern for what was initially still specified as the 'natural environment' or the 'human environment', as the first United Nations Conference in 1972 on the issue was called. Informed by ecological ideas and the compelling images of 'spaceship earth' (Höhler 2015), contemporaries viewed these problems as extending beyond borders and being of global scope.

The emergence of EEC environmental policy cannot exactly be traced back to the oft-mentioned breakup of the oil tanker Torrey Canyon oil 1967 between France and the UK (e.g. Zito, Burns and Lenschow 2019), which is credited to have raised environmental awareness, but to a similar ecological catastrophe with cross-border implications in the summer of 1969. The release of a pesticide in Germany poisoned the fish in the river Rhine and threatened drinking water resources downstream in the Netherlands. Dutch Members of the European Parliament (MEPs) made a public scandal of this disaster, and the river's pollution more generally with chemicals, untreated sewage and sodium. They also flagged up the anticipated thermal and radioactive pollution of the river's water due to the planned 'pearl necklace' of nuclear power plants upstream in Switzerland, France and West Germany. The Committee of Public Health and Social Affairs drew up an own initiative report, one of the few instruments the powerless parliament actually had. The MEPs not only demanded urgent European action on this main European watershed, and rivers more generally, but they also planned for widening the scope of the problem, by projecting a similar report on air pollution, as a 'stepwise' procedure to demand policy action on the environment. They self-confidently even suggested suitable legal bases to justify such 'task expansion' (Meyer 2021; Zito 2002).

Whereas traditionally nature conservation had been left to the non-binding texts of the Strasbourg Council of Europe, by 1970/71, the Commission became increasingly interested in the nascent issue of environmental policy, as other IOs, such as the North Atlantic Treaty Organization (NATO) and the Organization for Economic Cooperation and Development (OECD), sought to carve out their part of setting environmental norms. Next to such inter-organizational competition, two further factors played a key role. Firstly, as mentioned above, environmental rules were highly relevant as standards in the EECs main project, the Common Market (Lambert 1972); secondly, for Spinelli and others, the ambition to make the EEC relevant to European citizens, and demonstrating its worth to common people and contributing to their well-being, played an important role at a time when various attempts were undertaken for 'deepening' and 'completing', next to 'widening', the European Communities, as the summit of the Hague in 1969 had famously phrased it (Van de Grift 2018; Meyer 2009).

Under the auspices of Spinelli, in 1971, the European Commission set up a small task force and tested the ground with two detailed Communications (European Commission 1971, 1972a) outlining the justification for and the scope of the new policy and actual measures the EEC could undertake. These documents were intensely discussed by the EEC institutions, with the EP, for instance, making concrete suggestions regarding the inclusion of certain issues, such as bird protection. The EP's Legal Committee even drew up a report on the potential legal bases (Armengaud 1972). Business and agricultural lobby groups submitted comments (COPA 1972; UNICE 1972). While the French government was initially very hesitant to accept developing a new policy at the EEC level, they finally caved in to the reasoning that common environmental rules were indispensable for the functioning of the Common Market. Thus by the October 1972 Paris Summit the ground was effectively already well paved for an environmental action programme, which was negotiated and finalized during 1973 (Council 1973). Along with the action programme, the heads of state and government agreed to notify the Commission of any environmental legislation they were planning. This allowed the Commission to respond and propose European-level solutions. For member states this provided an opportunity to advance their own environmental policy priorities, while ensuring a level playing field in the Common Market.

The action programme outlined a number of policy principles, including the polluter pays principle, which the OECD also promoted at the time (Meyer 2017a). Most importantly, it specified a legislative programme of anti-pollution measures primarily on water and air pollution and waste. A substantial number of directives were enacted during the 1970s. Unexpectedly, environmental action also came to encompass nature protection, where the link to the Common Market was much harder to establish and other European organizations were traditionally responsible, such as the Council of Europe (Van de Grift and Meurs 2021). The issue was advanced by a coalition of activist MEPs and bird protection groups, whose concerns about bird hunting in Southern Europe met a receptive Commission, which in turn relied on scientific, ecological expertise the environmentalists were happy to provide. Joint lobbying efforts by the bird protection groups of their national governments helped overcome the threshold of a unanimous Council decision. Thus Europe's migrant birds and their habitats came to be protected by the 1979 Birds Directive (Meyer 2010b), which paved the ground for an even more ambitious nature conservation by the Habitats Directive of 1992 (Jackson 2018).

The development of European environmental policy was thus more strongly linked to societal concerns and debates than we tend to assume, in particular, when they related to issues with cross-border, thus more self-evidently European, implications. Not all of these eventually led to legislation. The debate about nuclear power, a major area of societal conflict in the 1970s, also arrived at the European level (Figure 11.2). In 1976, MEPs demanded Community competences for coordinating the siting of nuclear plants near national borders (Meyer 2022), but the subsequent Commission proposals did not find sufficient member-state support. Environmentalists also convinced the Commission to hold public hearings on nuclear power underneath the Brussels Atomium, and to discuss the use and promotion of alternative, renewable energy sources, and energy savings, which in the long run paved the way for our current energy transition (Meyer 2013).

Environmental scandals and catastrophes continued to shape the development of EEC environmental policy usually mediated via the EP or the Commission, or governments, as policy entrepreneurs, seeking to use the windows of opportunity the events provided. In the wake of the chemical plant disaster at Seveso, Italy, 1976, the Commission proposed legislation on industrial accidents. The debate on the forest dieback in West Germany in the early 1980s led to national efforts to introduce catalytic converters in cars, which quickly led to Community-level legislation, in order to prevent new obstacles on the common market for cars (Warlouzet 2021; Zito 2000).

FIGURE 11.2 *In the wake of the Three Mile Island nuclear accident in the United States, European citizens turning out for environmentalist protest in front of the newly elected European Parliament, 1979.* Photo: 20 July 1979, Demonstration by environmentalists at the entrance to the Parliament building. Courtesy of European Communities, 1979.

When barrels of toxic waste from Seveso went missing in 1983, the EP responded by demanding not only to improve relevant legislation but to actually enhance and control implementation on the ground. Against this backdrop, DG Environment set up a legal unit, which started to pursue member states for not having implemented environmental legislation, and if necessary, took member states to court for infringement of their treaty obligations. During late 1980s and early 1990s, the media-savvy Italian Commissioner for the Environment Carlo Ripa di Meana fully supported such Commission self-assertion, which a number of member states came to resent (Haigh and Lanigan 1995; Meyer forthcoming).

International factors contributed to some policy change in the 1990s. First, the sustainability agenda – which sought to reconcile economic and environmental objectives, and had been promoted by the World Commission on Environment and Development, the so-called Brundtland-Commission – took centre stage and continues to do so (Seefried 2021), as the wording of the European Green Deal suggests. Secondly, neoliberal and ecomodernist ideas – promoted internationally even more forcefully after the end of state socialism in 1989/91, and the dissatisfaction with implementation problems, induced the Commission to advocate new policy instruments. Thirdly, since the UN conference on environment and development at Rio de Janeiro in 1992, climate change increasingly became the most important environmental issue. It was on climate issues that the new policy instruments were tried out first. While the proposal of a carbon tax failed to win member-state support (Zito 2000), the subsequent introduction of carbon trade in the EU became an international model (Bradford 2020), even if its effectiveness for emissions was undermined by over-generous handouts of free carbon certificates by national governments trying to protect their national industries.

More generally, observers have noted that in the new millennium environmental policy was 'displace[d]' by other EU priorities and 'perhaps los[ing] direction' (Zito et al. 2019, 198) – in the face of renewed EU efforts to improve economic competitiveness with the Lisbon agenda (2000, for 2010) and combating a whole series of economic crises since 2008. The Juncker Commission (2014–19) was frequently criticized for seeking to water down and rescind existing environmental rules, or cynically only talk the environmental talk, while not taking measures (Knill, Steinebach and Fernández-i-Marín 2020; Schmitz 2014). Hence, even if there continues to be evidence of greenwashing, for instance, regarding the 'sustainability' of nuclear energy and natural gas (Economist 2022), the more pro-actively pro-environment approach of the von der Leyen presidency might be suggestive of a return to more forceful environmental action, and of the EU as a – frequently self-declared – environmental leader by both words and deeds. This would seem highly appropriate to many of the young people criticizing decades wasted with too little action.

# 3. Origins and development of consumer policy

Consumers were affected by the creation of the Common Market from the early days of European integration starting with the common agricultural policy (CAP). This flagship policy was shaped by the Commission in negotiations with the member states who prioritized agricultural producer interests in the 1960s (Chapter 9). Thus, the CAP's design implied relatively high consumer prices. Nevertheless, the Commission's DG for Agriculture was the first to reach out to consumer organizations. Following an initiative by Commissioner Sicco Mansholt (1958–67), a 'contact committee for consumer questions' was created in DG Agriculture in 1962. The committee comprised several Community-level consumer organizations, including the BEUC. While it had only a consultative function, the committee advised the Commission on agricultural prices and directives relating to specific foodstuffs (European Commission 1976).

Consumers were also affected by the creation of the common market for industrial products, which relied on the development of a European-level competition policy (Articles 85–86 EEC Treaty). The Commission recognized the interests of consumers in the common market for industrial products by establishing a special consumer department in DG Competition in 1968. Creating the Common Market involved competition policy and changes resulting from legal harmonization (based on Article 100 EEC Treaty). The institutionalization of consumer interests at the EEC level in DG Competition was to balance a transfer of relevant law making to the EEC during the creation of the Common Market, namely, first, the completion of the customs union in 1968 and, second, the end of the transition period of the Rome Treaty in 1970. The end of the transition period was especially pertinent to consumers because it gave immediate effect to a set of treaty articles relating to the free movement of goods and services (Articles 30–34 EEC Treaty). These articles required the Commission to tackle national legislation preventing the free circulation of goods, *potentially* including laws protecting consumers in the member states (Leucht 2022).

Consumer protection thus originated in two different DGs – Agriculture and Competition. This in turn gave rise to two competing views on consumer interests. The 'Social Democratic view', reflecting Agricultural Commissioner Mansholt's political affiliation (Chapter 9, Figure 9.4), included a preference for price fixing to protect consumers, which was anathema to DG Competition's approach. Instead, DG Competition posited that consumer interests were ultimately best served by the wider choices and lower prices resulting from market integration. This reflects German Christian Democratic Commissioner Hans von der Groeben's (1961–7) 'ordoliberal view' on competition policy (Van Zon 2020).

The Commission was not alone in starting to acknowledge the significance of consumers in European market integration, however. From 1969, the EP also began pushing the Commission to strengthen the special consumer department in DG Competition with a view to reinforcing the position of consumers in the Common Market. For sure, the timing of introducing consumers and consumer policy into the EEC portfolio in the 1970s owed to the progress in the economic integration of the Common Market. But, corresponding to the emerging environmental portfolio, the increasing attention EEC institutions paid to consumers was also in line with developments in other IOs and European states. So far, governments and IOs had focused almost exclusively on production and producers as the key to fostering growth in the post-war period. From the late 1960s, increasing technological progress, combined with growing mass production, increasing individual purchasing power and the expansion of markets led to a broader shift towards consumers and consumption (Frey and Warin 1974; Leucht 2022).

The origins of consumer policy *before* the Paris summit of 1972 created important path dependencies. To begin with, the 'pre-history' of the policy shows that the different tools used by the Community to advance economic integration had a direct impact on consumers. Even before the Commission had a mandate to develop consumer policy, it issued directives in agriculture and attempted to harmonize member-state laws to achieve a common market in industrial goods. The connection between consumers and Community legislation therefore preceded the development of EEC consumer policy. Crucially, EEC policymaking impacting on consumers *outside* of the area of consumer policy strictly speaking did not end, when the Paris summit gave the go-ahead for the Commission to develop a consumer policy for the Community. To the contrary, it was in the very nature of consumer interests that they remained diffused and consumer policy and law have continued emanating from different sources in the treaty, resulting in a somewhat disjointed body of law relating to consumers (Weatherill 2013).

Furthermore, from the beginning, the Commission framed consumers within the dynamics of market integration (see also Chapter 8). This had important implications for EEC consumer policy. Consumer interest groups increasingly viewed consumers as needing protection in the emerging Common Market, in the face of the 'dialectics of open borders, protectionism, and bona fide intervention of the Member State to protect legitimate societal values and goals even if at the expense of interrupting the free flow of goods on which the idea of the common marketplace is postulated' (Cappelletti, Seccombe and Weiler 1986a, vi). They thus highlighted that consumers could at the same time benefit *from* and lose *because of* European market integration. They would clearly benefit from access to wider product choice and competitive, lower prices. However, they were also increasingly exposed to the risk of losing legal protection previously enjoyed in the member states.

The 'preliminary programme for consumer protection and information policy', which was adopted by the Council of the EEC in 1975 (Council 1975; Davies 2011), was to address the contradictions between open borders supported by an effective competition policy and consumer protection. As in the case of the environment (Meyer 2017a), the EEC borrowed from the Council of Europe and the OECD in developing consumer policy (European Commission 1972b). The 'five basic rights' of the preliminary programme, for example, were taken over from the Council of Europe's Consumer Protection Charter (1973). These rights included the right to protection of health and safety; the right to protection of economic interests; the right of redress; the right to information and education; and the right of representation (the right to be heard). The five basic rights of the Council of Europe's Consumer Protection Charter, in turn, were imported from the United States. They reflected US President John F. Kennedy's 1962 special message to Congress, in which he had called for strengthening existing consumer protection and establishing new legislation (Kennedy 1962a).

Consumer policy was off to a much slower start than environmental policy. This was perhaps due to the lack of advocacy for a separate consumer policy within Community institutions prior to the Paris 1972 summit. Under Spinelli's leadership the Commission had stirred the discussion on environmental policy, but consumer protection was only taken out of the social policy portfolio and moved into a separate policy following a proposal by the Danish government in the summer of 1973 (Leucht 2022).

Following the adoption of the 1975 preliminary programme by the Council, the Commission immediately embarked on several activities to harmonize divergent legislation in the member states. Priority areas included consumer credit, misleading advertising and product liability (Council 1975). For example, the Commission proposed a directive concerning the liability for defective products in 1976. It is illustrative of the slow progress of consumer policy that it was only finally adopted, following protracted negotiations with member-state governments, by the Council in 1985 (Directive 85/374/EEC 1985). While this directive covers rather technical grounds, it is significant as an early example of member states' 'uploading' (Börzel 2002) domestically controversial issues to the European level. The West German government – a coalition between Social Democrats and more pro-business Liberals – had moved the potentially divisive decision over liability legislation to the EEC (Micklitz 2015).

Overall, the 1975 programme, the Community's first stab at a consumer policy for the emerging Common Market, cannot be considered a success from the point of view of consumer interest groups, including the BEUC. It was followed by a second and a third programme in 1981 and 1986, respectively. Formally speaking, the Council resolutions on the three consumer programmes were not binding legislative acts, but 'soft law' (Abbott and Snidal 2000). The legal foundation for the new consumer policy began changing in 1979 with the *Cassis de Dijon* decision (Case 120–78 *Rewe-Zentral AG v. Bundesmonopolverwaltung für Branntwein*; Albors-Llorens, Barnard and Leucht 2021). In this seminal judgement, the Court of Justice of the EU (CJEU) introduced the doctrine of mutual recognition, according to which goods produced and marketed in one member state could be marketed and sold in all member states. This doctrine provided an entrepreneurial Commission with a tool to develop a 'new approach' to creating the Common Market. It could now contribute to free trade within the Community *without* having to adopt legislation in the area (via the cumbersome process of legal harmonization). At the same time, the CJEU crucially recognized national consumer legislation as a legitimate barrier to trade. *Cassis de Dijon* is regarded as 'the shining beacon of EU law's image of the consumer even two generations later' (Lezcykiewicz and Weatherill 2016, 3; Weatherill 2021). In 1990, in the *GB Inno* case (Case 362–88 *GB-INNO-BM v. Confédération du commerce luxembourgeois*), the Court also recognized the first preliminary programme for consumer protection and information policy as well as its successor programmes (Weatherill 2013).

The case law of the Court fed into a wider prioritization of the 'completion of the common market' as the EEC's main political project from the 1980s. The 1986 consumer programme already presented the policy within the context of internal market policy from which consumers were to benefit too. The Court's *GB Inno* decision, in turn, established the right of private consumers to move freely across member-state borders, purchase for their own consumption and return home with their purchases. Consumers' de-facto rights had thus already improved before the *legal* basis for EEC consumer policy changed in the Maastricht Treaty.

The treaty came into force in 1993 and for the first time added a provision explicitly empowering EU action in the consumer protection field. Title XI on 'Consumer Protection' held:

> The Community shall contribute to the attainment of a high level of consumer protection through:
>
> (a) measures adopted pursuant to Article 100a [on harmonization] in the context of the completion of the internal market;
> (b) specific action which supports and supplements the policy pursued by the Member States to protect the health, safety and economic interests of consumers and to provide adequate information to consumers.

Formally, the Maastricht Treaty represented a breakthrough for consumer policy by transforming non-binding soft law (Council resolutions) into legislative competences. The possibilities for the Community to act on its legislative competences in the consumer field were limited by the introduction of the subsidiarity principle, however. This principle ensured that the debate on the appropriate aims and intensity of EU action in the consumer field would continue. The *practical* impact of the treaty change was therefore limited. Consumer policy would continue being developed through the tools that were there from the days of early European integration: the application of the rules on competition and the free movement, on the one hand, and legislative harmonization, on the other (Weatherill 2013).

As environmental policy, consumer policy has remained a shared competence of the EU and the member states. If we attempt to assess the success of the policy over time, it seems that consumer policy has in many respects remained in the shadow of the Common Market. The historical origins of the policy in DG Competition and the development of consumer policy in the framework of opening markets privileging producer interests over those of consumers would suggest such a reading. What is more, lobbying attempts by consumer groups at the European level, including the institutionalized lobbying of the European Commission by the European Consumer Organization, have been hampered by financially powerful producers with an interest in cross-border trade (Kleis 2019). However, thinking about consumer policy in a more contemporary context, at least two examples come to mind that do not simply serve producer interests but significantly advance the protection of consumers. First, Europeans are protected by EU rules when travelling by plane, including compensation for cancellations, delays and overbooked flights. Second, European consumers also enjoy advantageous conditions for using their mobile phones abroad and cannot be hit by excessive roaming charges. The respective rules underpinning consumer protection in these examples are *detrimental* to the economic interests of the airlines and mobile network operators. To explain the protection of consumer interests in areas that do not fit the rationale of producer-serving market integration, Christian Rauh (2016) has argued that the increasing politicization of European integration from the 1990s has allowed the European Commission to push relevant EU regulation.

This argument also explains advances made in another area at the crossroads of consumer protection and environmental policy, namely food safety. As in the case of the carbon trade model for EU environmental policy, EU food safety regulation has had a global impact: external producers need to comply with EU regulation to penetrate EU markets (Bradford 2020). As a result of the development of the common agricultural market, food is one of the first policy areas that fell under EU competence (see Chapter 9). Calls to regulate the food industry at EU level also responded to several scandals ranging from the BSE ('mad cow disease') in the 1990s to the horsemeat scandal in 2013. The latter was triggered when the Irish food safety authority identified undeclared animal species, including horse, in beef burgers and ready meals of major supermarket chains. These scandals attracted considerable publicity and media interest, and as the earlier environmental scandals, they crucially mobilized European citizens providing the European Commission with political legitimacy to address these issues at the European level. This can also be seen in the widely shared aversion of Europeans to genetically modified organisms (GMO), which represented one important obstacle to the successful conclusion of the Transatlantic Trade and Investment Partnership (2013–16). In recent years, consumer protection has also embraced the digital single market and financial services. In conclusion, a broader view on consumer policy shows that, the limited success following the changes in consumer protection in the European treaties notwithstanding, European consumers enjoy considerable protection based on EU rules.

# Conclusion

Which role did environmental and consumer policies play within the history of European integration? Both policies emerged at a specific moment in time, in the wake of the 1969 summit of the Hague and the progress in integration associated with it and the first enlargement. Indeed, Denmark and the UK had a keen interest in both new policies. The UK was even one of the first countries to have established a government minister for the environment; and both countries had strong traditions of consumer protection. Societal and value changes, a growing awareness of the downsides of consumer society and corporate power, and the international debate about the quality of life were mediated by the European institutions too. Public scandals – such as the pollution of the Rhine or the unregulated use of hazardous chemicals (Van Zon forthcoming) – were picked up and translated into demands for political action by the otherwise powerless EP, which pushed for consumer as well as for environmental policies since 1969. All this induced the European Commission to take action and convince the member states that this was a concern best addressed at EEC level, because these issues were closely intertwined with the Common Market, the EEC's raison d'être. Interestingly, these policies were introduced informally without a legal base in the 1970s, when treaty change was not on the agenda, and only formalized with the 1986 Single European Act.

As opposed to the traditional policies of the common market in industry and agriculture, which work in favour of concentrated producer interest, both policies address diffuse interests, the common good. They aim at (re) regulating the Common Market, with a view to harnessing market forces in a way that they do not harm those whose interests are more difficult to organize – such as consumers – or who cannot speak for themselves – such as nature and human beings relying on clean air and water, products that are not harmful or wasteful, for their well-being, health and survival. Hence, non-governmental organizations play an important role in the aggregation and representation of such diffuse interests – notably the BEUC, which even predates the arrival of consumer policy, and the EEB, which emerged right after the creation of environmental policy.

Both policies strongly relied on regulatory policy, with directives that set new rules, standards and norms for products and on production. Hence, they established standards for a growing and more integrated European market. While initially ideas and standards for consumer and environmental protection had been imported, particularly from the United States (Vogel 2003), the EEC and, later, the EU with its large internal market became a global standard setter, and a self declared leader, notably in climate policy, such as in the Kyoto Protocol of 1997 and the Paris Agreement of 2015. European norms were unilaterally respected elsewhere, because it was much more efficient in terms of industrial economies of scale to abide by them than to set up one's own rules. Thus, one of the unanticipated successes of these two policies lies in their global export (Bradford 2020; Chapter 14). This might be a lesson Brexit-Britain with its scepticism towards Brussels-made rules might slowly be realizing, especially in the face of difficulties to negotiate comprehensive bilateral trade deals outside of the EU Single Market.

# Five key questions

1. Why did consumer and environmental policies only emerge in the 1970s?
2. How did these policies connect to – but also perhaps contradict – the EEC's main project, the Common Market?
3. What are the main common features, and what are the main differences between the two policies?
4. In which ways have environmental and consumer policies impacted on the lives of European citizens?
5. What has been the role of EU regulatory policy in shaping the EU's global power?

# Ten key readings

## Consumer policy

Leucht, B. (2022), 'Beyond 1973: UK Accession and the Origins of EC Consumer Policy', *Global Policy* 13(Suppl. 2), 20–9.
Van de Grift, L. (2018), 'Representing European Society. The Rise of New Representative Claims in 1970s European Politics', *Archiv für Sozialgeschichte*, 58: 263–78.
Van de Velde, C. (2014), 'Environmental and Consumer Protection', in É. Bussière, et al. (eds), *The European Commission 1973–86: History and Memories of an Institution*, 385–92, Luxembourg: Publications Office of the European Union.
Van Zon, K. (2020), 'A Consumers' Europe? Common Market Governance between Consumers and Commerce, 1960s–1990s', *Journal of European Integration History*, 26 (2): 203–28.
Weatherill, S. (2013), *EU Consumer Law and Policy* 2nd ed., Elgar European Law, Cheltenham: Edward Elgar.

## Environment

Meyer, J.-H. (2020), 'Responding to the European Public? Public Debates, Societal Actors and the Emergence of a European Environmental Policy', in C. Wenkel et al. (eds), *The Environment and European Public Sphere: Perception, Actors, Policies*, 221–40, Winwick: White Horse.

Meyer, J.-H. (2021), 'Pushing for a Greener Europe. The European Parliament and Environmental Policy in the 1970s and 1980s', *Journal of European Integration History*, 27 (1): 57–78.

Van de Grift, L., and W. P. v. Meurs (2021), 'Europeanizing Biodiversity: International Organizations as Environmental Actors', in A.-K. Wöbse and P. Kupper (eds), *Greening Europe: Environmental Protection in the Long Twentieth Century – A Handbook*, 419–46, Berlin: De Gruyter Oldenbourg.

Warlouzet, L. (2021), 'A Social Europe with a Greener Perspective: The Evolution of the Delors Commission around 1989', *Studi storici*, 62 (1): 189–210.

Zito, A. R. (2000), *Creating Environmental Policy in the European Union*, Basingstoke: Macmillan.

# 12

# A European society? Social policy and migration

## Simone Paoli

## Introduction

In the past thirty years, there has been an increasing tendency in literature to offer alternatives to the hitherto dominant interpretations of the European integration as a primarily diplomatic process rooted in the period after the end of the Second World War. This literature tends to embed European integration into longer-term efforts to stabilize industrial societies (Milward et al. 1993). The complex relationship between the development of the capitalist system, the search for political stability and the social integration of local and foreign workers was and continues to be at the centre of these interpretations (Varsori and Kaiser 2010).

Another more recent trend in the historical literature, and one that followed from political science and law, is to draw on the concept of Europeanization, which, in its top-down version, refers to the impact of the European Economic Community (EEC) and later the European Union (EU) on national policies, societies and cultures (Conway and Patel 2010). While recognizing the persistence of national peculiarities, these studies highlighted the importance of the European integration process in establishing and diffusing rules, practices, paradigms and styles and in shaping common identities and models; the emergence and development of the 'European social model' was particularly investigated and discussed (Vaughan-Whitehead 2014).

Drawing on these interpretative approaches, this chapter analyses, from a long-term perspective going back to the nineteenth century, the historical evolution of the EU's migration and social policies. The chapter will place special emphasis on the triangular relationship between, firstly, the reconstruction of European economies and democracies after the Second World War and, later, the Cold War; secondly, the European integration process; and, thirdly, the construction, evolution and crisis of European welfare states.

# 1. The origins of the European welfare state

Welfare policies were born within the nineteenth-century European nation state. They slowly emerged in Great Britain in the context of the First Industrial Revolution in the 1830s and in continental Europe in the context of the Second Industrial Revolution in the 1880s. Building on a tradition of social programmes that began in Prussia and Saxony in the 1840s, the German Empire was the first continental European country to implement a coherent system of measures comprising retirement schemes, and health, accident and unemployment insurance. Although national differences were significant, welfare policies generally aimed at similar purposes, namely stimulating economic growth while simultaneously reducing overseas emigration, preserving social order and preventing a socialist revolution (Hennock 2007).

In the 1910s, Great Britain gave birth to the first modern welfare state, whose main aim was to prevent the working class from searching for more radical solutions to their poor living conditions. This came on the eve of the First World War, which further strengthened the role of workers and the power of their representative organizations. Meanwhile, the success of the 1917 Bolshevik Revolution in the Russian Empire helped to radicalize European labour movements. It was against this backdrop that the Allied Powers agreed to introduce social clauses into the 1919 Peace Treaty of Versailles. These provided for the protection of trade unions and workers' rights. They also established the International Labour Organization (ILO), a tripartite body bringing together representatives of governments, employers and workers. The reasons behind these decisions were of humanitarian, political and economic nature. Awareness of the exploitation of workers was increasing at the time when social injustice began to be perceived as a threat to the liberal-democratic order and international peace. There was also growing understanding of the international economic interdependence and the need for cooperation to establish similar working conditions in countries competing for markets (Mechi 2012).

The Great Depression between the late 1920s and early 1930s provided a further incentive to implement social measures, reorganize industrial relations and strengthen the role of the state in the economy. Significantly, both democratic and authoritarian regimes of different ideological colouring were compelled to deal with the social question, though with different instruments and from different perspectives.

The Second World War saw the further strengthening of the role of workers and the spread of pro-labour ideas. In the aftermath of the war, Britain was again in the vanguard. The 1942 Beveridge Report promised rewards for workers' sacrifices in the war in the form of a comprehensive policy of social emancipation and protection. After the victory in the 1945 general election, the Labour Party adopted, and to a great extent implemented, those proposals. The Clement Attlee government reformed the education system, expanded the national insurance, financed new housing and created a publicly funded healthcare system. It also nationalized public utilities and strategic industries and used public policies to achieve and maintain full employment. The Keynesian welfare state was thus established: for the first time in a capitalist democracy, a rather stable institutional framework was founded, which generated an unprecedented combination of economic growth and diffusion of prosperity and social security in the broad mass of the population (Boyer 2019).

Britain was not alone in pursuing such a policy. Though at different stages, with distinct characteristics and to different extents, all democratic countries in Western Europe strengthened and reformed their social policies, gradually transforming their poor care systems into modern welfare states. This process, which was a pillar of the post-war settlement, reflected the willingness to safeguard capitalism while stabilizing European societies and dampening social tensions. With the outbreak of the Cold War, in Western Europe these aims went hand in hand with the vital need to reduce the popularity of the Soviet Union and the appeal of Communist ideologies and parties.

Although this tendency was visible in all Western European countries, the establishment of welfare states was the result of distinctly national compromises, which were embedded in the institutional forms of national sovereignty. Social policies were negotiated, decided, financed and implemented at the national level, since they were considered fundamental to legitimize or relegitimize nation states and to build and maintain consensus on national governments. E. H. Carr (1945) defined this phenomenon as a simultaneous socialization of nationalism and nationalization of socialism.

# 2. Keynes at home, Smith abroad, 1951–69

The national nature of welfare states in post-war Europe does not mean that they did not have a crucial international dimension. On the contrary, the 1944 Bretton Woods Agreement created a system whereby multilateral free trade could coexist with the discretionary capacity of individual states to intervene in the economy to ensure welfare goals, full employment in particular. Similarly, the European Coal and Steel Community (ECSC) and the EEC, whose founding treaties were signed in 1951 and 1957, respectively (Chapter 1), were committed to internal trade liberalization while allowing member states to autonomously create their welfare states.

When Federico Mancini (1988) spoke of the 'social frigidity' of the founding fathers of the ECSC and the EEC, he hit a nerve: in both treaties social issues played a relatively minor role. Nonetheless, as emphasized by Robert Gilpin, this was not due to the laissez-faire ideology of the leaders of the Six; nor it was due to their disregard for the social question. On the contrary, the scarce attention to the social dimension in the original treaties was due to a sort of division of tasks. The European Communities were charged with helping to promote economic growth by liberalizing trade. The member states, meanwhile, were free to redistribute their economic benefits through state intervention. This mechanism was summarized in the well-known formula 'Keynes at home, Smith abroad': welfare state within national borders, free trade at the Community level (Gilpin 1987; Chapter 8).

At the same time, although the Communities were to play a subordinate and auxiliary role in the social realm, the importance of social aspects in the founding treaties should not be underestimated. On the basis of the treaty provisions, the ECSC implemented significant measures to improve working conditions (Figure 12.1), retrain workers and build new houses for coal and steel workers and their families. The main aim was to show the social sensitivity of the Community, thereby replying to the anti-European propaganda of Communist parties and unions.

Though to a lesser extent, the EEC Treaty, too, made provisions for social policies. The Six established the Economic and Social Committee, a consultative body bringing together representatives of employers, employees and other interested groups. Under pressure from France, preoccupied with social dumping, they also agreed on cooperation and harmonization of social legislation, especially of the equality of pay between women and men. Moreover, at the insistence of Italy, the EEC Treaty included the founding of a European Investment Bank, whose main aim was to provide loans for infrastructure projects, as well as a European Social Fund (ESF) to improve the possibilities of employment for workers and to contribute to the raising of their standard of living and gradually ensure freedom of movement for Community workers. The Italian government attached special importance to freedom of movement, the main aim being to overcome the limitations of bilateral agreements and encourage exportation of surplus workforce: this, in turn, was considered crucial to defuse social tensions and get rid of potential Communist supporters (Romero 1991).

However, it is fair to say that between the late 1950s and late 1960s, the Six lacked the willingness to make substantial progress in the social field. The Economic and Social Committee was given very limited powers. Meanwhile, cooperation in, and harmonization of, the social legislation lagged behind, and the ESF was provided with scarce resources; despite

FIGURE 12.1 *Image of a coal worker in a French mine with a mechanized coal-cutting machine in the 1960s. Courtesy of Centre historique minier (CHM), Lewarde (France).*

pressure from Italy, a regional policy was not developed. The only significant progress was made in the context of the freedom of movement. By the late 1960s, any discrimination between workers of member states on the grounds of nationality was abolished and the right to the same social and tax benefits as local workers was ensured. In addition, family members of migrant workers were allowed to reside and work in the host country. The very provisions for family reunification brought a new dimension to the concept of free movement; in particular, they highlighted new social issues, which went well beyond the sphere of economically active workers (Paoli 2016).

While recognizing the importance of the freedom of movement, Patrick Ireland pointed out its contradictory role in the establishment of Social Europe. One major reason for promoting the social dimension of the European integration process was to remove obstacles to intra-European mobility. At the same time, in his opinion, the decision to exclude non-EEC nationals from Community legislation represented the ultimate threat to efforts to forge a fully fledged and fully inclusive Social Europe (Ireland 1995).

# 3. The birth of Social Europe, 1969–84

Momentum towards a Social Europe built in the late 1960s and early 1970s in the context of the 1968 workers' movement and other protest movements as well as the shift to the political left in all the main Western European countries (Warlouzet 2018a; Andry 2019). At the summit in the Hague in 1969, the heads of state and government of the member states of the EEC committed themselves to reforming the ESF within the framework of a closely concerted social policy. At another summit meeting in Paris in 1972 they went even further, stating that economic growth should not be considered as an end in itself but as a means to enhance quality of life and standards of living and to reduce socio-economic inequalities. Social goals, in this context, should receive as much attention as the achievement of the Economic and Monetary Union (EMU), another aim the European leaders focused on at this summit (Chapters 8 and 10).

This commitment was followed up with concrete measures, not least because in the meantime economic and social conditions deteriorated in all the member states of the EEC due to the 1973 oil shock (Chapter 3). The relaunch of social policies at Community level was also linked to political considerations. The growing popular disaffection towards the Community made it urgent to develop initiatives to reconcile the public with European integration (see also Chapter 11). Growing social disorder, in addition, might be addressed more effectively through enhanced cooperation in the social field. In the context of the relative economic decline and reduced appeal of the United States, moreover, social values were proposed as distinctive features of the emerging European model: in the 1973 Declaration on European Identity, social justice was defined as the 'ultimate goal of economic progress' and was recognized as a fundamental principle on which the European identity should be based (Declaration 1973).

In the mid-1970s, attempts to regulate multinationals were made and the first Social Action Programme was adopted (Petrini 2013). The 1974 Social Action Programme, in particular, aimed at attaining full and better employment, improving living and working conditions, increasing involvement of employers' and employees' organizations in the Community's decision-making and the participation of workers in the management of their enterprises. The Social Action Programme also aimed at achieving equality between men and women in the labour market and protecting young and aged persons, disabled workers and migrants (Mechi 2010).

On this basis, the Community revived the recently established Standing Committee on Employment, and in 1975 it created both the European Centre for the Development of Vocational Training in West Berlin and the European Foundation for the Improvement of Living and Working Conditions in Dublin. Under pressure from Britain and Italy, in the same year, the Community also founded the European Regional Development Fund (ERDF), whose main aim was to support regions dependent on agriculture or affected by industrial restructuring. While the recently reformed ESF concentrated on assisting people to gain new skills, the ERDF focused on developing regional infrastructures (Hall 2014). The Community, finally, implemented actions to help women and the most vulnerable categories of people in the Community.

Special attention was devoted to migrants, a category of persons that during the 1960s had dramatically increased in size and assumed growing importance and visibility. The Action Programme in favour of migrant workers and their families, proposed by the Commission in 1974 and adopted by the Council in 1976, was the first attempt ever to establish a comprehensive strategy on migration at Community level. After three decades of foreign labour recruitment policies, in the mid-1970s Western European countries unilaterally suspended bilateral agreements with sending countries as a response to increased anti-immigration sentiments and the economic and social repercussions of the 1973 oil shock; in exchange, they increased efforts to incorporate foreign nationals already settled in the host societies. The Community, accordingly, suggested to combat regional and global imbalances that caused migration and to conduct a common fight against illegal immigration. At the same time, it proposed to humanize the free movement of Community workers and adopt common solutions to improve the social and educational conditions of migrants. This was necessary not only for humanitarian motives but also for public security considerations: the presence of large unassimilated groups of foreigners in European societies was considered as degrading for the migrants and dangerous for the Community. Despite efforts by the Commission, non-Community migrants continued to remain largely excluded from Community provisions and actions (Geddes, Hadj-Abdou and Brumat 2020).

The development of Social Europe, despite great ambitions, met with formidable obstacles. The member states were generally reluctant to give up their sovereignty in the social field and the richer Northern members of the Community resisted transferring significant resources for common social goals, as clearly shown by the tense negotiations on the budget of the ERDF. In addition, the election of British Prime Minister Margaret Thatcher in 1979 increased ideological opposition to the development of social policies at both national and regional levels: for the first time in the post-war period, neoliberalism became a credible challenge to the 'Social Democratic compromise' (Warlouzet 2018a and 2023).

# 4. Towards a social model, 1984–93

The turning point in the historical development of Social Europe coincided with the decision to complete the Single Market in the mid-1980s (Chapters 3 and 8). Jacques Delors, appointed president of the European Commission in 1985, was convinced that the free movement of goods, capital, services and people was crucial for Europe to withstand international competition and resist decline in the context of the globalization and the third industrial revolution. German Chancellor Helmut Kohl and French President François Mitterrand agreed with Delors that social policies and legislation at the European level would be necessary to compensate for the potential increase of imbalances due to the unification of European markets. This strategy was the fruit of a compromise between neoliberal tendencies, Social Democratic legacy and Christian leftist ideas (Bitumi 2018). Jean Degimbe, the director general in the Directorate-General for Employment and Social Affairs of the Commission, went as far as to say that this was the real founding moment of Social Europe (Degimbe 1999).

Despite initial scepticism from social partners, Delors launched the Val Duchesse Dialogue, named after a castle in Brussels where the meetings took place. This process brought together representatives of the European Trade Union Confederation (ETUC), the Union of Industrial and Employers' Confederations of Europe (UNICE) and the European Centre of Public Enterprises (CEEP). The Commission and its president considered the social dialogue as a key to boost social policies at the European level and legitimize the Single Market project as a whole. Meanwhile, the member states signed the Single European Act in 1986, committing to strengthen the economic and social cohesion of the Community and, in particular, to reduce disparities between regions and the backwardness of the least-favoured areas. They also agreed to promote improvements of health and safety of workers and foster dialogue between employers and employees at the European level. On this basis, the Council adopted a directive on the safety and health of workers.

The process of completion of the Single Market, combined with the Southern enlargement of the Community (Greece joined the EEC in 1981, Portugal and Spain in 1986), also stimulated a reform and a significant budget increase of both the ERDF and the ESF. The ERDF continued to be focused on industrial development and environmental plans while the ESF was still concentrated on the improvement and updating of workers' skills; the European Agricultural Guidance and Guarantee Fund (EAGGF), meanwhile, was directed at promoting employment and the diversification of production in rural areas. What was new was that the management of the ERDF, the ESF and the EAGGF Guidance Section became centralized, and their budgets were brought together under a single budgetary framework. Their activities were concentrated on a limited number of objectives, and the financial resources at their disposal were increased to one-third of the EEC's overall budget; by 1992, the contribution of the so-called Structural Funds was expected to double in real terms (Cavallaro 2019).

This had a major impact in poorer countries such as Greece, Spain and Portugal, as well as in Ireland and later in the ex-Communist countries in Central and Eastern Europe and Cyprus and Malta. They benefited various poor regions, including Southern Italy and the old coal basins in the UK (Figure 12.2). The plan for Economic and Monetary Union provided a further incentive to strengthen cooperation in the social field.

FIGURE 12.2 *Map of the Swansea seafront in Wales displaying the European Union's circle of stars and the dragon, symbol of Wales. They indicate several EU co-financed projects in and around Swansea. Courtesy of European Union, 2012.*

EMU, together with the Single Market, had the potential to aggravate socio-economic imbalances in the EU. The Commission, supported by the European Parliament and the Economic and Social Committee, agreed that a stronger European social dimension could counteract such developments. This was also seen as a way to make EMU more socially acceptable. ETUC pulled in the same direction, and Mitterrand gave his crucial support. In 1989, all member states except Britain adopted the Community Charter of the Fundamental Social Rights of Workers. This was a declaration that, for the first time at Community level, set out the main principles on which the European labour legislation should be based. The Charter was followed up with an Action Programme aimed at implementing it, making headway in areas such as health and safety of employees as well as workers' right to information and consultation. The collapse of Communist regimes in Central and Eastern Europe played an important role in the adoption of both the Charter and the Action Programme: it galvanized the Community institutions and the member states into more integration, and it temporarily increased cohesion and power of trade unions.

Between the late 1980s and early 1990s, however, the socio-economic situation in the member states again became precarious: stock markets crashed in 1987; oil prices increased due to the Gulf War in 1990–1; German reunification in 1990 proved unexpectedly costly. With the significant exception of Britain, the member states agreed that the time had come to give even more prominence to the social dimension, at least rhetorically.

The Maastricht Treaty (1992), accordingly, included a Social Chapter, based on an agreement between social partners (Box 12.1). This intergovernmental protocol re-emphasized the need to collaborate in the social field. It also prioritized the commitment to promote the social dialogue at the European level: the Commission was obliged to consult social partners before submitting proposals, and the dialogue between management and labour could lead to European contracts. Equal pay without discrimination based on sex was given special attention. Fearing the imposition of social rights and benefits from Brussels that it had abolished domestically after difficult struggles, British Prime Minister John Major, Thatcher's successor, maintained the same position as Thatcher on the issue and was granted an opt-out clause (Chapter 17).

## BOX 12.1  ARTICLE 1, SOCIAL CHAPTER, TREATY ON EUROPEAN UNION (MAASTRICHT TREATY)

The Community and the Member States shall have as their objectives the promotion of employment, improved living and working conditions, proper social protection, dialogue between management and labour, the development of human resources with a view to lasting high employment and the combatting of exclusion. To this end the Community and the Member States shall implement measures which take account of the diverse forms of national practices, in particular in the field of contractual relations, and the need to maintain the competitiveness of the Community economy.

By introducing the citizenship of the Union, granting the right to move and reside freely to every EU citizen, the Maastricht Treaty also redefined the boundaries of the political community and laid the foundations for a European social citizenship (Maas 2007). This came as the culmination of a long process in which the Court of Justice of the EU played a great role in overcoming the reluctance of member states to fund social welfare for Community migrants and their families and, more generally, developing the principle of free movement into overall European social citizenship (Comte 2018). As a response to increasing immigration from the South and from Central and Eastern European countries, meanwhile, migration from third countries was regarded for the first time as a matter of common interest; significantly, however, it was not considered as an economic and social issue but as an aspect of cooperation in the fields of justice and home affairs (Huysmans 2006).

Unsurprisingly, trade unions supported developments in the social policy sectors. However, it soon became clear that this process was taking place in an apparently paradoxical context. The consolidation of Social Europe and the parallel ambition to shape and promote a European social model came at the time when all member states, though to different extents and in different ways, were reforming and reducing social spending. Moreover, they were coming at a time when the completion of the Single Market and the gradual implementation of EMU were threatening the ability of national governments to intervene in the economy and fulfil social goals.

# 5. Reconciling competitiveness and social protection, 1993–2000

The Maastricht Treaty paved the way to a series of important projects, actions and directives in the social field. Among the main directives were improvements in the safety and health at work of pregnant women and the establishment of European Works Councils. On the basis of a framework agreement concluded by UNICE, ETUC and CEEP, an important directive on parental leave was also adopted.

As shown by the controversial and bitterly disputed directive on the organization of working time, however, this process was far from easy and peaceful. The UK government not only voted against the directive in the Council in 1993, it also denounced it as an illegitimate attempt to bypass the British opt-out from the Social Chapter and as an illegitimate interference in the autonomy of states and individuals.

With an aim to reconcile economic and social cohesion with the planned EMU, in 1993 the EU further reformed and increased resources devoted to the Structural Funds (on EMU, see Chapter 10). In the same year, it created the Cohesion Fund, whose main aim was to assist the poorest members of the EU in overcoming the difficulties they faced in moving towards EMU, especially through environmental and transport infrastructure projects.

Meanwhile, the EU committed to protection of workers: in 1994, the European Agency for Safety and Health at Work was instituted in Bilbao. More importantly, it increased emphasis on the promotion of workers' skills. Against the backdrop of the acceleration of globalization processes and the revolution in communication media and technologies, the member states of the EU were experiencing an economic recovery but one that failed to create sufficient employment. The fight against unemployment thus became an absolute priority. Lifelong learning, financed through the renewed ESF and a new generation of action programmes combining education and training, was conceived of as the main instrument to pursue that priority. Lifelong learning, in addition, should contribute to make European economies more competitive and European workers more adaptable to ever-changing and increasingly flexible labour markets (Paoli 2010).

The fight against unemployment was also at the centre of the 1993 White Paper on Growth, Competitiveness and Employment, the most ambitious attempt made by the Delors Commission to reconcile the need to meet the challenge of international competition, re-establish growth in employment and safeguard the European social model. In this view, social policy was not so much a way to redress the failures of the market economy as an instrument to accompany its necessary transformation; social policy, meanwhile, was considered as an instrument to legitimize the Single Market and EMU (Masini 2019; Warlouzet 2023).

These ideas inspired both the 1994 White Paper on European Social Policy and the new 1995 Medium-Term Social Action Programme. They also inspired the negotiations leading to the 1997 Amsterdam Treaty, which gave the fight against unemployment an unprecedented centrality. On a proposal from the French Socialist Prime Minister Lionel Jospin, the Amsterdam Treaty signed in 1997 officially gave the EU the aim to promote high levels of employment and introduced a new title specifically devoted to employment. According to this chapter, the Union and its member states should have worked towards developing a coordinated strategy for employment: special emphasis, in this context, was given to the need to prepare workers and labour markets to cope with the new economic and technological challenges facing them.

Meanwhile, significantly, Britain gave up its opt-out from the Social Chapter. In so doing, Britain's newly elected Labour Prime Minister Tony Blair (1997–2007), wanted to stress the difference from his conservative predecessors. Unlike them, Blair was committed to the EU and European integration. Despite his distance from traditional socialism and the decision to maintain the bulk of Thatcher's reforms, he was also supportive of progressive social policies, albeit in a very moderate way.

This trend culminated with the strategy announced at the European Council meeting in Lisbon in 2000. The explicit aim of the heads of state and government of the member states of the EU was to make Europe the most competitive and dynamic knowledge-based economy in the world, capable of sustainable economic growth with more and better jobs and greater social cohesion. This strategy well represented the political convictions of centre-left parties and politicians who were then leading the main European countries and the main EU institutions. The strategy also reflected the mixture of anxiety and optimism characterizing Europe at the turn of the century.

The EU was concerned with instability at its borders, new threats to its security, social problems, an ageing population, international economic competition and difficulties with reforming its own institutional structure. At the same time, there was a widespread sense of self-confidence and hope in the future. The EU had established a fully fledged Single Market in 1993 and introduced a single currency in 1999: the euro. The Schengen system of open borders, which was rooted in two intergovernmental agreements signed by France, Germany and the Benelux countries in 1985 and 1990, became fully operational and incorporated into the mainstream of EU law with the Amsterdam Treaty; after long resistance due to a combination of mistrust and political calculations, all the Southern member states of the EU – Italy, Spain, Portugal and Greece – were eventually admitted to being part of Schengen (Zaiotti 2011). The heads of state and government of the member states meeting in Tampere in 1999, meanwhile, adopted a comprehensive approach to migration and asylum and launched concrete actions to deal with them.

The EU was also preparing for its Eastern enlargement, after having helped former Communist countries in Central and Eastern Europe to alleviate their difficult and painful transition to democracy and market economy (Chapter 15). The PHARE programme, in particular, was the first large instrument used by the EU to channel economic, technical and infrastructural expertise and assistance to those states, the ultimate aim being to make them ready to assume the obligations of membership (Ther 2016). EU member states, finally, were experiencing appreciable economic and employment growth. The EU seemed not only able to meet the challenges it was facing but also capable to protect and project a model: social values were at the heart of that.

The Charter of Fundamental Rights of the EU, adopted in 2000, provided evidence of that. It enlarged beneficiaries and scope of the 1989 Community Charter of the Fundamental Social Rights of Workers (Box 12.2). Despite the exclusion of controversial rights such as the right to work and the right to an equitable wage and criticism from the most progressive sectors of the civil society, the EU seemed to continue to believe in the importance of safeguarding its own social model; it also seemed to continue to agree on its main characteristics.

## BOX 12.2 SELECTED ARTICLES FROM THE CHARTER OF FUNDAMENTAL RIGHTS OF THE EUROPEAN UNION

| | |
|---|---|
| Article 27 | Workers' right to information and consultation with the undertaking |
| Article 28 | Right of collective bargaining and action |
| Article 30 | Protection in the event of unjustified dismissal |
| Article 31 | Fair and just working conditions |
| Article 32 | Prohibition of child labour and protection of young people at work |

# 6. Challenges to European social models, 2000–21

In 2001, the 9/11 terror attack marked a turning point in Europe and the West. The ensuing decline in optimism affected the prospects of further developing Social Europe. The Commission slowed down its initiatives in the social field. The implementation of the Social Agenda, adopted to put the Lisbon strategy into practice, lagged behind. The Lisbon strategy itself met with unexpected obstacles and difficulties.

The member states took the opportunity of the treaty establishing a Constitution for Europe, signed in Rome in 2004, to re-emphasize the centrality of the social dimension and to put it within a broader, well-defined socio-economic model. The Union, in particular, should work for the sustainable development of Europe based on balanced economic growth and price stability. It also committed itself to combating social exclusion and discrimination, promoting social justice and protection and ensuring equality between women and men, solidarity between generations and respect for the rights of the child; it also announced the aim to achieve full employment. In addition, for the very first time in history, the EU made an official decision on the system to be implemented: the Union was to establish a highly competitive 'social market economy', which was meant as a form of capitalist welfare state. The Constitutional Treaty, too, introduced a horizontal social clause, which imposed on the EU to take into account social requirements in shaping and implementing all EU policies and activities.

The rejection of the Constitutional Treaty in referenda in France and the Netherlands in 2005 led to the temporary abandonment of these changes. It also showed that social policy was dramatically failing to legitimize the EU and to create consensus on its institutions. On the contrary, despite EU actions in the social field, there was a widespread conviction that the Union as a whole represented a threat to national welfare systems (Chapter 8). EMU and the Single Market, combined with the Eastern enlargement of 2004, were considered by many citizens and voters in Western Europe as factors that jeopardized and undermined the protection of their rights and their living and working conditions. In this context, the Maastricht convergence criteria to join the EMU and the 1997 Stability and Growth Pact, which was to ensure that fiscal discipline would be maintained and enforced also after the adoption of the euro, attracted particular concern and criticism. To many, the EU seemed not only unable to protect citizens from globalization but also as one of globalization's main components and determinants (Chapter 18).

The EU tried to react. In 2007, it created the European Globalization Adjustment Fund for Displaced Workers in order to help workers made redundant from structural changes in world trade. In the same year, the

Lisbon Treaty resumed all social contents of the Constitutional Treaty and gave the Charter of Fundamental Rights of the EU binding value. The EU institutions were then required to comply with the provisions of the Charter, subject to the principle of subsidiarity. The member states were also bound to meet them, though only when they were implementing EU law.

Through the European Citizens' Initiative, finally, the Lisbon Treaty gave EU citizens the right to ask the Commission to propose a legal act in a policy sector that was within the scope of the EU. The Minority SafePack, a complex package of law proposals for the protection and promotion of national minority rights presented in 2013, showed the potential impact that this bottom-up instrument could make on EU social and migration legislation. At the same time, the long and so far unsuccessful trajectory of this initiative showed shortcomings and contradictions of the European Citizens' Initiative as a whole.

In the meantime, the Great Recession in 2007–8 badly affected economic and social conditions in most member states. The austerity measures adopted to respond to the crisis, in turn, ended up further worsening the employment and socio-economic situation, aggravating inequalities and exacerbating social and political tensions, especially in Southern Europe. This, in turn, contributed to strengthening the idea that the EU was working to reduce rather than increase social justice and security; it also contributed to spreading the conviction that the EU was more interested in the winners rather than losers of economic and technological change (Martin and Ross 2004).

With the aim to improve the image of the EU and the deteriorating socio-economic situation, the Commission proposed Europe 2020, a ten-year strategy intended to establish smart, sustainable and inclusive growth with closer coordination of member states' policies. Despite criticism from business groups and reluctance from Germany, the plan and its ambitious targets of employment, research and development, environmental protection, education and poverty reduction were officially adopted in 2010.

Following on this path, in 2017, the Commission presented the Reflection Paper on the Social Dimension of Europe, which was aimed at contributing to the debate on how to adapt European social systems to internal and external challenges and how to strengthen cohesion and restore consensus on EU institutions; after the EU's poor performance during the Great Recession and the shock of the 2016 Brexit Referendum, social policy was considered as vital to safeguard confidence in European integration. The Migrant and Refugee Crisis in 2015, when an exceptionally high number of asylum seekers and migrants came to Europe from Africa and the Middle East, also contributed to cast doubt upon the EU and its ability and willingness to protect European borders and citizens (Dinan, Nugent and Paterson 2017). The problem was that agreement on the European social model and the role that the EU should play in it was rapidly vanishing. The enlarging gulf between Northern and Southern members, the increasing agency of

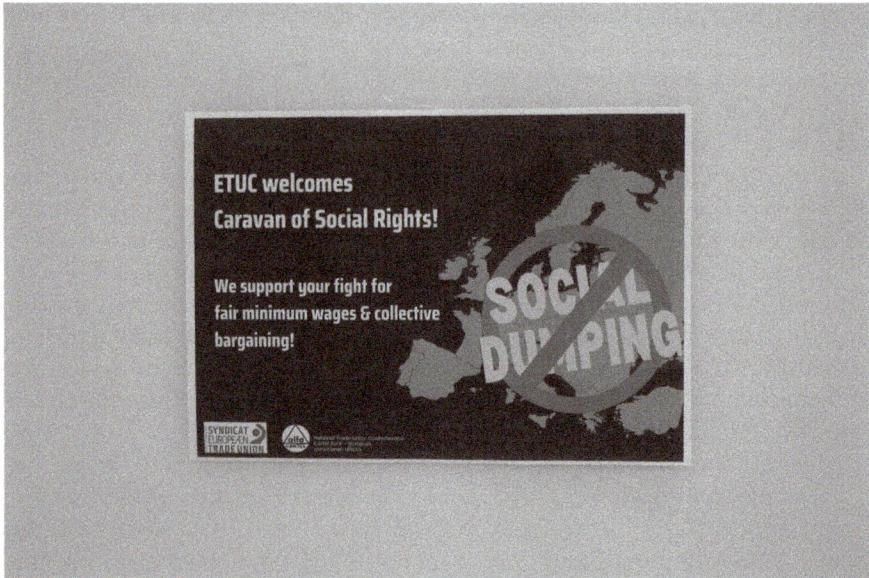

FIGURE 12.3 *'Social Dumping'. Caravan of Social Rights, meeting with Romanian trade unionist at the International Trade Union House (Brussels, Belgium), 2020. Courtesy of ETUC.*

Central and Eastern European countries, the political and electoral rise of Eurosceptic parties and the strong polarization of the social debate made it more and more difficult to reach an agreement.

In 2017 the Commission launched the European Pillar of Social Policy, which was adopted by all member states of the EU. Its aim was to promote social rights by stimulating convergence and collaboration between EU institutions, national governments, social actors and partners and organizations of the civil society. Despite lack of clear implementation rules, financial resources and penalties for non-compliant member states and in spite of criticism from sectors of the civil society, the Social Pillar was a valuable symbol of the renewed commitment of the EU to develop a social dimension (Vandenbroucke, Barnard and De Baere 2017). Meanwhile, the European Trade Union Confederation stepped up its campaign to fight against 'social dumping', notably by reaching out to trade unions in the poorest EU countries (Figure 12.3).

The willingness to relaunch social policies was confirmed by the establishment of the European Labour Authority in Bratislava in 2019 and the adoption of the European Pillar of Social Rights Action Plan two years later, in 2021. The Action Plan, in particular, aimed at implementing concrete actions to create an economy with a human face and address the dramatic socio-economic consequences of the Covid-19 pandemic.

Also, the EU's 2021–7 long-term budget, complemented by NextGenerationEU, announced the intention of the EU to help repair the economic and social damage caused by the pandemic. Accordingly, the funds for the cohesion policy increased from 371 billion euros in 2014–20 to 372.6 billion euros in 2021–7. That said, significantly, the share allocated to economic, social and territorial cohesion is now smaller, having decreased from 34 per cent in 2014–20 to 30.5 per cent in 2021–7; it is the smallest share since 1988–92. On the other hand, the EU budget allocated to migration and border management is not inconsiderable: €22.7 billion euros (2018 prices). This, however, will not necessarily lead to stronger social support for migrants. The greatest part of this budget chapter will be devoted to external border management. Meanwhile, the Asylum, Migration and Integration Fund, whose resources have tripled when compared with 2014–20, will be used not only to promote the social inclusion of non-EU nationals and initial reintegration into non-EU countries but also to enhance return and readmission of illegal migrants.

# Conclusion

In the post-1945 period, Western Europe gradually became the region with the highest levels of social protection in the world. This was not due to direct intervention from Brussels. The European Community, however, was important in supporting its member states in the formation and development of their welfare states, not least by helping them generate the financial resources to support social policies. By ensuring freedom of movement for Community workers and later citizens, the EEC contributed to establishing a European social space, which challenged the social sovereignty of its member states. At the same time, it excluded from legislation the growing mass of non-Community nationals, creating a dangerous fracture in European societies and a contradiction in Social Europe.

The development of Community social policies between the late 1960s and mid-1970s did not undermine the role of the state as the main decision-maker and provider of social protection for its citizens. Yet, the Community recognized for the first time the utmost importance of the social dimension in its mission and identity; it also launched a series of actions and agencies, which significantly contributed to shape the so-called European social model. Although many different doctrines influenced this model, it is clear that Social Democratic political convictions were the main driving force.

Between the mid-1980s and early 1990s, the completion of the Single Market and subsequently the establishment of the Economic and Monetary Union came together with the decision to strengthen the social dimension of the EEC. The development of social policy and dialogue at Community level was to legitimize the new course of Community politics and to accompany the redefinition of the European economy: the aim was not only to mitigate the adverse consequences of the Community economic policies but also to prepare the ground for the transformation of labour markets in the context of globalization and the technological revolution.

In the 1990s, the attempt to keep together market liberalization and social protection seemed likely to succeed. However, unlike in the 1950s, when liberal strategies at the European level were perfectly compatible with the development of welfare states at the national level, the result was now a two-speed process. While the Single Market and EMU made quick progress, the strengthening of the social dimension of the EU did not compensate for the weakening of national social policies. This weakening was mainly due to globalization, the crisis of the Keynesian consensus and EU economic policies themselves (Beckfield 2019).

The Great Recession reduced the resources to be redistributed and dramatically showed contradictions and tensions between EU rules for macroeconomic stability and Social Europe. More recently, the ongoing health and socio-economic crisis due to the Covid-19 pandemic has made this dilemma even more pressing. The suspension of the Stability and Growth Pact in 2020 and the Next Generation EU, adopted in conjunction with the 2021–7 Multiannual Financial Framework, seem significant efforts to put new emphasis on growth and social concerns. This strategy, however, will have to face serious challenges of sustainability and consensus; in addition, contrary to predictions, it will probably have to deal with divergence rather than convergence of political preferences and national models (Piotrowska and Rae 2018).

# Five key questions

1.  Why was social policy so marginal in the EEC Treaty?
2.  What was the link between freedom of movement and the establishment of Social Europe?
3.  How can we explain the relaunch of European social policies between the late 1960s and early 1970s?
4.  What was the relationship between the completion of the Single Market, the establishment of the EMU and the development of European social policies in the 1980s and the 1990s?
5.  In which ways has the EU social policy responded to political and socio-economic crises in the 2000s?

# Ten key readings

Cavallaro, M. E. (2019), 'Regional Policy: A New Source of Europeanisation', in V. Dujardin, E. Bussière, N. P. Ludlow, F. Romero, D. Schlenker and A.

# 13

# Ideas and movements in favour of European integration from the nineteenth century until today

## *Katja Seidel*

## Introduction

Ideas are powerful mental constructs that can inspire people and drive change. However, they do not always translate into concrete results and political action. How important were ideas of European unity for shaping European integration in the twentieth century? Some scholars argue that European integration after 1945 was the result of rational decision-making by politicians pursuing national (economic) interests (Milward 1992; Moravcsik 1998). Others see it as a response to pressures of the United States for European states to unite (Lundestad 1998). A third group of scholars argues that ideas have indeed been one of the driving forces for European integration (Lipgens 1982; Heater 1992; Parsons 2003), while a more recent strand in the historiography emphasizes the role of empire and colonialism in driving European integration (Pasture 2018; Hansen and Jonsson 2014). While it is difficult to measure the impact of ideas, there is no denying that ideas of European unity have been around for a long time and have inspired intellectuals, politicians, civil servants and citizens.

This chapter explores some of the ideas and movements that have contributed to conceptualizing and shaping European integration. It

will focus on ideas in favour of European unity, while the chapter on
Euroscepticism in this volume (Chapter 18) covers ideas of resistance
against European integration or certain forms of integration. It is
important to note that no single idea was able to take precedence and
completely determine the shape of European cooperation and integration.
The European organizations that emerged after 1945 contain elements
of different, and often competing, ideas, interests and approaches. This
chapter will first discuss the origins of ideas for European unity in the
nineteenth century and the context in which they emerged. It will then
focus on initiatives for other forms of international cooperation that had
an impact on European integration, notably in science and technology,
before exploring ideas of European cooperation and unity in the interwar
period. The fourth section will focus on the period after the Second World
War, discussing different variants of one political idea – federalism. The
final part looks at how federalists tried to influence the course of European
integration since the 1980s.

# 1. The origins of the European idea

The idea of European unity goes back to the Middle Ages. Aims for a
peaceful unification of the continent have existed since at least the
fourteenth century (Heater 1992; Hay 1968). European unity was defined
as a cultural and religious one, based on a shared Greco-Roman cultural
heritage, the Christian religion (ignoring for the most part the Jewish
heritage and the legacy of Arab culture on the Iberian Peninsula) and,
later on, cultural and intellectual phenomena such as the Renaissance
and the Enlightenment. Such ideas also tended to define Europe against
various 'others', be they the Muslim-ruled Ottoman Empire or, much
later, the Communist Soviet Union.

The idea that the European continent is characterized by a shared
cultural and religious heritage has been advanced for a long time and has
continuously been used by different individuals and movements advocating
European unity. This set of ideas has been incorporated into the value set of
the EU to the point that it shaped the EU's international relations, including
enlargement policy, where the organization sees itself as a normative power
(e.g. Krotz, Patel and Romero 2019; see also Chapter 14).

## Nineteenth-century internationalism

In the nineteenth century the idea of European unity became more firmly
associated with some form of shared European political organization as well
as the aim of achieving a permanent state of peace in Europe. Maintaining

peace became a foreign policy aim of European powers in the aftermath of the Napoleonic Wars (1803–15) against French Emperor Napoleon I. The Concert of Europe, established in 1815, was a coalition of great powers (Britain, Russia, Prussia, Austria and later France) that has since been interpreted as the first institutionalized framework for conflict avoidance and achieving collective security. Concurrently, a civil society driven transnational peace movement emerged in the early decades of the nineteenth century, though this was not limited to the European continent. The nineteenth century therefore gave rise to a first phase of internationalism, with the idea of European unity being one of the many expressions of this internationalism.

The French writer and politician Victor Hugo (1802–85), whose works encompassed the novel *Les Misérables*, was a prominent member of the mid-nineteenth-century peace movement. In a speech at the opening of the Paris Peace Congress on 21 August 1849, Hugo outlined his vision for a united Europe, which he based on the model of states organized along federal lines, Switzerland and the United States of America:

A day will come when war will seem as absurd between Paris and London, between Petersburg and Berlin, between Vienna and Turin, as it would today between Rouen and Amiens or between Boston and Philadelphia. A day will come when you – France, Russia, Italy, England, Germany – all you nations of the continent will merge, without losing your distinct qualities and your glorious individuality, in a close and higher unity to form a European brotherhood. (Hugo 1849)

Peace and democracy were at the heart of Hugo's vision of a politically united Europe. Similar to mid-nineteenth-century proponents of free trade, such as the English liberal politician Richard Cobden, Hugo saw trade as a means to peacefully link the people of Europe and the Western world more generally. The seemingly ever closer relations between Europeans through trading, transport and communication networks led many intellectuals in the nineteenth century to believe that peace through political unity would necessarily follow. While the First World War put an end to such optimistic assessments about the changing nature of mankind, in his speech, Hugo anticipated three of the main aims of European integration in the post–Second World War period: peace, democracy and economic prosperity. However, during Hugo's lifetime, these ideas remained marginal and failed to inspire politicians or the wider population.

# 2. Cooperation in science and technology

While for a long time ideas for a politically united Europe remained vague, cooperation among Europeans in practical matters such as health, science and technology was much more developed (Kaiser and Schot 2014). This cooperation took shape in the nineteenth century when technological advances such as the expansion of the railway network and the invention of the telegraph not only brought European societies closer together but also necessitated more systematic cooperation of transnational experts in non-state organizations such as the International Telegraph Union (1865) or the Universal Postal Union (1874).

Generally, industrialization, improvements in transport and communication and, not least, European colonial expansion required transnational solutions to shared problems (Schipper and Schot 2011). Different national or even regional systems of weights, measurements and railroads required standardization; trans-border trade and fluvial navigation needed to be regulated. Crucially, practical cooperation therefore predated political integration in Europe by a long while.

After the First World War, technological cooperation between experts from different European countries continued, as it was often possible to rebuild or revive earlier contacts and plans. However, a new centralization of economic policy by European states meant that perceived national interests as well as protectionism in the form of tariffs, exchange controls and import and export quotas prevented economic internationalism from thriving in the interwar years. In the political and economic sphere interstate cooperation thus did not reach the heights it had in the period before the war. Instead, the League of Nations, founded in 1920, became a focal point for what some authors have termed a 'technocratic internationalism', for instance, planning European networks for motorways or electricity. Vincent Langendijk and Johan Schot wrote: 'At the heart of technocratic internationalism was a concern for creating prosperity and peace through the establishment of an optimised international economy' (2008, 198). Such ideas and initiatives for technological cooperation remained popular throughout the twentieth century. The European Atomic Energy Community (Euratom, founded in 1957) and the European Space Agency (ESA, founded in 1975) are just two examples of integration through technocratic expertise that ran alongside political and economic attempts of European integration.

# 3. The European idea in the interwar period

The First World War gave rise to a new wave of internationalism among politicians and citizens who were concerned with the question of how to maintain permanent peace. The old-style internationalism of the Concert of Europe, concerned with holding the balance between great powers, appeared to have failed. Two new proposals for international order took its place: the Leninist world-view of a Communist-inspired global brotherhood of the working classes and the Wilsonian view of liberal internationalism, including a system of collective security. The Soviet Union embodied the former, the United States of America the latter solution. In his fourteen-point programme for peace of January 1918 US President Woodrow Wilson proposed a League of Nations. The Covenant of the League of Nations was incorporated into the Treaty of Versailles, signed on 28 June 1919 (Covenant 1919). The League was not an organization restricted to European countries, but, as the United States decided not to join, it was dominated by European powers, in particular Britain and France. The League was a new type of international organization and has to be seen as one of the models for post-1945 European organizations as well as the United Nations founded in 1945. Not least, it provided a vital experience in international administration. Based in Geneva, Switzerland, the League's institutional set-up was original as it featured a permanent international secretariat with a staff of independent international civil servants (Gram-Skjoldager and Ikonomou 2019). The limited membership (Germany and the Soviet Union, established in 1922 after the 1917 Russian Revolution, were not admitted at first) and the inability of Britain and France as the leading members of the League's Council to agree on key issues, such as disarmament and later on dealing with crises such as Japan's invasion of Chinese Manchuria in 1931 and Italy's invasion of Ethiopia in 1935, ultimately weakened the League. Faced with determined aggressors such as Nazi Germany's leader Adolf Hitler and Italy's Fascist dictator Benito Mussolini, it was unable to maintain peace. The League thus did not 'make the world safe for democracy' (Wilson), but Wilson's liberal internationalism enjoyed a lasting legacy after the Second World War, giving birth to the United Nations in 1945.

## Richard von Coudenhove-Kalergi and the Paneurope movement

Whilst the League of Nations became the first experiment for a new global order of peace and cooperation, the European idea also gained traction in the interwar period. The First World War led to a more widespread realization among Europeans of the need to cooperate in order to safeguard the peace and to counter a perceived decline of the European continent vis-à-vis the seemingly inexhaustible economic resources of the United States. To the east, the Communist Soviet Union was seen as a major threat to capitalism, democracy and a liberal economic order.

The Paneurope movement, founded in 1923, was arguably the most important initiative in the interwar period. Its founder, Count Richard von Coudenhove-Kalergi, was a cosmopolitan who had Austro-Hungarian as well as Japanese heritage. Coudenhove initially had high hopes for the League of Nations but soon saw it as ineffective in keeping the peace. He therefore reflected on the necessity of a united Europe for security, political and economic purposes: firstly, to ensure the continent's survival in the face of the powerful United States and the Communist Soviet Union; secondly, to improve the economic performance of European states and thus increase the general welfare of its citizens; thirdly, to achieve reconciliation of European nations, particularly France and Germany (Ziegenhofer-Prettenthaler 2004; Bond 2021).

In 1923 Coudenhove published his ideas in a book titled *Paneurope*. It became the manifesto for the movement of the same name, the Paneurope movement. In the book, Coudenhove argued that the world was divided into five power blocs: the United States and Latin America, the British Empire, the Soviet Union, East Asia and finally the weakened and divided European countries (Figure 13.1). While Coudenhove did not exclude the UK from his united Europe, he envisaged Britain and its Empire and Commonwealth as an independent bloc, associated with, rather than a full member of, Paneurope. At the time, Britain seemed more detached from continental European affairs both in terms of politics and economic relations whereas, for example, the continental powers France and Germany shared a border and a bloody history of war and enmity which Coudenhove and others sought to overcome (Chapter 16).

The Paneurope movement quickly gained support and opened branches in numerous European countries as well as the United States. Coudenhove's book *Paneurope* was translated into many languages and sold sixteen thousand copies in 1926 alone. The relative success of the Paneurope movement (relative as membership never exceeded eight thousand members) also has to be seen in the context of the improved situation in Europe in the 1920s,

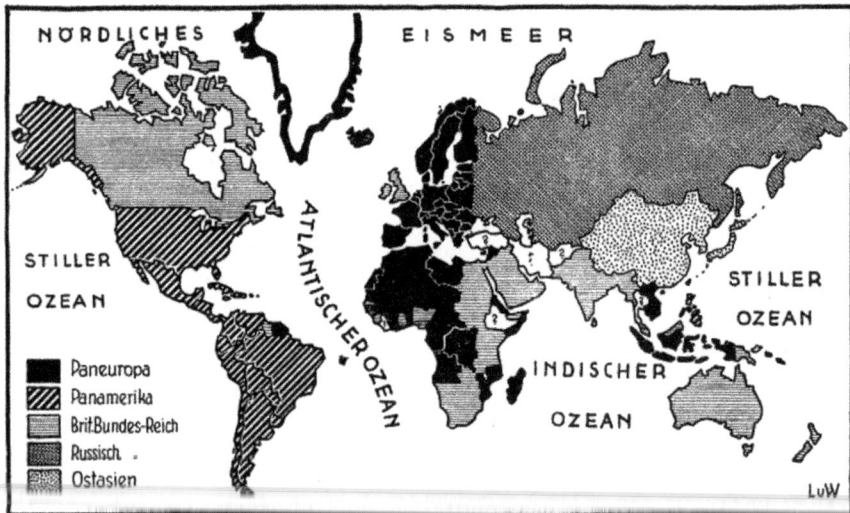

FIGURE 13.1 *World map from the 1925 German edition of Paneurope, showing the division of the world into spheres of influence: Paneurope with its colonial possessions, Panamerica, British Empire, Russian Empire and East Asia. Courtesy of Paneuropa-Verlag GmbH Augsburg.*

coinciding with the 'golden years' of economic recovery and international reconciliation. Reconciliation was embodied in the Dawes Plan of 1924 ending the occupation of the German Ruhr area by allied troops and reducing Germany's war reparations payments, and the Locarno Treaties of 1925.

The Locarno Pact, a series of agreements between France, Belgium and Germany on the inviolability of these states' Western borders, opened a new, albeit short-lived, chapter of Franco-German rapprochement in the interwar period. Germany joined the League of Nations in 1926. The Paneurope movement had many prominent members; among them were French Prime Minister (and at times Foreign Minister) Aristide Briand as honorary president, and future West German Chancellor Konrad Adenauer, then mayor of Cologne. However, the movement lacked firm ideas about the institutional set-up of Paneurope; was it to be a federation, a confederation or even the United States of Europe (Orluc 2007)? In the 1930s Coudenhove's commitment to democracy and parliamentarianism seemed doubtful. Never embracing Nazi racism, he nevertheless advocated a form of 'popular authoritarianism' and flirted occasionally with Mussolini's Fascism as a potential ally against Bolshevism and Hitler's National Socialism. Not only the hostility of the German Nazi regime towards Coudenhove but also this political opportunism contributed to the (temporary) end of the Paneurope movement in 1938.

# Eurafrica: Imperialism and the European idea

One issue historians are bringing to the fore is the link between imperialism and European integration. Racist ideas of the superiority of Europeans over other races were common and largely uncontested in the nineteenth and early twentieth centuries. It was normal for individuals across the political spectrum, from conservatives to liberals to socialists, to hold imperialist and racist views, justifying the conquest of Africa and other parts of the world with the 'civilizing mission' Europeans allegedly had (Hansen and Jonsson 2014). For example, Hugo's speech on peace and European unity, cited above, also hailed imperial conquest as a valid enterprise designed to unite Europeans. 'In place of conspiring for revolution, men would combine to establish colonies!', Hugo exclaimed excitedly. In the interwar period, ideas of Eurafrica, that is, unity between Europe and parts of Africa, were dreamt up to counter fears of European decline. African colonies were to help Europe recover from the war economically and to help maintain its global influence and relevance (Hansen and Jonsson 2014). It was also thought that a joint effort and cooperation in Africa would bring Europeans together. In this sense a cooperative imperialism seemed preferable to the competitive one that had characterized the period leading up to the First World War. Coudenhove and many others at the time thus advocated the inclusion of North Africa and other European colonies in Asia into Paneurope (Figure 13.1). Ideas of Eurafrica continued to influence European integration, at least as long as European states still had colonies. For example, the term featured in the Schuman Plan of 1950, was advocated by British Foreign Minister Ernest Bevin and influenced the European Economic Community's (EEC) association policy with African and Caribbean countries in the late 1950s and early 1960s (Chapters 1 and 2).

## The Briand Plan, 1929–30

The Paneurope movement inspired French politician Aristide Briand to present a plan for European unity in 1929. Briand had been an advocate of Franco-German rapprochement and had been instrumental in negotiating the Locarno Pact. Briand's German counterpart, Gustav Stresemann, had also kindled the idea of a European customs union with France and Germany at their core. Briand presented his 'Briand Plan' to the League of Nations Assembly on 5 September 1929. His more detailed 'Memorandum on the Organization of a Regime of European Federal Union' was published in May 1930. In terms of its objectives for European unity, the memorandum proposed a confederation of European states and emphasized that a loss of national sovereignty was out of the question and that 'complete political independence' of the participating states must be maintained. Political union should have precedence over economic union.

This reluctance to embrace an economic union before a political union has to be understood in the context of the economic and also political resurgence of Germany in the mid-1920s and Briand's wish to maintain the balance of power between the two countries. The theme of Franco-German relations and binding Germany into an international arrangement to control it, which would be a vital component of post-war European integration, was thus already present in the interwar years. Most League members, particularly Britain, were reluctant to commit to the plan. Stresemann's untimely death in 1929 as well as the onset of the Great Depression in the same year and the ensuing rise of nationalism put an end to those lofty ambitions.

# 4. The Second World War and the birth of European federalism

During the Second World War, the idea of Europe was taken up by the Fascist powers. Nazi Germany advocated a 'new order' in the parts of Europe they occupied. However, the Nazi new order was not based on voluntary engagement and cooperation, let alone equality among its members, but was geared towards supporting the German war effort. When much of Europe was occupied by the Nazis, resistance movements were not only engaged in fighting the German occupiers, but they were also making plans for Europe's future. For many of these groups, a united Europe became the answer to the question of how to avoid another war. In their view, nationalism as expressed through the sovereign nation state had lost its legitimacy given that it had led to two world wars.

To safeguard peace and prosperity, the future of Europe was unity. European federalism, the idea that is expressed here, was popularized with the so-called Ventotene manifesto 'For a Free and United Europe. A Draft Manifesto', written in 1941 by the Italian left-wing politicians Altiero Spinelli, Ernesto Rossi and Eugenio Colorni (see Boxes 13.1 and 13.2 and Figure 13.2). The authors argued that returning to the old system of nation states after the war was futile as this would merely lead to another war. They wrote: 'The question which must be resolved first, ... is the definitive abolition of the division of Europe into national, sovereign States ... Feelings today are already far more disposed than they were in the past to accept a federal reorganization of Europe' (Spinelli, Rossi and Colorni 1941). The text became the founding manifesto of the European Federalist Movement.

## BOX 13.1 FEDERALISM

Federalism refers to a mode of governance that advocates the division of power between a central authority or government and provincial authorities or governments. The United States, Switzerland and Germany are examples of states organized on federal principles. In fact, the term was first used in the political sense to refer to the US Constitution signed in 1776. In countries organized on federal principles, government is shared between a central government, for example, in the United States the federal government of the United States located in Washington DC, as well as the state governments of federal states such as Texas or California. In federal systems regional governments take independent decisions in a range of areas, for instance, education, healthcare or environmental protection, while the central government usually has authority over foreign and defence policy. In the European Union federalism then refers to the division of power between the central Brussels-based institutions, member states' governments and member states' regional authorities.

## BOX 13.2 ALTIERO SPINELLI

Altiero Spinelli (1907–1986) was an Italian politician, European commissioner and Member of the European Parliament (MEP). As a young man he joined the Italian Communist party and was arrested and detained by Mussolini's Fascist regime, serving a sixteen-year sentence. Confined on Ventotene, an island off the Italian coast, in 1941, he co-wrote the so-called Ventotene Manifesto which proposed a federal organization of Europe. After the war Spinelli turned his back on Communism and instead pursued his vision of a federal Europe. In the 1970s, he became a member of the European Commission before serving as an MEP in the European Parliament (1979–86). In 1980 he founded the 'Crocodile Club', with other federalist MEPs, named after a restaurant in Strasbourg where they met, to advocate for a new European treaty. The European Parliament then established a special committee to work on the treaty, and the 'Draft Treaty Establishing the European Union' was adopted by the parliamentarians in 1984. It became an inspiration for further developments of the European Community such as the Single European Act of 1986 and the Maastricht Treaty establishing the European Union of 1992 (see Chapter 7).

FIGURE 13.2  *Altiero Spinelli. Courtesy of European Communities, 1970.*

Federalism became a popular idea in Europe, especially in the immediate post-war period, and a number of federalist movements emerged, though a unified movement with a set of agreed aims never came into being. In December 1946 the Union of European Federalists (UEF) was founded to coordinate the different federalist movements that had sprung up, such as the European Federalist Movement but also the Federal Union founded in the UK in 1938 by Lord Lothian, Lionel Robbins and William Beveridge. The latter had a strong influence on continental federalist thinking, particularly in Italy. Federalism had a wider appeal among the elites but also citizens of European countries in the immediate post-war period.

# Winston Churchill and European federalism

In 1945 British Prime Minister Winston Churchill lost the general election to Clement Attlee of the Labour Party. As leader of the opposition, Churchill became a prominent figure in the European federalist movement. On 19 September 1946, he gave a speech at Zurich University in which he called for a United States of Europe and particularly the close cooperation between the former archenemies, France and Germany (Churchill 1946). European unity, he argued, provided the only chance for Europe to recover from the damages of war, avoid another war and play an important role in world affairs. Due to his international standing and reputation as Britain's successful wartime leader, Churchill's powerful endorsement of the idea for European unity gave impetus to the case of the federalists.

In 1947, on Churchill's initiative, the United Europe Movement was founded in Britain. Churchill also became involved in the federalist Congress of The Hague in 1948, serving as its honorary president. Crucially, however, Churchill did not intend for the UK to be part of such a united Europe. His stance was to support such initiatives for closer European integration and establish close ties between Britain, the British Commonwealth and such a European federation. After he had been re-elected as prime minister in 1951, Churchill resisted calls for a closer association of Britain to Europe, for example, by joining the European Coal and Steel Community (ECSC) founded that year.

# The Congress of Europe, 1948

The Congress of Europe at The Hague in the Netherlands marked the peak of the post-war federalist movement. It took place from 7 to 11 May 1948 and was an opportunity to demonstrate the unity of federalist activists which had organized themselves in a multitude of groups and organizations. The objective of the Congress was to: firstly, show that in all 'free countries of Europe', that is non-Communist countries, public opinion was supportive of European unity; secondly, to discuss the issues of European unity and present practical solutions to governments; thirdly, to instil vigour and enthusiasm into the international federalist campaign (Guieu 2009). The Congress was attended by about eight hundred men (and a few women), politicians and parliamentarians but also intellectuals, businessmen, trade unionists and scientists, selected by the Joint International Committee of the Movements for European Unity (comprising several federalist organizations) for their representativeness of their respective countries. Attendees debated the future of Europe and agreed to advocate the founding of a European assembly.

Coudenhove-Kalergi was also present, thus providing continuity with the interwar European movement.

Federalism was a broad church that lacked a unified organization with well-defined aims and those attending the Congress can be divided into 'unionists' and 'federalists'. The two factions differed regarding how far they wanted integration to go and how quickly the integration of Europe should be completed. Federalists favoured a far-reaching transfer of national sovereignty to European institutions and the immediate drafting of a European constitution, while unionists advocated a slower pace towards European unity, starting with organizations that were limited in scope and were based on intergovernmental decision-making in which participating nation states did not have to abandon national sovereignty.

The Congress concluded with a Political Resolution, a compromise but one weighted in favour of the unionists who were in the majority at The Hague. The resolution called for economic and political union, a European assembly, a charter of human rights and a European court. It was now up to the politicians to decide on the remit of this assembly. In the end, a compromise was agreed which saw the setting up of a Ministerial Committee and a Consultative Assembly whose members were appointed by a procedure decided on by each government.

On 5 May 1949 ten European states (France, UK, Belgium, Netherlands, Luxembourg, Italy, Denmark, Ireland, Norway and Sweden) signed the treaty founding the Council of Europe. Greece and Turkey joined shortly afterwards. Federalists had high hopes for the Council of Europe, based in Strasbourg, to transform into a government of Europe. These hopes were soon dashed as Britain, backed by the Nordic countries, would only agree to intergovernmental decision-making and was not prepared to grant more powers to the new organization. The limited progress and limited possibilities for development of the Council of Europe meant that it failed to become the political centre of European integration.

For federalists the Council of Europe was a disappointment. However, federalism had made deep inroads into Christian-Democratic parties in continental Europe, then in government in France, Italy and Germany. Politicians of such parties worked towards closer integration, even with the danger of excluding Britain from any such scheme (Kaiser 2007). The French government finally took the initiative with the Schuman Plan of 9 May 1950 (Chapter 1). The Schuman Plan, drafted by Jean Monnet, gave birth to a different kind of European integration, not a European (constituent) assembly or even a constitution establishing the United States of Europe in one daring leap of faith, but by creating a strong institutional setting in a narrow area – coal and steel – that had the potential to serve as the basis for developing closer cooperation and integration over time. Following the establishment of the ECSC in 1951, Monnet's institutional Europe became the blueprint for future integration initiatives, but constitutional federalism continued to exist and would occasionally influence European integration.

# 5. Ideas of Europe in the age of European institutions

Scholar of federalism Michael Burgess argues that federalist ideas 'have been an ever-present, indeed integral, part of the European Community's continuous political and constitutional development' (1989, 1). Federalism has influenced European integration in two ways since the 1950s: the incremental federalism of Monnet and others, notably Walter Hallstein, aiming to achieve a European federation through an evolution of existing institutions, and Spinelli's constitutional federalism, which aimed at immediate change through a constitutional event such as a Constituent Assembly.

While the aims of Monnet and Spinelli were similar in that both strived to achieve a United States of Europe, though the end-point of European integration has never been clearly defined, they diverged in the means to achieve such close state of integration. Monnet adopted a gradual way to integration. In his memoirs he called it the 'pragmatic method ... [that] would also lead to a federation validated by the people's vote' (2015, 367). The evolution of the European Union (EU) and its economic, social, political and legal integration has shown that his method works – at least to an extent.

Spinelli, on the other hand, criticized the 'Monnet method' of integration and its incremental nature. According to Spinelli, Monnet failed to confront the realities of organized political power in the member states and its tendency to preserve the status quo. A 'big bang' event, such as a new treaty, rather than incrementalism was needed, he felt. In the early 1980s, a period when European integration appeared to have stalled, Spinelli and others tried to revive the federalist idea of a constitutional treaty for Europe. The European Parliament (EP) adopted the 'draft Treaty establishing the European Union' in February 1984 (Box 13.2 and Figure 13.3).

The treaty took the existing Community system as a point of departure and provided for its gradual extension to the fields of intergovernmental cooperation, extended the powers of the EP, which would become the key initiator of legislation, and the Commission, whose executive role would be strengthened. The member states would be represented in a second chamber of the EP and in the Council of Ministers. The treaty enshrined the subsidiarity principle, meaning that the union would only take on tasks that could be more effectively executed jointly in the union, rather than individually in a member state. Foreign policy and defence remained off-limits and were confined to intergovernmental cooperation, at least initially.

The treaty was presented to national parliaments, not governments. It was not seriously considered by the member states, but the question of a European union, and what it should look like, remained on the table. To an extent then, Spinelli's draft treaty gave momentum to member states and the

Commission to tackle treaty reform and re-energize the integration process. However, this was, again, done incrementally, first with the Single European Act of 1986 and subsequent treaty revisions negotiated at intergovernmental conferences (IGCs) among member states.

## The Constitutional Treaty of 2004

Federalist influence came to bear more strongly on European integration at specific points in time. Since the 1960s, one common aim of federalist activism was the democratization of the EEC. This was seen as essential for the EEC/EU's transformation into a federation with strong and representative central institutions but also establishing a clear division and hierarchy of competences between the Union and its member states. One example of federalist influence on the development of the EU was the European Convention leading to the signing of the treaty establishing a Constitution for Europe on 29 October 2004.

Treaty changes until 2001 had been piecemeal reactions to emerging problems, for instance, the inadequacy of the institutional framework of the EU to deal with events such as enlargement of the EU with Central and Eastern European countries (Chapter 4). In the late 1990s many had become frustrated with the difficult process of treaty reform, the cumbersome and undemocratic process of IGCs and summit meetings. New impetus to a federal initiative came from various directions. In 2000 German Foreign Minister Joschka Fischer gave a speech at Humboldt University in Berlin entitled 'From confederation to federation' (Fischer 2000). He diagnosed that a dead-end had been reached by the 'Monnet method', that is, the incremental evolution of the EU. A year later at the Laeken European Council in December 2001, EU leaders formally agreed to launch a far-reaching consultation process, the European Convention, that should draft proposals which would then be negotiated at an IGC. The new treaty project was given the ambitious name of European Constitution.

The Convention on the Future of Europe was an exercise between March 2002 and July 2003, chaired by former French President Valéry Giscard d'Estaing. Though Giscard was not known to be a fervent federalist, federalist influence on the Convention and the draft treaty was considerable. Members of the convention were delegates from national parliaments, the European Parliament, national governments of the fifteen member states as well as the thirteen applicant states and the European Commission. Views of civil society, for example, NGOs, business and academia, were also heard in a 'public forum'. Federalist organizations such as the Union of European Federalists lobbied the Convention to get their views across through their 'Campaign for a European federal Constitution' (Federalist letter 2003).

The majority of the members of the Convention, particularly among its twelve-member-strong steering committee, were federalists (Shaw 2003).

'It was clear from the outset of the Convention that a formal federal constitutional construct was in the minds of key leaders' (Delaney 2019, 83). This does not necessarily mean that a radical departure, a 'big constitutional bang' in the spirit of Spinelli, was realistic. As this chapter has so far shown, federalism was a broad church. The European People's Party (EPP), the transnational party group in which Christian Democratic parties were organized in the European Parliament, made an important contribution to the Convention. Their document contained a vision of Europe that was based on social market economy, with strong federal elements but a sharing of sovereignty between the EU and the member states based on the principle of subsidiarity. While the EPP document made far-reaching claims, calling for 'a constitution for the Union addressed to all its citizens', its solutions were still wedded to the existing institutional framework of the EU and to developing this (European People's Party Congress Document 2002). It is thus hardly surprising that the outcome of the Convention was not a new institutional structure, given that the members of the Convention were not working from a clean slate but had existing institutions and policies to contend with.

Among the member states it was mainly the British government that opposed the use of federalist terminology since the political establishment, and the British public, saw federalism with suspicion. The most serious confrontations during the Convention concerned institutional questions. French President Jacques Chirac, British Prime Minister Tony Blair and Spanish Prime Minister José María Aznar aimed to strengthen the intergovernmental elements of the union, calling for a permanent European Council president, a European foreign affairs chief and a less powerful Commission. In contrast, the Germans had a preference for strengthening the president of the Commission. Belgium, the Netherlands and Luxembourg even wanted the Commission president to be elected by the EP and wanted them to chair the Council of Ministers.

The Convention presented federalists with the opportunity to achieve a federal European state in one 'constitutional moment', as opposed to the incremental process of developing institutions and policies to advance European integration (Delaney 2019). Despite this, the Convention was not a clean slate from which to draft a completely new Europe. Instead, its members were bound by the achievements of incremental federalism and by powerful member states resisting a federalist 'big bang'. Although it was meant to make the EU more democratic, ironically in the end the European Constitutional Treaty failed to gain the support of the European citizens. Put to a vote in a referendum in France and the Netherlands in 2005, in both countries the majority of voters rejected the treaty (but it was accepted in popular referendums in Spain and in Luxembourg). As all member states needed to ratify a new treaty before it could enter into force, these referenda proved the treaty's death-knell, though some elements of it were rescued in the Treaty of Lisbon of 2007.

# Conclusion

Though dating back centuries, ideas for European cooperation and even unity became more concrete in the nineteenth and early twentieth centuries as part of a wider trend of internationalism. In this respect, European unity as an idea was a regional variant of global ideas of and attempts for closer international cooperation. At the same time, ideas for European integration also gained traction as a response to specifically European issues: economic weakness, competition with emerging powers such as the United States and the Soviet Union and, last but not least, maintaining peace.

It is therefore not surprising that the post-war years, after 1918 and 1945, respectively, were particularly prolific for spawning ideas for the future of Europe. It was only after 1945 that such ideas fell on more fertile ground and were more widely supported by European citizens and crucially political elites. While many politicians were supportive of the European idea, most of them favoured Monnet's incremental federalism over Spinelli's 'big bang'. Monnet and Spinelli were united in their aim of having 'more Europe' and 'better Europe'. They differed in the methods used to achieve this goal. They also differed in their views of the involvement of the European citizens. Monnet's incremental building of Europe relied on elites and institutions, and Spinelli's and the federalists' constitution was very much about a democratization of the European project.

Even though sceptics of federal European integration such as French President Charles de Gaulle or British Prime Minister Margaret Thatcher had influenced European integration in important ways (Chapters 2 and 3), Eurosceptic and anti-European ideas were not prominently represented at these formal and informal debates about the future of Europe. Voices arguing in favour of repatriating powers to national governments were thus marginalized even though such forces were able to increase their influence, for example, in the EP but also in the media, leading to the Brexit vote in the UK. After the Brexit referendum, however, the European idea has experienced something of a revival, particularly among younger EU citizens.

# Five key questions

1. Why did internationalism prosper in the nineteenth century?
2. What political and economic concerns underpinned the European idea in the interwar period?
3. Why did federalism become a popular idea in the post-war years?
4. To what extent has the idea of federalism influenced European integration since 1945?
5. How can it be argued that ideas matter in European integration?

# Ten key readings

Burgess, M. (2000), *Federalism and the European Union: The Building of Europe, 1950–2000*, London: Routledge.

Burgess, M. (2006), *Federalism and European Union: Political Ideas, Influences, and Strategies in the European Community 1972–1986*, London: Routledge.

Delzell, C. (1993), 'Altiero Spinelli and the Origins of the European Federalist Movement in Italy', *History of European Ideas*, 16 (4–6): 767–71.

Geyer, M., and J. Paulmann (eds) (2001), *The Mechanisms of Internationalism: Culture, Society, and Politics from the 1840s to the First World War*, Oxford: Oxford University Press.

Hansen, P., and S. Jonsson (2014), *Eurafrica: The Untold History of European Integration*, London: Bloomsbury Academic.

Hewitson, M., and M. D'Auria (eds) (2015), *Europe in Crisis: Intellectuals and the European Idea, 1917–1957*, New York: Berghahn.

*Journal of Modern European History* (2008), 'Technological Innovation and Transnational Networks: Europe between the Wars', Special Issue, 6 (2).

Kaiser, W., and J. Schot (2014), *Writing the Rules for Europe: Experts, Cartels, and International Organizations*, Basingstoke: Palgrave Macmillan.

Pagden, A. (2002), *The Idea of Europe: From Antiquity to the European Union*, Cambridge: Cambridge University Press.

Parsons, C. (2003), *A Certain Idea of Europe*, Ithaca, NY: Cornell University Press.

# 14

# The European Union in international politics and trade: A global power in the making?

## *Brigitte Leucht*

## Introduction

This chapter traces the role of the European Union (EU) and its predecessors in international politics and trade. What makes the Union a 'global power'? From the beginning, the policies of the European Coal and Steel Community (ECSC) shaped global markets in coal and steel beyond the Six. Once the institutions of the European Economic Community (EEC) began operating in 1958, the organization's executive, the European Commission, tackled advancing the Community's supranational policies. Here, we can distinguish *external* supranational policies, including a common commercial (trade) policy, development and enlargement, from *internal* supranational policies with an external impact. The common agricultural policy (CAP), competition policy and the single market, economic and monetary coordination and environmental policy all have been shaping international (economic) governance. Chapters 8–11 dealing with these policies have discussed their external impact and highlighted how the European Community, and then the Union, interacted with a range of actors in the international arena – from other international organizations (IOs), to state, most importantly, the United States, and non-state actors. In terms of the supranational policies this chapter therefore focuses on the ensemble of trade, development and enlargement policies. Having said this, a neat public policy approach does not match the complexity of history, and it is impossible to discuss trade policy without reference to the EEC's common agricultural market, for example. The chapter will show that the EEC/EU has been a 'trade power' from the early days of the Community.

We will also discuss the development of the Community's foreign policy, which was coordinated along intergovernmental lines. Foreign policy was first developed through the establishment of the European Political Cooperation (EPC) in 1970. Against the backdrop of structural changes in the international system, including the dynamics of the transatlantic relationship, the EEC was able to develop its role as a 'normative' power. This role was first tied to enlargement and the accession of Greece, Portugal and Spain to the Community. In a formal sense, candidate states must accept the *acquis communautaire*, the cumulative body of EU law, as a condition for accession, including incentivizing future member states to comply with the principles of the rule of law, democracy and human rights. But the EU has over time also functioned as a normative power resulting from the more informal 'pull' of its regulatory framework, that is, countries and companies outside of the EEC/EU have had to adopt the standards of the Common Market to engage with and penetrate it (Bradford 2020). Second, the EEC owed its (self-) perception as a normative power to making their political position felt internationally through the coordination of the member states' foreign policy positions in the EPC. We will discuss the Helsinki peace process in the early 1970s and, later, the issuing of economic sanctions against the Soviet Union and Argentina in the 1980s to illustrate this point. The chapter therefore combines a roughly chronological with a thematic approach highlighting the development of different actor roles the EEC/EU has played over time.

# 1. A trade power in the making? Trade, development and enlargement in the 1960s

## Representing markets: The limitations of 'provincialization'

By means of sketching the *pre*-history of the EEC/EU as a trade power, it is important to note that the Community began playing a role in international politics and economic relations from the early days of the ECSC. Market conditions for third countries were impacted by the High Authority's decision to tolerate the anti-competitive practices of the so-called Brussels Entente. The Entente resembled the International Steel Cartel of the interwar period and began fixing the prices for steel exports when the common market in steel came into being in 1953 (Spierenburg and Poidevin 1994; Rosen 1958; Barthel

1993). The High Authority's lenient attitude towards the steel producers' export cartel also threatened the American steel industry; and it seemed to confirm the US government's worst fears when they were presented with the Schuman Plan prior to its launch in May 1950, namely that the planned community would advance a European super cartel. The High Authority's approach to tolerating the steel export cartel challenged the principled support for core European integration by the US government and created tensions between European market integration and the transatlantic relationship.

The relations between the ECSC/EEC and the United States were crucially important in the Cold War, and European integration and the Atlantic Alliance regarded as mutually reinforcing. At the same time, European market integration also led to tensions in transatlantic relations. Table 14.1 presents a chronology of key developments in transatlantic relations between the Community and the United States, which are discussed in this chapter.

**Table 14.1** *The relationship between the ECSC/EEC and the United States in historical perspective*

| | |
|---|---|
| 1953 | Establishment of the common steel market and formation of steel producers' export cartel threaten US economic interests |
| 1954–5 | Failure of the European Defence and European Political Communities, followed by West Germany's integration into NATO (Chapter 1) |
| 1958 | US Mission to the European Communities opens |
| *1960s*: Continuing its support for European integration in principle, the US government is challenged by the CAP and France's self-assertion in nuclear policy as part of the wider defence of the West. | |
| 1960–1 | GATT Dillon Round: arrival of EEC as a trade power in international politics |
| 1962–3 | 'Chicken wars': the first economic dispute in transatlantic relations |
| 1963 | French challenge to US leadership in nuclear policy and first veto against British accession to the Common Market |
| 1964–7 | GATT Kennedy Round |
| 1966 | France leaves the integrated military command of NATO (but remains a member of the Alliance) |
| *1970s*: The US government develops a more 'hands-off' approach to Western Europe and pursues detente, which enables Western European states to step out of the shadow of the 'benevolent hegemon' and act more independently. | |

(continued)

**Table 14.1** *(continued)*

| | |
|---|---|
| 1969 | Beginning of *Ostpolitik* accepting the division of Germany while casting doubt on the permanence of the post-1945 Cold War division of Europe |
| 1971 | Nixon's unilateral decision to stop the dollar's convertibility into gold sends shockwaves among European currencies |
| 1972–5 | European Political Cooperation assumes a role independent of the United States in the Helsinki Process |
| 1973 | Tensions around Kissinger's 'Year of Europe' initiative (see also Chapter 18) |
| 1973–9 | GATT Tokyo Round |

*1980s*: The changed quality in the transatlantic relationship continues with the EEC focusing on Southern enlargement and the single market programme to tackle competitiveness issues. The US government meanwhile deploys nuclear weapons on European territory (in West Germany, Italy and the UK) in a move highly contested in these states.

| | |
|---|---|
| 1981–2 | Conflict over the Soviet pipeline and EEC economic sanctions against the Soviet Union (in relation to developments in Poland) and Argentina (Falklands War) |
| 1986–94 | GATT Uruguay Round |
| 1987 | Reagan and Gorbachev sign the Intermediate Range Nuclear Forces Treaty initiating the progressive dismantling of missiles and signalling US-Soviet rapprochement |

*1990s–early 2000s*: The end of the Cold War leads towards a transatlantic partnership between equals in the economic field, but less so in foreign, security and defence policy.

| | |
|---|---|
| 1989 | Group of Seven (G7) Summit tasks the European Commission with coordinating economic assistance to the countries of the former Soviet bloc |
| 1991–5 | First test of the CFSP in the wars in Croatia and Bosnia |
| 1995 | New Transatlantic Agenda for creating a transatlantic marketplace |
| 1998–9 | EU unable to broker peace in Kosovo, leaves military initiative against Serbia to NATO |
| 2003 | US-led war against Iraq leads to a crisis in the transatlantic alliance and highlights the lack of cohesion within the EU: while the UK joins the United States, Germany and France remain opposed to the war |

From 1952, the High Authority was represented alongside member-state governments in several IOs, including the Organization for European Economic Cooperation (OEEC), charged with the implementation of the Marshall Plan (1948–52) and later transformed into the Organization for Economic Cooperation and Development (OECD) (1961). When the first president of the European Commission, the German Walter Hallstein, travelled to the United States in 1961, his trip very much resembled the visit of an elder statesman representing an important partner of the Americans – an impression of his office and of the Community Hallstein nurtured in several talks he gave during his US tour, including the speech at Georgetown University (Figure 14.1).

FIGURE 14.1 *Speech by Walter Hallstein on the prospects and problems of the European Common Market before a Georgetown University gathering, 16 May 1961. Courtesy of European Communities, 1961.*

Hallstein's approach to embedding the EEC within an international framework reflected his approach to the internal management of the institution, where the different directorates-general (DGs) in the Commission were modelled after national ministries (Chapter 5), including two DGs for external relations (focusing on trade policy) and for overseas development. The refined organization of the DGs in 1968 accentuated the increasing significance of the EEC's external economic relations, which now made up the portfolio of three DGs: for external relations (including a series of delegations, for example, to the UK and to IOs in Geneva), for development aid and for external trade (Organisation Charts 2007, 565–71). Clearly, the self-understanding and the self-presentation of the ECSC/EEC resembled that of a government on the international scene. This approach – while temporarily challenged from *within* by the Dutch and French governments – was reciprocated by important players, including the US government, which opened the US Mission to the European Communities in 1958 (Bossuat and Legendre 2007; Krumrey 2018b). These choices indicate that there was something different about the Communities, something that distinguished the EEC from other IOs even in the early days. Examining the external relations of the EC therefore suggests that there are limitations to the wider call of 'provincializing' the EU (Patel 2013; Chapter 19) and approaching it as *one* IO alongside other IOs competing for global influence. Indeed, one of the characteristics distinguishing the early EEC from purely intergovernmental IOs was the commitment to establishing a customs union (Patel 2020), which the next section will discuss.

## Trade policy

The Six regarded the establishment of a customs union as the first step in the creation of the Common Market. To realize a Common Market – based on the free movement of goods and a common competition policy – first entailed the progressive removal of all internal tariffs (taxes on goods circulating between the member states) and the setting up of a common external tariff. A common trade policy would further strengthen the internal cohesion of the Six, while enabling them to be perceived as a single customs union internationally (Bussière 2007). The EEC therefore from the beginning had exclusive competence for trade policy based on Article 113 EEC. This treaty article also empowered the Community to 'speak with one voice' in the multilateral trading system of the General Agreement on Tariffs and Trade (GATT), the predecessor of the World Trade Organization (WTO) established in 1995.

From the 1960s, the European Commission represented the EEC and negotiated on behalf of the member states in consecutive GATT negotiation rounds. Initially, GATT negotiations between the 'contracting parties' focused on lowering and eliminating tariffs (taxes on imports) and quotas (quantifying how many products are allowed into a country) to liberalize trade. Only from the 1970s did the negotiations also tackle non-tariff barriers to trade, including subsidies for domestic producers, voluntary restraints to deter (foreign) competitors, product specifications and administrative regulations. In the Dillon Round (1960–1), named after US Secretary for the Treasury Douglas Dillon (1961–5), Belgian Commissioner for External Relations Jean Rey (1958–67) and his team for the first time successfully defended the joint EEC position in a multilateral context (Loth and Bitsch 2007; Coppolaro 2013). The Dillon Round focused on negotiating the impact of the EEC's common external tariff and arguably represents the arrival of the EEC as a trade power on the international stage.

The Kennedy Round (1964–7) in turn focused on the impact of EEC trade policy and the CAP on the developed world. Before the second round of multilateral trade negotiations the Community also clashed with its 'benevolent hegemon' (Patel 2017), the US government. The parallel development of European *and* Atlantic institutions in the 1950s led to both synergies and tensions in transatlantic relations. While the progressive integration of Western European economies through the EEC contributed to stability in Western Europe, meeting a core objective of US support for core European integration (Chapter 1), it also represented a threat to US economic interests on the global marketplace. The John F. Kennedy administration's (1961–3) principled continuing support of Western European integration was challenged with the development of the protectionist CAP. Crucially, the EEC's new agricultural policy represented a threat to US agricultural interests. Agriculture made up one-third of total US exports to the EEC. And while agricultural exports to the EEC were growing in absolute numbers, they were declining relatively.

The Kennedy administration was therefore concerned when the Six started to work out the CAP, which they agreed on in January 1962 (Chapter 9). The CAP also contained a regulation on establishing a common poultry market that would threaten US export interests in that sector. Rising duties on chicken imported from the United States directly challenged the expansionist and powerful US poultry industry. The 'chicken wars' could not be resolved by diplomacy, and in 1963, Kennedy's successor, President Lyndon B. Johnson, imposed a 25 per cent tariff on potato starch, dextrin, brandy and light trucks imported to the United States, which became known as the 'chicken tax' (Coppolaro 2013). The 'chicken wars' challenged the notion that European market integration would benefit the US economy and were the first of many economic disputes in transatlantic relations.

In the GATT, the objective of the US government was to negotiate acceptable access of US agricultural exports to the EEC market. Full liberalization of the sector would have caused domestic problems in the United States (Coppolaro 2009). The importance of transatlantic relations continued to characterize the third GATT round of negotiations, the Tokyo Round (1973–9). In the Uruguay Round (1986–94), which led to the internal reform of the CAP in 1992, other players started becoming important too (Seidel 2019; Chapter 9).

The EEC was a true rival to the United States based on internal trade liberalization and the external trade policy in the GATT during the Cold War. This (self-)perception of the EEC has given rise to its characterization as a 'trade power' (Bretherton and Vogler 2006) affecting the policies and strategies of other players in international economic governance through altering the conditions for market access. The EEC/EU has not only exercised power *in* trade, however, acting on its exclusive trade competence, but also *through* trade (Meunier and Nikolaïdis 2006). According to this view the EEC/EU has used trade policy as a substitute for a 'real' foreign policy, which was only developed from 1970 through the EPC (De Ville 2020).

# Development policy

If EEC trade policy was a spin-off of the customs union and the Common Market, development policy emerged out of the colonial, later decolonization, policies of some of the founding member states. When the Treaties of Rome were negotiated, some of its signatory states still held colonies (Chapter 1). Against the backdrop of the further disintegration of the French and Belgian colonial empires in Africa, the Community's relationship with the 'overseas countries and territories' (OCTs) continued being important during its formative years. According to the EEC Treaty, the OCTs were to be linked to the development of the Community and should profit from a European Development Fund (EDF), which was to be established and managed by the European Commission. Against the backdrop of decolonization, this Community mechanism was transformed to give aid to former colonies in Africa, culminating in the first Yaoundé association agreement between the EEC and eighteen independent African states (1963–4). Further milestones in the Community's development and cooperation policy included its first food aid programme (1968) and the renewal of the Yaoundé agreement (1969) as well as the developments leading to the signing of the Lomé Convention (1975) by the EEC, then nine member states and forty-six African, Caribbean and Pacific independent states (Migani 2014b; see also Chapter 2).

As a result of the different historical trajectories of the member states, development policy brought to the fore differences in their approaches to relations with the developing world. For France, EEC development policy represented a chance to spread the cost of development assistance, while continuing to profit from economic rewards. The provisions for the 'association' for all dependencies in Articles 131–6 of the EEC Treaty owed to French insistence at the negotiations. With its colonial ties, including French West Africa, French Equatorial Africa and island dependencies in the Pacific and elsewhere, France benefitted most from the 'special relations' status granted to these territories. Arguably, Articles 131–6 thus perpetuated member states' colonial ties. This was contrary to the objectives of the West German government that wanted to support Third World countries and benefit from its role in the EDF without, however, nurturing post-colonial dependency (Rempe 2012). Furthermore, the decision to treat member states and colonial dependencies similarly regarding trade access, investment and the progressive dismantling of customs duties also had 'unintended consequences' in discriminating against other third countries in the Global South.

Véronique Dimier has argued that important path dependencies for development policy were created during the formative years of the European Commission originating in French colonial rule. Portraying 'Brussels' as 'the last French colony' (Dimier 2014, 22) she shows how French former colonial officials first staffed and then shaped the DG for Overseas Countries and Territories, later Development Aid. In the process, the DG even gained some independence vis-à-vis the main beneficiary of the association agreements, namely France, by playing off member-state interests against each other. The accession of the UK with its different institutions, policies and post-colonial legacies in 1973 represented a shock to (the French-dominated) DG Development Aid. The former French and British Empires clashed over the Lomé Convention, which, on British insistence, introduced a programming system assessing priorities and objectives of recipient countries over a five-year period (Dimier 2014; Migani 2014b).

Overall, achieving coherence in the development field remained challenging for the EEC. Not only did DG Development Aid have to manage tensions within the Commission – vis-à-vis the DGs for trade and agriculture, for example – but the Community found it difficult to agree on a joint position in the United Nations Conference for Trade and Development with the Global South (UNCTAD) from 1964 (Garavini 2012). Further, development was a 'crowded' field, in which the EEC competed with other IOs, including the OECD, the International Bank for Reconstruction and Development, and UNCTAD, for influence. Arguably, the EEC/EU's role as a 'development and humanitarian' actor (Bretherton and Vogler 2006), the latter based on human rights promotion vis-à-vis the Global South, has therefore gained less traction than that of the Community as a trade power in international politics.

# Enlargement policy

Just like trade and development, enlargement policy is enshrined in the Treaty of Rome. The Community's potential to expand by means other than coercion was inscribed into Articles 237 and 238 of the EEC Treaty. Article 237 articulated the potential to accept new member states, and Article 238 stipulated the procedure for the EEC to enter into international agreements. Enlargement policy gave the EEC the capacity to generate external collective action through admitting new member states and expanding the Community providing it with an instrument of foreign policy before EPC was launched. What is more, enlargement policy developed prior to the first enlargement of the EEC in 1973, when the UK, the Republic of Ireland and Denmark joined the Community. Association agreements in preparation for membership were signed with the Mediterranean countries of Greece (1961), Turkey (1963), Malta (1970) and Cyprus (1972) (Kaiser and Elvert 2004; Leucht 2012).

These initiatives notwithstanding, the first decade of the Community's enlargement policy was characterized by the failure of 'widening'. To begin with, unlike in trade, the Commission did not have a clear mandate to speak for the Community in accession negotiations. Formally, the Commission was only granted advisory capacity by the member-state governments for negotiations with the UK, Ireland, Denmark and Norway. Once negotiations had started in 1961, the Commission could exercise more power than formally granted, however; and monthly private dinners, including Commission President Hallstein and the head of the British delegation, Edward Heath, helped in advancing progress in the negotiations informally (Ludlow 1997; Van der Harst 2007). All of this came to a halt when, in January 1963, French President Charles de Gaulle vetoed the British entry into the Common Market putting a spanner into the process of European integration (Chapter 18). It is debatable if de Gaulle's veto was driven by attempts to restore France's 'glory' against the backdrop of Algerian independence, or if it was guided by the objective to secure economic advantages for France.

Crucially, the French president's veto went hand in hand with his simultaneous refusal to take part in any kind of integrated nuclear scheme with the United States on the same basis as with the British (Winand 1993). Voluntarily or involuntarily, de Gaulle established a link between British accession to the Common Market and the role of nuclear policy in transatlantic relations, between European integration and the Atlantic Alliance. Military integration through the North Atlantic Treaty Organization (NATO) was generally accepted and even desired by Western European states during the Cold War. Building on the failure of the European Defence Community (EDC) initiative in 1954 and the integration of West Germany into NATO in 1955 (Chapter 1), the EEC's security and defence policies were developed within the framework of the integration of the EEC into the West. Against this backdrop, the French president in 1963 challenged the US administration's vision of an 'Atlantic partnership of equals' promoted by Kennedy in 1962, with a united and *integrated* Europe as America's (somewhat junior) partner. It is evocative that de Gaulle's solo in blocking EEC enlargement and challenging US control in nuclear policy coincided with the 'chicken wars' in which the Six *jointly* contested US hegemony in economic matters. Questioning America's role in the defence of Western Europe in 1963 backgrounded de Gaulle's decision to withdraw from the integrated military command of NATO in March 1966. Ultimately, the impasse created by de Gaulle's unilateral approach to enlargement backfired and, in the end, it strengthened pro-enlargement arguments.

Following de Gaulle's departure from office, the agenda of 'widening', 'deepening' and 'completing' was introduced at the Hague summit in 1969, facilitating the successful conclusion of accession negotiations with the UK, Ireland, Denmark and Norway. Following a vote against accession to the EEC in 1972, Norway did not join the Community. The EEC would expand further with the Southern enlargement against the backdrop of significant structural changes in the international system in the 1970s.

# 2. A normative power in the making? Southern enlargement and EPC in the 1970s and 1980s

## The structural crisis of the 1970s

Two major developments framed change in the 1970s, the first of which consists of significant economic developments, with long-term repercussions for the international system. The Bretton Woods system that had linked the dollar to the value of gold and fixed transatlantic exchange rates broke up (1971/73). Unlike his predecessors, the new US President Richard Nixon (1969–74) was not prepared to continue supporting the US dollar in the face of an ongoing dollar surplus caused by military spending and foreign aid. Nixon's announcement of a 'new economic policy' for the United States signalled a turn to economic nationalism and the end of the Bretton Woods system. When the Arab members of the Organization of Petroleum Exporting Countries (OPEC) sanctioned an oil export embargo, this led to the oil crises of 1973–4. Contemporaries and analysts have conceived of the 1970s as a period of crisis and have examined Europe's 'shock of the global' (Ferguson et al. 2010). Charles Maier has characterized the crisis of the 1970s as a 'crisis of industrial society'. In this view, the crisis of the 1970s is the third of three systemic crises of the twentieth century. The first two crises led to global war: the 'crisis of political representation' preceded the Great War and the 'crisis within capitalism' the Second World War. In contrast, the crisis of the 1970s triggered the transformation of industrial societies in East and West, including shifting the focus from manufacturing to the services industry and attaching heightened significance to science and technology (Maier 2010; Leucht 2012). For Western Europe, the 'shock of the global' came with the rise of new competitors, including Japan in the global marketplace, causing a period of 'soul searching' for the best way to reorient Western Europe's political economies (Warlouzet 2018a).

These changes, triggered off in the economic sphere, went hand in hand with important developments in the Cold War. The abandonment of US leadership in the international monetary coordination of the West made the Nixon administration appear fragile. This fragility was confirmed by the United States' struggle in Vietnam – an engagement that finally collapsed in 1975 (Hanhimäki 2004). At the same time, Nixon and his national security advisor, the future US Secretary of State Henry Kissinger (1973–7), pursued a successful policy of detente. This major reorientation of US foreign policy peaked with President Nixon's visit to Moscow in May 1972. Cold War detente was not to last, and it ended with the Soviet invasion of Afghanistan in 1979. However, some of the bridges built between East and West during the detente of the 1970s outlasted the return of global superpower rivalry in the early 1980s. As an international system, the Cold War had not one but many endings reaching as far back as the 1970s. In Europe, the Cold War began 'crumbling' in the 1970s, putting into perspective the watershed moment of 1989/91 (Westad 2005).

The structural crisis of the 1970s opened several windows of opportunity for change in Europe. Crucially, the US administration's more 'hands-off' approach vis-à-vis Western Europe allowed Europeans to act more independently of the United States. This approach backgrounded the establishment of EPC and the development of EC monetary cooperation (Chapter 10). Kissinger's 'Year of Europe' initiative (1973) invited the US administration's European partners to refocus on transatlantic cooperation. But the initiative, which had not previously been coordinated with European leaders, generated division and resentment in Western Europe, not least as it seemed to undermine the momentum of European integration after the accession of the UK, Ireland and Denmark earlier in the year (Gfeller 2012; Chapter 18). Detente facilitated the steady but slow perforation of the Iron Curtain in Europe. West German Chancellor Willy Brandt's *Ostpolitik* accepted the division of Germany, while casting doubt on the permanence of the post–Second World War division of Europe. The durability of post-1945 arrangements was further undermined by the Helsinki process, in which the Community played an important role through coordination in the EPC (Romano 2009). In the Helsinki process and in the further pursuit of enlargement policy the EEC developed a new role as a promoter of democracy and human rights. This role as a 'normative power' in international politics (Manners 2002) did not replace but began complementing that of the trade power role.

## Southern enlargement

After the first enlargement, the EEC of the Nine had 256 million inhabitants, making it more populous than both the United States (with 207 million inhabitants) and the Soviet Union (with 245 million inhabitants) (Dujardin 2014, 17). If we further consider, with Britain, a former empire and major European economic and military power had joined the EEC, and this increased the importance of the Community in global politics. In 1975, Greece submitted its application for membership, following the collapse of the military regime. In 1974/75, the dictatorships in Portugal and Spain ended, and the two Iberian states applied for membership in 1977 (Pinto and Teixeira 2009). For Greece, Spain and Portugal, accession to the EEC was part of a wider political, economic and social transformation departing from autocratic rule and economic underdevelopment. In terms of the transformation of their economies, the three candidate countries did not start from scratch. Greece and Portugal were founding members of the OEEC/ OECD and Spain joined the organization in 1959 already. Although they were under autocratic rule for decades, economic liberalization preceded the membership applications of all three countries; arguably, it also played a role in ending the autocratic regimes. Regarding the link between political change and the application for EEC membership, the Southern enlargement served as a precursor to the Eastern enlargements, which would follow the end of the Cold War (Leucht 2012).

The Southern enlargement, unlike the 1973 enlargement, produced tensions within the EEC. The Community was committed to stabilizing the new democracies through the promotion of democracy and human rights and through fostering economic growth. At the same time, this commitment was accompanied by concerns about how well the enlarged Community would be able to cope with the economically underdeveloped new members states. The accession of Greece (1981) and Portugal and Spain (1986) therefore proved a test for solidarity between richer and poorer countries within the Community. To meet some of the reservations articulated against the accession of the three Southern European states, the EEC developed the tool of 'conditionality'. Accordingly, candidate countries should meet several democratic and market economy conditions prior to accession. At their 1978 summit in Copenhagen the EEC heads of state and government issued a 'Declaration on Democracy' for the first time stating that 'respect for and maintenance of representative democracy and human rights in all member states constitute an essential element of membership in the European Communities' (Erklärung 1978). While issued in the run-up to the first direct elections to the European Parliament in 1979, this message also clearly addressed concerns member states harboured regarding Southern enlargement (Leucht 2012).

In the 1978 Copenhagen declaration the Community presented itself as a promoter of democracy and human rights. But this was not the first time the EEC used norms and values to shape its environment. The Community had already done this in the Helsinki process, which we will now turn to.

# EPC and the Helsinki process

The idea of European political cooperation was first advanced in the supranational European Political Community, which, together with the EDC, failed in 1954. In the early 1960s no other than de Gaulle picked up the concept of a political community, but from an intergovernmental angle. For the French president, regular meetings between representatives of the member-state governments at several levels represented a way forward in building a Europe of States. Following de Gaulle's initiative, the 'Fouchet Plans' (1960–1) were developed. They failed, however, because other member states were opposed to strengthening the intergovernmental dimension with a set of institutions controlling the Community institutions and did not want to complicate ongoing accession negotiations with Britain. Another issue causing disagreement was the absence of any reference to NATO in the second Fouchet Plan (Chapter 2; Ferrari 2016).

The concept of political cooperation came back with a vengeance at the Hague summit of 1969, following de Gaulle's departure from office. The 'Davignon Report', developed under the guidance of the Belgian diplomat Etienne Davignon, proposed the establishment of foreign policy coordination called European Political Cooperation. The EPC report was adopted by the six foreign ministers at their meeting in Luxembourg in October 1970 and then officially shared with the four EEC applicant countries (UK, Ireland, Denmark and Norway). The report focused on the harmonization of the foreign policies of the EEC member states by institutionalizing biannual meetings of the foreign ministers of the Six. The EPC had two major flaws. First, it was not legally binding and was only given a treaty base in the Single European Act (1986). Second, the institutionalized intergovernmental cooperation in foreign policy issues was insufficiently coordinated with the European Commission's pursuit of supranational external policies (Viñas, Ramírez-Pérez and Bussière 2014). The two-track structure for external relations and foreign policy made it difficult for the Community and the member-state governments to reach agreement on such key issues as the relationship between the Community and the United States and NATO.

But EPC produced positive results. A case in point is the 'Helsinki process', which originated with the Soviet-inspired call for an all-European security conference. In 1969, the Finnish government invited the two superpowers, Canada and European countries on both sides of the Iron Curtain to Helsinki to work out arrangements and the framework for such a conference. In a changed international setting the EEC was for the first time able to assume a role independent of the United States. Through coordination in the EPC, the Nine shaped and contributed to facilitating the conclusion of the 1975 Helsinki Accords (Romano 2009). The agreement was signed by thirty-five countries, including the two superpowers and the European neutral states, and represented a milestone in the Cold War detente in Europe. It promoted human rights and economic, social and cultural cooperation between East and West. What is more, the successful operation of EEC member states in international negotiations provided evidence for the possibilities opened by the intergovernmental coordination of their foreign policies through EPC in assuming a more pronounced international presence (Möckli 2008). The Community was no longer simply a trade power but increasingly assumed a normative power role in international politics.

Figure 11.2 shows US President Gerald R. Ford during his visit to Brussels, where he attended the NATO summit meeting in May 1975. Later in the same year, Ford attended the opening session of the Conference on Security and Cooperation and signed the Final Act of the Conference on 1 August 1975.

FIGURE 14.2 *Meeting between Gerald Ford, president of the United States (on the right), and François-Xavier Ortoli, president of the European Commission (second from right), in Brussels, 30 May 1975. They are accompanied by US Secretary of State Henry Kissinger (on the left) and European Commissioner for External Relations Christopher Soames (second from left). Courtesy of European Communities, 1975.*

## Economic sanctions

Helsinki was only the beginning of the EEC's global promotion of democracy and human rights. On the one hand, the promotion of these values shaped (supranational) enlargement policy from the 1970s. The exception to this trend was the 1995 enlargement, when the three neutrals, Austria, Finland and Sweden, joined the EU. On the other hand, in 1982, the Community for the first time issued economic sanctions against Argentina based on Article 113 EEC on the common commercial policy to back up a foreign policy preference developed in the EPC. We need to contextualize this episode within two partly overlapping developments, the first of which relates to calls for EPC reform. The failure of the EPC to react immediately to the Soviet invasion of Afghanistan in 1979 led to calls for reforming the intergovernmental foreign policy coordination mechanism. In January 1981, the German and Italian foreign ministers, Hans-Dietrich Genscher and Emilio Colombo, respectively, paired up to develop a common foreign policy led by a shared vision rather than a narrow focus on procedural reform of the EPC. The Genscher–Colombo initiative was not supported by the French government, and it was met with criticism from several member states who were not willing to agree to the proposal's call to extend EPC to security and cultural issues. Despite its failure, one of the outcomes of the initiative was the admission of the European Commission to participate fully in the EPC, improving the coordination of the intergovernmental and supranational dimension of the Community's foreign policy (Nuttall 1992). This helped the policy coordination of the Community after Argentina occupied the Falkland Islands in April 1982. In this context, the member states decided that a decision in the EPC would be a precondition for using Article 113 EEC on the common commercial policy to issue economic sanctions against states outside of the Community (Viñas, Ramírez-Pérez and Bussière 2014).

The second development concerns the changes in Polish domestic politics. From the summer of 1980, the social movement Solidarność began challenging the Communist regime under General Wojciech Jaruzelski and, by extension, its Soviet protectors. The European Council, created in 1974 as an institution fostering informal discussion between the heads of state and government of the member states, addressed tensions in Poland in its 'Declaration on East-West Relations' in December 1980. The declaration 'expressed its sympathy for Poland' and emphasized the Nine's commitment to the UN Charter and the principles of the Helsinki Final Act (European Council 1980). Following the imposition of martial law in Poland in December 1981 and the issuing of sanctions against Poland and the Soviet Union by the US government, the EEC retaliated with economic sanctions against the Soviet Union (Ludlow 2021). At this point, transatlantic relations were tense, as the new Ronald Reagan administration (1980–8) had criticized Western European states, eager to bolster up their energy supplies in the aftermath of the crises of the 1970s, for negotiating a pipeline deal with the Soviets (1981–2). Reagan imposed sanctions on European companies involved in the deal, only to rescind them when the European Community reacted strongly and unanimously against him (Warlouzet 2018a). The use of economic sanctions against the Soviet Union by the EEC preceded the Falklands War and shows that the boundaries between intergovernmental cooperation relating to foreign policy and integrated community policy (trade) became increasingly blurred. When martial law in Poland was lifted, in July 1983, EEC sanctions were lifted as well.

The EEC continued acting as a normative power and issued economic sanctions, including against the white minority regime in South Africa – one of only two cases (the other being Rhodesia) in which the UN Security Council was able to reach necessary agreement to apply sanctions during the Cold War. The effectiveness of economic sanctions has been debated, especially its humanitarian impact on the societies of the targeted countries. For purposes of this chapter, however, it illustrates the EEC's choice to deal with norm violations abroad and to promote specific political, economic and social values through economic means.

# 3. Beyond the end of the Cold War: Outlook and conclusion

The division into integrated community policies and intergovernmental cooperation was formalized in the Maastricht Treaty on EU in 1991 introducing Pillar 1 (supranational policies/EEC) and Pillar 2 (intergovernmental Common Foreign and Security Policy [CFSP]) (Chapter 4). At the same time, the United States, not the EU, continued to play the leading role in transatlantic security. To the surprise of many observers at the time, NATO outlived the Cold War. The organization founded in the early Cold War to defend the West against the Soviet Union even extended its membership and integrated Poland (1999) and other Eastern European states. CFSP did not establish the EU as a 'second Western voice' next to the United States in international politics. Its first test came with the collapse of the Federal Republic of Yugoslavia. Because the member states of the Community could not develop a coherent response, the EU was sidelined early on (1992), and worked alongside the UN and then the multilateral diplomatic task force composed of the United States, Russia, the UK, France and Germany. While the EU's role became more important during the reconstruction process, it was not able to broker peace when Serbia attacked Kosovo (1998), and in the end, it was NATO leading the military initiative against Serbia (1999). Similarly, EU member states did not develop a coherent position regarding the US-led Iraq war (2003), leading to the UK's joining the war, on the one hand, and France and Germany opposing it bitterly, on the other. Russia's invasion of Ukraine on 24 February 2022 not only prompted Sweden and Finland to apply for NATO membership, but it also catapulted security and defence policy back on to the top of the EU's agenda.

In the economic field, the EU began looking more and more like an equal partner to the United States consolidating its (self-)perception as a trade power. Beginning in the 1990s, the EU and the United States negotiated outside the GATT/WTO framework pursuing several initiatives to coordinate trade and agree on sectoral arrangements. Initiatives included the Transatlantic Declaration of Cooperation (1990); the New Transatlantic

Agenda (1995), which set out the creation of a 'transatlantic marketplace' while also promoting links between the US and EU legislators; and the CEO-led Trans-Atlantic Business Dialogue (1995).

The successful management of the Eastern enlargement (2004/7) gave rise to yet another type of actorness – that of the EU as a 'regional power' using its enlargement policy to foster stability in its environment. In a recent contribution, moreover, Anu Bradford (2020) has conceptualized the EU's global power with the catchy phrase of the 'Brussels effect'. According to this view, the EU shapes other international actors by enacting a regulatory framework (e.g. in technical and environmental standards), which is then disseminated globally. We have discussed examples of this type of exercise of power, including the EU carbon trade model and EU food safety regulation in relation to EU environmental and consumer policies (Chapter 11). The argument developed in this chapter is that the economic policies of the EC/EU indeed have served as the main source for its actorness in international politics and trade. Even if the coordination of the member states' foreign policies has sometimes yielded results, it is through its economic base that we can best capture what makes the Union a global power.

## Five questions

1.  How has the EEC shaped global politics as a 'trade power' and a 'normative power'?

2.  How can we characterize Western Europe's 'shock of the global'?

3.  What has been the role of supranational policies and intergovernmental coordination in having the EEC's voice heard in international politics?

4.  To what extent has transatlantic cooperation during the Cold War hindered the development of an independent EEC foreign policy?

5.  To what extent can it be argued that the EPC and CFSP influenced states outside the EEC/EU?

## Ten key readings

Coppolaro, L. (2013), *The Making of a World Trading Power: The EEC in the GATT Kennedy Round Negotiations, 1963–1967*, London: Routledge.

Dimier, V. (2014), *The Invention of a European Aid Bureaucracy: Recycling Empire*, Basingstoke: Palgrave Macmillan.

Garavini. G. (2012). *After Empires: European Integration, Decolonization and the Challenge from the Global South, 1957–1986*, Oxford: Oxford University Press.

Gfeller, A. E. (2012). *Building a European Identity: France, the United States, and the Oil Shock, 1973–74*, New York: Berghahn.

Leucht, B. (2012), 'Actorness and Enlargement in Historical Perspective', in B. Arcidiacono, K. Milzow, A. Marion and P.-E. Bourneuf (eds), *Europe Twenty Years after the End of the Cold War. The New Europe, New Europes?*, 115–29, Brussels: PIE Peter Lang.

Manners, I. (2002), 'Normative Power Europe: A Contradiction in Terms?' *Journal of Common Market Studies*, 40 (2): 235–58.

Meunier, S., and K. Nicolaïdis (2006), 'The European Union as a Conflicted Trade Power', *Journal of European Public Policy*, 13 (6): 906–25.

Romano, A. (2009), *From Détente in Europe to European Détente: How the West Shaped the Helsinki CSCE*, Brussels: PIE Peter Lang.

Seidel, K. (2019). 'The External Dimensions of the Common Agricultural Policy: From Developed to Developing Countries', in U. Krotz, K. K. Patel and F. Romero (eds), *Europe's Cold War Relations: The EC towards a Global Role*, 165–84, London: Bloomsbury.

Warlouzet, L. (2018a). *Governing Europe in a Globalizing World: Neoliberalism and its Alternatives following the 1973 Oil Crisis*, London: Routledge.

# 15

# Eastern Europe in the history of European integration: From the periphery to the centre?

## *Ferenc Laczó and Vera Scepanovic*

## Introduction

Mainstream histories of European integration tend to accord Eastern Europe a marginal position. When today's Eastern members of the European project do make an appearance, it is usually in the context of enlargement, as test cases for narratives about the European Union's (EU) transformative power. This externalizing perspective on the 'other Europe' is perhaps unsurprising, since the predecessors of today's EU originated exclusively within Western Europe and did so in the context of the Cold War fought against the Eastern bloc countries. Yet this very fact also points to a much more constitutive, if asymmetric, role the eastern part of the continent has played in the history of European integration: as a mirror, a rival, a pupil, a new frontier, a partner, an experiment ground, a reservoir of growth or an internal 'other'.

This chapter argues that putting the East–West entanglements at the centre provides an exciting new perspective on the history of European integration. A more inclusive historical approach is certainly long overdue in a Union in which eleven and a quarter (counting the territory of the former East Germany) of twenty-seven member states can be understood as 'post-Eastern'. More importantly, it also promises to open new avenues for thinking about the choices and blind spots of the European integration project, as well as its ongoing contestations.

The chapter explores Eastern Europe's changing role in the post-war history of European integration and the political, economic and cultural dimensions of Eastern and Western Europe's asymmetric relationship over three periods. It focuses on those countries that used to be part of the socialist block and have since become members of the EU, even though 'Eastern Europe' – much like 'Europe' or 'the West' – is a contested designation that changed meaning and membership over the course of the long twentieth century. The first section covers the Cold War decades which were characterized by separation, rejection and mirroring between Eastern and Western Europe in the early years, followed by deepening entanglements during the decades of detente. The next section then looks at Eastern Europe's complex post-Communist transformation and the almost entirely consensual Europeanization of former Soviet satellite states in Europe. It highlights the special historical moment after 1989 when the two sides trusted the benefits of European unification across the former Iron Curtain – although for very different reasons – and explores how the mismatch of expectations planted seeds of later mutual disappointments (Laczó and Lisjak Gabrijelčič 2020a). The final section turns to the years since the EU's big bang enlargement in 2004 with a focus on the EU's new challenges that are directly connected to the East–West dynamics.

The objective of this chapter is to offer a corrective to the usual treatment of Eastern Europe in European integration history, which starts with the enlargement process in the 1990s and is preoccupied mainly with the successes or failures of their supposed 'Europeanization'. Instead, we argue that the coevolution and rapprochement of the 'two halves of the continent' started prior to 1989, but also that the processes of 'Europeanization' or 'Westernization', which seemed so consensual in the 1990s, were in fact the product of a historically highly specific moment after the Cold War. Seen through a longer historical lens, Eastern Europe's Occidentalism is revealed to be less of a uniform yearning for a 'return to Europe' but rather a deeply held tension between hopes and resentments towards Western models of modernity. It is this tension that continues to shape not only the political and economic processes in these countries but also the struggles over the present and the future of the EU.

# 1. From mutual rejection to deepening entanglements before 1989

The post-1989 narrative of a 'return to Europe' paints the picture of East European nations as having been hijacked by 'Soviet totalitarianism' from their 'true European path'. It is certainly true that the political concept of Eastern Europe we employ today is still largely shaped by the legacy of the Iron Curtain, and that immediate post-war attempts to revolutionize economies and societies in this region were imposed by violent Stalinist-style dictatorships. Yet it is also undeniable that the ideology of state socialism drew on a host of home-grown ideas about the region as a semi-periphery whose political and economic development required separation from the dominant 'West'. In a region consisting of diverse parts of the former German, Habsburg, Ottoman and Russian Empires, the notions of dependency as an obstacle to development and the 'double exploitation' of peasantry by the cities and of the cities by a transnational capitalist elite resonated with both sides of the political spectrum during the tumultuous post-war period.

As an economic project, state socialism was heavily based, especially in its post-war Stalinist guise, on centrally planned, import-substituting industrialization as the path to development. Separation from the more industrially advanced economies to the West did not, however, mean autarchy: from early on, East European countries engaged in their own project of regional integration. The Council for Mutual Economic Assistance (COMECON), led by the Soviet Union, was launched in 1949 with the aim of facilitating exchange of goods and technology, as well as coordinating investment plans across the Soviet realm.

Though it partly mirrored integration initiatives in the Western part of the continent, COMECON's ideology and methods were different. Originally founded by six members – the Soviet Union, Bulgaria, Czechoslovakia, Poland, Hungary and Romania – its membership soon expanded even beyond Europe, with the accession of Mongolia, Cuba and Vietnam in the 1960s and 1970s. Unlike the European Coal and Steel Community (ECSC), founded in 1951, or the European Economic Community (EEC), founded in 1957, COMECON possessed no supranational authority that would have overseen the implementation of investment decisions agreed by the Council. Crucially, it was a forum for cooperation among sovereign states that gave few individual rights to their citizens or companies. Individual travel between participating countries was limited, although study trips were encouraged. Member countries were not expected to liberalize their trade or maintain freely convertible currencies to facilitate trade flows; rather, exchanges were arranged through centrally negotiated clearing accounts. Technology sharing, on the other hand, was practiced in a remarkably 'liberal' manner. At an early meeting in 1949 COMECON members rejected the Western systems of patents and licenses and were thereafter able, at least in theory, to access one another's technology for the mere price of copying technical documentation.

If the Eastern bloc's methods explicitly rejected those of the 'imperialist West', its vision of modernity remained inspired by a certain image of Western development. In Eastern Europe, this included not only advanced levels of industrialization and social welfare but also the Western model of an ethnically and linguistically homogeneous nation state. Up until the Second World War the Eastern part of the continent was in fact the ethnically much more diverse one – even states with relatively large titular majorities such as Poland or Romania still had about 30 per cent minority populations in the interwar years. Nazi genocidal violence, ethnic cleansing and even early post-war international support for expulsions and 'population exchanges' all contributed to a radical reduction of diversity after the Second World War – paradoxically just as Western Europe was itself starting to become more ethnically and linguistically diverse (Gatrell 2019).

By the 1970s, several new developments were again pushing Eastern Europe's ambivalent Occidentalism from rejection to attraction. Politically, the de-Stalinization process launched in the mid-1950s opened some space for experimentation in both economic and foreign policy. West Germany's new *Ostpolitik* from the 1960s onwards and the start of negotiations within the Conference for Security and Cooperation in Europe that culminated in the Helsinki Accords in 1975 reduced security and territorial concerns. They allowed for growing detente and deeper entanglements between the competing Cold War parties (Romano 2009; Cotey Morgan 2018). To be clear, there were limits to how far the satellite states could stray, as was brutally demonstrated by military 'solutions' to the East German uprising in 1953, the Hungarian revolution in 1956, the reform attempt in Czechoslovakia in 1968 and the mass mobilization in Poland in 1980–1 (Judt 2005). Yet these tragic events too fed the attraction of the West, not only among the dissidents but also among the younger members of the Communist elites. Frustrated by a system that lacked a properly institutionalized mechanisms of internal power transfer, and concerned that the West European economic train was pulling ahead while their countries remained shackled to yet another stagnant empire with its increasingly anachronistic model of modernity, many of these 'reform Communists' attempted to revive economic connections with the West (Romano and Romero 2020).

Soviet-type central planning had proven capable of extensive growth in earlier years, rapidly closing the industrialization gap with the more advanced economies and becoming competitive in a range of heavy industries, production of military equipment and, famously, space exploration. It was much less apt at developing successful light industries and satisfying growing consumer demand of the new urban classes whose numbers had soared as a result of successful industrialization. For the countries on the Western edge of the Eastern bloc, which had few natural resources of their own, even the relative advantages of the COMECON trading system, such as preferential access to the energy and mineral resources of the Soviet Union, began to be viewed as counterproductive, as they further reinforced reliance on traditional heavy industry. At the same time, investments in new industries – above all electronics and consumer goods – required access to capital and technology that could only be found in the West and would necessitate repayment in currencies earned on Western markets.

The response was a growing network of contacts that emerged between state-owned enterprises and state officials in the East and their counterparts in Western Europe. In 1980, Romania became the first Socialist country to sign a preferential trade agreement with the EEC. The fact that the same country could be a maverick when it came to changing Cold War alignments as well as a country with an increasingly despotic 'national Stalinist' regime (Tismaneanu 1999) is a useful reminder of the ambivalence with which the East European Communist elites viewed their countries' place in between the two poles. The impact in trade terms was minimal, but Romania's move broke an important taboo on bilateral relations between COMECON members and the EEC, and agreements with Hungary, Poland and even the Soviet Union followed in 1988 and 1989.

The attraction was also cultural. Softening travel restrictions, partly prompted by the desire to increase earnings from tourism, brought more contact between ordinary citizens living on the opposite sides of the Iron Curtain. Western music, lifestyle and consumer habits formed an aspirational horizon for young generations in the East just as their countries' ties to the developing world began to weaken (Mark et al. 2019). It certainly helped that citizens of Eastern European countries, were welcome in the West in this period. Unlike post-colonial and other, often more economically motivated, migrants from outside Europe who frequently encountered cultural bias and racist prejudice in Western Europe, the emigrees from the Soviet realm tended to be embraced and even celebrated, both as martyrs of a 'struggle for freedom' and as actors from across the Iron Curtain who could offer precious evidence of the West's own superiority. For those eager to escape socialist oppression and persecution, their very freedom-loving 'Europeanness' – contrasted with the 'Eastern despotism' they had to endure – became a claim on the goodwill of the West.

The partial softening on the political, cultural and economic fronts of the Cold War created different patterns of connections in different countries. As economic connections deepened, so the foreign debt towards Western creditors began to rise across the region, and the new entanglements took on a sinister tinge of past dependence. Some of the pioneers of economic opening got cold feet: partly inspired by the perception of economic threat and partly by revolutionary elan that had already faded in other parts of the Eastern Block, the Ceauşescu regime in Romania turned into a notoriously hard-line dictatorship. In the interest of gaining 'true independence', the megalomaniac dictator attempted to pay off all his country's external debt, which was accomplished through draconian austerity measures that plunged Romanian society into deep economic misery. Others, like Hungary, long known as a staunch Soviet ally in foreign policy terms (after all, János Kádár, the country's leader for decades, was catapulted into power by Soviet tanks in 1956), gradually abandoned ideological commitment to the Soviet model in favour of an ever more pragmatic and flexible economic policy. In sharp contrast to Romania with which its relations gravely deteriorated in the 1980s, the Hungarian regime in fact encouraged consumerism in order to prop up its legitimacy – at the price of spiralling foreign debt, a problem it shared with other Eastern bloc states, such as Poland and East Germany.

The largely peaceful collapse of the socialist regimes took most observers by surprise, not least because the Western view of the Soviet regimes as 'totalitarian' made it difficult to notice, or even imagine, that these countries could undergo internal change. In reality, by the time the Berlin Wall fell in the autumn of 1989, the Soviet side under Mikhail Gorbachev had already stopped fighting the Cold War, and Hungary had already removed its fortified border fence towards neutral Austria (Spohr 2019; Taubman 2017). The key foundations for the East European revolutions (or, in Timothy Garton Ash's apt phrase, *refolutions* – reform packages with revolutionary consequences) have been laid over many years through gradual efforts that perforated the Iron Curtain (Garton Ash 1990; Villaume and Westad 2010).

Yet one sees only fragments through the holes in a curtain. East Europeans' disaffection with Soviet Communism may have been rooted in a repressive political and cultural environment and a malfunctioning economy, but their expectations of how far they could go once liberated from the straitjacket of the socialist model were made unrealistically high by the vertiginous post-war economic successes of the countries bordering the Iron Curtain – such as West Germany, Austria or Finland. Members of East European societies may have resented political impositions and economic mismanagement of the one-party states, but they also cherished their stability and their commitment to social welfare. By 1989, they were eager to 'return to Europe'; but the European future they had in mind was drawn from an overly airbrushed and rapidly aging picture of economically prosperous, social democratic and culturally familiar continent.

If the previous decades had mellowed the one-time fierce competitor into a reluctant partner, 1989 had turned it into an eager pupil hoping to join the distinguished club of its former enemies as a full member. First, however, it was going to have to learn some lessons.

# 2. Europe as the future of Eastern Europe, 1989–2004

The end of the Cold War, the independence and the liberal democratic turn of most of Eastern Europe in 1989–91, the unification of the two Germanies in 1990, the foundation of the EU in 1992 and the 1993 plan to eventually enlarge the Union eastward were all part of the same historical moment and intimately connected to one other. The Cold War had divided Europe in more ways than one. Nearly all of the 'neutral' European states had remained not only outside of the North Atlantic Treaty Organization (NATO) but also outside the EEC, forming an 'outer club' of members of the European Free Trade Association (EFTA) (Chapter 2), and many alternative organizations flourished on the European continent (Patel 2020). In a suddenly unipolar world, however, the European integration project looked poised to become the only game in town. This was also an opportunity to reimagine its scope and borders, the internal social contract on which the Union was based, as well as its relationship with the rest of the world.

The early post–Cold War moment did indeed bring several momentous changes. The intention to safely embed an enlarged Federal Republic of Germany into European structures had a key impact on the negotiations at Maastricht, including the decision to introduce the euro. The early 1990s also saw more emphasis on the European Social Model, a project to give a European dimension to its members' welfare states and constitutionalize – through the European Social Charter – the principles of social cohesion that were likely to come under pressure with the future accession of so many less-developed countries (Chapters and 12). Under the leadership of Commission President Jacques Delors, himself a staunch supporter of European social policies, the European Commission moved quickly to offer support packages to East European countries as early as 1989.

At the 1993 Copenhagen summit, the EU for the first time specified the conditions for becoming a member, and with that spelled out its own foundational principles. European institutions, and especially the European Commission, became an important contact point for East European countries (Figure 15.1). In a myriad of smaller and more mundane ways, this process continued throughout the subsequent enlargement process. As the EU confronted the challenge of making post-socialist economies and administrative structures compatible with its own policies, it was forced to make explicit its political and legal values, economic principles and administrative traditions and even rethink its own institutional frameworks. The enlargement process itself, often branded the EU's most successful foreign policy, thus redefined the character of the EU and raised hopes and beliefs that it could transform external actors through the attraction of its fundamental values and its large single market (Bradford 2020; Chapters 8 and 14).

In hindsight, this momentous historical change was nonetheless accompanied by poverty of political imagination. The decisions resulting in the Treaty of Maastricht may have been precipitated by the events around 1989–90, but for the most part they were shaped by processes that had been under way for years and even decades. The momentum to reimagine European social policy quickly petered out, partly out of fear of having to contend with major gaps in social standards between 'old' and 'new' Europe. In fact, much support for enlargement came precisely from those actors who opposed further expansion of EU's powers such as the United Kingdom: 'widening' the project could also be a way not to 'deepen' it. Even the institutional reforms made in anticipation of the accession of the Eastern states, such as those of the voting rules in the Council of Ministers, were made defensively to ensure that the increased heterogeneity of preferences did not upset established compromises.

FIGURE 15.1 *Visit of the Polish leader Lech Wałęsa to the EEC. From left to right: Lech Wałęsa, the interpreter of the Polish delegation and Jacques Delors, 3 April 1991. Photographer: Christian Lambiotte. Courtesy of European Communities, 1991.*

It is perhaps unsurprising that the West showed so little appetite for systemic reflection – after all, its political and economic system had just won the Cold War. For the post-Communist countries, however, 'the end of history' (a term coined by the American scholar Francis Fukuyama to describe the end of the Cold War and the 'victory' of the West) meant only the beginning of a complex transformation away from a single-party system, a regimented society and a centrally planned and nominally collectively owned economy. That all this was supposed to take place in the context of democracy was both an opportunity and a risk: indeed, many authors considered such a 'dual transition' to be nearly impossible and almost certain to break down under the pressure of political instability (Przeworski 1991). The bloody dissolution of former Yugoslavia offered a most vivid illustration of the ways in which the transition could go wrong and painfully highlighted the complete lack of mechanisms in the European Community to deal with such events on its doorstep.

In these circumstances, the prospect of EU membership for other countries on the EU's eastern borders became the key instrument in securing stability and avoiding major reversals. The promise of integration into the EU came to be seen as an international shelter for those fearing the lingering influence of Russia, an anchor for domestic politics that strengthened the influence of centrist parties and a blueprint for reforms. It also helped to dampen public discontent and sustain the reform momentum even as the shock of the systemic collapse plunged these countries into the deepest peacetime recessions in modern European history.

Nevertheless, replacing domestic politics with external conditionality also meant that the complexity of the transformation was replaced by a teleological notion of 'transition' towards some ideal-typical Western liberal model, and that many central questions of national political life were answered before more substantial debates could have taken place. This had several important consequences for the region's politics. First, introducing liberal democracy to Eastern Europe with external models and Western standards of measurement in mind was always likely to remain a top-down process, even in countries where democratization was a result of mass mobilization, as in East Germany or Czechoslovakia. This, together with the emphasis on stability and continuity of reforms, gave the citizens very little sense of control over politics and provided fertile ground for the later populist narrative of 'unfinished' or 'stolen' revolutions (Mark 2011).

Second, transposing new political and institutional frameworks went much faster and proved much easier to do than creating a Western-style society where substantial numbers of people were economically secure and truly independent of the state (Dahrendorf 1990). This made the new institutions – from judiciary to parliaments – less effective and more pliable to informal political influence, which in turn undermined popular trust in them. These factors combined to make the countries vulnerable to grave trends of de-democratization even in nominally consolidated democracies.

The mismatch between the 'imitation imperative' (Krastev and Holmes 2018) and the realities of the transformation was possibly even broader in the economic sphere. Converting into functional capitalist economies systems which for decades had functioned without private property and with administratively set prices was a challenge comparable in scale to the original agenda of Sovietization. Yet the triumphant liberal economic narrative made the task seem straightforward: markets worked best when they were left free of state intervention, so all the East European countries had to do was to ensure the state retreated from the economy, reversing nationalizations, price controls and central planning. In practice, as a contemporary joke went, the attempt rather resembled trying to turn fish soup back into an aquarium (Ther 2016).

Different decisions taken early on over the method of privatization and the lengths to which the state was willing to go to protect the citizens and industries crystallized over time into different models of capitalism in the East. The spectrum ranged from the radical neoliberal economies in the Baltic States, Estonia, Latvia and Lithuania, to the more 'embedded neoliberalism' in East Central Europe (Bohle and Greskovits 2012). More neo-patrimonial forms of capitalism emerged in countries where aspiring local capitalists managed to align with political power, as in much of Southeast Europe and

the former Soviet Union. In countries closest to the EU where the pull of
membership remained strong these patterns could at times be reversed. This
was most visible in the case of Slovakia, and to a lesser extent in Romania,
where the threat of being left out of the EU galvanized the opposition into
overthrowing semi-authoritarian post-Socialist governments and launching
a second, at the time uniquely radical, wave of neoliberal reforms in the
early 2000s.

Despite the differences, the East European capitalist varieties also
share a number of commonalities. All of them broadly fall within a more
neoliberal capitalist variant, with lower levels of labour market protection,
less generous welfare states and weaker social partners than in most of the
'old' EU member states. They are also heavily dependent on foreign capital,
which dominates not only the export-oriented manufacturing sectors but
also private services such as banking and retail. Foreign investment emerged
early on as the most straightforward solution to building capitalism in
the former lands of workers. It was often less contentious than building a
domestic capitalist class, it facilitated the arrival of new technologies and
opened up access to West European export markets and, at least early on, it
was also seen as a way to geopolitically anchor the region to the West and
keep Russian economic and political interests at bay. It was also heartily
supported by the EU, which readily invested in building up investment
promotion agencies in these countries, and facilitated attraction of foreign
firms through exemptions from its otherwise rigorous competition policy
(Drahokoupil 2009).

This reliance on foreign investment shaped the institutional environment
of East European economies well beyond the narrow purview of industrial
policy. Attempts to attract investors resulted in competitions for the lowest
corporate tax rate or the most 'competitive' labour law as well as in policies
to ensure currency stability, which imposed additional constraints on public
spending. Private actors, including investors themselves but also policy
advisors and transnational communities of technocrats, such as central
bankers, also joined in to promote policy ideas that were at the cutting edge
of liberal economic thinking but would have been unimplementable in the
'core' states, such as flat taxes, privatization of pensions and extreme forms
of monetarism (Appel and Orenstein 2018; Johnson 2016). If they were
not all directly exportable to the Western core, some of these experiments
nevertheless served to shore up the argument of the neoliberals there too,
and certainly to increase the pressure on organized labour in industries
that came to directly compete with newly established 'Eastern' affiliates
(Ther 2016).

As they emerged out of socialism and into their European future, the East
European states grappled with a number of deep ambiguities. They were
jealous of their newly regained sovereignty, yet eager to surrender it in order
to join the EU. They were economically unusually open but often nationalistic
in terms of their political and cultural outlooks. They eagerly accepted

foreign advice and capital in order to become like 'the West' but instead became neoliberal experiment fields. They were praised internationally as the miracles of economic transformation: between 2000 and 2008, GDP in what were to become new EU member states grew on average 4–6 per cent per year, comparable to the golden age of the East Asian 'tigers'. These soaring rates of growth drew a sharp line between the new EU members and countries further east whose economies continued to decline or stagnate. Whereas in 1989 Poland and Ukraine had comparable per capita GDP, by 2010 Poland's was nearly 2.5 times greater. Within the EU, however, this was only enough to regain the status of semi-periphery: in the same period, Polish average wages only caught up to about 30 per cent of those in the 'old' EU members. Even the wealthiest East European members – the Czech Republic and Slovenia – are only about as well-off as the poorest Western ones, Portugal and Greece. Inequality also rose vertiginously: within the three decades since the collapse of socialism, these societies became some of the most unequal in Europe.

Despite these contradictions, and despite the hardships of transition, the 1990s were also a period of mutual trust between Eastern and Western Europe and of confidence in a common European future. This mutual trust was also, in part, based on mutual ignorance and wishful thinking. The West Europeans embraced the Eastern enlargement hoping that little would change; the eleven East European 'accession states' put all of their hopes in an epochal transformation that would allow them to escape the semi-periphery. In the end, enlargement changed much more than the former expected but less than the latter desired, laying the path to a series of mutual disappointments.

# 3. A less-balanced union and a new East–West divide since 2004

The 'big bang enlargement' of 1 May 2004 brought the first eight East European countries into the EU (if we disregard the special case of the German Democratic Republic): Czech Republic, Estonia, Hungary, Latvia, Lithuania, Poland, Slovakia and Slovenia. They were followed by Bulgaria and Romania in 2007 and Croatia in 2013 (Figure 15.2). While nearly every second member state of the EU could thus be called East European, in demographic terms the 'newer' account for only about one-fifth of the Union's population. With continuing socioeconomic disparities between the Western and the Eastern 'halves' of the continent, their economic share is even lower.

In the EU's largely confederal system, this means that since 2004 an economically underdeveloped semi-periphery consisting of numerous smallish nation states came to play a disproportionately large political role.

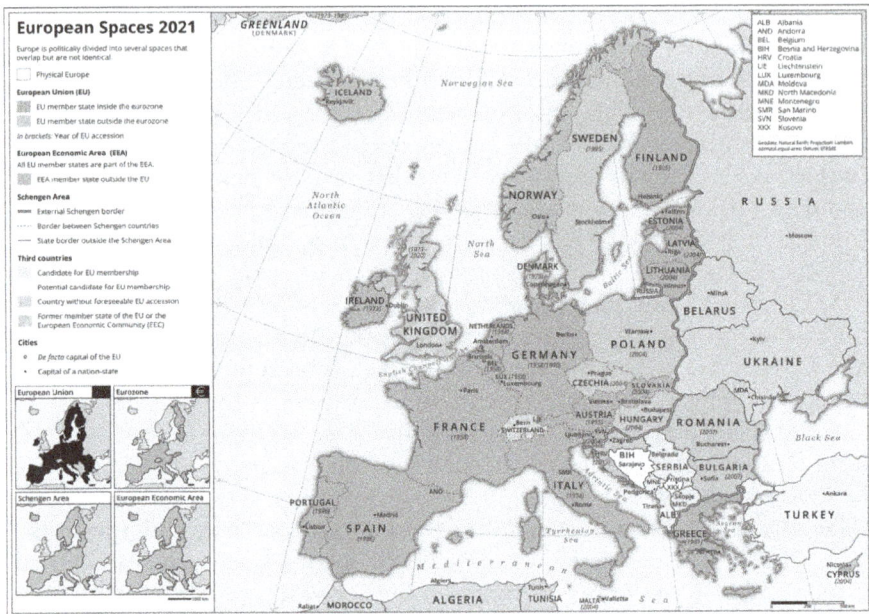

FIGURE 15.2 *Map of the European Union, indicating in which year countries joined the EU. Courtesy of Domser, CC BY-SA 4.0 https://creativecommons.org/ licenses/by-sa/4.0, via Wikimedia Commons.*

Taken together, these countries were suddenly responsible, among others, for nearly half of the votes in the European Council and every second European commissioner. The relative underdevelopment of East European member states also meant that a substantial share of EU structural funds started to flow in their direction just as their citizens began to emigrate in droves. By the end of the 2010s, millions of East Europeans moved West for work, with emigration rates reaching over 10 per cent of the working-age population in Latvia, Lithuania, Bulgaria and Croatia and 20 per cent in Romania (Eurostat 2018). Beyond the level of political representation, the entry of eleven East European states has thus come to reshape the composition of the European budget and the functioning of the large and borderless internal market.

The expansion of political representation at the EU level was not, however, accompanied by similarly proportional representation of the citizens of the 'newer' member states in the EU's technocratic, administrative and business elites. In other words, East Europeans have come to command disproportionate influence in the Union via the intergovernmental channels while having an almost negligible presence in its transnational networks of power and influence. This situation, rooted in multiple and persisting discrepancies between East and West, has bred an intergovernmentalist bias even among the European-minded members of East European elites. In the succession of crises that buffeted the

Union since 2008, this bias occasionally flared up in ways that appeared as direct challenges to the EU's constitutional order. In the context of East–West dynamics, three such crises stand out: the financial and economic crisis starting in 2008–9, the so-called migrant and refugee crisis that – temporarily – peaked in 2015 and the worsening crisis related to democracy and the rule of law within member states (see also Chapters 4 and 18).

The financial and economic crisis had a major impact on East–West relations for three main reasons. First, while East European countries chalked up impressive growth rates and the late 1990s and early 2000s brought them somewhat closer to the EU average, the protracted crisis halted this convergence. Foreign investment flows wobbled and even reversed: since 2008, foreign companies have been taking out of the region in profits at least as much as they bring in investment (Scepanovic and Bohle 2018).

Second, the crisis laid bare the fact that membership of the EU was in itself no guarantee of convergence: in fact, during the very period in which East European countries joined the EU – and partly as a by-product of their integration – some of the Southern members have been falling behind the North and benefiting unevenly from the Union (Chapter 10). The crisis arguably affected the Eastern members – most of which were not in the eurozone at the time it stuck and had relatively little public debt – much less than the Southern ones. It nevertheless laid bare the fact that the benefits of integration could also turn into liabilities as their export markets wobbled, the foreign-owned banks ceased local lending and the currency speculators set their sights on countries such as Slovakia, Estonia, and Latvia, and Lithuania, whose promise to eventually join the European Monetary Union now meant they had to refrain from using monetary policy to ease the recession. Smaller countries decided they could not afford currency instability and rushed to adopt the euro amidst the crisis, often at the cost of radical austerity. Figure 15.3 shows an example of Estonia's campaign for introducing Euro, conducted amidst radical austerity to preserve currency stability during the crisis. Larger ones, such as Poland, the Czech Republic and Hungary, have postponed their plans to join the eurozone indefinitely, for the first time intentionally keeping out of a European integration project.

Third, either way, the crisis did much to dispel the naive trust that the West had all the answers and that integration would inevitably increase prosperity. Some East European political actors began to question whether imitating the West and playing by liberal democratic rules was truly their best course of action. In a broader context of the rising influence of other global players – China and Russia, above all – this once again made the idea of hedging and cultivating alternative alliances more appealing.

The so-called migration crisis that peaked in 2015 when over a million people fled across the Mediterranean in an attempt to reach the EU precipitated another rift between East and West. While the EU and its 'core' member states struggled to tread a fine line between demonstrations of humanitarianism and international solidarity, on the one hand, and the insistence on the rules

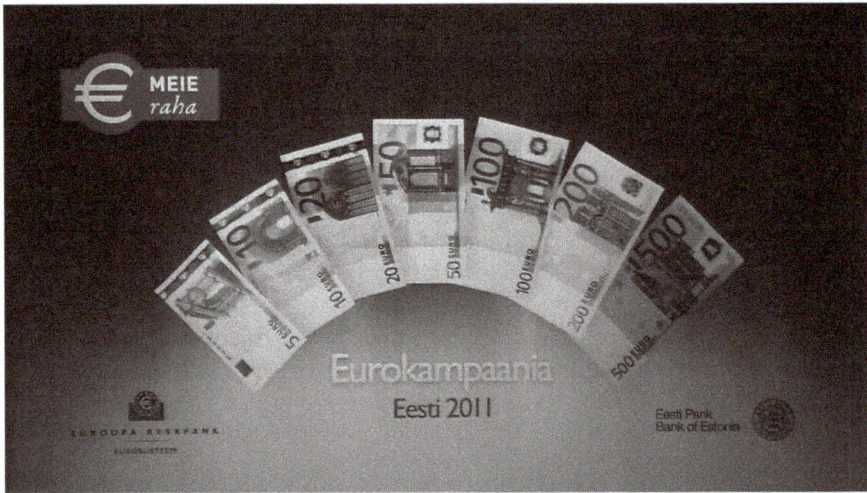

FIGURE 15.3 *Euro Information Campaign Estonia 2010. On 1 January 2011, the euro became legal tender in Estonia. Photographer: Karli Saul. Courtesy of European Union, 2010.*

and procedures, on the other, the East European states – Hungary most vocally – flat out refused calls for solidarity amidst an emergency and even questioned the very right to asylum. To be sure, this was less a conflict of underlying values and policy preferences than of political culture: while the East Europeans openly challenged refugee relocation quotas, others merely quietly disregarded them. Still, even if they played the role of 'useful idiots' whose intransigence could be used to justify a policy that emphasized control and securitization over humanitarianism and solidarity, they drew the ire of the West European political elites for breaking long-standing taboos of mainstream European politics by letting the genie of white, Christian nationalism out of the bottle from the highest level of government.

The crisis of the rule of law and democracy within the Union – acute in the case of Hungary throughout the 2010s and in Poland since the second half of the decade and increasingly also in Bulgaria and Slovenia – has shown just how little European institutions could and would do to protect, let alone promote, liberal democracy in member states (Kelemen 2020). The paucity of existing instruments and of political will to defend liberal democracies came as a negative surprise, especially for those East Europeans who had come to trust the EU's transformative power during the accession process and were now experiencing de-democratization first hand. As the most notorious backsliders – Poland and Hungary – continued to receive major funding from the EU, and Hungary's ruling party Fidesz, probably the most vocal challenger of liberal democratic standards, remained an influential member of the European People's Party throughout the 2010s, many wondered whether the EU was in fact enabling, rather than constraining, illiberal regimes in its midst.

It is remarkable that precisely those two East European countries that have been the first and most eager to Westernize around 1989 ended up electing and re-electing governments propagating authoritarian forms of nationalism and exclusionary visions of Europe two to three decades later. What makes this all the more remarkable is that Poland has been the single most successful national economy in Europe during recent decades and the only one in Europe to escape recession during the global financial crisis. The already fragile Hungarian economy, on the other hand, was severely hit in 2008–9, which was the main reason Viktor Orbán managed to capture an electoral supermajority in 2010. This contrast between the two countries makes it difficult to argue for any facile connection between economic performance and politically motivated revolt against the European mainstream. Yet it would also be wrong to ascribe the success of their illiberal projects to some deep-set flaw in the East European political culture without taking note of how the unbalanced patterns of Europeanization created spaces for resentment and opportunities for resource capture by authoritarian-minded elites.

Much like the process of enlargement, successive crises and the recurring conflicts between Eastern and Western European states are once again forcing the EU to clarify its character and values. The old neoliberal model is losing traction, including in the West itself, while the contours of the one to replace it are being fiercely contested. The debates surrounding the current Polish and the Hungarian regimes have also brought to the fore an older and deeper polarization between two self-understandings of the West – the West as a normative, liberal-progressive project, on the one hand, and the West as a nostalgic, culturalist-racial one, on the other. East European populists, emboldened by their membership of the EU, appear ready to reject the former, but they do so at their own peril since – as debates in the UK around Brexit have amply demonstrated – the latter is still ready to reject them.

# Conclusion

Disappointed expectations, institutional imbalances within the Union and discursive polarization around key concepts such as 'Europe' or 'the West' have been accumulating in recent years to create the sense of a new East–West divide. Mainstream interpretations of this process tend to speak about successful-then-failed 'Europeanization of Eastern Europe'. This chapter has presented arguments that show how East–West dynamics have been a lot more layered, multidirectional and embedded in a much longer history between the two parts of the continent.

This chapter has set the process of formal integration of East European members into the EU against a longer trend that sees Eastern Europe as internally conflicted over its semi-peripheral status and torn between attraction to and rejection of Western models of modernity. We have also argued that the relations between East European countries and the European integration project started prior to 1989 and that the subsequent consensual 'Europeanization' or 'Westernization' of these countries emerged out of a very specific context of the post–Cold War moment of mutual trust.

This mutual trust has enabled the profound reshaping of Eastern Europe since 1989, bifurcating the post-Communist region into members and non-members of the EU and transforming the former in ways that brought them closer to the ideal end point of post-Communist transition but could also leave them disappointingly far from it. Eastern Europe has contributed in crucial, though often indirect, ways to the evolution of the EU as it is today: as a rival during the Cold War, offering an ideological alternative against which to shape one's politics; as an eager pupil during its post-Communist transformation, forcing the EU to clarify its own positions and values; as an experiment field to test out new ideas and radical reforms; and as an internal other in more recent years, holding up a mirror, or rather a mocking glass, to the buried but undead dark sides and prejudices of the West.

# Five key questions

1.    What various roles have Eastern European countries played in the history of European integration since 1945?

2.    What was detente, and how did the relationship between the Soviet and Western models of modernity evolve in the late decades of the Cold War period?

3.    In what ways has Eastern Europe co-determined the European Union since the end of the Cold War?

4.    What have been key asymmetries and imbalances in East–West relations within the EU since the 'big bang enlargement' of 2004?

5.    What roles did Eastern European countries play during the major crises of the post-2004 years, and how did these crises impact them?

# Ten key readings

Bohle, D., and B. Greskovits (2012), *Capitalism Diversity on Europe's Periphery*, Ithaca, NY: Cornell University Press.

Kelemen, R. D. (2020), 'The European Union's Authoritarian Equilibrium', *Journal of European Public Policy*, 27 (3): 481–99.

Krastev, I., and S. Holmes (2019), *The Light That Failed: A Reckoning*, London: Penguin.

Laczó, F., and L. Lisjak Gabrijelcic (eds) (2020a), *The Legacy of Division: East and West after 1989*, Budapest-Vienna: CEU Press-Eurozine.

Mark, J., B. Iacob, T. Rupprecht and L. Spaskovska (2019), *1989: A Global History of Eastern Europe*, Cambridge: Cambridge University Press.

Melegh, A. (2005), *On the East-West Slope: Globalization, Nationalism, Racism and Discourses on Central and Eastern Europe*, Budapest: CEU.

Romano, A., and F. Romero (eds) (2020), *European Socialist Regimes' Fateful Engagement with the West: National Strategies in the Long 1970s*, London: Routledge.

Schenk, B. (2017), 'Eastern Europe', in D. Mishkova and B. Trencsényi (eds), *European Regions and Boundaries: A Conceptual History*, 188–209, New York: Berghahn.

Ther, P. (2016), *Europe since 1989: A History*, trans. Charlotte Hughes-Kreutzmüller, Princeton, NJ: Princeton University Press.

Villaume, P., and O. A. Westad (eds) (2010), *Perforating the Iron Curtain: European Détente, Transatlantic Relations, and the Cold War, 1965–1985*, Copenhagen: Museum Tusculanum Press.

# 16

# The Franco-German relationship at the heart of EU history

## *Carine Germond and Katja Seidel*

## Introduction

The close relationship between France and Germany has been described as a driving force for European integration. In this narrative, France and Germany acted as Europe's 'motor' or 'engine'. The terms 'couple', 'tandem' or 'duo' have been applied to their leaders. In the history of the European Union (EU) the Franco-German relationship stands out as the most constant, talked about and effective, but also the most criticized bilateral relationship in the Union. If, as many claim, the EU has a leadership problem, the Franco-German relationship has at times, though not always and not consistently, provided that leadership (Paterson 2008).

Krotz and Schild (2013) have coined the term 'embedded bilateralism' to conceptualize how the bilateral Franco-German relationship interacts with the multilateral EU. They posit that France and Germany form a core of established bilateral cooperation that has close links with European integration but also exists separately from the EU. As both countries and their governments are generally in favour of European integration, their cooperation has frequently resulted in joint European integration initiatives or provided joint solutions in periods of crises. Conversely, the European integration process itself has provided more opportunities for these two countries to work together and thus deepened their cooperation. Given the importance of France and Germany in the EU in terms of their geography, demographic size, economic power, political clout and history as founding member states, it is not surprising that their joint initiatives are bound to carry weight in the EU.

This chapter firstly explores the historical background of how Germany and France came to be viewed as 'hereditary enemies'. Secondly, it analyses how they became reconciled after the Second World War and why their relationship became central to European integration in the 1950s and 1960s. Thirdly, the chapter discusses the institutionalization of the Franco-German relationship with the Elysée Treaty of 1963. Fourthly, it discusses the Franco-German 'couples' from 1974 to 1995, often considered the high-point of Franco-German cooperation. Finally, the chapter highlights the more recent pressures on the Franco-German relationship in an enlarging Union since the early 1990s. Within the chronological sections, we study factors which affected the effectiveness of the Franco-German relationship such as the respective national leaders, the state of the bilateral relationship as well as the European and global context which they tried to shape or which influenced their actions. The chapter also considers the challenges this close bilateral relationship poses in a multinational setting such as the EU.

# 1. France and Germany: Hereditary enemies and rivals

Before 1945 Franco-German relations were characterized by 'long-lasting antagonism feeding on rivalry for territory and hegemony on the European continent, as well as humiliated national sentiments and revenge discourses' (Germond and Türk 2008, 1). In the early nineteenth century, the occupation of German territory by French Emperor Napoleon I's troops and the subsequent wars of liberation from Napoleonic rule established France as Germany's principal enemy and rival.

The French developed their own deep-seated hatred towards Germany when the two countries went to war with each other again in 1870, resulting in defeat for France and the annexation of the French Eastern provinces Alsace and Lorraine by Germany. To add insult to injury, in January 1871 the German empire was proclaimed in the Hall of Mirrors in the castle of Versailles, the former residence of French kings. In the First World War, the brutal fighting in the trenches further entrenched the enmity. Purposely, the negotiations to the peace treaty in 1919 were held in Versailles in retaliation for the humiliation France had experienced at the hand of Germany over forty years earlier. The Versailles peace treaty imposed harsh reparations on Germany and was geared towards permanently weakening the country to safeguard French security as well as its political and economic superiority in Europe.

In the interwar period some politicians in both countries, like German Foreign Minister Gustav Stresemann and French Foreign Minister Aristide Briand, understood that lasting peace in Europe could only be achieved if France and Germany came to an understanding. European integration, organized around a Franco-German partnership, was to be a means to that end. The Locarno Treaties of 1925 were a first step towards a normalization of relations between Germany and France as in these agreements Germany formally accepted the Western borders as they were drawn in the Treaty of Versailles. Later, the Briand Plan, an initiative by French Foreign Minister Briand in 1929, proposed a federal union of European countries with France and Germany at its core (Chapter 13). Bilateral relations developed across the diplomatic, economic and cultural fields too.

Relations broke down again when the Nazis came to power in Germany. France's defeat in June 1940 ushered in a new period of hostility between the two countries that would affect their relationship in the immediate post-war period. After the war, France, alongside the United States, Britain and the Soviet Union, became one of the four allied powers that decided on the fate of defeated Germany. Understandably, at first, the quest for security dominated the post-war French governments' policy towards Germany. Tellingly, the instructions sent to the French commander in Germany in July 1945 were: 'The essential target is the military, economic, and financial disarmament of the ancient Reich' (Gavin Munte 2008, 165).

# 2. On the path to reconciliation since 1945

French policy towards Germany evolved gradually after 1945. At first, the French set up a comparably harsh regime in their occupation zone in Germany, set to benefit France economically and avoid any kind of German military resurgence. In 1946 the French separated the coal-rich Saar region from the rest of their occupation zone and attributed it the status of an autonomous region, integrating it into the French economy. The French Saar policy became a major obstacle to improving relations between the two countries. It was only resolved in 1955 when the majority of the Saar population opted in a referendum for rejoining Germany which it did in 1957.

Immediately after the war the French government had also advocated a separation of the Ruhr region, the heart of German heavy industry, from the rest of Germany, but under pressure from Britain and the United States it settled for an alternative plan. An International Ruhr Authority was set up in 1949 to devise and manage production quotas for German heavy industry. The high-quality Ruhr coal became crucial for French steel works across the border as France was an importer of coal. French economic post-war reconstruction thus relied partly on the continued limitation of

Germany's economic potential. Similar to the early interwar period, the French government was convinced that a new war in Europe could only be avoided if France became both politically and economically stronger than its German rival. But this strategy soon reached a dead-end. It was criticized by France's allies, the United States and Britain, who understood that European economic reconstruction had to include the economic reconstruction and reintegration of Germany into the West European economy.

Other factors explain why the French government changed its attitude towards Germany. Firstly, the catastrophe of the Second World War, the Holocaust and the scale of destruction and disruption the war left in Europe made it necessary to durably pacify relations between both countries. Secondly, the war ended with two superpowers dominating world affairs: the liberal-democratic capitalist United States and the Communist Soviet Union. As the two superpowers' relationship deteriorated, Europe became drawn into the Cold War. The Iron Curtain separating the Communist Eastern Europe from the democratic western part of the continent came down between West and East Germany. The political and economic stability of West Germany as a border state in the Cold War thus became essential to the US government which contributed to West European reconstruction with Marshall Aid from 1948 and put pressure on France to improve its relations with West Germany.

Finally, although many French politicians remained wary of Germany, French Foreign Minister Robert Schuman, together with his German counterpart Konrad Adenauer, then chancellor and foreign minister, were prepared to embark on a new relationship between their countries. Schuman came from the Lorraine border region, once heavily contested between France and Germany, and was fluent in both French and German. Both men became convinced of the importance of the Franco-German relationship for the prosperity of Western Europe as a whole and the maintenance of peace on the continent. In a speech at the University of Zurich on 19 September 1946, Winston Churchill had already linked the future of Europe, and the success of European integration, with the necessity for a close relationship between France and Germany:

> The first step in the re-creation of the European family must be a partnership between France and Germany. In this way only can France recover the moral and cultural leadership of Europe. There can be no revival of Europe without a spiritually great France and a spiritually great Germany. (Churchill 1946)

Adenauer understood too that West Germany's sovereignty, its international role and its economic strength could only be regained in close partnership with France and in the context of a united Europe.

# The Europeanization of the German problem in the 1950s

Pressured by the United States to improve its relationship with Germany and to advance European integration, the French government soon realized that European integration could in fact help solve its 'German problem'. The Schuman Plan launched on 9 May 1950, named after Foreign Minister Schuman, envisaged a pooling of French and German coal and steel resources (Figure 16.1).

The plan was geared towards maintaining a certain amount of (indirect) control over West German economic sovereignty and recovery. The French government was prepared to relinquish a portion of its national sovereignty to achieve this aim when it suggested placing the control over a

FIGURE 16.1 *Cartoon 'Runaway Romance over the Anvil'. Robert Schuman and Konrad Adenauer are depicted as the happy couple. Behind them is British Foreign Minister Ernest Bevin, and US Secretary of State Dean Acheson is standing behind the anvil. Cartoon by David Low, Daily Herald, 12 May 1950. Courtesy of Solo Syndication London.*

common European coal and steel market into the hands of an independent
supranational body, the High Authority. Simultaneously though, this plan
would secure French supplies in German coal, which under the plan would
be accessible to all member states on equal terms. The German government
under Adenauer was willing to surrender sovereignty in the coal and steel
sector to regain sovereignty and equality as one of the member states of
the new European organization, the European Coal and Steel Community
(ECSC). The Schuman declaration emphasized the Franco-German
dimension of this first step in supranational European integration and thus
underscored the importance of this bilateral relationship for Europe's future
development (see also Chapter 1).

When the issue of German rearmament and membership in the North
Atlantic Treaty Organization (NATO) came onto the agenda with the outbreak
of the Korean War in 1950, the French government applied the same method: to
Europeanize the problem. A German army only five years after the war was
inconceivable for the French. Prime Minister René Pleven, in collaboration with
Jean Monnet who had also drafted the Schuman Plan, proposed a European
army in the form of a European Defense Community (EDC). The German
government, along with the other four member states of the ECSC, agreed and
in 1952 signed a treaty to form the EDC and a European Political Community.
However, this time a majority in the French National Assembly did not tolerate
the loss of national sovereignty in such a key area as security and defence and
rejected the treaty in 1954. Instead, Germany had its full sovereignty restored
and its military forces became integrated into the Western alliance when it
joined NATO and the Western European Union in 1955.

While these were the most obvious attempts by the French government to
Europeanize the German problem, the precondition of all future major steps
in European integration was a necessary, viable compromise between France
and Germany's often diverging positions. How was it then possible that since
the 1950s these two countries, who held very different views on a multitude of
issues due to the different political, economic and cultural traditions in their
countries, were able to agree and become a 'motor' of European integration?
One reason both countries were often, but not always, able to overcome these
differences was the gradual institutionalization of a close working relationship
between France and Germany through the Elysée Treaty that allowed for
regular discussions, exchanges of views and a coordination of positions.

## 3. The Elysée Treaty and the institutionalization of the Franco-German relationship

While Schuman and Adenauer can be considered as the first Franco-
German 'couple', it was Adenauer's close relationship with French

President Charles de Gaulle that facilitated the emergence of embedded bilateralism between the two countries. When de Gaulle came to power in 1958, he was well known for his scepticism about supranational European integration. When he became president just as the European Economic Community (EEC) started working in Brussels, Adenauer and others feared that he would withdraw France from the organization and thus spell doom for the Common Market project (Chapter 2). To their surprise, de Gaulle kept France in the EEC and recognized the advantages that it held for France. The common agricultural policy was advantageous for French farmers, and the customs union encouraged the modernization of the French economy.

As to the Franco-German relationship, to Adenauer's surprise de Gaulle was keen to establish a close and privileged relationship with the German chancellor. Several symbolic acts underscore this fledgling 'special relationship': in September 1958 de Gaulle invited Adenauer to visit him at his private home, an honour he granted no other foreign leader. Both leaders also shared a deep Catholic faith. Another symbolic act was their meeting in 1962 when they attended mass together at Reims Cathedral, site of the coronations of French kings and linked to the medieval Emperor Charles the Great, who both countries claim as an ancestor. The cathedral, intentionally damaged by the Germans in the First World War, strikingly symbolizes past divisions, shared history and the active policy of both leaders of overcoming these divisions.

The close relationship was maintained even though many of de Gaulle's policies were contrary to German interests, notably his quest to distance himself from NATO, which he thought was too dominated by the United States, and his emphasis of a European third way, independent of the United States. It was in this context that de Gaulle advocated a Franco-German partnership at the heart of Europe. However, Germany was dependent on NATO and US support, and many Germans felt a close affinity with the United States.

Another point of contention was de Gaulle's attempt to increase the role the EEC member states would play in European integration at the expense of the European Commission. De Gaulle's initiative in the early 1960s to establish an intergovernmental European political union and to curtail the power of the Commission failed, not least as smaller member states feared French and German domination (Chapter 2). Adenauer went along with these plans, but he did not have the majority of his cabinet behind him. Once the negotiations had failed in the summer of 1962, a frustrated de Gaulle proposed to Adenauer to form a Franco-German union. Finally, de Gaulle's unilateral decision to end accession negotiations with the UK in January 1963 drew the wrath of the other member states, including members of the German government. It was thus in a context of crisis that de Gaulle and Adenauer decided to deepen and institutionalize the Franco-German relationship with a friendship treaty (Box 16.1).

## BOX 16.1  EXTRACT FROM THE JOINT DECLARATION BY ADENAUER AND DE GAULLE, 23 JANUARY 1963

Convinced that the reconciliation of the German people and the French people, ending a centuries-old rivalry, constitutes a historic event which profoundly transforms the relations between the two peoples,

Conscious of the solidarity uniting the two peoples from the point of view of both their security and their economic and cultural development,

Aware in particular that youth has recognised this solidarity and is called upon to play a decisive part in the consolidation of Franco-German friendship,

Recognising that increased co-operation between the two countries constitutes an indispensable stage on the way to a united Europe, which is the aim of the two peoples:

Have agreed to the organisation and principles of co-operation between the two States as set out in the treaty signed today.

*Source*: Joint declaration (1963)

The Elysée Treaty of 1963 was an ambiguous construct and greeted with suspicion by France and Germany's partners in the EEC. With the treaty, de Gaulle transferred his ambitious aims for European political union to the bilateral level. However, as a condition for adopting the Elysée Treaty, the German parliament, the Bundestag, insisted on adding a preamble to the treaty which emphasized Germany's continued commitment to NATO and the close relationship with the United States. In de Gaulle's eyes, this made the treaty almost worthless.

That the Elysée Treaty would turn into an important instrument of Franco-German cooperation was thus not immediately foreseeable, not least as the new German Chancellor Ludwig Erhard (1963–6) was much less taken by Gaullist ideas than Adenauer. So ironically the signature of the friendship treaty was followed by a period of deteriorating relations between the two countries. However, the terms of the treaty were respected, and a regular working relationship between politicians and civil servants was established independently of who led the two countries. The treaty prescribed a strict schedule for regular meetings between ministers, civil servants and even the chiefs of staff of the two countries' armies. Regarding foreign affairs, the treaty stipulated: 'The two Governments shall consult each other, prior to any decision, on all important questions of foreign policy and in the first place on questions of common interest, with a view to reaching, as far as possible, an analogous position.' This included the countries' positions on questions of European integration. Another section specified collaboration in security and defence. The final section sought to promote relations in the areas of culture and youth, giving rise to a multitude of civil society links between the two countries and founding the Franco-German Youth Office in 1963 which funds exchange, cultural and language programmes for young people and quickly became a driving force of bilateral rapprochement.

The treaty provided a new impetus for the deepening of cultural and societal relations between France and Germany, but it was only possible because much work had already been achieved. After 1945, a few pioneering individuals actively promoted cultural and societal contacts as a linchpin to reconciliation between the two countries. The town partnerships, the first of which was established in 1950, were the most emblematic examples of these efforts. Contrary to the 1920s when Franco-German contacts had been supported by only a small intellectual and economic elite, post-war cultural and societal exchanges encompassed the two countries' societies. This popular support was instrumental to the acceptance and success of the political process of rapprochement initiated in the 1950s.

In the late 1980s, four new Councils for Defense and Security, Economics and Finance, Culture and the Environment were added. Since 2003, the biannual summit meetings have been called 'Franco-German Ministerial Councils', and both countries have established the post of 'General Secretaries of Franco-German Cooperation' to prepare the meetings (Krotz and Schild 2013). In 2001, the French president and German chancellor agreed to meet informally every six to eight weeks. More recently, in January 2019, Chancellor Angela Merkel and President Emmanuel Macron signed the Treaty of Franco-German Cooperation and Integration. While it did not provide much in terms of new and visionary policies, it can be deemed important as a reaffirmation of the basic values of the embedded bilateralism. The institutionalization of the Franco-German relationship through the Elysée Treaty made it easier for the two governments to sound out opinions and coordinate positions before presenting them to their European partners. In reality consultation did not always take place on all important issues and, if it did, did not always result in agreement and joint action.

# 4. The era of 'the Franco-German couples' from the 1970s to the 1990s

## The meeting of minds: Valéry Giscard d'Estaing and Helmut Schmidt

Valéry Giscard d'Estaing and Helmut Schmidt, whose years as president and chancellor stretch from 1974 to 1981 and 1982, respectively, are usually considered one of the most successful Franco-German 'couples'. This is due to a number of factors: firstly, they led their countries in a period characterized by economic recession, high unemployment and inflation rates and international monetary turbulences that favoured close bilateral cooperation to address those shared problems. Secondly, they had an excellent personal chemistry and shared a strong interest and expertise in economic and financial matters. Thirdly, the increasingly volatile relationship between the United States and Europe – Schmidt and US President Jimmy Carter (1977–81) were particularly at odds with each other – made Germany refocus attention on its relations with France and Europe. Fourthly, the loosening transatlantic relations and the monetary turbulences instilled in Giscard and Schmidt the aim of establishing the European Community as an international player and using it to improve economic and monetary cooperation between member states. Fifthly, relatively weak Community institutions opened the door for a strong bilateral leadership role for France and Germany. Both men were reluctant to strengthen the Community institutions, particularly the Commission, and preferred to deal directly with the other member states. Finally, both benefited from the institutionalized cooperation established by the Elysée Treaty. This close coordination of the Franco-German position was then crucial for convincing their Community partners of their initiatives.

Among their achievements were the establishment of the European Council in 1974 and the European Monetary System (EMS) in 1978. However, not all developments in the Community were due to Franco-German leadership. Individuals from other member states could equally have an impact on how the Community developed. For example, European Political Cooperation (EPC) became a new Community instrument for foreign and security policy coordination of the member states. EPC had been proposed by the Belgian Foreign Minister Etienne Davignon in 1970. This new instrument suited France and Germany as they were keen to establish a forum to discuss foreign and security affairs without creating formal powers for the Community in this sensitive area where nation states' sovereignty was keenly defended. National leaders thereby sought to increase Europe's weight in the world both economically and diplomatically (see also Chapters 3 and 14).

The establishment of the European Council was something French President Georges Pompidou (1969–74) and his successor Giscard had pushed to enhance the role national leaders were playing in the Community. The EEC Treaty had not given a role to national leaders as a 'motor' of the development of the Community. Summit meetings were thus the exception rather than the rule. The summit in Paris in 1972 took place as a result of a Franco-German initiative. Two years later, in December 1974, the heads of state and government decided to meet three times a year as the 'European Council' to give direction to the Community.

As demonstrated above for the 1950s, if France and Germany played a leading role in European integration, it was often to solve an issue in the bilateral relationship. France's support for integration initiatives such as EPC and Economic and Monetary Union (EMU) in the 1970s was also geared to bind Germany further into the Community. France had become concerned about German Chancellor Willy Brandt's (1969–74) 'new *Ostpolitik*', his policy towards the Communist East, which had resulted in a number of bilateral treaties with countries such as the Soviet Union and East Germany. This normalization of relations with the East gave Germany new clout as an independent actor on the international scene but also raised concerns in France. Chancellor Brandt therefore tried to reassure President Pompidou that Germany was still committed to European integration and the Franco-German relationship: 'Ostpolitik starts in the West' Brandt said to Pompidou in 1970. This meant that Ostpolitik could only be developed against the backdrop of a solid relationship between Germany and its Western partners.

As it was the case for many policies, France and Germany held very different views on how to achieve EMU (Chapter 10). For Germany, monetary union could only be achieved after a long period of domestic fiscal reforms, for example, curbing inflation, controlling public spending and the convergence of economic policies. The French government, on the other hand, advocated close monetary cooperation to support the weak franc but otherwise wanted to remain flexible in its economic policy decisions, generally more geared towards spending to stimulate growth as opposed to Germany's preferred stability policy, which emphasized low inflation rates and sound public finances. This controversy persisted until the negotiations to achieve EMU in the 1990s.

To this day, French and German governments disagree over the advantages of an economic government for the Eurozone, an idea cherished by the French government but rejected by Germany, most recently by Chancellor Angela Merkel, who feared that Germany would incur much of the costs for such an economic programme and supporting the economies of the weaker eurozone members. The EMS Giscard and Schmidt worked towards in the late 1970s did not pose a problem in this respect as it focused solely on monetary stability.

## The era of Kohl and Mitterrand

With President François Mitterrand and Chancellor Helmut Kohl Franco-German relations and influence in the Community reached a high point. Like Giscard and Schmidt, they stood on different sides of the political spectrum – Kohl was a Christian Democrat, Mitterrand a Socialist – and were keen to deepen Franco-German friendship. Both were convinced of the crucial role of Franco-German cooperation for Europe and had a keen awareness of history and the 'oft-tragic – community of destiny that united their countries' (Germond 2013, 3). Both were also early and keen supporters of European integration. While Schmidt and Giscard had been more pragmatic, Kohl

FIGURE 16.2 *Helmut Kohl (right) and François Mitterrand (left) holding hands at Verdun, 22 September 1984. Courtesy of Presse- und Informationsamt der Bundesregierung.*

and Mitterrand followed in de Gaulle's and Adenauer's footsteps and staged highly symbolic encounters, underscoring their understanding of their countries' shared past and its relevance for Europe's future. For example, in 1984, the two statesmen held hands at a ceremony commemorating the fallen of the First World War on the battlefields of Verdun (Figure 16.2). Their gesture had turned a symbol of past hatred and violence into one of hope for the future.

However, this display of a shared memory and celebration of Franco-German friendship masked their often diverging views on European policies, including on the development of EMU on which Mitterrand was keen, on economic policy, on the desirability of free trade versus Mitterrand's more protectionist view, on agriculture and the institutional development of the EEC. How were they able to reconcile these diverging positions? First, both leaders had a strong conviction of the importance of their historic relationship and of driving European integration which helped to find common ground. In addition, the breakdown of Communism in Central and Eastern Europe, and, of particular relevance for their relationship, in Eastern Germany in 1989/91, challenged the leaders to seek a solution that was acceptable to both countries.

Not surprisingly, it happened to be a European solution as France (and Germany) sought deeper integration of a united Germany into European structures: the German problem was (again) Europeanized. Kohl, submerged in the turmoil of domestic problems and adopting the stance of a quick unification of the two countries, eventually understood and accepted the French concerns over German unification. He then agreed to deeper European integration in the form of political union and fully accepted EMU. The idea that Kohl sacrificed Germany's strong currency, the deutschmark, for German unification is not entirely correct as the agreement to proceed with EMU had been taken in the summer of 1988 at the Hanover European Council, before the fall of the Berlin Wall. However, the German commitment to EMU, which was still only lukewarm in the summer of 1989, and the speed with which it was implemented were certainly affected by the events of autumn 1989. It was only then, in December 1989, that Kohl agreed to set the date for an intergovernmental conference (IGC) on Monetary Union and Political Union, not least to signal that a larger united Germany would not pose a threat to its European neighbours.

German unification therefore became a driving force for European integration resulting in the creation of the EU, including EMU and a common foreign and security policy. EMU was also a typical Franco-German compromise. The Germans conceded on the issue of monetary union itself but obtained an independent central bank modelled on the German Bundesbank as well as strict economic stability criteria for states before they could join the euro. More generally, Franco-German proposals were crucial for shaping the Treaty of Maastricht signed in 1992.

The Franco-German relationship suited both sides. France remained the dominant partner in the relationship. German chancellors tolerated their French counterparts claiming the senior role in their partnership. Europe became France's power base after the loss of its empire and its world role. Germany, keen to regain international recognition and status and to overcome the old antagonism with its neighbour across the Rhine, was pleased to join. It can be argued that at first France and Germany were partners of necessity, but later also of choice.

# 5. The Franco-German relationship since German unification

German unification and the end of the Cold War triggered shifts, if not a recalibration, in the Franco-German relationship (Germond 2022). A unified Germany was a larger, economically stronger and potentially politically more influential and assertive state and threatened to unbalance the 'tandem'. In the longer term, Germany's economic might and increased political influence meant that it was no longer the junior partner in the

Franco-German relationship. The enlargement with ten Central and Eastern European countries in 2004 and 2007 further strengthened Germany's position in the centre of the enlarged Union. Germany supported eastern enlargement for historical and political reasons but also for the economic benefits it would bring to the German economy. The French government was less supportive of Eastern enlargement and worried about the shifting balance of power in Europe and its own loss of power.

Franco-German leaders after Kohl and Mitterrand were less close. One reason for this might be the generational shift, with the new generation of politicians lacking personal experience of the Second World War. Kohl's successor, the Social Democrat Gerhard Schroeder, was born at the end of the Second World War, unlike Kohl, Mitterrand and Jacques Chirac who had lived through the war. When in 2003 Schroeder and French President Chirac, a neo-Gaullist, decided to renew the Elysée Treaty on the occasion of its fortieth anniversary, it was a joint effort to bring closer together these two allies who had become estranged. Schroeder had not been set on a close relationship with Chirac but had sought to deepen Germany's relationship with the UK. Chirac and Schroeder had clashed publicly at the summit of EU leaders in 2000 in Nice over the voting weights in a new EU treaty then under negotiation (Nice Treaty 2001; Chapter 4). Schroeder thought German unification and its increase in population needed to be acknowledged through increasing the weight of the German vote in the Council of Ministers. Chirac insisted on continued parity of the French and the German votes. A complicated compromise formula was found, but the negotiations had been concluded in a hostile atmosphere. In 2003 they agreed on opposing military intervention in Iraq, issuing a joint declaration, but failed to forge a united EU position in this crucial foreign and security policy issue. The UK, Spain, Portugal, Poland and Italy and four other member states sided with the United States in favour of military intervention in Iraq, signalling that an enlarged EU would be more diverse in the interests it represented with member states less prone to align with French and German positions.

The relationship between German Chancellor Angela Merkel (2005–21) and President Nicholas Sarkozy (2007–12), successors of Schroeder and Chirac, respectively, also got off to a rocky start. Instead of focusing his attention on Germany, Sarkozy tried to establish a multilateral leadership for the EU by seeking a close partnership with the UK, Italy, Spain and Poland, with France in a leadership role. However, the financial crisis that broke out in 2008 required the cooperation of France and Germany as the two largest member states using the euro even though they did not always see eye to eye. By 2010 the Merkel–Sarkozy couple was known as 'Merkozy', and their relationship had improved. Both leaders agreed on measures and policies to resolve the crisis and improve governance of the eurozone. These included new treaties to improve eurozone governance and reform (in 2010, a European Financial Stabilization Mechanism and, in 2012, the Treaty on Stability, Coordination and Governance in the EMU; Chapter 10).

Since the 1990s, France's economic decline and competitiveness problems compared to Germany's continued economic strength meant that Germany became the strongest economy in the eurozone and a crucial power broker in the financial crisis. However, during the eurozone crisis Germany's role of the creditor insisting on deep and painful reforms in the debtor countries was often badly received. A German hegemony in the Union would arguably be unacceptable for many member states and is something Germany does not wish for, not least for historical reasons.

In President Emmanuel Macron (2017–27) France has a leader who has reaffirmed the historic nature of the two countries' close relationship and has presented Merkel with plans for deep and ambitious reforms of the EU and the eurozone, not all of which were to the liking of the German chancellor. Despite very different personal styles and temperament, Macron's and Merkel's views coincided more often than they diverged. But Merkel's decision not to run for a fifth term and the make-up of the governing coalition limited Germany's ability to take major European decisions, much to Macron's disappointment. Despite deep divergences over the EU's direction, the Franco-German engine sprung back to life in the face of the Covid-19 crisis, which struck Europe in spring 2020. Franco-German close cooperation was instrumental in brokering a historical agreement on an EU rescue and bailout package that provided financial assistance to struggling European governments and laid the groundwork to closer fiscal integration. In contrast, there has been little Franco-German coordinated response to the war in Ukraine.

# Conclusion

The relationship between France and Germany is unusual, not to say unique, due to its depth, longevity and the level of its institutionalization. Politicians from both countries have continued to emphasize to this day the necessity of Franco-German understanding and the importance of this relationship for stability in Europe and beyond. With regard to those two countries, therefore, bilateralism in Europe clearly mattered. The Franco-German bilateral relationship 'is integration of a particular kind, which on the one hand takes place outside of the multilateral, Brussels-centred EU frame, and on the other hand undergirds such wider multilateral integration' (Krotz and Schild 2013, 234).

Their influence on Europe as an 'internal federator' has varied according to political fields and time. It was decisive for the founding acts such as the ECSC and EEC Treaties but also for moments of relaunch, such as the decision to enlarge the Community in 1969, the founding of the European Council in 1974, the EMS in 1978/9 and EMU and Political Union in the 1990s. Their method of influencing varied from 'agenda setting, compromise building [to] crisis management' (Krotz and Schild 2013, 237). The inability to form a joint position on the Iraq War with all EU member states shows, however, that in particular in the areas of foreign, security and defence policy Franco-German leadership has been less successful.

The Franco-German 'tandem' thus did not exert a consistent and continued leadership role in the Community. The Franco-German couple rarely showed a consistent level of unity. Rather, it was often the diverging interests between the two countries that had to be overcome that were important for the development of the Union: if a compromise between these two countries could be reached, it often satisfied the needs and interests of the other member states. One should not overstate the influence of France and Germany as policymaking in the Union takes place in a complex interplay between member states, the Commission and the European Parliament. But it is clear that in the Union nothing can happen against the wishes of France and Germany.

The future of the Franco-German relationship and its firm link and commitment to European integration are uncertain. Both countries have seen rising support for the French Rassemblement National and the German Alternative for Germany – two nationalist, populist, anti-immigrant Eurosceptic parties. Brexit might strengthen Germany's standing in the Union if France cannot overcome its economic difficulties. At the same time, the departure of the UK weakens the group of countries wedded to market liberalism, deregulation and free trade within the EU, of which Germany is one, and is set to strengthen those, France among them, more in favour of protectionism and state intervention in the economy. For now, Franco-German agency in the EU is set to continue since in late 2021 Germany elected the pro-European Social Democrat Olaf Scholz as its leader while France in April 2022 elected Macron for a second term against the Eurosceptic candidate Marine Le Pen. After Brexit, France and Germany are set to remain in the inner circle of EU policymaking. Brexit may even re-energize the relationship between the two countries and their leadership role in the EU (Krotz and Schild 2018). Even so, a more assertive tandem post-Brexit may not be so easily accepted by their EU partners.

# Five key questions

1.  Why did the Franco-German relationship become central to European integration?

2.  How can we account for the effectiveness of the Franco-German couple within the EU?

3.  What factors limit the ability of France and Germany to exert influence within the Union?

4.  How can we explain the longevity and adaptability of the Franco-German relationship in Europe?

5.  To what extent was the Franco-German couple about 'Europeanizing' problems and issues?

# Ten key readings

Cole, A. (2000), *Franco-German Relations*, London: Routledge.

*German Politics & Society* (2013), 'The Elysée Treaty at Fifty', Special Issue, 31 (1): https://www.jstor.org/stable/i23744591.

Germond, C. (2013), 'Dynamic Franco-German Duos: Giscard-Schmidt and Mitterrand-Kohl', in E. Jones, A. Menon and S. Weatherill (eds), *The Oxford Handbook of the European Union*, Oxford: Oxford University Press.

Germond, C. (2022), 'Franco-German Relations and the European Integration Process since German Reunification', in K. Larres and H. Moroff (eds), *Oxford Handbook of German Politics*, 491–508, Oxford: Oxford University Press.

Germond, C., and H. Türk (eds) (2008), *A History of Franco-German Relations in Europe: From 'Hereditary Enemies' to Partners*, New York: Palgrave.

Hendriks, G., and A. Morgan (eds) (2001), *The Franco-German Axis in European Integration*, Cheltenham: Edward Elgar.

Krotz, U., and J. Schild (2013), *Shaping Europe: France, Germany, and Embedded Bilateralism from the Elysée Treaty to Twenty-First Century Politics*, Oxford: Oxford University Press.

Krotz, U., and J. Schild (2018), 'Back to the Future? Franco-German Bilateralism in a Post-Brexit Union', *Journal of European Public Policy*, 25 (8): 1174–93.

Paterson, W. E. (2008), 'Did France and Germany Lead Europe? A Retrospect', in J. E. Hayward (ed.), *Leaderless Europe*, 89–110, New York: Oxford University Press.

Sangar, E. (2020), *Diffusion in Franco-German Relations: A Different Perspective on a History of Cooperation and Conflict*, Cham: Palgrave Macmillan.

# 17

# In or out? Britain and the European project

## Mathias Haeussler

## Introduction

In 2016, 51.89 per cent of the British people voted to leave the European Union (EU) in a nationwide referendum, a process that quickly became known as 'Brexit'. To many observers, however, the British vote merely marked the culmination of the country's notoriously difficult relationship with European integration since 1945. In the immediate post-war years, Britain first declined to take part in the nascent European Communities, since it deemed membership as being incompatible with its global interests and trade relationships. During the 1960s, it then applied twice for membership – only to be rebuffed each time by the French President Charles de Gaulle. Having finally entered the EC (the European Communities made of the EEC, Euratom and the ECSC) in 1973, Britain remained a difficult partner: it sought to 'renegotiate' its terms of membership, in particular as regards the country's contributions to the EC budget, and remained outside key integrationist projects such as the Economic and Monetary Union (EMU). In the 1990s, the political scientist Stephen George therefore described Britain as an 'awkward partner' of Europe, a term that has since become notorious in the political discourse. In light of that well-known history, one is tempted to ask: did Britain ever manage to come to terms with the realities of EC/EU membership?

This chapter traces Britain's role in the European integration process from the end of the Second World War right up to 'Brexit'. But it rejects the idea that Britain has always been negatively predisposed towards

European integration, or that 'Brexit' was the seemingly inevitable result of the country's difficult role inside the European Communities. Instead, the chapter argues that British European policy was based primarily on pragmatic and rational considerations of the country's national interests, and that it significantly modified its positions towards European integration as circumstances changed. The chapter also shows how Britain played a positive – in some cases even proactive – role towards key integrationist projects, above all the completion of the Single Market from the mid-1980s onwards. To establish this, the chapter is structured in three main chronological sections: the period from the end of the Second World War to British EC entry in 1973, Britain's time as an EC member from 1973 to the early 1990s, and from the creation of the EU in 1992 to today.

# 1. 1945–73: The long way in ...

In 1945, Britain was still an imperial power with global reach. Its colonial possessions and dominions stretched across Africa, Asia and Australia, and over seven hundred million people were citizens of the British Empire and Commonwealth. Although the Second World War had put a massive strain on the country's finances, over half of the world's trade was still conducted in pounds sterling, and the UK produced around one-third of Western Europe's industrial output in 1950 (Deighton 2010; Self 2010; Reynolds 2000). The country's heroic role in the Second World War had also reinforced a sense of national pride and belief in national identity. It is therefore no surprise that the UK pursued a decidedly global, rather than European-oriented, national strategy in the immediate post-war years, trying to maximize the many 'great but short-term advantages' of its position (Milward 2002, 2). That meant first and foremost the exploitation of Commonwealth trade preferences and the pursuit of a one world system based largely on pound sterling as a reserve currency, coupled with the closest possible relationship with the United States in intelligence, security and defence matters (Reynolds 1985). Britain's European role, by contrast, remained rather limited. Although Labour's Foreign Secretary Ernest Bevin briefly toyed with the idea of a European 'third force' between the communist Soviet Union and the capitalist United States, the intensification of the East–West conflict in the late 1940s eventually made him abandon such plans and instead work towards binding the United States as closely as possible to the defence of Europe through the North Atlantic Treaty Organisation (NATO) (Greenwood 1992).

In May 1950, the Schuman Plan – which proposed to pool Europe's coal and steel resources under a joint supranational authority – put the British government in a dilemma. On the one hand, it appreciated the French scheme as a major contribution to the post-war European order, not least because it offered a constructive short-term solution to the 'German question' that had plagued the Allies for much of the late 1940s (Chapters 1 and 16). British policymakers also feared that non-participation might exclude the country from an emerging new power centre in Western Europe. On the other hand, however, there were little economic incentives for British participation, given that its coal and steel production still far surpassed that of the other West European countries. Britain also did not like the supranational principle at the very heart of the scheme, as the Labour government feared that it might lose control over some industries it had only recently nationalized. 'It's no good, we cannot do it', the deputy Prime Minister Herbert Morrison famously declared in cabinet, 'the Durham miners won't wear it' (Young 1998, 31). There was also some diplomatic snubbing involved: although France had consulted the Americans and the West German Chancellor Konrad Adenauer in advance of the plan, it had apparently not done so with the British. A few weeks later, the French government also issued a 24-hour deadline for Britain to make up its mind while Prime Minister Attlee was on holiday and Foreign Secretary Ernest Bevin sick in hospital.

Faced with the French ultimatum, the British cabinet therefore made the fateful decision to abstain from the conference that resulted, in 1952, in the foundation of the European Coal and Steel Community (ECSC). With the benefit of hindsight, some historians have therefore claimed that Britain's abstention constituted a major missed opportunity in Britain's relationship with post-war Europe: by rejecting participation, Britain had voluntarily excluded itself from a major new power bloc on the European continent, was unable to shape the emerging institutions according to their own interests and ultimately handed over the leadership of post-war Europe to France and West Germany (Dell 1995). Such views, however, should be treated with caution because of their ingrained teleology: at the time, the Schuman Plan was only one of many possible schemes for post-war European cooperation, one that seemed unlikely to succeed, and one that clearly ran counter to Britain's political and economic objectives as well as global strategy.

Importantly, Britain's rejection of the Schuman Plan did not automatically exclude the country from future plans for closer European cooperation. In 1955, Britain was again invited to take part in the deliberations of the so-called Spaak Committee, which was set up to explore the opportunities for the creation of a European common market and the joint European use of atomic energy. Although Britain accepted the invitation, it did so reluctantly: rather than sending an official delegation, it merely seconded the Under-Secretary at the Board of Trade Russell Bretherton as a 'representative', hoping that he might be able to guide the discussions in directions that were more favourable to British interests. However, when it became apparent that the other participants were set on the establishment of a customs union with a common external tariff and had no interest in abandoning the principle of supranationalism either, Bretherton soon withdrew from the committee. Following the Treaties of Rome in March 1957, the EEC was established in January 1958 without British participation.

Why exactly did Britain decide to abstain? While politicians and officials did consider the arguments seriously, there were powerful considerations against British membership. The proposed customs union, for example, clearly ran counter to the country's economic interests: while Britain liked the idea of a free trade area, the proposed common external tariff would have irrevocably jeopardized its significant extra-European trade and Commonwealth preferences. Politically too, the British government appreciated the scheme's potential contribution to inner-European peace, but it remained sceptical about the principle of supranationalism as a prerequisite for closer European integration. Above all, however, there was a widespread belief amongst British policymakers that the proposed scheme was simply too ambitious and that the whole thing was unlikely to succeed. When it became clear that the other countries were actually pushing ahead with their plans, Britain hastily launched a complementary proposal of a Europe-wide free trade area (FTA) encompassing both EEC and non-EEC members, but the initiative was vetoed by the incoming French President de Gaulle in November 1958 (Warlouzet 2011; Lynch 2000; Ellison 2000a). The quickly composed alternative European Free Trade Area (EFTA, 1960), consisting of Britain and six other non-EEC European states (Austria, Denmark, Ireland, Norway, Portugal, Sweden), proved a poor and ineffective substitute. At the time, the resulting split of Western Europe into two rival economic spheres was commonly described as the 'Outer Seven' EFTA members against the 'Inner Six' of the EEC.

While British non-participation in the Schuman Plan had been of little consequence, the British rejection of the EEC membership proved a lot more fateful in the long run. Already in the late 1950s, Britain felt the negative effects of its self-exclusion. Not only did the EEC member states' quick economic progress contrast with Britain's comparatively sluggish performance at the time, but there were also frequent signs that the EEC's economic strength would eventually translate into political power. 'For the first time since the Napoleonic era', Prime Minister Harold Macmillan wrote in an internal note in October 1959, the major European powers were 'united in a positive grouping, with considerable political aspects, which ... may have the effect of excluding us both from European markets and from consultation in European policy' (qtd in Ellison 2000b, 179). Such fears of exclusion were compounded by the simultaneous erosion of the other pillars of Britain's global strategy at the time: decolonization had eroded most remaining parts of the British Empire by the early 1960s, and the Commonwealth had also not turned into the powerful economic bloc Britain had hoped for. To add insult to injury, the United States too now made it clear that they preferred Britain to be inside rather than outside the EEC.

Eventually, it dawned on British policymakers that there were few alternatives left to seeking full EEC membership. On 31 July 1961, Prime Minister Macmillan therefore declared Britain's first application in the House of Commons. Yet the British government did not apply outright: it made its application conditional on the obtainment of special conditions for Commonwealth trade and the protection of British agriculture. Such conditionality meant that the entry negotiations soon got bogged down in long and protracted talks between Britain and the other EEC member states (Ludlow 1997). At home too, public opinion was divided: while some regarded British membership as an opportunity for the country's economic modernization and to foster a new post-imperial identity, others denounced it as the surrender of national sovereignty and the abandonment of overseas partners (Haeussler 2014). Ultimately, however, it was French President de Gaulle who put the nail in the coffin by vetoing the British application on 14 January 1963. 'England in effect is insular, she is maritime, she is linked through her exchanges, her markets, her supply lines to the most diverse and often the most distant countries', he famously declared in a press conference; 'the nature, the structure, the very situation [conjoncture] that are England's differ profoundly from those of the continentals'. While the French president had always been ill-disposed towards British membership, the inflexibility displayed by the British delegation in the entry negotiations, as well as an Anglo-American nuclear deal concluded the month before, gave him the perfect political excuse to actually do so (Ludlow 1997; Kaiser 1996).

Whatever the ultimate reasons for de Gaulle's veto, the result was that Britain found itself locked out of the EEC and without a constructive European policy for much of the 1960s. Although the subsequent Labour government of Harold Wilson, who served as prime minister from 1964 to 1970, initially displayed little enthusiasm for European integration, it too saw few alternatives to full EEC membership. In May 1967, Wilson and his Foreign Secretary George Brown tabled Britain's second EEC application – this time without any special conditions attached – and campaigned energetically for membership with high-profile visits to key EEC capitals (Parr 2005). Yet again, however, the British were rebuffed by Charles de Gaulle, who issued his second veto in November that same year. While other EEC member states such as West Germany were dismayed by French obstructionism, they ultimately acquiesced because of the overriding importance they attributed to Franco-German reconciliation and France's general indispensability to the European integration process. Nonetheless, the British application was not withdrawn but left on the table so that it could be picked up easily should circumstances change.

It was only after de Gaulle's departure in 1969, however, that British EC membership became a realistic prospect again. The new French President Georges Pompidou was determined to revitalize the EC, and he felt that British entry might boost the Community's political and economic standing. In Britain too, the newly elected Conservative Prime Minister Edward Heath (1970–4) was an ardent supporter of EC membership, having already acted as Britain's chief negotiator during the first application in 1961–3. In May 1971, Heath and Pompidou met for a high-profile summit in Paris, where they broke the deadlock on many protracted issues surrounding British membership and thus paved the way for the subsequent negotiations. Yet

FIGURE 17.1 *Agreement late in the night (with journalist sleeping rough) at the Council of Ministers on the British enlargement, 22 June 1971. Photograph: Karel van Milleghem. Courtesy of European Communities, 1971.*

progress was also helped by Heath's acceptance of several pieces of EC legislation that were clearly unfavourable to the British, particularly as regards the financing of the EC's budget and the common agricultural policy (CAP). Once inside the Community, so Heath hoped, Britain could still gradually improve its position through the skilled use of regular EC mechanisms and policies (Aqui 2020) (Figure 17.1).

More than a decade after Britain's first application, then, British EC membership was finally achieved, but the delay came at a price: not only had Britain missed the EC's 'honeymoon years' in which the founding member states were able to adjust to the new realities of membership in a largely benevolent political and economic climate but it also had to join an institution whose institutions, rules and mechanisms were not of its own making and did not necessarily reflect British preferences. More generally, the British decision to seek membership was largely driven by negative motivations, above all by the belief that Britain could not afford to stay outside, rather than by a more positive rationale for joining. There was no cross-party consensus for EC membership either: the House of Commons debate lasted an entire six days, and it took a secret collusion between Labour and the Conservative Party to get the Bill over the line the following year (Ludlow 2015; Young 2000). All of these factors would shape Britain's role inside the EC for many years to come.

# 2. 1973–90: Awkward or influential? Britain inside the EC

Britain officially joined the European Communities on 1 January 1973, and it did so with great fanfare: the Heath government organized a two-week festival with over three hundred events, including a gala at the Royal Opera House and concerts by the Kinks and Slade, as well as a friendly football match (Saunders 2018). The realities of membership, however, proved rather less exciting than these initial celebrations suggested. The deteriorating world economy, Britain's unfortunate standing in the EC's financing system, the lack of a cross-party consensus on membership, as well as severe domestic problems all proved significant obstacles for Britain's first years inside the Community. Yet Britain's widely publicized problems of adjusting to EC membership have often overshadowed its positive contributions in many areas of European integration.

The most immediate development in Britain's EC membership, however, was the British government's decision to renegotiate the country's terms of entry, and then conduct a nationwide referendum over continuing EC membership. The decision was driven largely by Prime Minister Harold Wilson, who had returned to Downing Street following Edward Heath's defeat in the February 1974 elections. Wilson's strategy was driven overwhelmingly by party-political considerations: although he was personally in favour of British EC membership, the Labour Party was deeply divided over the question. In order to prevent an irrevocable rift within his party, Wilson therefore tried to outsource the debate from party politics into the national realm. In the short term, his strategy succeeded: although the final result of the renegotiations amounted to little substantial improvements, Wilson nonetheless proclaimed them to be a great victory and recommended continuing EC membership on these newly negotiated terms to the British people. In the subsequent referendum on 5 June 1975, 67.23 per cent voted in favour of EC membership, even if the vote seemed to signify the British peoples' resigned acceptance of a lack of alternatives rather than a whole-hearted endorsement of the European project (Saunders 2018). In the long run, however, the renegotiations had not only failed to adequately improve Britain's position in the EC's financial structures but they had also antagonized Wilson's European counterparts such as the French President Valéry Giscard d'Estaing or the West German Chancellor Helmut Schmidt (Haeussler 2015).

There were also other problems in Britain's relationship with its European partners. Although the Labour governments of Harold Wilson

(1974–6) and his successor James Callaghan (1976–9) repeatedly professed their desire for Britain to play its full part inside the EC, scepticism over future integrationist projects persisted nonetheless. The debates over direct elections to the European Parliament (EP) in the mid-1970s are a case in point (Chapter 7). Although the Labour Party had abandoned its blockade and finally sent off delegates to the EP after the referendum, it remained at best half-hearted over the idea of direct elections. Although Wilson eventually accepted direct elections in principle, there remained protracted disputes over precise voting mechanisms and dates. Again, the British position was bound up with domestic politics: not only did British public opinion remain sceptical about direct elections, fearing that it might contribute to a strengthening of the EP vis-à-vis the British Parliament and thus to a gradual erosion of national sovereignty, but the Labour Party had also recently lost its majority in the House of Commons and was kept in power only by a pact with the Liberals, who tied their support of direct elections to the principle of proportional representation. All of this meant that Britain kept delaying a decision on the issue, leading to the eventual postponement of the first direct elections from 1978 to June 1979.

More consequential was the British rejection of the European Monetary System (EMS) in 1978–9, which tied together European currencies within a fixed band of exchange rates in order to provide greater intra-EC stability and to offer better protection against external currency shocks. Although Prime Minister Callaghan clearly appreciated the scheme's potential value for European economies, he also saw a number of obstacles. First, and despite repeated reassurances to the contrary, Callaghan and some of his key advisers never quite overcame their belief that the EMS was designed to rival the US dollar, and that British participation might thus jeopardize the country's relationship with the United States in the long run. The British public's strong emotional attachment to the pound sterling as a symbol of national identity also played some part. Most importantly, however, Britain was suffering from severe domestic difficulties at the time: the Callaghan government had just failed to renew its 'social contract' with the British trade unions and now faced the prospect of inner-party rebellion as well as widespread industrial action and strikes. Faced by the combination of all these factors, Callaghan therefore decided not to take part in the scheme, and the EMS came into being without British participation (Mourlon-Druol 2012a; Haeussler 2019).

While these examples show the limits of how far British governments were prepared to go towards further European integration, Britain simultaneously proved a constructive EC member in many other policy areas. Regarding the EC as a potential vehicle for its post-imperial international influence, Britain played a particularly active role in trying to foster closer European cooperation in the fields of security and defence, not least within the newly established mechanisms for European Political

Cooperation (EPC). Following the US Secretary of State Henry Kissinger's ill-fated call for a 'Year of Europe' in 1973–4, for example, Britain coordinated its diplomatic response closely with the other West Europeans, and throughout the 1970s and 1980s it worked actively towards the creation and preservation of inner-European detente that was often at odds with the United States (Romano 2017). The stimulus of British influence was also felt inside the EC's supranational institutions: from 1977 to 1981, the high-profile Labour politician Roy Jenkins served as first British president of the European Commission and offered a new sense of direction and leadership for the embattled institution; the entry of British delegates into the EP also served to inject the country's lively and entertaining debating culture into the EP's proceedings (Ludlow 2016; Roos 2021a).

The arrival of Margaret Thatcher as British prime minister marked yet another break in Britain's relations with Europe. Although Thatcher, who had campaigned in favour of EC membership during the 1975 referendum, was determined that Britain should play its full part in the European integration process, she also insisted that, in order to do so, the country's disadvantageous standing in the EC's financing system had to be remedied first. The main problem was a structural one, caused by Britain's historically different trading and agricultural patterns: Britain traditionally imported large quantities of food and other goods from non-EC countries, for which levies and taxes went directly into the EC budget under the 'own resources' principle, whereas it had a comparatively small agricultural sector, into which, however, 70–75 per cent of EC expenditure went at the time. Simply put, Britain was paying a lot more into the EC budget than it got out of it. With the transitionary period of membership running out, Britain would soon be exposed to the full force of the system: by 1980, it was likely to become the largest or second largest net contributor to the EC budget even though it was also the third poorest member state at the time (Ludlow 2016; Seidel 2020b).

It was style, rather than substance, that made Thatcher's battle over the British Budgetary Question (BBQ) – or the Bloody British Question, as some called it – such a long and acrimonious one. Whereas Thatcher's predecessors had all sought to tackle the structural problem in a more or less communitarian way, for example by trying to offset Britain's high budget contributions with receipts from the European Regional Fund, Thatcher decided to address the issue in a much more confrontational way, tirelessly banging her handbag at European Council meetings and declaring that she wanted 'my money back'. While such performances surely propped up Thatcher's image as an uncompromising defender of British interests at home, it also alienated her European counterparts such as the French President Mitterrand or the West German Chancellor Helmut Schmidt and his successor Helmut Kohl. After many years of protracted haggling, Thatcher eventually achieved satisfaction: in June 1984, the Fontainebleau

European Council decided the so-called UK rebate which reduced Britain's net contribution to the EC budget by around two-thirds. It was a significant success in purely financial terms – but it also came at the cost of having yet again severely undermined the trust and confidence of Britain's European partners (Ludlow 2020).

Yet it would be a mistake to reduce Thatcher's European policy to such one-sided obstructionism. Even at the height of tensions over the BBQ, for example, Thatcher at the same time worked hard to foster common European positions in the realm of foreign and security policies against the background of worsening East–West relationships. Trying to preserve the political and economic interdependencies created by inner-European detente, Thatcher coordinated British policy closely with her European counterparts, not least by resisting US calls for far-reaching economic sanctions following the Soviet invasion of Afghanistan and the declaration of martial law in Poland (Colbourn and Haeussler 2021). Thatcher also frequently joined ranks with her European partners to tackle US President Ronald Reagan over the United States' high-deficit spending and its effects on West European interest rates, even if her pleas went largely unheard in Washington, DC (Basosi 2013; Haeussler 2019).

Thatcher's most significant contribution to the European integration process, however, came in the form of her energetic support for the Single European Act (SEA) (Warlouzet (2018a and 2018b). Although the creation of a truly single market had long been on the EC's agenda, the persistence of numerous non-tariff trade barriers still compromised significant parts of intra-EC trade. Together with the new Commission President Jacques Delors and the support of key member states such as France and Germany, Thatcher thus worked energetically for the further liberalization of intra-EC trade. The SEA matched both Thatcher's economic philosophy and her vision of the EC as a largely intergovernmental grouping of West European states to counter the effects of globalization and the technological advances of the United States and Japan. At the same time, however, the final version of the SEA was not entirely consistent with Thatcher's vision, particularly given the treaty's expansion of qualified majority voting (QMV) over harmonization. She also resisted attempts to complement the liberalization of intra-European trade with the establishment of common social policies or attempts to foster a greater sense of European identity. On 20 September 1988, Thatcher therefore reiterated her support for the SEA and closer intergovernmental cooperation in a speech at the College of Europe in Bruges. But she also warned against the creation of some 'identikit European personality' and famously declared that she had not 'successfully rolled back the frontiers of the state in Britain, only to see them re-imposed at a European level with a European super-state exercising a new dominance from Brussels'. It foreshadowed some of the rhetoric that eventually came to dominate the British discourse over European integration from the 1990s onwards.

FIGURE 17.2 *Visit of Margaret Thatcher, prime minister of the UK, at the European Parliament in Strasbourg, 1 December 1986. With a group of Members of the European Parliament supporting the removal of border controls. From left to right: Christiane Scrivener, Basil de Ferranti, Karl von Wogau, Margaret Thatcher, George Benjamin Patterson, Dieter Rogalla, Thomas Raftery and Fernand Herman. Courtesy of European Parliament Multimedia Center.*

# 3. 1990–2016: … the long way out?

The changes in the international landscape triggered by the end of the Cold War, such as the erosion of the Soviet Empire in Central and Eastern Europe and the reunification of Germany, had profound effects both on the European integration process and on British attitudes towards it. Whereas key EC member states such as France and Germany regarded the deepening of European integration as a reassurance against the potential political and economic power of a reunified Germany, many British politicians by contrast feared that it might actually constitute a mechanism for the potential revival of German power. These different strategic outlooks manifested themselves in the virulent debates over the Treaty of Maastricht, and they also stimulated the more general rise of Euroscepticism in British politics from the 1990s onwards.

The most acrimonious debates crystallized around the establishment of EMU, which had already been set in motion during the late 1980s and now received a strong political boost by the geopolitical changes in Europe. Whereas many European politicians, including the French President François Mitterrand as well as the German Chancellor Helmut Kohl, saw EMU as an opportunity to bind the reunified Germany irrevocably tight into larger European structures, Thatcher instead thought that the common currency might ultimately contribute to German political and economic dominance over its partners (Moore 2019). The most vocal articulation of such British views came from Thatcher's long-standing Secretary of Trade Nicholas Ridley, who famously declared in an interview with the conservative weekly *Spectator* that EMU was 'a German racket designed to take over the whole of Europe ... This rushed take-over by the Germans on the worst possible basis, with the French behaving like poodles to the Germans, is absolutely intolerable'. He also spoke out strongly against political union, declaring that he was 'not against giving up sovereignty in principle, but not to this lot. You might just as well give it to Adolf Hitler, frankly' (Lawson 1990, 8). Although Ridley's gaffe caused a huge outcry and ultimately led to his resignation, few observers doubted that his views reflected Thatcher's own feelings on the matter.

By 1990, the British government had become deeply split over the European question. Whereas Thatcher continued to resist moves towards EMU with often hostile appearances at European Council meetings, key ministers like the Chancellor of the Exchequer Nigel Lawson or Foreign Secretary Geoffrey Howe now openly advocated a more positive European policy, including above all British participation in the European Exchange Rate Mechanism (ERM). On 1 November 1990, Thatcher's former ally Howe resigned as deputy prime minister. In a devastating resignation speech, Howe roundly condemned Thatcher's European policies, which eventually triggered her fall from office a few days later. Her successor John Major promised to adapt more constructive positions in the intergovernmental conferences preparing the Treaty of Maastricht, but his position was severely compromised by Conservative in-fighting over European policy. He too proved ultimately unable to hold the competing fractions of his party together, resulting in Britain's half-hearted support for the Treaty of Maastricht and the insistence on British opt-outs from EMU and the social chapter. Major's efforts did little to slow the rise of Euroscepticism within his party, as well as the wider public: the British tabloid press had by now turned almost uniformly Eurosceptic, and the period also saw the establishment of the United Kingdom Independence Party (UKIP) and James Goldsmith's Referendum Party (Daddow 2012; Chapter 18).

If the Conservative Party slowly but surely came to embrace Euroscepticism from the late 1980s, then the opposite holds true for the Labour Party. In 1983, the party's left-wing leadership had still called for a complete British withdrawal from the Community, claiming that membership made it impossible to pursue socialist policies in Britain. By the early 1990s, however, Labour had reversed its position on Europe almost completely, a process that reflected the party's transformation into a more moderate, centre-left party at the time. From 1997 onwards, Labour Prime Minister Tony Blair endorsed British EU membership enthusiastically, signing Britain up to the social chapter of the Maastricht Treaty and even musing about the country's potential participation in the common currency. Yet significant differences over European policy within the government, including with the Chancellor of the Exchequer Gordon Brown, as well as the real or perceived constraints of public opinion, often led to more cautious British European policies than Blair may personally have liked. In 2002–3, some bigger strategic differences came to the fore when Blair strongly supported the US invasion of Iraq, but several EU member states such as France and Germany refused to follow the American lead.

When David Cameron was elected prime minister in 2010 after the Conservative Party's thirteen-year hiatus from government, a lot of pressure had built up within his party to address the European question. The pro-European stance of his coalition partner the Liberal Democrats, however, prevented Cameron from pursuing any more than symbolic moves, such as taking the Conservatives out of the European People's Party (EPP) group in the EP as it was considered too pro-European, or issuing a largely non-consequential British veto of the Fiscal Stability Treaty at a European Council meeting in December 2011 (Smith 2016). More significantly, however, Cameron also made the fateful decision to promise a renegotiation of the UK's relationship with the EU and then conduct a nationwide in/out referendum over continuing membership in case of a Conservative victory at the next elections. When the 2015 elections unexpectedly handed Cameron a full majority, he promptly embarked upon the renegotiations, in which he achieved some limited changes, including an 'emergency brake' on social benefits for EU immigrants and a largely symbolic opt-out from the EU's commitment to 'ever closer union'.

The 2016 referendum, however, soon became dominated by debates that had little if anything to do with the renegotiations. The proponents of continuing EU membership, above all Prime Minister Cameron and Chancellor of the Exchequer George Osborne, focused their arguments largely on the economic advantages of membership, strongly warning against the dangers of a potential withdrawal. By contrast, the opponents of membership stirred up fears over an erosion of British national sovereignty, which they often tied to concerns over EU immigration. Their strategy was helped by the existence of several different anti-EU campaigns, whose messages complemented each other well: whereas the official *Vote Leave* campaign focused its message primarily on the alleged constitutional and economic implications of membership, a message famously put across in its dubious claim that EU membership cost UK taxpayers £350 million a week, unofficial campaigns such as *Grassroots Out* and *Leave.EU* used street rallies and marches to stir up populist and often xenophobic fears over border control and immigration (Clarke, Goodwin and Whiteley 2017). In so doing, the Leave campaigns managed to successfully instrumentalize wider anti-immigration, anti-elite populist sentiments, and then project them onto the question of EU membership (Haeussler 2022).

Although Britain finally left the EU on 31 January 2020, the country's future relationship with European integration is still uncertain. After over forty years of membership, it proved difficult to disentangle the countless ways in which Britain had become interwoven with the EU's institutions and the other member states. Although Cameron's successor Theresa May formally triggered Article 50 of the Lisbon Treaty to initiate the withdrawal soon after the referendum, Britain proved unable to negotiate a satisfactory withdrawal agreement, let alone a post-exit trade agreement, within the envisioned time frame of two years. In particular, the British insistence on ending the free movement of workers, to avoid being subject to the Court of Justice of the EU, as well as on its future ability to strike independent trade deals ruled out most options for a so-called soft Brexit, such as continuing membership of the customs union. It also raised the very real possibility of a 'hard border' in Ireland, which would severely threaten the 'Good Friday' agreement and was thus unacceptable to the EU. While the Brexit Withdrawal Agreement was passed in January 2020 and the EU-UK Trade and Cooperation Agreement came into force the following year, key questions over the UK's future relationship with the EU still remain.

# Conclusion

Between 1945 and 2016, Britain came full circle in its relationship with European integration. Having first refused to join, it then applied twice for membership in the 1960s, only to be rejected each time by French President de Gaulle. Once inside, Britain found it hard to adjust to the realities of membership, not least regarding its high contributions to the EC budget and several initiatives for closer integration. Nonetheless, it played an important part in shaping the EC's transformation into a more coherent and visible actor in the 1970s and 1980s, working towards the completion of the Single Market and strongly supporting closer cooperation in foreign and security policies. From the 1990s onwards, however, the growing divisions over Europe within the Conservative Party increasingly compromised Britain's European policies and were ultimately at the heart of Cameron's decision to call a second referendum on EU membership in the 2010s. What broader lessons can be drawn from this story?

First, it is evident that Britain's late entry severely compromised both the country's standing within the Community frameworks and the wider public's attitudes towards the integration process. To be sure, this is not to say that late entry was a mistake, at least not based on the information available at the time: the British decision was based on serious (if perhaps short-sighted) considerations of Britain's interests in light of its global post-war strategy (Milward 2002). Nonetheless, the fact of British non-membership meant that the European Communities were built according to the preferences of the founding member states such as France and Germany, and that Britain eventually had to join institutions whose rules and regulations were not of its own making. It also meant that Britain was not part of the EEC during its unexpectedly rapid political consolidation and economic growth in the 1950s and 1960s. These two factors are part of the reason why there never emerged a solid cross-party consensus over Community membership in Britain, and why the European question always remained a playing card of domestic party politics.

The path dependencies resulting from Britain's belated membership also compromised Britain's role once inside the EC, where its attempts to readjust its own position within the EC framework often overshadowed its manifold positive contributions in many other areas of European integration. Given the structural disadvantages of Britain's standing within the EC framework, British politicians like Margaret Thatcher saw no contradiction between fighting aggressively for an improvement of Britain's standing within the EC institutions while at the same time still contributing proactively in other policy areas. Britain's European partners, however, increasingly came to regard British haggling over the basic rules and mechanisms of the EC as symptomatic of a British inability or unwillingness to come to terms with the very foundations of European integration. This led to a far-reaching erosion of trust in British European policy amongst its partners, which Britain never really managed to overcome.

Finally, however, it is also important to stress the role of contingency and chance in the history of Britain and European integration. While it is tempting to interpret the 'Brexit' vote of 23 June 2016 as the seemingly inevitable result of Britain's uneasy relationship with the EC/EU, there were many points in that history where the story could have taken a different turn. Personalities played an important part: Margaret Thatcher's confrontational and uncompromising negotiating style, for example, eventually came to overshadow her constructive engagement in many other areas, and the 'Brexit' vote too may have turned out rather differently had it not been for Boris Johnson's decision to campaign for a British withdrawal. The longer-term history of Britain and European integration can tell us much about why the European question became such a contested and virulent issue in British politics – but it cannot fully explain the outcome of the June 2016 referendum.

# Five key questions

1. Was it a mistake for Britain to not join the ECSC and/or the EEC from the outset?

2. Was French President Charles de Gaulle right to veto British membership in the 1960s?

3. To what extent, if at all, can Britain be seen as an 'awkward partner' of Europe during the 1970s and 1980s?

4. How important was Margaret Thatcher for the evolution of British attitudes towards European integration?

5. In what ways can the history of British attitudes towards European integration since the Second World War help us explain the 'Brexit' vote of 2016?

# Ten key readings

Aqui, L. (2020), *The First Referendum: Reassessing Britain's Entry to Europe, 1973–75*, Manchester: Manchester University Press.

Ellison, J. (2000a), *Threatening Europe: Britain and the Creation of the European Community, 1955–58*, Basingstoke: Macmillan.

George, G. (1994), *An Awkward Partner: Britain in the European Community*, Oxford: Oxford University Press.

Haeussler, M. (2019), *Helmut Schmidt and British-German Relations: A European Misunderstanding*, Cambridge: Cambridge University Press.

Ludlow, N. P. (1997), *Dealing with Britain: The Six and the First UK Application to the EEC*, Cambridge: Cambridge University Press.

Milward, A. S. (2002), *The Rise and Fall of a National Strategy, 1945–1963: The UK and the European Community*, vol. 1, London: Whitehall History. In association with Frank Cass.

Saunders, R. (2018), *Yes to Europe! The 1975 Referendum and Seventies Britain*, Cambridge: Cambridge University Press.

Warlouzet, L. (2018b), 'Britain at the Centre of European Co-operation (1948–2016)', *Journal of Common Market Studies*, 56 (4): 955–70.

Young, H. (1998), *This Blessed Plot: Britain and Europe from Churchill to Blair*, London: Macmillan.

Young, J. W. (1999), *Britain and European Unity 1945–1999*, 2nd ed., Basingstoke: Macmillan.

# 18

# Integrating or breaking up Europe? Euroscepticism and opposition to Europe

## *Carine Germond*

## Introduction

In November 2020, the non-partisan fact tank Pew Research Centre, based in the United States, published a survey showing that Europeans had a very favourable opinion of the European Union (EU). Ironically, this trend was even more conspicuous in the UK after Brexit, where positive views of the bloc climbed to a historic high, with 60 per cent saying they had a favourable opinion of the EU. A Eurobarometer survey conducted a year earlier had similar findings: 68 per cent of those polled felt EU countries had benefited from being part of the bloc while 61 per cent believed their country's EU membership was a good thing (European Parliament 2019). While these positive results may reflect a sense that the EU offers better protection against mounting social uncertainties and economic upheavals, they are astonishing as they come after years of rising scepticism about, contestation of and opposition to the EU.

Nevertheless, concluding from these two polls that opposition to European integration or the EU is receding would be hasty. Instead, they lay bare the current paradox at the heart of Europe: even though public support for the EU is at record highs, Euroscepticism is thriving. Many EU member states, including traditionally pro-European ones, have EU-critical or EU-hostile political parties that have been electorally successful. The 2016

Brexit vote illustrates the popular success and appeal of Euroscepticism to voters. The growing traction and public support that Eurosceptic parties have gained has contributed 'to both the democratization and legitimation of the EU as well as its potential disintegration' (Leruth, Startin and Usherwood 2018, 9).

Euroscepticism is a multifaceted and elusive phenomenon. Endeavours to conceptualize and categorize its myriad dimensions have resulted in a wealth of taxonomies, each attempting to capture the nature of Euroscepticism. The best known and most cited is by Aleks Szczerbiak and Paul Taggart, who identified 'hard' and 'soft' strains of Euroscepticism (Szczerbiak and Taggart 2008). They produced a two-by-two matrix of possible party positions on European integration structured along an EU pessimist/optimist and a Europhobe/Europhile axis.

Similarly, Petr Kopecký and Cas Mudde (2002) distinguished between specific and diffuse support for integration and European integration in general and offered a two-dimensional typology with four categories: Euro-enthusiast, Euro-pragmatic, Eurosceptic and Euro-reject. Deliberately avoiding the term 'Euroscepticism', Chris Flood (2009) developed a six-point continuum covering the entire range of party positions towards the EU ranging from rejectionists (opposition to EU membership or to participation in some institutions or policies) to maximalists (strong advocacy of further integration).

This chapter charts the origins and historical development of Euroscepticism. Contrary to popular opinion, European integration has been a contested process ever since its inception. The chapter first explores early contestation of European integration in a period (1950s–1980s) traditionally characterized by a tacit and largely indifferent support of integration by European public opinions. Secondly, it examines the shift to an increasing dissensus in the wake of important integrationist advances from the 1990s to the 2000s. Lastly, it discusses the growth of Eurosceptic attitudes in the wake of the multiple crises that have recently affected the EU.

# 1. A tacit consent? Early contestation and competing visions, 1950s–1980s

In 1949, a poster drawn by a Dutch artist Reyn Dirksen depicted a 'Europe' ship surfing the waves. This poster captured the strong pro-European spirit of the post-war period at a time when European countries rebuilt their economies and organized their cooperation. Yet, this positive image concealed the fact that European integration was – then and now – a conflict-laden, contentious process. This is principally demonstrated in the evolution of two of the principal forerunners to the modern EU. These were the European Coal and Steel Community (ECSC), founded in 1951, and the European Economic Community (EEC), founded in 1957. These were neither uncontroversial nor were they the guaranteed institutional solutions to the problems of the time (Gilbert 2008).

In the formative years of the ECSC and EEC, three central premises served to legitimize the existence and institutional form of European integration (Schrag Sternberg 2013). The first was the necessity to safeguard peace, security and economic recovery in Europe following the Second World War and in the context of the emerging Cold War. While some would later argue the cultural approach as a superior motivator for integration, a major success of the early advocates of European integration was to make economic integration the obvious and natural choice in seeking to achieve these objectives. This was ultimately a prioritization of a functionalist approach based on integrating economies over the promotion of other integration alternatives.

Secondly, while an environment of peace and prosperity was naturally desirable and uncontested, how it could be achieved was much more controversial. To this effect, the promotion of the post-national ideal of an indivisible, common European good, welfare and interest served to draw the attention away from the more contested nature of European integration. Accordingly, the founding treaties remained sketchy about the exact nature and goal of European integration, beyond the core, but vague, objective of an 'ever-closer union' enshrined in the Rome Treaty of 1957. The successive European treaties essentially established institutions whose purpose was to change the ways in which national, sectoral or particular interests would be achieved. The aim was to substitute historical rivalries – primarily between France and Germany – for a common destiny, which would make war materially impossible (Chapters 1 and 16).

Thirdly, the premise of a widely applicable legal structure served to direct the institutional form that European integration took. This priority also benefited integration by further depoliticizing the process of integrating, with law and legality eventually becoming cornerstone principles of the incipient Communities. A fundamental credo of the EU – and its forerunners, the ECSC and EEC – is that it is a rule- and law-based organization and a community of law (Chapter 6).

Yet, this idea of economic and supranational integration as the only way to peace and prosperity was never uncontested. Competing visions often centred on the crucial questions of how these objectives should be achieved and how the costs and benefits of integration should be divided (Schrag Sternberg 2013). Contrary to the 'founding fathers' of the EEC, the proponents of alternative integration projects deliberately politicized these questions at different historical junctures.

In the 1950s, the first group drew on federalist and national arguments, and primarily considered democracy as a vital condition for the Communities' legitimacy. In the 1960s, the second group supported an intergovernmental, rather than a supranational, counter-vision of integration as the better means of protecting nation states' sovereignty.

One of their most prominent proponents was Charles de Gaulle, a former French resistance leader and president of the French Republic (1958–69). The intergovernmental – and mainly Gaullist – challenge of the Communities' supranational elements was at the heart of the crises of the 1960s (Chapter 2). The final challenge to the Communities' legitimizing narrative of economic prosperity arose from the difficulties in finding appropriate European solutions to the financial and economic crises of the 1970s.

During the formative years of the EEC, opposition was generally limited to the political class. But instead of originating from a single party or member state, it arose from multiple disparate sources. In France, nationalist right parties and the French Gaullists opposed integration on the basis that it threatened national sovereignty. Communists and some socialists were among the most uncompromising opponents, often for ideological reasons. The former rejected European economic integration as a capitalist venture, while the latter were critical of the liberal economic and supranational principles on which it rested. These early 'Eurosceptics' were responsible for the failure of the European Defence Community (EDC) and the project of a European Political Community (EPC), which were voted down in the French parliament by a motley coalition in 1954.

Even in the strongly pro-European Federal Republic of Germany (FRG), the Social Democratic Party (SPD), the main West German opposition party, criticized the pro-integration policies pursued by the Christian Democratic Union (CDU)-led government of Chancellor Konrad Adenauer and voted against the establishment of the Council of Europe, the ECSC and the EDC. The party rejected the FRG's integration into Western Europe, fearing that it would be detrimental to achieving the aim of German unity. It also opposed the supranational and capitalist elements of the Communities and their poor democratic credentials. By the end of the 1950s, however, the SPD moved from opposing to supporting European integration and, in 1957, voted in favour of the ratification of the Rome Treaties. But unanimity was far from being prevalent in Adenauer's government. Prominent political personalities publicly adopted integration-sceptic positions. For example, Economics Minister and later Chancellor Ludwig Erhard, who is also credited with bringing about the German economic miracle, fought publicly and internally against the founding of the EEC. Erhard and the SPD joined forces in 1963 to impose a preamble to the Franco-German Elysée Treaty, which they felt threatened Germany's (and Europe's) close ties with the United States.

Across Europe in the later 1950s, an alternative idea of integration underlined Euroscepticism, rather than outright opposition to the principle of European solidarity. While a unified and powerful Europe was a central element of de Gaulle's thoughts, his alternative vision to supranational integration was the creation of a loose intergovernmental union or confederation of European nation states, in which France could project its influence. For him, sovereign nation states, not supranational, technocratic institutions, should take centre stage.

Although Erhard was principally in favour of European unity, he was also deeply sceptical of supranational integration within a small Community endowed with strong supranational institutions. Instead, he envisioned a much looser and larger free trade area which would include the UK and could serve as a framework for European economic cooperation. Socialist parties criticized first and foremost the capitalist, liberal and supranational aspects of integration and defended a vision of European cooperation resting on economic planning, rapprochement with Britain and mistrust of Germany.

While most of the political class supported European integration, an often indifferent and uninformed public opinion consented tacitly to European integration. This tacit consent was facilitated by the obvious advantages that integration brought during the post-war years, a period of unprecedented economic growth and prosperity with low unemployment, high average wages and mass consumption, highly developed welfare systems and upward social mobility. While these were not a direct consequence of European integration, the stability the Communities provided constituted a congenial environment for post-war economic expansion. This tacit consent has been described as a 'permissive consensus', a term first coined by two US political scientists, Leon Lindberg and Stuart Scheingold, in 1970 to describe the popular consensus support for the European Community (Lindberg and Scheingold 1970). This permissive consensus became a characteristic of the decades from the Treaty of Rome (1957) to the Maastricht Treaty (1992).

Up until the 1980s, despite occasional appearances in the EEC member states, Euroscepticism, as a rejection of European integration, remained predominantly confined to the UK. Before and even shortly after the accession of the country to the Community in 1973, the Labour Party, which had refused to participate in the Schuman Plan in 1950 and demanded renegotiations of the UK's accession treaty in 1974, was the main opponent of European integration. In the 1980s, this role was taken over by the Conservative Party whose position evolved from a pragmatic pro-Europeanism to a pragmatic Euroscepticism. Prime Minister Margaret Thatcher (1979–90) both embodied and brought about this change. She had occupied a ministerial function in the government that took the UK into the Communities, campaigned in favour of the 'yes' side in the referendum held in 1975 to validate Britain's EEC membership and signed the Single European Act (SEA) in 1986. But during her prime ministerial tenure, she adopted increasingly Eurosceptic and integration-hostile positions, such as her iconic 'No, No, No' to Economic and Monetary Union (1990).

A key moment of the shift in thinking among British Tories and the drift towards Euroscepticism was Thatcher's Bruges speech of 20 September 1988 (Box 18.1). In this speech, she clearly identified her preference for cooperation between sovereign states, her rejection of any control exerted by the Community supranational institutions and promoted a Thatcherite agenda of deregulation, openness and competition that went far beyond the free-market principles of the SEA. The speech was also a response to Commission President Jacques Delors's speech at the British Trade Unions Congress eight days before, on 12 September 1988, in which he defended his project of Social Europe precisely to address the perceived democratic deficit (Warlouzet 2022; Zaccaria 2021). Thatcher's Bruges speech was widely interpreted as legitimizing Euroscepticism in Britain.

## BOX 18.1 MARGARET THATCHER'S BRUGES SPEECH, 20 SEPTEMBER 1988

The Community is not an end in itself. Nor is it an institutional device to be constantly modified according to the dictates of some abstract intellectual concept.

Nor must it be ossified by endless regulation ...

Willing and active cooperation between independent sovereign states is the best way to build a successful European Community. To try to suppress nationhood and concentrate power at the centre of a European conglomerate would be highly damaging and would jeopardise the objectives we seek to achieve ...

Community policies must tackle present problems in a practical way, however difficult that may be. If we cannot reform those Community policies which are patently wrong or ineffective and which are rightly causing public disquiet, then we shall not get the public support for the Community's future development ...

My third guiding principle is the need for Community policies which encourage enterprise. If Europe is to flourish and create the jobs of the future, enterprise is the key. The basic framework is there: the Treaty of Rome itself was intended as a Charter for Economic Liberty. But that it is not how it has always been read, still less applied ...

Europe should not be protectionist. The expansion of the world economy requires us to continue the process of removing barriers to trade, and to do so in the multilateral negotiations in the GATT. It would be a betrayal if, while breaking down constraints on trade within Europe, the Community were to erect greater external protection ...

*Source*: Thatcher MSS (digital collection). Courtesy of Crown copyright (1988), Open Government Licence v.3.0.

It is not accidental that the Eurosceptic vocabulary enriched considerably during the Thatcher era. Although the terms 'anti-marketeers' and

'Eurosceptics' were often used interchangeably in the British press, a range of different variations ('Euro-phobes', 'Euro-rebels', etc.) emerged.

Opposition to European integration also came from outside Europe. Ever since the foundation of the ECSC, the Soviet Union had condemned European integration, which Soviet leaders regarded as a spawn of US capitalism. They were also concerned about the military threat it represented, both in facilitating the rebirth of German militarism and expanding the reach of the North Atlantic Treaty Organization in continental Europe as a direct threat to the Communist bloc. In the 1970s–1980s, the United States, formerly an active supporter of European integrationist efforts, reacted increasingly negatively to the desire of Europeans to assert themselves on the international scene. Growing economic, trade and diplomatic competition and rivalry between the United States and the Community elicited this change in attitude. In a speech delivered in New York in April 1973 (Box 18.2), Secretary of State Henry Kissinger proposed to rebuild transatlantic relations, which would be defined in an Atlantic Charter giving the United States a global role while relegating the Nine EEC countries to a strictly regional role.

## BOX 18.2  HENRY KISSINGER'S 'YEAR OF EUROPE' SPEECH, NEW YORK, 23 APRIL 1973

The problems in Atlantic relationships are real. They have arisen in part because during the fifties and sixties the Atlantic community organized itself in different ways in the many different dimensions of its common enterprise.

– In economic relations the European Community has increasingly stressed its regional personality; the United States at the same time must act as part of, and be responsible for, a wider international trade and monetary system. We must reconcile these two perspectives.

– In our collective defence we are still organized on the principle of unity and integration, but in radically different strategic conditions. The full implications of this change have yet to be faced.

– Diplomacy is the subject of frequent consultations but is essentially being conducted by traditional nation states. The United States has global interests and responsibilities. Our European allies have regional interests. These are not necessarily in conflict, but in the new era neither are they automatically identical.

...

No element of American postwar policy has been more consistent than our support of European unity. We encouraged it at every turn. We knew that a united Europe would be a more independent partner. But we assumed, perhaps too uncritically, that our common interests would be assured by our long history of cooperation. We expected that political unity would follow economic integration and that a unified Europe working cooperatively with us in an Atlantic partnership would ease many of our international burdens. It is clear that many of these expectations are not being fulfilled.

Source: *The Department of State Bulletin*. Dir. of publ. Department of State. 14.05.1973, n° vol. LXVIII. Washington: US Government Printing Office. 'The Year of Europe', pp. 593–8. Courtesy Department of State (public domain).

The administrations of Presidents Richard Nixon (1969–74) in particular and to a lesser extent Jimmy Carter (1977–81) regularly attempted to impede the international actions of the Nine through deliberate attempts to undermine European coordination on foreign policy matters. Effectively disrupting integration in this area, such US opposition would become a recurring feature of American politics in the following decades.

## 2. The emergence and consolidation of a constraining dissensus, 1990s–2000s

There is wide acceptance that the post-Maastricht period saw a growing proportion of the EU population opposing further integration, with increasing numbers of Europeans either hostile to or ambivalent about further integration. The permissive consensus which had prevailed in first three decades of the EU's existence was replaced by what Lisbeth Hooghe and Gary Marks (2008) termed a 'constraining dissensus'. In essence, the term means that political leaders can no longer take for granted acceptance and support but must rather make room for a more Eurosceptic public. The rising salience of European issues, including economic and social benefits (and losses), immigration and national sovereignty, in some respects explain this increased politicization of European integration in elections and referendums.

Treaty revisions have provided a fertile ground for the politicization of European matters and the expression of Eurosceptic views. Treaty reform was necessary to adapt the framework of European legislation and policies to prepare for the accession of new member countries, introduce new areas of cooperation – such as the single currency – or improve the decision-making capabilities of an enlarging union. The drawn-out process of treaty revisions resulted in five major amendments: the Maastricht Treaty (1992), the Amsterdam Treaty (1997), the Nice Treaty (2001), the Constitutional Treaty (2004) and the Lisbon Treaty (2007). In some countries, the constitutional requirement to hold popular consultation as part of the ratification process enabled Eurosceptics to draw attention to and popularize their views. The referendums and the 'No' vote in certain member states unveiled the growing gap between broadly EU-supportive political elites and an ever more sceptical public. Through this process, three main fault lines emerged.

The first of these highlights the protest-based nature of Euroscepticism and relates to a growing malaise vis-à-vis democratic institutions and/or the political class. The continued decrease in voter turnout at European Parliament (EP) elections (Figure 18.1) reflects in part this democratic discontent. The highest ever achieved turnout occurred in the first EP direct elections, held in 1979, but voter turnout declined in every subsequent election.

Although the EP is the only directly elected EU institution, European elections continue to be perceived as 'second-order' elections. Moreover, the EP still has a reputation for being a weak body, although it is an equal co-legislator with the Council since 2007. Yet there is also a specifically Eurosceptic dimension to those who do not vote in EP elections. Abstainers come predominantly from the electorate of anti-establishment parties and particularly extreme-right, anti-European parties. They are more likely to be dissatisfied with the way representative democracy works in their countries or defiant of the political establishment and opposed to further European integration. In addition to abstention in EP elections, low trust in democratic institutions and scepticism towards the political class were major motives behind the no-vote in the 2005 referendums in France and the Netherlands and the 2008 referendum in Ireland.

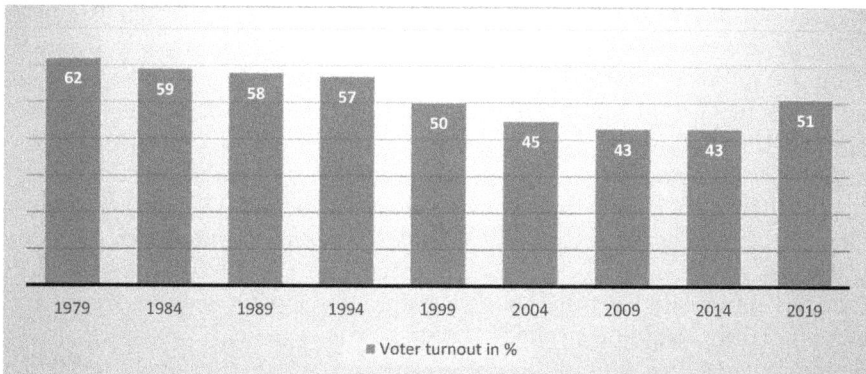

FIGURE 18.1 *Voter turnout in the European Parliament elections, 1979–2019.*
*Source*: Author's own compilation based on various issues of the Eurobarometer.*

* Percentages rounded up or down to the closest full number.

A second characteristic of the post-Maastricht Eurosceptic debate concerned the redistributive benefits of European integration. Although confrontations over the social and economic dimension of European integration were not new, the completion of the Internal Market raised fears among certain segments of the population. Eurobarometer surveys from the period revealed a growing gap between the better educated/ skilled who were more supportive and the less educated/skilled who tended to be less supportive. Accordingly, no-voters in referendums on European integration or treaties were often found among the manual workers and the less educated citizens, a population notably more directly affected by the economic recession of the 1990s. Demands for a greater social integration remained, even as popular opposition to a form of neoliberal integration that put market and corporate interests before those of workers expanded. In conjuring up images of a Europe as a Trojan horse for unregulated neoliberal globalization, the simultaneous rise of the anti-globalization movement bolstered anti-EU sentiments. These issues, among others, were especially key for French no-voters in the 2005 referendum.

As the third component of Euroscepticism in the period, the loss of national identity, representation and national sovereignty ranked high in the concerns of sceptical Europeans. In the first Irish referendum, worries about a fair representation of smaller countries were central for explaining the Irish no-vote to the Nice Treaty in 2001. Similarly, a poll conducted in 2005 before the referendum on the Constitutional Treaty showed that a large portion of the Dutch population thought that smaller member states would lose influence. These fears often crystallized around diminished voting powers in the Council and the possible loss of a commissioner.

Enlargement has provided another source of discontent. Since its creation, the EU has expanded continuously from the original six member states to the present-day EU of twenty-seven. Each enlargement widened the Union's geographical scope and policy remit with the largest and most challenging being the accession of the twelve former Communist countries in Central and Eastern Europe after the fall of the Berlin Wall. Long considered one of European integration's most prominent success, the successive enlargement rounds brought Europe back together and exemplified the effectiveness of the EU's transformative 'soft power' in delivering stability, democracy and prosperity to its new members (Chapters 14 and 15). Yet, since the last and biggest enlargement, this positive assessment has given way to scepticism. Enlargement fatigue, a generic term for EU citizens' and member states' hesitancy vis-à-vis the Union's geographic expansion and fear of its economic and social impact, has become a critical issue. It prompted Jean-Claude Juncker, president of the European Commission from 2014 to 2019, to express doubts over whether the EU would continue to expand after Croatia joined in 2013.

The elitist nature of the enlargement process – except for the French referendum on British membership in 1972 citizens have not been consulted on the accession of new members – accounts partially for the disaffection of the public. The political and historical necessity of enlargement was deemed more important than any active engagement with the European public on the matter. Ultimately passive dissatisfaction gave way to more active popular questioning of the success and benefits of enlargement, particularly in the 'older' member states. The negative reactions to and protests against the controversial Directive on Services in the Internal Market, the infamous 'Bolkestein Directive' (2003–5), highlighted mounting social anxieties linked to enlargement. Likewise, sovereigntist, anti-EU parties in the context of the debate on the Constitutional Treaty used the popular image of the 'Polish plumber' as a symbol emphasizing the threat of social dumping and the EU's alleged dismantling of social protection systems.

Enlargement furthermore spurred a debate about the nature and limits of European integration: could an enlarging Union still achieve the goal of closer political union? If so, how? Should it include all the member states or only those willing and able to move forward? What should the EU's borders be? In the context of Turkey's EU membership application, this last question had particular salience. Associated with the EU since 1963, the Turkish government had applied for EU membership in 1987. Accession negotiations began in 2005 but stalled in 2007 due to opposition from certain member states and increasing concerns about Turkish President Recep Erdoğan's clampdown on media freedom and democracy. The prospect of the accession of a Muslim country fuelled enlargement-sceptic discourses about the Union's identity and its Christian heritage. Besides, were it to join, Turkey would be the most populous state, bringing with it considerable weight in the Council of Ministers and in the EP. To reassure an ever more enlargement-sceptic public, the French government introduced in 2007 a clause in its Constitution that instituted an obligatory referendum on future EU enlargements.

Lastly, the EU's failure to develop a new narrative beyond peace and prosperity further fuelled critics of enlargement. Persisting institutional flaws, economic recession and war in Yugoslavia, and a perceived lack of democratic legitimacy and accountability – the infamous 'democratic deficit' – provided a fertile ground on which Eurosceptic rhetoric could prosper, even more so since crisis hit European shores in the late 2000s.

# 3. Crisis Europe and the rising tide of Euroscepticism, 2000s–2020s

Since 2008–9, the EU has been mired in a polymorphous crisis which has galvanized opposition to Europe. The financial and economic crisis called into question one of its central legitimizing pillars: the economic prosperity it promises to deliver its citizens. The migration crisis highlighted the profound division of European leaders and their blatant inability to find appropriate solutions to the continent's biggest humanitarian crisis since the Second World War (Chapters 4 and 12). Worse, it has emboldened sovereignist parties, which advocate for closed borders and a return to the nation state, in a direct challenge of the EU's core principles of solidarity and free movement. Moreover, the EU is facing a crisis of values with member states where governments overtly undercut liberal democracy, for example, in Hungary with the return to power of Viktor Orbán in 2010 and in Poland since 2015. Democratic backsliding and the rise of neo-authoritarian, Eurosceptic governments in these countries thus pose a serious existential threat to the EU (Van Middelaar 2021).

These multifaceted crises question the EU's nature and purpose and have nurtured a growing popular discontent. As a result, the past two decades have seen the rise of Eurosceptic, often radical right, and populist political movements in several EU member states – old and new. Euroscepticism has grown into a mainstream element of European politics. Anti-EU rhetoric and arguments opposing or rejecting European integration or, in a milder form, demanding far-reaching reforms often requiring the repatriation of powers from the EU to the national level have become more commonplace, including among mainstream political parties.

The growing electoral appeal of Eurosceptic parties is particularly visible in some member states. One of the most significant far-right parties is the French Eurosceptic National Rally (RN), a party that has made substantial electoral gains since its current leader, Marine Le Pen, took over. Within a decade, it has gone from a relatively marginal, sulphurous party lacking any presence in parliament to obtaining seats in both the National Assembly and the Senate, presiding in regions and cities and expanding its traditional voter base to new groups. During the 2017 presidential elections, Le Pen campaigned with a nationalist, anti-immigration, anti-EU electoral platform, advocating in favour of a referendum on 'Frexit', a return to the French franc, stricter controls of borders and immigration and, more broadly, the return of the nation state. She finished second in the elections. Running again (unsuccessfully) in the French presidential race in 2022, she has meanwhile abandoned her (unpopular) plans for leaving the EU and the euro. Yet, that mainstream parties on both the left and the right have adopted some of her rhetoric on national identity or immigration illustrates the appeal of a brand of nationalist-populist Euroscepticism.

Brexit remains undeniably the most prominent success for Eurosceptic parties. Promoted originally as a single issue by Nigel Farage's United Kingdom Independence Party (UKIP), it resulted in the rejection of European integration by a (slim) majority of Britons. The negative outcome of the 2016 referendum – 51.9 per cent voted to leave the EU, 48.1 per cent voted to remain – owed to several factors. In addition to a deeply Eurosceptic public and an influential EU-hostile press, there were high levels of citizen uncertainty regarding the economic benefits of integration and EU freedom of movement. These concerns were successfully exploited by UKIP in controversial campaign posters picturing immigration as a direct threat to British jobs or as reaching 'breaking point'. Deep divisions among mainstream political parties on the EU, including David Cameron's Conservative Party, played into the hands of the Eurosceptics. But it also had specific domestic origins: British EU membership was traditionally understood and evaluated in terms of costs-benefits rather than by emotional attachment or historical responsibility (Chapter 17). Yet Brexit did not have the disintegrating domino effect many feared. For the time being, the protracted and difficult Brexit negotiations seem to have softened Eurosceptic attitudes in some of the more traditionally Eurosceptic EU member states, such as Denmark.

Eurosceptics have not only been successful domestically but have also established a presence in the EP itself. Ironically, it is this arena that has served as a political platform for some of the most notorious adversaries of the EU. That said, even with the first Eurosceptic group formed in 1992, the Eurosceptic family has never been united; Eurosceptic forces often share no other ties than their common opposition to the European integration project. Rather, it is a motley group of left to centre-right, conservative to far-right, sovereigntist parties with soft to hard Eurosceptic stances. Since they first entered the EP, Eurosceptic parties have formed various political groups to reflect their Eurosceptic preferences (Table 18.1).

This being the case, the Eurosceptic vote is often divided. In the EP, the Austrian Freedom Party (FPÖ), the German Alternative for Germany (AfD), the French RN, the Italian Northern League (Liga) and the Dutch Party for Freedom form a right-wing and strongly Eurosceptic front. On the left, however, a more moderately anti-EU grouping features the Italian Five Star Movement, among others. Finally, a collection of right-wing and moderate anti-EU parties includes the Hungarian Fidesz as well the Polish Law and Justice party, although these two have moved closer to more radical Euroscepticism in recent years. These parties also strongly diverge on several important issues, such as relations with Vladimir Putin's Russia, immigration, economic and monetary policies and EU membership. Yet, their presence in the EP (Table 18.2) illustrates the Europeanization of Euroscepticism, which has become a transnational and pan-European phenomenon.

Although the 2019 EP election witnessed the highest voter turnout in thirty-five years, Euroscepticism remains a significant political phenomenon across the EU. The economic and migration crises have undermined the EU as a political project legitimized by its performance and achievements. The Eurozone members that have been hit hardest by the eurozone crisis, such as Italy and Greece, have become deeply critical of the EU. In other traditionally pro-European members such as France and Italy, Euroscepticism has also taken deep root. Moreover, a rampant Euroscepticism mixed with nationalist and populist tendencies has emerged in some of the newer member states,

**Table 18.1** *Eurosceptic political groups in the European Parliament, 1979–2024*

| Name | Acronym | Ideology | Period |
|---|---|---|---|
| Identity and Democracy | ID | Right-wing to far-right, nationalist Euroscepticism Successor of MNEL | 2019–pres. |
| Europe of Nations and Liberties | MNEL | Nationalist, right-wing populist and Eurosceptic | 2014–19 |
| European Conservatives and Reformists | ECR | Conservative, anti-federalist, right-wing, Euroscepticism | 2009–pres. Known as the Alliance of Conservatives and Reformists in Europe (2016–19) and Alliance of European Conservatives and Reformists (2009–16) |
| Independence and Democracy group | ID/DEM | Successor group of EDD | 2004–9 |
| Europe of Democracies and Diversities | EDD | Sovereigntist Euroscepticism | 1999–2004 |
| Europe of Freedom and Democracy | EFD | Right-wing Euroscepticism | 2009–14 |
| Alliance of European National Movements | AENM | Far-right, ultra-nationalist, sovereigntist, Euroscepticism | 2009–14 |

| Name | Acronym | Ideology | Period |
|---|---|---|---|
| Europeans United for Democracy – Alliance for a Europe of Democracies | EUDemocrates | Reformist Euroscepticism Centre-left faction of the IND/DEM | 2005–9 |
| Alliance of Independent Democrats in Europe | AIDE | Nationalist, sovereigntist, Euroscepticism Centre-right faction of the IND/DEM group | 2005–8 |
| Alliance for Europe of Nations | AEN | Conservative and national-conservative Euroscepticism | 2002–9 |
| Union for Europe of the Nations | UEN | National-conservative Euroscepticism | 1999–2009 |
| European Democrats | ED | Liberal-conservative Euroscepticism | 1994–2009 (associated with EPP) 1979–92 (independent group) |

*Source*: Author's compilation.

**Table 18.2** *The main Eurosceptic parties and their political groups in the European Parliament, 2019–2024*

| Country | Party | EP political group |
| --- | --- | --- |
| Germany | AfD (Alternative for Germany) | ID |
| France | National Rally | ID |
| Italy | 5 Stars | Non-attached (NI) |
| | Northern League | ID |
| Sweden | Swedish Democrats | ECR |
| Austria | Austrian Freedom Party | ID |
| Netherlands | Forum for Democracy | ECR |
| Denmark | Danish People's Party | ID |
| Finland | True Finns | ID |
| Greece | Golden Dawn | Non-attached (NI) |
| Poland | Law and Justice | ECR |
| Hungary | FIDESZ Hungarian Civic Alliance | ECR (joined in Spring 2021 after leaving the EPP) |

*Source*: Author's compilation based on https://www.europarl.europa.eu/election-results-2019/en/
breakdown-national-parties-political-group/2019-2024/.

although the population remains more sympathetic towards the EU than its political class.

The outbreak of the Covid-19 pandemic in Europe in early 2020 brought European economies to their knees. Although the EU provided generous recovery plans to help address the economic and social fallouts from the pandemic and purchased vast quantities of vaccines, Eurosceptic forces have been quick to gleefully point to flaws in the EU's response. These criticisms include the absence of a truly unified EU-level approach to the lockdowns, the introduction of temporary border controls and quarantine measures and vaccine roll-out hiccups. Yet Euroscepticism in Covid times looks more divided than ever. Some, such as the Italian Northern Liga, have toned down their anti-Brussels rhetoric and face growing competition from the national conservative 'Brothers of Italy', a party with roots in the neo-fascist right. The far-right 'Brothers of Italy', which dominates the conservative alliance of right-wing parties, won a majority in both houses of the Italian Parliament in the September 2022 elections. A few others, such as the German AfD, are still positioning themselves as favourable to their country's exit from the EU, while others advocate for an alternative European project. Which of these path(s) Eurosceptic parties will ultimately choose when post-crisis normality returns is likely to depend on how effectively the socio-economic consequences of the Covid-19 crisis and the war in Ukraine are managed within the EU.

# Conclusion

The history of Euroscepticism is in essence a story of the struggle between different conceptions and visions of what Europe should be and how (or at what pace) it should integrate. Critical attitudes, competing visions or even active contestation have been an intrinsic part of the European integration process, although opposition to it was traditionally viewed as marginal or exceptional until the 1980s. Tacit consent and broadly positive attitudes towards the EC prevailed in most European states, while opposition among the elite remained marginal, temporary or sectoral (Leconte 2010). European integration was predominantly seen as a non-issue for the public. The deliberately imprecise character of the European project helped the emergence and consolidation of the permissive consensus in the post-war era.

A discernible change occurred in the context of the SEA that prompted increasingly diverging views among the elites. Since the Maastricht Treaty in 1992, a crucial crystallization point of opposition to European integration, Euroscepticism has grown in extent and scope to become a mainstream phenomenon that encompasses a broad diversity of sceptic and oppositional attitudes and political ideologies. With the growth of EU competences in areas of 'high politics' – economic and monetary union, foreign relations, security, defence, immigration, asylum and policing – the lives of Europeans and national states' sovereignty are more directly impacted. In this light, public consensus on the EU has eroded and political contestation has increased. This shift is accompanied by a growing polarization of public opinions and political parties on the EU.

The roots of Euroscepticism are multifarious and complex, but they are not mutually exclusive. Some of the Eurosceptic frustration focuses particularly on 'Brussels' as the incarnation of an EU that is aloof and incomprehensible. The Commission is regularly accused of regulating too much, of being a technocratic, opaque, unelected and dissipative body. But even the EP is not immune to criticism. The record-high level of abstention for EP elections exemplifies the diffusion of Euroscepticism across EU member states. Moreover, when treating the EU as a scapegoat for the ills affecting member states, national governments often play unwittingly into the hands of Eurosceptics.

Opposition to enlargement and immigration also feature strongly in Eurosceptic discourse and feed into concerns for economic stability and identity solidarity. Such concerns are directly linked to further economic arguments against deeper integration, primarily citing the topics of unfair economic competition and an unbridled liberalism that undermines domestic welfare and social protection systems. European integration has therefore been perceived increasingly in terms of oppositions between an economically and socially regulated Europe and a Europe of the free trade and globalization (Chapter 8). This neoliberal EU exacerbates the divides between the 'winners' and 'losers' of globalization, between those who benefit the most from the opportunities arising from the Internal Market and those who do not.

Furthermore, fears for the nation state as an independent and sovereign entity with a unique national character have been historical fixtures of Eurosceptic discourses. Opposition to Europe thus remains characterized by the tension between the nation states and Europe along with the conflicting dichotomy of proponents for strengthened national competencies and the advocates of expanding powers for European supranational institutions.

Finally, Euroscepticism is not confined to the EU. It can also originate from third countries who might fear that a strong united Europe would become an economic and/or political rival or even a menace for its partners or opponents. They might dislike the EU's attempt to disseminate its shared values and principles and thus try to undermine the process of European integration.

As has been demonstrated in this chapter, Euroscepticism is not a one-dimensional phenomenon. Rather it refers to a whole array of positions towards the practical ways of integration, from reservations to outright hostility and rejection. When Eurosceptics call the EU into question, it is not always to abolish it altogether. Sometimes they promote alternative visions of European integration to make it closer to EU citizens, more democratic and more social or, on the contrary, more liberal and more respectful of national sovereignty. Only time will tell how its identity will evolve with a new crises or popular movement.

# Five key questions

1.   What is Euroscepticism?
2.   Why is Euroscepticism a contested concept?
3.   What are the main drivers of Euroscepticism in the EU?
4.   How have Eurosceptic attitudes evolved since 1951?
5.   How are Eurosceptic parties represented in the EU?

# Ten key readings

Brack, N. (2018), *Opposing Europe in the European Parliament: Rebels and Radicals in the Chamber*, London: Palgrave Macmillan.
Flood, C. (2009), 'Dimensions of Euroscepticism', *Journal of Common Market Studies*, 47 (4): 911–17.
Gilbert, M., and D. Pacquinucci (eds) (2020), *Eurosceptiscisms: The Historical Roots of a Political Challenge*, Leiden: Brill.
Kopecký, P., and C. Mudde (2002), 'The Two Sides of Euroscepticism: Party Positions on European Integration in East Central Europe', *European Union Politics*, 3 (3): 297–326.
Leconte, C. (2010), *Understanding Euroscepticism*, Basingstoke: Palgrave Macmillan.
Leruth, B., N. Startin and S. Usherwoods (eds) (2018), *The Routledge Handbook of Euroscepticism*, Abingdon: Routledge.
Levi, G., and D. Preda (eds) (2019), *Eurosceptiscisms: Resistance and Opposition to the European Community/European Union*, Bologna: Il mulino.
Schrag Sternberg, C. *The Struggle for EU Legitimacy: Public Contestation 1950–2005*, Basingstoke: Palgrave Macmillan.
Szcerbiak, A., and P. Taggart (eds) (2008), *Opposing Europe? The Comparative Party Politics of Euroscepticism*, 2 vols, Oxford: Oxford University Press.
Taylor, P. (2008), *The End of European Integration: Anti-Europeanism Explained*, Abingdon: Routledge.

# Websites

Eurobarometer: https://europa.eu/eurobarometer/screen/home.
Provides access to the EU's regular public opinion surveys.
The PopuList: https://popu-list.org/.
A peer-reviewed website offering an overview of populist, far right, far left and Eurosceptic parties in Europe since 1989.

# 19

# Interpretations of European integration history and introduction to research tools

## Brigitte Leucht, Katja Seidel and Laurent Warlouzet

## Introduction

This chapter discusses the historiography of European integration. Reflecting the approach of our book, we do not equate the history of European integration with that of the European Union (EU), narrowly defined as the development of an international organization (IO) over time. As the contributions to this book demonstrate, European integration history encompasses more than the history of a series of public policies ranging from agriculture to competition and trade. The history of the EU also analyses the impact of political, economic and legal integration on the member states making up the 'Europe' of the EU; it tells the story of the development of European societies from 1945; and it tries to understand how these changes are embedded in a wider set of processes, including the Cold War, decolonization, social and societal struggles and the upheaval in Europe's political economies stirred by globalization and the rise of neoliberalism from the 1980s (Patel 2020). From this wider perspective – transcending a focus on institutions and policymaking – the history of European integration is nothing less than the history of how we came to be where we are: as Europeans, as EU citizens, even as citizens of states associated in various forms with the EU and all of this within an increasingly global context. If we add to this argument that European integration has impacted on all aspects of life ranging from the exercise of political rights to consumption and to the challenges of our time, including the threat to the environment and social inequality, then we need to ask ourselves the crucial question of how historians have defined, approached and explained 'European integration' as the object of their study over time.

The chapter will first outline the origins and institutionalization of EU history. Nowadays the historiography of European integration is extremely varied (Gehler 2016) but it had its origins in two approaches that were more narrowly concerned with explaining the phenomenon of European integration itself. These two approaches, usually termed the 'federalist' and the 'nation-state' perspective, will be outlined in the second part of the chapter. These early debates offered all-encompassing explanations regarding the drivers, processes and objectives of European integration. From the early 2000s, historians have become more reluctant to advance overall explanations of European integration presenting instead a wider and more complex field of study. While this trend complicates the categorization and presentation of the field, in the third part of the chapter we will argue that this historiography can be characterized by a few partly overlapping trends, focusing on (1) adopting an interdisciplinary perspective and (2) embedding EU history within a wider historiography. The chapter concludes with an overview of online archives and other web resources.

# 1. The origins and the institutionalization of EU history

Generally speaking, historians were latecomers to the study of European integration, a field that was first pioneered by political scientists, International Relations (IR) scholars, economists and lawyers in the 1950s, describing the emergence of the European Coal and Steel Community and studying the founding treaties (Diebold 1959). In 1958 Ernst Haas, a US scholar of international relations, published his seminal *Uniting of Europe* ([1958] 2004), advancing the European integration theory of 'neo-functionalism'. Neo-functionalist theory anticipates that European states would slowly disappear. European integration is conceptualized as a gradual process in which the notion of 'spillover' represents an important element. Accordingly, integration in one policy sector – a 'low politics' sector such as trade rules – creates pressures for integration in other, related sectors. As the functional areas of government become more integrated, the political and bureaucratic or technocratic elites administering these policies would increasingly switch their loyalties, expectations and goals from the national government arena to the overall aims of the integration agencies. Spillover of integration from one sector to others, driven by an elite socialized into the European integration project, would therefore ultimately lead to political community (Haas [1958] 2004; Leucht 2017).

The 'set-back' to European integration symbolized by the Empty Chair Crisis and the Luxembourg compromise (1966) appeared to (temporarily) discredit the explanatory value of neo-functionalism. The theory was given a new lease of life from the 1990s in the context of the 'completion' of the single market (Sandholtz and Stone Sweet 1998). Neo-functionalism gave way to intergovernmentalism, which highlighted the role of (large) member states (Germany, France and, from 1973, the UK) in driving European integration (Milward 1984 and 1992; Moravcsik 1998). Historians did not engage with theory at this time. However, in explaining European integration, the theory of neo-functionalism shares important assumptions with early 'federalist' historiography which would be developed from the 1960s by the German historian Walter Lipgens. The theory of intergovernmentalism on the other hand shared many assumptions with historians adopting an approach that sought to demonstrate the importance of nation states and national interests in the development of European integration, such as the British historian Alan Milward (the contributions of both historians are discussed in the next section). See Table 19.1 for the affinities and overlaps between theoretical and historical approaches.

But how can we account for the historians' late arrival to the study of European integration? One important reason is that most historians rely on the availability of archival material for their work. Most archives, including those of governments and the archives of EU institutions, have

**Table 19.1** *Neo-functionalism/federalism versus intergovernmentalism/nation-state approach*

| Theory/ approach | Neo-functionalism | Federalism | Intergovernmentalism | Nation-state approach |
|---|---|---|---|---|
| Key scholars of European integration | Ernst B. Haas, Leon Lindberg, Stuart Scheingold | Walter Lipgens | Stanley Hoffman, Andrew Moravcsik | Alan S. Milward |
| Driving forces of European integration | Non-state actors (e.g. interest groups, businesses, European institutions) | Non-state actors (resistance movements) | Nation-states | Nation-states (mostly economic interests but not always) |
| How is European integration advanced? | 'Spillover' from one policy area to the next | Influence of ideas on people and leaders | Grand bargains at intergovernmental conferences | Inter-state bargaining |

a thirty-year embargo before they are able to release documents. This is both an advantage and a disadvantage. Compared to other disciplines that rely on published material such as speeches, interviews, published official documents, newspapers and observations, historians often wait a long time before approaching a subject. The advantage of using archival material is that those documents often reveal some of the real motivations of actors that are usually missing in public documents. Historians can therefore achieve a more nuanced narrative, in particular if they opt for a multi-archival and multi-perspective approach, which most EU historians do. They are also not driven by the urge of establishing and then proving a theory or grand narrative. The disadvantage is that EU historians' work is sometimes piecemeal, narrow and remains overlooked by other disciplines, for example, political scientists who are looking for a grand narrative and bold interpretations of EU history and the driving forces of European integration.

Given the delay on the release of archival documents from governments and EU institutions, it is not surprising that the first historians of EU integration, for instance, the aforementioned Walter Lipgens, started their investigation into the origins of the European idea and subsequently European institutions only in the late 1960s. Crucially, this historiography was not impacted by the thirty-year rule, as it focused on transnational pressure groups and built its accounts on non-governmental archival sources (Lipgens 1968; 1977). The lasting impact of this historiography is to have established the professional study of European integration as a field in its own right (Kaiser 2002; Loth 2012). In contrast, limited access to governmental sources 'delayed' historians who approached the study of European integration from the perspective of the member states, including examining the motivations of member-state governments for concluding international treaties (1951 and 1957) and negotiating new policies such as agriculture in the early 1960s.

From the 1980s, the history of European integration has become institutionalized and also better funded. The European University Institute (EUI), a European institution independent from the European Economic Community (EEC)/EU, was created in 1972 in Florence. It hosts a chair of European integration history, whose rotating system (the tenure is eight years) has ensured a regular flow of scholars, among them some of the most renowned historians of the field, starting with Walter Lipgens and Alan Milward and, more recently, Kiran Klaus Patel and Federico Romero.

In 1982, an association of historians from the EEC member states, the European Community Liaison Committee of Historians (today called EU Historians), was established and benefited, for the first two decades of its existence, from some financial support from EEC institutions (Calligaro 2013). This group created the *Journal of European Integration History* in 1995, which still exists and helps to structure the field. Other networks were established outside of the Liaison Committee and its activities, including the Research Group on European Identity in the Twentieth Century (1988), initiated by René Girault and then managed by Robert Frank. This group focused on examining the *forces profondes* and mentalities in Europe in the twentieth century, an indication of the breadth of the field. In parallel, in the 1990s, the Commission created so-called Jean Monnet programmes and chairs to promote the teaching of European Studies, notably in law and political science, but also in history. Lastly, in the early 2000s, two postgraduate student networks of historians were established, HEIRS and RICHIE. After having established a common website and mailing-list (see Guide to web resources), they have helped to circulate information and knowledge among new generations of researchers.

The institutionalization of the field in turn led to the accusation of historians of European integration being too supportive of EEC/EU institutions, and too narrowly centred on them. Arguably, the European institutions have indeed sought to promote a history of European integration with broadly positive undertones. For example, many European institutions have commissioned historians to write the history of their institution (Larat, Mangenot and Schirmann 2018). This approach is not specific to the EU though, but has been followed by many governments, IOs, companies and civil society organizations (such as trade unions) around the world. For example, the British government commissioned a history of *The United Kingdom and the European Community*, whose first volume was written by the historian Alan Milward (2002) and the second and third by the diplomat Stephen Wall (2013; 2019).

Paradoxically, criticism of the discipline's lack of a critical view on European integration came from within the field itself. In 1992, Milward castigated the federalist historians and their tendency to overestimate the idealistic commitment of the 'Fathers of Europe' in a chapter provocatively entitled 'The Lives and Teaching of the European Saints' (1992). For Milward, Monnet, Schuman, Adenauer or Spaak did not act out of an idealistic commitment to federalist ideas but simply out of self-interest as European integration was seen as the best way to promote their nation state's geopolitical and economic interests. Later, in 2008, Mark Gilbert, himself a prominent historian of European integration, criticized the teleological tendencies of certain EU historians whose narratives, he argued, were influenced by an end point ('telos' in Greek) of the story (Gilbert 2008). Some historians indeed indulged in an ECSC/EEC/EU-centred view, which considers any step towards strengthening EU institutions as 'progress' towards the brighter future of a united Europe. In some respect this is also a generational issue as Gilbert tended to direct his criticism at an older generation of historians, exempting the new generation (such as Piers Ludlow) of this flaw. Later, Wolfram Kaiser and Kiran Patel also criticized the tendency of some historians to write narrow historical accounts, ignoring for the most part important social science debates and approaches to the EU (Kaiser 2008). In a final step, such criticism aimed at the idea of 'EU history' as a separate field, urging historians to 'provincialize Europe' and consider global perspective as well as other IOs that have shaped the European continent (Patel 2013). All considered, the mere fact that those

critics come from within the discipline is evidence of EU history being a
dynamic, self-reflective and ever-changing field.

# 2. The classical debate: Federalist versus nation-state perspectives on European integration

The first seminal question about the history of European integration
concerns the relationship between European institutions and the member
states. Historians (and political scientists acting as historians) have tried
to understand if European integration would overcome or strengthen the
nation state. The second question historical research has examined is that
of the driving forces behind European integration. This question requires
exploring the structural conditions that made possible or encouraged
European integration. For example, to explain the origins of European
integration in Europe after the Second World War, historians would address
the role the emerging Cold War played in this process. Equally, historical
research has tried to address which individual and collective actors were
responsible for European states giving up part of their sovereignty. Two
actors, or agency constellations, have assumed a special role in driving
forward integration, namely first the US government as an 'external
federator' and the Franco-German relationship as an 'internal federator'
(e.g. Chapters 1, 2, 14 and 16).

Historians developed two main perspectives to answer these research
questions: the federal and the European nation-state perspective. The
federal perspective was pioneered by the German historian Walter Lipgens
who regarded the transnationally networked elites among the European
resistance movements during the Second World War as the driving forces
for post-war European integration. His approach was characterized by
a distinctly normative direction, which reflected his personal belief in a
federalist system (Kaiser 2002). As a historian of ideas, Lipgens (1968; 1977)
explored the concepts and plans for post-war integration that these elites
developed, promoted and circulated during the war. The unification of post-
war (Western) Europe represented the solution to a threefold problem for
Lipgens: the political and economic decline of Europe during the interwar
period and the accompanying rise of the Soviet Union and the United States;
the devastating effects of nationalism and the fascist and National Socialist
regimes; and the perceived anachronism of the nation state (Wurm 1995).
Together these developments caused a profound change in the political
consciousness of European leaders. As a result, European states agreed to
surrender sovereignty to a supranational European union leading to the
disappearance of the nation state. While Lipgens focused on the ideational
motivations of transnational elites, including the European Movement in

triggering European integration, he did not examine how these ideas were translated into post-war policies of national governments, for example, at the interstate conference on the Schuman Plan.

From the 1980s, in line with the opening of governmental archival sources, historians began challenging key assumptions of Lipgens's appraisal of (the origins of) European integration. Adopting a nation-state perspective, they argued that European integration would strengthen states, not lead to their disappearance; and that member-state governments would control and influence the integration process. These historians turned the focus from ideas to decision-making, actions and decisions; and to intergovernmental bargaining of nationally defined material interests. One of two approaches developed under the nation-state perspective was a diplomatic history approach. This historiography focused on the analysis of (nation-)state foreign policies 'towards' Europe; and the role of political and security interests in foreign policy formulation. In this view, European integration (and EU) history represents the accumulation of the various national foreign policies.

The second approach is the 'revisionist' economic history approach, pioneered by the British historian Alan Milward. For Milward (1984; 1992), European integration represents a new, state-controlled regulatory framework for 'the European rescue of the nation-state'. From this perspective, the driving forces behind European integration are not ideas but domestically derived economic interests. Milward (1995) was the first historian to engage with integration theory, and he rejected neo-functionalism, while calling at the same time for more interdisciplinary work and more engagement of historians with conceptual debates. Milward's scholarship was certainly exceptional, given that he was able to master vast amounts of archival material from a range of archives written in many different languages. Using this material Milward developed a compelling narrative on what for him were the main driving forces of post-war European integration, encapsulated in the catchy title of his 1992 book: *The European Rescue of the Nation-State*. This volume interpreted the early years of European integration as part of member states' national strategies of reconstruction after the war. European integration for him was thus not the result of vague federalist ideas but tangible material interests, particularly economic ones.

Milward's approach also had limitations (Ramírez Pérez 2012). Due to the thirty-year embargo on archival sources Milward, who was writing in the 1980s and 1990s, spent much of his career studying the 1940s and 1950s. He therefore largely ignored the role of Community institutions in the development of European integration. When he did focus on the 1960s, it was to examine the EEC from the outside, assessing Britain's 'national strategy' towards the institution (Milward 2002). Ironically, the most renowned historian of European integration had hardly ever studied the EEC/EU! This opened the door for the political scientist Andrew Moravcsik to influence the field of European integration history. His book *The Choice for Europe*

(1998) is a comprehensive history of some of the critical junctures of EEC treaties between 1955 and 1992 promoting his 'liberal intergovernmental' interpretation. Moravcsik used very few primary sources and relied mostly on a review of a vast body of literature written in several languages.

His approach is intergovernmental as it posits, like Milward, that the main decision-makers are the nation states, and that EEC institutions are just agents, whose range of action is limited. In this narrative, the Commission and the Court of Justice of the EU (CJEU) are useful for the member states to create binding commitments, that is, to ensure that agreements will be enforced fairly and consistently, but they are not considered as independent driving forces of integration. Moravcsik called his theory 'liberal' as it relies on a two-stage approach to explain the decision-making process. In a first step, national actors such as political parties, businesses and trade unions compete for influence *within* nation states. Economic interdependence helps explain why actors support further steps in European integration. The national government then defines its position considering the balance of power between those groups (notably electoral considerations and economic opportunities). Then, in a second step, national governments interact with each other at European-level negotiations and strike up compromises that allow them to achieve at least some of the aims defined in step one. National leaders agree to create relatively strong European institutions in order to achieve 'credible commitments', that is a consistent implementation of complex rules and agreements, but ultimately, Moravcsik argues, nation states remain at the core of the system.

While Milward and Moravcsik's approach has been hugely influential, they have also attracted criticism for their disregard of supranational institutions and transnational networks. Besides, even though both considered geopolitical considerations (indeed, they argue that they played a major role for some actors such as West Germany), they put a strong emphasis on economic factors, thus neglecting other explanatory factors contributing to the development of European integration.

Despite their differences in accounting for the drivers and motivations of European integration, Lipgens and Milward assigned crucial importance to the consequences of the interwar period and the Second World War; they emphasized the watershed of 1945. Both the federal and the nation-state perspective also offer wide-ranging explanations of European integration. This would not be the case for the generation of historians working on the subject from the early 2000s.

## 3. New directions: Broadening the scope of EU history

Over time, historians have gained access to, and started taking an interest in, a wider collection of archival materials, not only of national governments but also of supranational institutions, the European Commission, the European Parliament and, more recently, the CJEU. In addition, archives of European non-state actors, such as European political parties, consumer associations, the European Trade Union Confederation (ETUC) and others have also been made accessible. Lastly, vast troves of private papers and oral archives of former decision-makers have been collected and made available to the general public, notably on the website of the Historical Archives of the EU. This trend towards increasing and diversifying the flow of primary sources, has been accompanied by two major developments resulting in the broadening of the field of EU history, namely, first, an openness towards interdisciplinary research and cooperation and, second, a drive to integrate EU history within a wider historiography. The first trend on interdisciplinarity will be discussed in the sections on: the transnational approach; the European institutional system; and Europeanization. The remaining sections will embed EU history more broadly within other historical fields by introducing: the cultural turn; the global turn; a wider chronological approach; and the themes of capitalism and neoliberalism.

# The transnational approach

In the early 2000s, the transnational dimension made a forceful comeback to historical research on European integration. This trend fed into both a growing interest of international historians in a transnational research perspective and a fresh awareness of transnational relations by political scientists, encapsulated by Thomas Risse-Kappen's (1995, 3) call to 'bring transnational relations back' into the study of international politics. These trends provided the basis for developing a conceptually refined transnational history of European integration, quite different from Lipgens's original version, even including important insights of Milward's emphasis on material interests (Leucht 2017).

This refined transnational history drew methodological inspiration from engaging with the social sciences. While previously historians – with the notable exception of Milward – shied away from social sciences concepts and theory, Wolfram Kaiser and others began promoting interdisciplinary dialogue. Their research agenda conceptualized the first decades of European integration as the beginnings of a European political system, without however arguing (like Lipgens did) that the EU would become a federation. Historical research also started using social science concepts to reflect on and revise the field's research questions and to enhance the analysis of archival materials. Examples include the use of the network concept to examine the formation of a transnational European political society and engagement with different institutionalist theories to explore the emerging supranational European system (Kaiser, Leucht and Rasmussen 2009).

'Path dependency' has been another concept fruitful for refining historical analysis as well as for engaging in a dialogue with social scientists. This is part of a wider call by 'historical institutionalists' to theorize timing and sequencing in order to move from a 'snapshot view' of political life to 'moving pictures'. Initial institutional or policy decisions have the potential to become self-reinforcing over time. According to historical institutionalism, path-dependent processes therefore can shape and 'lock in' institutional change and policy developments (Pierson 2004). Warlouzet (2016), for example, has applied historical institutionalism to account for some surprising developments in the history of EEC competition policy, notably the adoption of the merger regulation in 1989, while Seidel (2010a; 2020a) studied path dependency regarding early decisions taken in policy areas such as agriculture, 'locking' the policy into a certain trajectory, accounting for why it was notoriously difficult to reform.

To be fair, not *all* historians of European integration engaged with these new methodological approaches in their work, at least not systematically. Piers Ludlow's (2006) work on the European Commission in the 1960s, for example, pioneered an archival approach, including different member-state governments *and* European institutions, greatly enhancing our understanding of this formative period of European integration without, however, resorting to interdisciplinary discussions. His approach of weaving together, seemingly effortlessly, multiple national perspectives and those of the supranational institutions has influenced a whole generation of scholars, and it has become standard practice. This multi-archival and transnational approach has since been used to revisit many of the EEC/EU's developments and policies. For example, studies on the common agricultural policy have punctured a traditional narrative, according to which France was the driving force behind this policy by putting an emphasis on other hitherto neglected actors such as the Dutch and German governments and the European Commission (Knudsen 2009a; Patel 2009c; Seidel 2010a), as well as on previous attempts such as the 'green pool' (Thiemeyer 2009). Recent studies on economic and monetary union have shed light on the interplay between the Franco-German debate and transnational networks of experts and of central bankers (James 2012; Mourlon-Druol 2012a; Dyson and Maes 2016), and sometimes even private banks (Drach 2020). The interaction between car companies, governments and European institutions (Ramírez Pérez 2020; Suzuki 2020), the role of multinational corporations (Ballor 2022) and of businesses more generally (Bussière, Dumoulin and Schirman 2009; Petrini 2014) have also been investigated.

An openness towards interdisciplinarity has also resonated with another recent trend leading to the broadening of EU history, namely examining EU institutions in context.

# The specificity of the European institutional system

In recent years, a range of studies revitalized the theory of neo-functionalism by focusing on 'supranational' institutions of the EEC/EU and their development and impact on European integration. Historians, but also political scientists and sociologists, have examined the European Commission. Such studies highlighted the peculiarity of the working methods of this unique international institution, its internal conflicts, the great variety of public policies it developed and, generally, its successes and failures. The creation and evolution of the European civil service and the question of its attitudes towards European integration has also been central to such research (Bussière et al. 2014; Dujardin et al. 2019; Dumoulin 2007b; Georgakakis 2017; Kassim et al. 2013; Ludlow 2016; Seidel 2010a).

More recently, historians have begun exploring the European Parliament (Roos 2021a; Patel and Salm 2021) while a range of studies has focused on the legal field and the idea of 'integration through law' (see Chapter 6; Cohen and Vauchez 2005; Davies 2012; Rasmussen 2012; Davies and Rasmussen 2012; Vauchez 2015). Finally, an important institutional innovation of the EEC/EU was the European Council, created in 1975. Interestingly, historians have only recently begun to pay attention to this institution assembling the heads of state and government, partly because historians of the federalist conviction felt the European Council encroached on the role of the supranational institutions and thus slowed down, or even unmade, the 'progress' of transferring ever more powers from the member states to the European level. As historians have moved away from such teleological interpretations, the history of the creation of the European Council has been studied in its own right, contextualizing it with the difficult economic and political situation of the 1970s, its role as agenda-setter, for instance, in economic and monetary union, and finally its position in the institutional interplay in the Community (Ludlow 2019; Mourlon-Druol 2012a, 2012b; Van Middelaar 2013).

The last trend characterizing the opening and broadening of EU history in terms of interdisciplinary research concerns works on Europeanization.

# Europeanization

The concept of Europeanization originated in political science and legal research analysing the effect of EU policies on the member states. Historians have taken a wider view, moving away from the EU and top-down institutional approaches towards a focus on the construction of 'Europe' through discourse and practice and experience. In this perspective, Europeanization is not a uniform process. It is not teleological, that is, in the sense that the direction is always towards 'more' Europeanization or more cooperation. The process is not even limited to the geographical entity of Europe broadly defined (von Hirschhausen and Patel 2010). Research about the shared European experience of empire-building, for example, demonstrates the extent to which non-European experiences have shaped Europe and its integration and ideas of Europe were both shared and similar across different geographical entities (Brown 2022; Greiner 2014; Hansen and Jonsson 2014).

Another aspect of Europeanization is the study of European societies to understand to what extent these societies are becoming more similar. The German social historian Hartmut Kaelble has explored possible convergences (but also divergences) in European societies to evaluate how homogenous Europe has become, analysing areas such as work, family, consumerism, values and religiosity (Kaelble 2007). While not an 'EU historian' per se – the book does not focus solely on EU member states – Kaelble proposes that European integration is one key factor that has induced further homogenization by encouraging the harmonization of social protection and education systems, for example.

Other historians have begun to study how European integration has affected European citizens' lives in terms of mobility. The Schengen Treaty opened borders, and progressively led to the right to live and work in another EU country, following earlier decisions fostering the mobility of workers since the 1960s, while mobility programmes developed by the EU, such as the university exchange programme Erasmus, are also meant to foster the emergence of a European society (Comte 2017; Paoli 2016). Even fields at the core of nation-state sovereignty, such as police counter-terrorism, have been concerned by a European intergovernmental cooperation since the 1970s (Oberloskamp 2016).

The last works discussed here indicate that EU history has been increasingly embedded within other 'histories' – a trend which will be developed in the following sections.

## The 'cultural turn'

In addition to work addressing European society formation and the lived experiences of Europeans, historians have parted with the earlier focus on political, economic and institutional history to examine whether European citizens 'feel' European. Cultural historians, for example, have explored the question of whether a European identity exists and what it could consist of. Collective identities are defined as shared social constructions derived, for example, from shared experiences or memories. Aline Sierp (2014) has argued that the Holocaust is one such experience shared by all Europeans, demonstrating that a shared Holocaust memory culture is emerging; and European institutions played an important role in the construction of this shared memory. Others are more critical of such a view arguing that collective memories of the two world wars would not be EU-specific but include European countries beyond the EU. Since the 2000s, the EU also includes member states that brought other collective memories into the Union, for example, that of Communism (Kaiser, Krankenhagen and Poehls 2016).

Another strand in this research on a European identity focuses on the analysis of (media) discourses, for example, analysing to what extent a European public sphere or public space exists (Frank et al. 2010). Meyer's (2010a) research, for example, has tended to confirm a slow Europeanization of the debates in several quality newspapers for the pre-Maastricht period. European institutions themselves, going back to the Organization for European Economic Cooperation, have sought to promote a European identity. Recent research has delved into the EEC/EU policies devised to foster a sense of identification, often calling into question the official institutional narrative (Calligaro 2013; Cohen 2007; Krumrey 2018). Another trend has focused on the (more or less) new member states, namely southern European and central and eastern European countries, and their specific relationship to European integration (Cunha 2019; Guirao 2020; Karamouzi 2014; Ther 2016).

The broadening of EU history further owes to an opening of the space and time in which to study European integration.

## The global turn: Provincializing Europe

In the context of a general critique of Eurocentric views of Western historiography and the growth of global history, calls to 'provincialize Europe' (Chakrabarti 2008) have led to a more critical assessment by EU historians regarding the 'uniqueness' of European integration and the EEC/EU over the past decade. Kiran Klaus Patel (2013) has called on historians to question the centrality of the EEC/EU and study the EU and its history by comparing it to alternative IOs. Several volumes have since adhered to this call and have demonstrated the interlinkage between various institutions of European and international cooperation (Kaiser and Patel 2018; Mechi, Migani and Petrini 2014). For example, Warlouzet (2018a) has approached the debate on the control of large companies in the 1970s–1980s from a global and multilayered perspective, integrating the European negotiations into a larger debate straddling many international institutions such as the Organization for Economic Cooperation and Development, the International Labour Organization and the United Nations. Left-wing actors – politicians and trade unionists – first engaged with IOs other than the EEC, as these were arenas that they were more familiar with. They only began turning to the EEC once they understood that the binding nature of Community law was more advantageous for them. In technological cooperation, too, international and European cooperation were often intermingled, with the latter being often carried out by non-EEC/EU institutions (Bouneau, Burigana and Varsori 2010).

The interaction between the EEC/EU and processes of globalization is at the heart of historical studies on trade negotiations, either through the Western framework of the General Agreement on Tariffs and Trade (GATT) (Coppolaro 2013; Seidel 2020a) or, more recently, through the North-South lens (see also Chapter 14). The protracted North-South negotiations of the 1970s, notably the 'New International Economic Order' declared in 1973 and its European response, the 1975 Lomé Convention between the EEC and forty-six former colonies, the so-called associated countries, led to several studies (Migani 2014b), including some based on archival sources of the South, still a rare accomplishment even in global history (Garavini 2012; Rempe 2012). Fledgling attempts at global governance have been studied through the simultaneous emergence of both the European Council and the G7 in 1975 (Garavini 2006; Mourlon-Druol and Romero 2014) and through the EEC/ASEAN negotiations (Kuroda 2019).

Studies on transatlantic networks are still emerging and have become more methodologically sophisticated using a multi-archival and multi-tiered approach (Bitumi 2018; Leucht 2010). In addition, the Community itself has attempted to become a geopolitical actor (Krotz, Patel and Romero 2019). Its global influence has remained rather weak, even though it played a useful coordinating role in specific circumstances, such as the Helsinki Conference on Security and Cooperation in Europe (Romano 2009; more generally on the 1970s: Varsori and Migani 2011).

## An expanding chronology

Just as the move to 'provincialize' Europe and European integration has resulted in studies comparing and contrasting the EU with other post-war IOs as well as analysing its interaction with these organizations, another trend in contemporary history has been to move back in time. As we have shown in the chapter on European ideas (Chapter 13), European cooperation and even ideas for European unity are not a post-1945 phenomenon. Institutionalized cooperation in areas such as fluvial navigation, communication and health has occurred since the early nineteenth century. The Central Commission for the Navigation of the Rhine, established in 1815 by the Congress of Vienna, is now considered the first modern form of European cooperation. Wolfram Kaiser and Johan Schot's (2014) history of European technical cooperation endeavoured to uncover the 'hidden integration of Europe'. Interestingly, their study confirmed the view that technical cooperation was especially strong in the interwar period among countries that would later become the 'core Europe' countries, notably France, Germany as well as the

Benelux states, leaving Britain on the fringes. It thus shows that European integration of the Six in the post-war period was built on strong roots of interwar cooperation between these countries.

Another predecessor of post-war integration both at global and at European level was the League of Nations, an organization that has recently attracted a lot of attention from historians who have also worked on European integration history (Gram-Skjoldager, Ikonomou and Kahlert 2020; Van Leeuwen and Rasmussen 2021). Rather than the organization that failed to prevent the Second World War, the history of the League is now examined in its own right and in the context of its time (Pedersen 2015). The League's independent civil service is also seen as the first of its kind and a model for post-war international bureaucracies (Gram-Skjoldager and Ikonomou 2019), thus bridging the divide between the interwar period and the post-1945 world.

From this perspective, the EU often *followed* other IOs in entering and shaping policy fields internationally as can be seen in the examples of transport policy and, in this volume, in the chapter on environmental and consumer policies (Patel 2013; Chapter 11).

A final trend broadening the history of European integration contextualizes this history within the wider historiography on capitalism and neoliberalism.

# European integration in the history of capitalism and neoliberalism

The EU as a capitalist market-driven entity eroding workers' rights has long been the bane of its left-wing critics. Recent historiography has returned its focus on the economic aspects of European integration. Some scholars have indeed argued that the 1970s were a kind of 'point of no return' when a more social Europe was discarded and the path to neoliberalism became irresistible (Andry 2019; Petrini 2013). Other scholars however have pointed out how versatile, flexible and multifaceted the EEC/EU has been in accommodating different economic ideas. Focusing on the history of ideas, Quinn Slobodian (2018) has shown how ordo-liberals, a German variant of economic liberalism, were at first very critical of European integration before fully engaging with the EEC. More generally, a recent historiographical review explains the historical contingency of the triumph of neoliberalism in the 1980s as being linked to the crisis of social democracy and failed attempts to reform the welfare state in the 1970s. Warlouzet (2018a; 2022; 2023) has interpreted European integration as a contest between three types of economic policies: the socially oriented, neomercantilist and market-oriented models, with neoliberalism being a radical version of the market-oriented model (chapter 8). Attempts at promoting European-level mercantilism were rife in the 1970s; except in the case of Airbus, they were largely unsuccessful. While neoliberalism has clearly been on the rise since the 1980s, it has coexisted with socially oriented policies (such as cohesion, gender and environmental policies). Environmental policy in particular has been the subject of recent research on the interplay between international, transnational and EEC/EU actors and institutions in complex negotiations over environmental protection, from bird protection to sustainable development (Bussière et al. 2020; Kaiser and Meyer 2017; Meyer 2010b; Warlouzet 2021). The recent definition of the EU as a 'social market economy' has been explored historically in a multidisciplinary perspective (Segers et al. 2019).

The EEC/EU thus remains embedded in a broader set of economic and social policies that are negotiated at national and international levels. It has never just adopted one model or vision.

# Conclusion

This overview has demonstrated how dynamic the field of European integration history has become over the past fifty years. From a new discipline narrowly focused on the federal idea on the one hand and nation-state interests on the other, the field has benefited both from inspiration and exchanges with neighbouring disciplines as well as developments in the wider field of history such as the history of ideas, memory studies, general European, global and environmental history. European integration is certainly on the path towards 'normalization', becoming part of the general history of Europe and beyond.

# Guide to web resources

## Official websites of EU institutions and other international organizations

Organization for Economic Cooperation and Development (OECD): https://www.oecd.org/

Successor organization of the Organization for European Economic Cooperation founded in 1948, this site gives access to information on its European member countries as well as on the organization itself.

Council of Europe: https://www.coe.int/en/web/portal/home

Official website of the Council of Europe, founded in 1949 and located in Strasbourg.

European Union: https://european-union.europa.eu/index_en

Council of Ministers of the EU: https://www.consilium.europa.eu/en/
Court of Justice of the EU: https://curia.europa.eu/jcms/jcms/j_6/en/
European Council: https://www.consilium.europa.eu/en/european-council/
European Commission: https://ec.europa.eu/info/index_en
European Parliament: https://www.europarl.europa.eu/portal/en
United Nations: https://www.un.org/en/

# Online archives and databases

Archive of European Integration (AEI), University of Pittsburg: aei.pitt.
  edu
  Founded in 2003 the AEI holds a digital collection of scholarly papers
and archival documents on European integration since 1945. Most
are official documents from European Union institutions. The AEI is
thus narrowly focused on the European Union and its predecessor
organizations.

Centre Virtuel sur la connaissance de l'Europe (CVCE): https://www.
  cvce.eu/en
  The CVCE is a research institute and digital archive. The project
initially received funding from the European Union (EU) and the
government of Luxembourg and is now part of the University of
Luxembourg. The centre engages in research, published on the site,
but the main advantage of the CVCE is the collection of multimedia
materials available through the site. This database contains a broad
range of digitized archival material sourced from European institutions
and archives in the EU's member states, oral history interviews, videos,
newspaper articles, photographs and cartoons. Most, but not all,
documents are translated into English.

Eur-Lex: http://eur-lex.europa.eu/homepage.html
  EUR-Lex is a database providing free access to the Official Journal
of the European Union (EU), EU law, preparatory acts, EU case-law,
international agreements, European Free Trade Association documents,
summaries of EU legislation and other public documents.

Eurobarometer: https://europa.eu/eurobarometer/screen/home
  Provides access to the European Union's regular public opinion surveys.

# Physical archives with at least some online material

Historical Archives of the European Union: https://www.eui.eu/en/acade
    mic-units/historical-archives-of-the-european-union
    The website of the Historical Archives of the European Union gives
access to some of the archives' collections. The archives hold the papers
of the European institutions as well as personal papers of individuals
such as former European civil servants, politicians and people engaged
in organizations, including the European movement. Some resources and
documents are digitized and available online, though most need to be
consulted on site in Florence, Italy. The website also offers access to a
rather vast oral history collection.

European Parliamentary Research Service (EPRS) Historical Archives,
    Luxembourg:
https://historicalarchives.europarl.europa.eu/home.html
    The EPRS holds digital copies of all proceedings of the European
Parliament and offers a library and issues its own publications. The
website also contains photos, videos, podcasts and other historical
material.

Fondation Jean Monnet pour l'Europe, Lausanne: https://jean-monnet.
    ch/en/
    Private archive of key personalities such as Jean Monnet, Robert
Schuman, Robert Marjolin and Jacques Delors.

United Nations and League of Nations Archives, Geneva: https://libra
    ryresources.unog.ch/leagueofnationsarchives
    Website of the archives of the League and the United Nations. Some
documents are digitized.

Foreign Relations of the United States (FRUS): https://history.state.gov/
    historicaldocuments
    Organized chronologically by US presidential administrations,
this collection makes accessible archival sources from a range of US
governmental archives such as the Departments of State and Defense,
National Security Council, Central Intelligence Agency as well as private
papers of key individuals involved in US foreign policy formulation. US
government involvement, assessment and reaction to European events
and developments can be studied using this collection.

## Research institutions and groups

HEIRS and RICHIE: HEIRS: https://heirsweb.wordpress.com/ and
www.europe-richie.org
These two networks aim to foster contacts between young researchers
in European history through a mailing list and the organization of annual
conferences and other events. They are run by teams of PhD students and
postdocs from several European countries.

EU Historians: https://eu-historians.org
Website of the group of EU historians giving free access to the *Journal
of European Integration History* and other publications.

Huygens-ING – The Netherlands and European Integration, 1950–
86: http://resources.huygens.knaw.nl/europeseintegratie/index_
html_en
Online database of documents from the Dutch Ministry of Foreign
Affairs relating to European integration. Most documents are in Dutch.

The PopuList: https://popu-list.org/
A peer-reviewed website offering an overview of populist, far right, far
left and Eurosceptic parties in Europe since 1989.

# Five key questions

1. How can we explain that approaches to the study of European
   integration have changed over time?
2. How did historians adopting federalist and nation-state perspectives
   view the drivers, processes and outcomes of European integration?
3. What was the 'transnational turn' in European integration history,
   and what has been its impact?
4. Is European integration history still dominated by federalist and
   teleological narratives?
5. What is meant by 'provincializing' Europe?

# Ten key readings

Gehler, M. (2016), '"Europe", Europeanizations and Their Meaning for European
   Integration Historiography', *Journal of European Integration History*, 22
   (1): 141–74.
Gilbert, M. (2008), 'Narrating the Process: Questioning the Progressive Story of
   European Integration', *Journal of Common Market Studies*, 46 (3): 641–62.

Kaiser, W. (2008), 'History Meets Politics: Overcoming Interdisciplinary Volapük in Research on the EU', *Journal of European Public Policy*, 15 (2): 300–13.

Kaiser, W., and A. Varsori (eds) (2010), *European Union History: Themes and Debates*, Chippenham: Palgrave Macmillan.

Ludlow, N. P. (2006), *The European Community and the Crises of the 1960s: Negotiating the Gaullist Challenge*, London: Routledge.

Milward, A. S., with the assistance of G. Brennan and F. Romero (1992), *The European Rescue of the Nation-State*, London: Routledge.

Moravcsik, A. (1998), *The Choice for Europe: Social Purpose and State Power from Messina to Maastricht*, Ithaca, NY: Cornell University Press.

Patel, K. K. (2013), 'Provincialising European Union: Co-operation and Integration in Europe in a Historical Perspective', *Contemporary European History*, 22 (4): 649–73.

Patel, K. K. (2019), 'Widening and Deepening? Recent Advances in European Integration History', *Neue Politische Literatur*, 64 (2): 327–57.

Warlouzet, L. (2018), 'European Integration History: Beyond the Crisis', *Politique Européenne*, 44 (2): 98–122.

# CHRONOLOGY

## Nineteenth century

| | |
|---|---|
| 1815 | Concert of Europe |
| 21 August 1849 | Victor Hugo's united Europe speech at the Paris Peace Congress |
| 1865 | International Telegraph Union |
| 1874 | Universal Postal Union |

## Early twentieth century up to the Second World War

| | |
|---|---|
| 1914–18 | First World War |
| 1917 | Russian Revolution |
| 8 January 1918 | US President Wilson's Fourteen Points Speech |
| 1919 | Treaty of Versailles signed |
| 1920 | Founding of the League of Nations |
| 1923 | Publication of Richard Coudenhove-Kalergi's book *Paneurope* |
| 1925 | Locarno Pact |
| 5 September 1929 | French Foreign Minister Aristide Briand presents his plan for a federal European union at the League of Nations |
| 1931 | Japan invades Manchuria |
| 1935 | Italy invades Abyssinia (modern-day Ethiopia) |
| 1936–9 | Spanish Civil War |
| 1 September 1939 | Nazi Germany invades Poland. Beginning of the Second World War |

## 1940s

| | |
|---|---|
| 1941 | Ventotene manifesto 'For a Free and United Europe' |
| 1944 | Bretton Woods agreement |
| 8 May 1945 | Second World War ends in Europe |

| | |
|---|---|
| 6 and 9 August 1945 | United States drop nuclear bombs on Japanese cities of Hiroshima and Nagasaki |
| 2 September 1945 | Second World War ends with surrender of Japan |
| 24 October 1945 | Founding of the United Nations |
| 5 March 1946 | Winston Churchill's 'Iron Curtain' speech delivered at Fulton, Missouri |
| 19 September 1946 | Winston Churchill's Zurich speech |
| 5 June 1947 | Marshall Plan speech |
| 15 August 1947 | India independence day |
| 25 February 1948 | Communist coup in Prague |
| 16 April 1948 | Founding of the Organization for European Economic Cooperation (OEEC) |
| 7–11 May 1948 | Congress of Europe at The Hague |
| 24 June 1948–12 May 1949 | Berlin blockade |
| 5 May 1949 | Founding of the Council of Europe |
| 1949 | International Ruhr Authority set up to manage West German heavy industry |

# 1950s

| | |
|---|---|
| 9 May 1950 | Schuman Plan Declaration |
| 25 June 1950 | Outbreak of the Korean War |
| 24 October 1950 | Pleven Plan for a European army |
| 18 April 1951 | Treaty of Paris signed establishing the European Coal and Steel Community (ECSC) |
| 27 May 1952 | Treaty of Paris signed establishing the European Defence Community (EDC) |
| 30 August 1954 | France fails to ratify the EDC Treaty |
| 1–3 June 1955 | Meeting of foreign ministers of the Six at Messina |
| 25 March 1957 | Treaties of Rome establishing the European Economic Community and Euratom |
| 1 June 1958 | Charles de Gaulle returns to power as head of government in France |

# 1960s

| | |
|---|---|
| 1959–62 | GATT Dillon Round |
| 4 January 1960 | Treaty of European Free Trade Association (EFTA) signed |
| 31 July 1961 | British Prime Minister Macmillan announces UK will apply to become EEC member |

| 14 January 1962 | Agreement on the common agricultural policy (CAP) |
| 14 January 1963 | French President de Gaulle vetoes Britain's EEC membership |
| 22 January 1963 | Elysée Treaty signed by France and West Germany |
| 20 July 1963 | Yaoundé Convention between the EEC and eighteen African states and Madagascar |
| 1964–7 | GATT Kennedy Round |
| 8 April 1965 | Treaty of Mergers of Executives of the three European Communities |
| 1 July 1965–30 January 1966 | Empty Chair crisis |
| 11 May 1967 | Britain's second EEC application tabled |
| 27 November 1967 | De Gaulle's second veto to UK membership in EEC |
| 1 July 1968 | Completion of the customs union |
| 1–2 December 1969 | Summit meeting of EEC heads of state and government at The Hague |

# 1970s

| 8 October 1970 | Werner Report on economic and monetary union |
| 15 August 1971 | US President Richard Nixon suspends the convertibility of the dollar into gold marking the end of the Bretton Woods system of fixed and stable exchange rates |
| December 1971 | Smithsonian Agreement |
| March 1972 | EEC countries create the currency 'snake' |
| 1 January 1973 | Denmark, Ireland and the UK join the European Communities |
| 1973–5 | Helsinki Conference on Security and Cooperation in Europe |
| 1973–9 | GATT Tokyo Round |
| October 1973 | Oil Shock |
| 9–10 December 1974 | Paris summit meeting, creating the European Council |
| 28 February 1975 | Lomé Convention between the EEC and forty-six associated states |
| 5 June 1975 | First UK referendum on EEC membership |
| 1975 | Tindemans report on European Union |
| 1975 | Marjolin report on economic and monetary union |
| 1975 | Founding of European Regional Development Fund (ERDF) |
| 15–17 November 1975 | First G7 meeting |

| | |
|---|---|
| 20 September 1976 | Act on the direct election of the members of the European Parliament |
| January 1978 | Iranian Revolution |
| 1979 | Second oil shock |
| 1979 | European Monetary System |
| June 1979 | First direct elections to the European Parliament |
| 24 December 1979 | Soviet invasion in Afghanistan leading to guerrilla war lasting until 1989 |

# 1980s

| | |
|---|---|
| 1 January 1981 | Greece joins European Communities |
| 13 December 1981 | Declaration of martial law in Poland |
| 2 April–14 June 1982 | Falklands War between Argentina and the UK |
| 26 June 1984 | Fontainebleau European Council agrees to British budgetary rebate and milk quotas |
| 14 June 1985 | Schengen Agreement signed by Belgium, France, Luxembourg, the Netherlands and Germany ending border controls between these countries |
| 1 January 1985–22 January 1995 | Commission presided by Jacques Delors |
| 14 February 1985 | The European Parliament adopts the Spinelli Treaty on the European Union |
| 1986–94 | GATT Uruguay Round |
| 1 January 1986 | Spain and Portugal join European Communities |
| 17 February 1986 | Single European Act signed |
| 13 February 1988 | Delors package |
| 2 May 1989 | Hungary cuts its border fence with Austria |
| 26–27 June 1989 | Madrid European Council approves the Delors report on the Economic and Monetary Union |
| 9 November 1989 | Fall of the Berlin Wall |
| 8–9 December 1989 | Strasbourg European Council decides to convene an intergovernmental conference on a new treaty |

# 1990s

| | |
|---|---|
| 3 October 1990 | German unification |
| 17 January–28 February 1991 | First Gulf War |
| June 1991–December 1995 | War in Yugoslavia (and in 1998–9 in Kosovo) |
| 26 December 1991 | Break-up of the Soviet Union |

| | |
|---|---|
| 7 February 1992 | Treaty on European Union (Maastricht Treaty) signed |
| 2 June 1992 | Danish referendum on the Maastricht Treaty (50.7 per cent 'No') |
| 20 September 1992 | French referendum on the Maastricht Treaty (51 per cent 'Yes') |
| 18 May 1993 | Second Danish referendum on the Maastricht Treaty (56.8 per cent 'Yes') |
| 28 November 1994 | Second Norwegian referendum refusing EU membership (52.2 per cent 'No') |
| 1995 | Austria, Finland and Sweden join the EU |
| 22 March 1996 | 'Mad cow' crisis; ban on British exports of bovine meat |
| 13–14 December 1996 | Adoption of the 'Stability and Growth' Pact |
| 2 October 1997 | Amsterdam Treaty signed |
| 1 January 1999 | Introduction of the euro as an accounting currency |
| 15 March 1999 | Resignation of the Santer Commission |

# 2000s

| | |
|---|---|
| 12 May 2000 | Joschka Fischer speech at Humboldt University 'From confederation to federation' |
| 1 January 2001 | Greece joins the eurozone |
| 26 February 2001 | Nice Treaty signed |
| 1 January 2002 | Introduction of euro coins and banknotes |
| 28 February 2002–13 June 2003 | Convention on the Future of Europe |
| 1 May 2004 | Czech Republic, Cyprus, Estonia, Hungary, Latvia, Lithuania, Malta, Poland, Slovakia and Slovenia join the EU |
| 29 October 2004 | Treaty establishing a Constitution for Europe |
| 29 May 2005 | Treaty establishing a Constitution for Europe rejected in referenda in France and the Netherlands (on 1 June) |
| 13 December 2007 | Treaty on the Functioning of the European Union (TFEU, Lisbon Treaty) signed |
| 2007 | Bulgaria and Romania join the EU |

# 2010s

| 9 May 2010 | Eurozone crisis; first rescue package to Greece, and then to other ailing countries in 2010–13 (Ireland, Portugal, Spanish banks, Cyprus) |
| 2 March 2012 | 'Fiscal Compact' or Treaty on Stability, Coordination and Governance in the Economic and Monetary Union |
| 26 July 2012 | 'Whatever it takes' speech of ECB President Mario Draghi |
| 2013 | Croatia joins the EU and the euro |
| 2015 | Threat of Grexit, overcome by a last rescue package |
| 23 June 2016 | In a referendum Britain's population votes to leave the European Union |
| 17 October 2019 | EU–UK Withdrawal Agreement; UK leaves the EU on 1 February 2020 |
| 21 July 2020 | Covid-19 EU Relaunch Plan |
| 30 December 2020 | EU-UK Trade and Cooperation Agreement |
| 24 February 2022 | Russia invades Ukraine |

# GLOSSARY

**ACP countries** African, Caribbean and Pacific countries; most of them former Belgian, British and French colonies.

**Briand Plan** Scheme launched by French Foreign Minister Aristide Briand in September 1929 at the League of Nations for an economic union of European states.

**COMECON** The Council for Mutual Economic Assistance, an economic organization founded in 1949. Dominated by the Soviet Union, it was designed to coordinate trade and economic cooperation between Communist countries in Europe and beyond. Dissolved in 1991.

**Commonwealth** Association of countries consisting mostly of former colonies of the UK.

**Concert of Europe** An international informal agreement formed at the Congress of Vienna in 1815 in the aftermath of the Napoleonic Wars to maintain a balance of power in Europe and ensure political stability. Sometimes seen as a precursor to modern international organizations.

**Council of Europe** European intergovernmental organization founded in 1949, based in Strasbourg to facilitate cooperation between European countries in various areas, such as human rights, culture and education. Currently comprising forty-seven member states.

**Economic and Monetary Union (EMU)** Formally established by the Treaty of Maastricht in 1992, EMU comprises a common monetary policy, a European central bank, a common currency, the euro and close coordination of economic and fiscal policies. Only nineteen of the EU's twenty-seven member states are participating in the monetary union, that is, have adopted the euro as their currency.

**European Atomic Energy Community (or Euratom)** Established in 1957 by the Treaties of Rome alongside the EEC, Euratom intended to establish a common market for nuclear materials and technology in Europe as well as supporting research into the peaceful use of nuclear power.

**European Coal and Steel Community (ECSC)** Established in 1951 by the Treaty of Paris, the ECSC established a common market for coal and steel among six member states: Belgium, France, Germany, Italy, Luxembourg and the Netherlands. The ECSC's institutional set-up became the model for subsequent organizations, the EEC and Euratom. The ECSC Treaty was concluded for fifty years. Thus, it expired in 2002, and the ECSC's functions were taken over by the EU.

**European Communities (EC)** Created in 1967 by the merger of the ECSC, the EEC and Euratom. Until the Maastricht Treaty came into force in 1993, establishing the European Union (EU), it was customary to refer to the European Communities (or, inaccurately, the European Community). The EEC was also still referred to when discussing economic integration.

**European Economic Community (EEC)** Established in 1957 by the Treaties of Rome, the EEC's main task was to create a customs union among its member states leading to closer economic integration as well as a common market for agricultural products. The EEC Treaty covered a wide range of areas which the EEC members could tackle, for instance, policy areas such as transport, development, competition policy and social affairs.

**European Free Trade Association (EFTA)** An intergovernmental organization formed in 1960 (Stockholm Convention) by Austria, Denmark, Norway, Portugal, Sweden, Switzerland and the UK to promote free trade and closer economic cooperation.

**European Political Cooperation (EPC)** Initially an informal agreement made by the EEC member states in 1970 to cooperate more closely in foreign policy matters and find common positions. EPC took the form of regular meetings of foreign ministers and became part of discussions in the European Council, established in 1974. In the Maastricht Treaty (1992), EPC became the second pillar of the treaty under the title 'common foreign and security policy'.

**European Round Table of Industrialists (ERT)** An informal forum for CEOs and leaders of European multinationals formed in 1983. The ERT was one actor among others which supported the creation of the Single Market in the late 1980s.

**European Union (EU)** The idea to develop the EEC into a European Union dates back to the 1970s (the leaders of the future Nine committed themselves to the long-term formation of a 'European Union' at the 1972 Paris Summit) and 1980s. The Treaty of Maastricht (1992), also called the Treaty on European Union, established the EU as a further step in the development of European integration. This Union consisted of three pillars, the EC pillar, consisting of the old EEC with increased competences in new areas, as well as two intergovernmental pillars, the common and security policy and justice and home affairs.

**Galileo** European global navigation system, running a civilian satellite and a control system network in Europe.

**General Agreement on Tariffs and Trade (GATT)** Signed in 1947 its signatory states vouched to establish free trade and to work towards dismantling tariffs and other barriers to trade. GATT negotiations have taken place at regular intervals in so-called GATT Rounds leading to further cuts in tariffs between members. In 1995 GATT was replaced by the World Trade Organization (WTO).

**German Democratic Republic (GDR)** East German Communist state created on 7 October 1949 out of the Soviet occupation zone in Germany. Part of the Soviet sphere of influence, the GDR collapsed following the fall of the Berlin Wall on 9 November 1989. The GDR was united with the Federal Republic of Germany on 3 October 1990.

**Great Depression** A worldwide economic recession that broke out following a stock market crash in October 1929 in the United States, spread to other parts of the world such as Europe and Latin America and lasted until the late 1930s.

The economic crisis led to a drop in industrial output and trade, high rates of unemployment and exacerbated political instability.

**Great Recession** Economic downturn triggered by a banking and economic crisis in the United States in 2007 and lasting until 2009. The crisis spread to other countries, including Europe, where it contributed to a sovereign debt crisis that started in late 2009, lasting until 2012.

**Group of 7 (G7)** Founded in 1975 as a forum for the seven (originally six until Canada joined in 1976) most advanced capitalist countries to discuss economic and political issues in annual meetings. It includes Britain, France, Germany, Italy, Japan, the United States and Canada.

**Intergovernmental/inter-governmentalism** Mode of cooperation between states, often in the context of international organizations, where states retain full control over whether or not they cooperate in certain matters. This can include using a veto to block a proposal or a decision.

**International Steel Cartel (ISC)** A 1926 agreement between steel producers from Belgium, France, Germany, Luxembourg and the Saar to work together to divide up market share and deal with competition from the UK and the United States. The ISC existed in various guises and extended membership until it was dissolved in 1939.

**League of Nations** Founded in 1920 as an international organization to preserve peace. Based in Geneva, Switzerland, it worked on wide-ranging issues such as disarmament, minorities, economic and financial matters, trafficking, health, refugees and colonial questions. Unable to prevent the Second World War, it

was dissolved in 1945 and replaced by the United Nations.

**Locarno Treaties** Also known as the Locarno Pact, these were a series of agreements concluded by Belgium, France, Germany, Italy and the UK in October 1925 at Locarno (Switzerland). In the treaties the German government gave security guarantees to Western European countries. Germany was subsequently allowed to become a member of the League of Nations.

**Lomé Convention** Agreement signed between the EEC and forty-six African, Caribbean and Pacific states in 1975. Preferential access to the EEC market for exports from the ACP countries as well as a price stabilization mechanism called Stabex. The Lomé Convention was renewed several times (Lomé II in 1979, Lomé III in 1984, Lomé IV in 1989) and replaced in 2000 by the Cotonou convention.

**Marshall Plan** A plan for recovery of Western European countries announced in a speech on 5 June 1947 at Harvard University by US Secretary of State George C. Marshall. Also known by its official name, European Recovery Program, the programme ran from April 1948 to December 1951 and distributed aid amounting to 13 billion USD to seventeen countries.

**Multi Fibre Arrangement** Signed in 1974 the agreement regulated global trade in textiles and garments, agreeing quotas on how much developing countries could export to developed countries. Expired in 1994.

**Neoliberalism** The term designates in this book a set of economic policies designed to liberalize markets and retrench the welfare state. It is associated with policies conducted by British Prime Minister Margaret

Thatcher and US President Ronald Reagan from 1979–80 onwards.

**Neomercantilism** Refers to a set of policies aimed at supporting the development of local industries by various protectionist measures such as state aids, custom duties and monopolies (hence the reference to early modern mercantilism) while at the same time shying away from 1930s-style blatant protectionism. Most European countries pursued active neomercantilist industrial policies from 1945 to the early 1980s, without reneging on their international obligation to abide by free trade rules.

**North Atlantic Treaty Organization (NATO)** Established after the North Atlantic Treaty signed on 4 April 1949 by Belgium, Canada, Denmark, France, Iceland, Italy, Luxembourg, Netherlands, Norway, Portugal, the UK and the United States. Membership increased subsequently; Greece and Turkey joined in 1952, West Germany in 1955, Spain gained full membership in 1982. Post–Cold War NATO was extended in 1999 to include Czech Republic, Poland and Hungary. More central and eastern European countries joined in 2004, including the three Baltic states, Estonia, Latvia and Lithuania.

**Organization for European Economic Cooperation (OEEC)** Created in 1948 as the umbrella organization of the Marshall Plan to promote the progressive liberalization of trade and payments within Western Europe. It included sixteen Western European states as well as the Western zone of occupied Germany. It was replaced by the Organization for Economic Co-operation and Development (OECD) in 1960, when the United States and Canada joined.

*Ostpolitik* Policy of West Germany towards the Soviet Union and Eastern Europe aiming to normalize relationship and ease tensions. Created in 1966 by the then German Foreign Minister Willy Brandt, *Ostpolitik* led to a series of bilateral treaties in the early 1970s.

**Protectionism** Refers to a policy designed to protect the local producers by erecting obstacles to free trade such as quotas, custom duties and more indirect tools, for example, standards and legal rules which effectively prevent foreign competition.

**Qualified majority voting** This is a voting method in the Council of Ministers of the EU. Since the 2007 Lisbon Treaty, a qualified majority is reached when 55 per cent of the member states representing 65 per cent of the EU's population vote in favour of a policy proposal from the Commission.

**Quantitative restrictions** Specific limits on the quantity or value of goods that can be imported (or exported) into a country during a specific time period. Synonymous to quota.

**Schuman Plan** Refers to the French plan unveiled on 9 May 1950 to set up a common organization of the coal and steel sectors, with supranational features, and which was open to other European countries. It sparked the creation of the ECSC, and then of the EC and of the EU. Thus, 9 May is remembered today as the 'Day of Europe' in the EU.

**Single Market** Whereas the 'Common Market' encapsulated in the 1957 Treaty of Rome was based on the removal of custom duties for goods, the 'Single Market' envisaged in the 1986 Single Act was predicated upon the removal of all obstacles to trade for goods, including non-tariff barriers such as standards. It also includes the freedom of movements for people, capital and services, albeit to a lesser extent than for goods in practice.

**Solidarity/***Solidarność* Founded in Gdansk (Poland) in 1980, it became the first independent trade union in Poland and Communist-led Eastern Europe, more generally. Several of its members were imprisoned after the 1981 crackdown, notably its leader Lech Wałęsa. Solidarity played a crucial role in the struggle for workers' rights and more freedom in Poland. In 1989 it negotiated an agreement with the Communist government for a democratic transition and the first free elections since 1947.

**Subsidiarity principle** The principle whereby the EU does not take action (except in the areas that fall within its exclusive competence), unless it is more effective than action taken at national, regional or local level (enshrined in Article 5, Treaty on European Union).

**Supranational/supranationalism** This is a principle and mode of functioning of an international organization referring to the controlled and limited abandonment of national sovereignty by its members. First mentioned in the Treaty of Paris in 1951, establishing the ECSC, it has since been associated with European integration and its quasi-independent institutions, the Court of Justice, the European Commission and the European Parliament.

**Unanimity** This is one of the voting rules applicable in the Council of Ministers. In certain policy areas regarded as sensitive, for example, foreign and security policy, all member states need to agree to a decision. Over time the Community has generally endeavoured to take more decisions by majority vote to increase efficiency and speed up decision-making.

**United Nations (UN)** A global international organization established in 1945 to replace the League of Nations. Based in New York it currently has 193 member states.

**Yaoundé Conventions** Association agreements between the EEC and the eighteen Associated African States and Madagascar. The first agreement was signed in 1963, the second in 1969. The agreements included a free trade arrangement and a European Development Fund.

# REFERENCES

## 1. Treaties

Please refer to the 'Chronology' for the founding treaties of the European Union and successive treaties.

## 2. Case law

### Court of Justice of the European Union decisions

Case 26–62 *NV Algemene Transport- en Expeditie Onderneming van Gend & Loos v. Netherlands Inland Revenue Administration.* ('*Van Gend*')

Case 6–64 *Flaminio Costa v. E.N.E.L.* ('*Costa*')

Case 11–70 *Internationale Handelsgesellschaft mbH v. Einfuhr- und Vorratsstelle für Getreide und Futtermittel.* ('*Internationale*')

Case 22–70 *Commission of the European Communities v. Council of the European Communities.* ('*ERTA*')

Case 41–74 *Yvonne van Duyn v. Home Office.* ('*Van Duyn*')

Case 43–75 *Gabrielle Defrenne v. Société anonyme belge de navigation aérienne Sabena.* ('*Defrenne* II')

Case 120–78 *Rewe-Zentral AG v. Bundesmonopolverwaltung für Branntwein.* ('*Cassis de Dijon*')

Case 44–79 *Liselotte Hauer v Land Rheinland-Pfalz.* ('*Hauer*')

Case 294–83 *Parti écologiste 'Les Verts' v. European Parliament.* ('*Les Verts*')

Case 362–88 *GB-INNO-BM v. Confédération du commerce luxembourgeois.* ('*GB Inno*')

### National Court decisions

*Frontini v. Ministero delle Finanze* [1974] 2 CMLR 372 (Italian Constitutional Court). ('*Frontini*')

2 BvL 52/71 – *Solange I*, 29 May 1974 – BVerfGE 37, 271 (German Constitutional Court). ('*Solange I*')

2 BvR 197/83 – *Solange II*, 22 October 1986 – BVerfGE 73, 339 (German Constitutional Court). ('*Solange II*')

## 3. Literature and primary sources

Abbott, K. W., and D. Snidal (2000), 'Hard and Soft Law in International Governance', *International Organization*, 54 (3): 421–56.

Acheson, D. (1969), *Present at the Creation: My Years in the State Department*, New York: W. W. Norton.

Albors-Llorens, A., C. Barnard and B. Leucht (eds) (2021), *Cassis de Dijon: 40 Years On*, London: Hart.

Allen, A. (2010), 'Cohesion Policy', in H. Wallace, M. Pollack and A. Young (eds), *Policy-Making in the EU*, 229–52, Oxford: Oxford University Press.

Alter, K. (2001), *Establishing the Supremacy of European Law: The Making of an International Rule of Law in Europe*, Oxford: Oxford University Press.

Alter, K. (2021), 'Big Decisions in European Legal and Economic Integration: What Have We Learned', in A. Albors-Llorens, C. Barnard and B. Leucht (eds), *Cassis de Dijon: 40 Years On*, 253–71, London: Hart.

Alter, K., and S. Meunier (1994), 'Judicial Politics in the European Community: European Integration and the Pathbreaking Cassis de Dijon Decision', *Comparative Political Studies*, 26 (4): 535–61.

Andry, A. (2019), 'Was There an Alternative? European Socialists Facing Capitalism in the Long 1970s', *European Review of History*, 26 (4): 723–46.

Appel, H., and M. Orenstein (2018), *From Triumph to Crisis: Neoliberal Economic Reform in Postcommunist Countries*, Cambridge: Cambridge University Press.

Aqui, L. (2020), *The First Referendum: Reassessing Britain's Entry to Europe, 1973–75*, Manchester: Manchester University Press.

Armengaud, A. (1972), 'Rapport fait au nom de la commission juridique sur les possibilités qu'offrent les traités communautaires en matières de lutte contre la pollution du milieu et les modifications qu'il faut éventuellement proposer d'y apporter PE 29179 def 17.04.1972 [CES 4011]', *European Parliament: Working Documents*, 1972–3 (15/72).

Armstrong, K., and S. Bulmer (1998), *The Governance of the Single European Market*, Manchester: Manchester University Press.

Asbeek Brusse, W. (1997), *Tariffs, Trade and European Integration, 1947–1957: From Study Group to Common Market*, New York: St Martin's.

Bailes, A., and G. Messervy-Whiting (2011), 'Death of an Institution: The End for Western European Union, a Future for European Defence?' *Egmont Paper*, 46, May, Brussels: Royal Institute for International Relations.

Bakker, A. (1996), *The Liberalization of Capital Movements in Europe: The Monetary Committee and Financial Integration 1958–1994*, Dordrecht: Kluwer Academic.

Ballor, G. (2022), 'CE Marking, Business, and European Market Integration', Business *History Review*, 96 (1): 77–108.

Barthel, C. (1993), 'De l'entente belgo-luxembourgoise à la Convention de Bruxelles. 1948–1954. Les maîtres de forges luxembourgois et la renaissance des ententes internationales au lendemain de la Seconde Guerre mondiale', in M. Dumoulin, R. Girault and G. Trausch (eds), *L'Europe de Patronat: De la guerre froide aux années soixante*, 29–62, Bern: Peter Lang.

Basosi, D. (2013), 'The European Community and International Reaganomics, 1981–1985', in K. K. Patel and K. Weisbrode (eds), *European Integration and the Atlantic Community in the 1980s*, 133–53, Cambridge: Cambridge University Press.

Beckfield, J. (2019), *Unequal Europe: Regional Integration and the Rise of European Inequality*, New York: Oxford University Press.

Bernier, A. (2012), 'Constructing and Legitimating: Transnational Jurist Networks and the Making of a Constitutional Practice of European Law, 1950–70', *Contemporary European History*, 21 (3): 399–415.

Billows, S., S. Kohl and F. Tarissan (2021), 'Bureaucrats or Ideologues? EU Merger Control as Market-Centred Integration', *Journal of Common Market Studies*, 59 (4): 762–81.

Bitumi, A. (2018), 'An Uplifting Tale of Europe. Jacques Delors and the Contradictory Quest for a European Social Model in the Age of Reagan', *Journal of Transatlantic Studies*, 16 (3): 203–21.

Boerger, A. (2012), 'Negotiating the Foundations of European Law, 1950–1957: The Legal History of the Treaties of Paris and Rome', *Contemporary European History*, 21 (3): 339–56.

Bohle, D., and B. Greskovits (2012), *Capitalism Diversity on Europe's Periphery*, Ithaca, NY: Cornell University Press.

Bond, M. (2021), *Hitler's Cosmopolitan Bastard: Count Richard Coudenhove-Kalergi and His Vision of Europe*, Montreal: McGill-Queen's University Press.

Börzel, T. A. (2002), 'Pace-Setting, Foot-Dragging and Fence-Sitting: Member State Responses to Europeanization', *Journal of Common Market Studies*, 40 (2): 193–214.

Börzel, T. A., A. Dimitrova and F. Schimmelfennig (2018), *European Union Enlargement and Integration Capacity*, London: Routledge.

Bossuat, G., and A. Legendre (2007), 'The Commission's Role in External Relations', in M. Dumoulin (ed.), *The European Commission, 1958–72: History and Memories*, 339–76, Luxembourg: Office for Official Publications of the European Communities.

Bouneau, C., D. Burigana and A. Varsori (eds) (2010), *Les trajectoires de l'innovation technologique et la construction Européenne: des voies de structuration durable?/Trends in Technological Innovation and the European Construction: The Emerging of Enduring Dynamics?*, Brussels: Peter Lang.

Boyer, G. (2019), *The Winding Road to the Welfare State: Economic Insecurity and Social Welfare Policy in Britain*, Princeton, NJ: Princeton University Press.

Bozo, F. (2009), *Mitterrand, the End of the Cold War, and German Unification*, New York: Berghahn.

Brack, N. (2018), *Opposing Europe in the European Parliament: Rebels and Radicals in the Chamber*, London: Palgrave Macmillan.

Bradford, A. (2020), *The Brussels Effect: How the European Union Rules the World*, Oxford: Oxford University Press.

Bradford, A., R. Jackson and J. Zytnick (2017), 'Is EU Merger Control Used for Protectionism? An Empirical Analysis', *Journal of Empirical Legal Studies*, 15 (1): 165–91.

Bressanelli, E., and N. Chelotti (eds) (2021), 'What Brexit Means for Europe: EU Institutions and Actors after the British Referendum', *Politics and Governance*, 9 (1) (special issue on Brexit): 1–89.

Bretherton, C., and J. Vogler (2006), *The European Union as a Global Actor*, London: Routledge.

Brown, M. (2022), The Seventh Member State. Algeria, France and the European Community, Cambridge, MA: Harvard University Press.

Brunn, G. (2004), 'Das Europäische Parlament auf dem Weg zur ersten Direktwahl 1979', in F. Knipping and M. Schönwald (eds), *Aufbruch zum Europa der zweiten Generation: Die europäische Einigung*, 47–72, Trier: Wissenschaftlicher Verlag Trier.

Bührer, W. (1986), *Ruhrstahl und Europa: Die Wirtschaftsvereinigung Eisen- und Stahlindustrie und die Anfänge der Europäischen Integration 1945–52*, Schriftenreihe der Vierteljahreshefte für Zeitgeschichte, vol. 53, Munich: R. Oldenbourg.

Bulmer, S., and W. E. Paterson (2017), 'Germany and the Crisis: Asset or Liability?', in D. Dinan, N. Nugent and W. E. Paterson (eds), *The European Union in Crisis*, 212–32, London: Palgrave.

Buonanno, L. (2017), 'The European Migration Crisis', in D. Dinan, N. Nugent and W. E. Paterson (eds), *The European Union in Crisis*, 100–30, London: Palgrave.

Burgess, M. (1989), *Federalism and European Union: Political Ideas, Influences and Strategies in the European Community, 1972–1987*, London: Routledge.

Burgess, M. (2000), *Federalism and the European Union: The Building of Europe, 1950–2000*, London: Routledge.

Burgess, M. (2006), *Federalism and European Union: Political Ideas, Influences, and Strategies in the European Community 1972–1986*, London: Routledge.

Bussière, E. (2007), 'Not Quite a Common Market Yet', in M. Dumoulin (ed.), *The European Commission, 1958–72: History and Memories*, 289–302, Luxembourg: Office for Official Publications of the European Communities.

Bussière, E., M. Dumoulin and S. Schirmann (2009), 'The Development of Economic Integration', in W. Loth (ed.), *Experiencing Europe: 50 Years of European Construction 1957–2007*, 45–102, Baden-Baden Nomos.

Bussière, E., V. Dujardin, M. Dumoulin, P. Ludlow, J. W. Brouwer and P. Tilly (eds) (2014), *The European Commission 1973–1986: History and Memories of an Institution*, Luxembourg: Office for Official Publications of the European Communities.

Bussière, E., A. Grisoni, H. Miard-Delacroix and C. Wenkel (eds) (2020), *The Environment and the European Public Sphere: Perceptions, Actors, Policies*, Winwick: White Horse.

Calligaro, O. (2013), *Negotiating Europe: EU Promotion of Europeanness since the 1950s*, Basingstoke: Palgrave Macmillan.

Cappelletti, M., M. Seccombe and J. H. H. Weiler (1986a), 'General Editors' Foreword', in T. Bourgoignie and D. M. Trubek (eds), *Integration through Law, Vol 3: Consumer Law, Common Markets and Federalism in Europe and the United States*, v–viii, Berlin: W. de Gruyter.

Cappelletti, M., M. Seccombe and J. H. H. Weiler (1986b), *Integration through Law: Europe and the American Federal Experience*, Berlin: W. de Gruyter.

Carr, E. H. (1945), *Nationalism and After*, London: Macmillan.

Cavallaro, M. E. (2019), 'Regional Policy: A New Source of Europeanisation', in V. Dujardin, E. Bussière, N. P. Ludlow, F. Romero, D. Schlenker and A. Varsori (eds), *The European Commission 1986–2000: Histories and Memory of an Institution*, 421–41, Luxembourg: Office for Official Publications of the European Communities.

Chakrabarti, D. (2008), *Provincialising Europe: Postcolonial Thought and Historical Difference*, Princeton, NJ: Princeton University Press.

Church, C., and D. Phinnemore (2016), 'From the Constitutional Treaty to the Treaty of Lisbon and Beyond', in M. Cini and N. Pérez-Solórzano Borragán (eds), *European Union Politics*, 30–49, Oxford: Oxford University Press.

Churchill, W. (1946), Speech delivered at the University of Zurich, 19 September. Available online: https://rm.coe.int/16806981f3 (accessed 7 January 2022).

Cini, M., and L. McGowan (2009), *Competition Policy in the European Union*, Basingstoke: Palgrave Macmillan.

Claeys, G. (2017), 'How to Build a Resilient Monetary Union? Lessons from the Euro Crisis', *Asian Development Bank Institute Working Paper Series*, no. 778.

Clarke, H. D., M. Goodwin and P. Whiteley (2017), *Brexit: Why Britain Voted to Leave the European Union*, Cambridge: Cambridge University Press.

Cohen, A. (2007), 'Le "père de l'Europe": La construction sociale d'un récit des origines', *Actes de la recherche en sciences sociales*, 166: 14–29.

Cohen, A., and A. Vauchez (2005), 'Les juristes et l'ordre politique européen', *Critique internationale*, 1: 97–9.

Colbourn, S., and M. Haeussler (2021), 'Once More, with Feeling: Transatlantic Relations in the Reagan Years', in J. R. Hunt and S. Miles (eds), *The Reagan Moment: America and the World in the 1980s*, 123–43, Ithaca, NY: Cornell University Press.

Cole, A. (2000), *Franco-German Relations*, London: Routledge.

Communauté européenne (ed.) (1958), 'Final Resolution adopted by the Delegations of the Six Member States of the European Economic Community (EEC)', *Recueil des documents de la Conférence agricole des Etats membres de la Communauté économique européenne à Stresa du 3 au 12 juillet 1958*, 219–24, Luxembourg: Service des publications des Communautés européennes.

Comte, E. (2018), *The History of the European Migration Regime: Germany's Strategic Hegemony*, New York: Routledge.

Conway, M., and K. K. Patel (2010), *Europeanization in the Twentieth Century: Historical Approaches*, Basingstoke: Palgrave Macmillan.

COPA (1972), 'Observations du Comité des Organisations Agricoles sur le programme en matière d'environnement, 10 November 1972, sent to Sicco Mansholt, European Commission, 16 November 1972', *Historical Archives of the European Commission*, BAC 244/1991 6: 7–18.

Coppolaro, L. (2009), 'The Six, Agriculture, and GATT: An International History of the CAP Negotiations, 1958–1967', in K. Patel (ed.), *Fertile Ground for Europe? The History of European Integration and the Common Agricultural Policy since 1945*, 201–19, Baden-Baden: Nomos.

Coppolaro, L. (2013), *The Making of a World Trading Power: The European Economic Community (EEC) in the GATT Kennedy Round Negotiations (1963–1967)*, London: Routledge.

Coppolaro, L. (2016), 'GATT, Inflation and Exchange Rate Instability: Liberalizing Trade in the Tokyo Round Negotiations (1973–1979)', in M.-P. Chélini and L. Warlouzet (eds), *Slowing Prices Down: European Inflation in the 1970s*, 323–41, Paris: Presses de Sciences Po.

Coppolaro, L. (2018), 'In the Shadow of Globalization: The European Community and the United States in the GATT Negotiations of the Tokyo Round (1973–1977)', *International History Review*, 40 (4): 752–73.

Corbett, R., F. Jacobs and M. Shackleton (2021), *The European Parliament*, 9th ed., London: John Harper.

Cotey Morgan, M. (2018), *The Final Act: The Helsinki Accords and the Transformation of the Cold War*, Princeton, NJ: Princeton University Press.

Council (1973), 'Declaration of the Council of the European Communities and of the Representatives of the Governments of the Member States Meeting in the Council of 22 November 1973 on the Programme of Action of the European Communities on the Environment', *Official Journal of the European Communities*, 16 (C 112, 20 December): 1–53.

Council (1975), 'Preliminary Programme for Consumer Protection and Information Policy', *Official Journal of the EC*, 18 (C 92, 25 April).

Council of Ministers (1966), 'Final Communique of the Extraordinary Session of the Council (January 1966)', *Bulletin of the European Economic Community*, March, no. 3, p. 9. Available online: http://aei.pitt.edu/54209/1/BUL063.pdf (accessed 21 March 2022).

'Covenant of the League of Nations' (1919), *The Avalon Project: Documents in Law, History and Diplomacy*. Available online: https://avalon.law.yale.edu/20th_century/leagcov.asp (accessed 7 January 2022).

Craig, P. (2013), *The Lisbon Treaty: Law, Politics, and Treaty Reform*, Oxford: Oxford University Press.

Crespy, A. (2016), *Welfare Markets in Europe: The Democratic Challenge of European Integration*, Basingstoke: Palgrave Macmillan.

Crump, L. (2015), *The Warsaw Pact Reconsidered: International Relations in Eastern Europe, 1955–1969*, New York: Routledge.

Cunha, A. (2019), 'A Welcome Incentive: Pre-accession Aid to Portugal within the Context of the Iberian Enlargement', *Journal of European Integration History*, 25 (2): 207–23.

Daddow, O. (2012), 'The UK Media and "Europe": From Permissive Consensus to Destructive Dissent', *International Affairs*, 88 (6): 1219–36.

Daddow, O. (ed.) (2016), *Harold Wilson and European Integration: Britain's Second Application to Join the EEC*, London: Routledge.

Dahrendorf, R. (1990), *Reflections on the Revolution in Europe*, London: Chatto & Windus.

Davies, B. (2012), *Resisting the European Court of Justice: West Germany's Confrontation with European Law, 1949–1979*, Cambridge: Cambridge University Press.

Davies, B. (2015), 'Resistance to European Law and Constitutional Identity in Germany: Herbert Kraus and Solange in Its Intellectual Context', *European Law Journal*, 21 (4): 434–59.

Davies, B., and F. Nicola (eds) (2017), *EU Law Stories: Contextual and Critical Histories of European Jurisprudence*, Cambridge: Cambridge University Press.

Davies, B., and M. Rasmussen (2012), 'Introduction: Towards a New History of European Law', *Contemporary European History*, 21 (3): 305–18.

Davies, B., and M. Rasmussen (2014), 'From International Law to a European *Rechtsgemeinschaft*: Towards a New History of European Law, 1950–1979', in J. Laursen (ed.), *Institutions and Dynamics of the European Community, 1973–83*, 97–130, Baden-Baden: Nomos.

Davies, J. (2011), *The European Consumer Citizen in Law and Policy*, Basingstoke: Palgrave.

De Ville, F. (2020), 'Trade Policy: Which Gains for Which Losses', in R. Coman, A. Crespy and V. Schmidt (eds), *Governance and Politics in the Post-Crisis European Union*, 278–93, Cambridge: Cambridge University Press.

'Declaration on European Identity (1973)', *Bulletin of the European Communities*, December 1973, No 12, 118–22, Luxembourg: Office for Official Publications of the European Communities. Available online: https://www.cvce.eu/content/publication/1999/1/1/02798dc9-9c69-4b7d-b2c9-f03a8db7da32/publishable_en.pdf (accessed 11 January 2022).

Degimbe, J. (1999), *La politique sociale européenne: du Traité de Rome au Traité d'Amsterdam*, Brussels: Institut syndical européen.

Deighton, A. (2010), 'Britain and the Cold War, 1945–1955', in M. P. Leffler and O. A. Westad (eds), *The Cambridge History of the Cold War, Vol. I: Origins*, 112–32, Cambridge: Cambridge University Press.

Deighton, D., and A. Milward (eds) (1999), *Widening, Deepening and Acceleration: The European Economic Community 1957–1963*, Baden-Baden: Nomos.

Delaney, E. F. (2019), 'The European Constitution and Europe's Dialectical Federalism', in N. W. Barber (ed.), *The Rise and Fall of the European Constitution*, 73–88, London: Hart.

Delcker, J. (2015), 'Merkel on Migration: We Will Manage', *Politico*, 8 October: https://www.politico.eu/article/merkel-on-migration-we-will-manage/ (accessed 15 September 2022).

Dell, E. (1995), *The Schuman Plan and the British Abdication of Leadership in Europe*, Oxford: Clarendon.

Delors, J. (1985), 'The Thrust of Commission Policy.' Statement by Jacques Delors, President of the Commission, to the European Parliament, Strasbourg, 14–15 January. Available online: http://aei.pitt.edu/8525/ (accessed 24 March 2022).

Delzell, C. (1993), 'Altiero Spinelli and the Origins of the European Federalist Movement in Italy', *History of European Ideas*, 16 (4–6): 767–71.

Diebold, W. (1959), *The Schuman Plan: A Study in Economic Cooperation 1950–1959*, New York: Frederick A. Praeger.

Dimier, V. (2014), *The Invention of a European Development Aid Bureaucracy: Recycling Empire*, Basingstoke: Palgrave Macmillan.

Dinan, D. (2014), *Europe Recast: A History of European Union*, Basingstoke: Palgrave Macmillan.

Dinan, D. (2021), 'The European Parliament: Moving to the Centre of Historical Interest in the European Union', *Journal of European Integration History*, 27 (1): 139–55.

Dinan, D., N. Nugent and W. Paterson (eds) (2017), *The European Union in Crisis*, London: Palgrave Macmillan.

Drach, A. (2020), 'Reluctant Europeans? British and French Commercial Banks and the Common Market in Banking (1977–1992)', *Enterprise and Society*, 21 (3): 768–98.

Drach, D. (2021), 'Removing Obstacles to Integration: The European Way to Deregulation', in A. Drach and Y. Cassis (eds), *Financial Deregulation: A Historical Perspective*, 76–100, Oxford: Oxford University Press.

Drahokoupil, J. (2009), *Globalization and the State in Central and Eastern Europe: The Politics of Foreign Direct Investment*, London: Routledge.

Drake, H. (2000), *Jacques Delors: Perspectives on a European Leader*, London: Routledge.

Dujardin, V. (2014), 'Building New Momentum: 1973–1986', in E. Bussière, V. Dujardin, M. Dumoulin, P. Ludlow, J. W. Brouwer and P. Tilly (eds), *The European Commission, 1973–1986: History and Memories of an Institution*, 15–30, Luxembourg: Office for Official Publications of the European Communities.

Dujardin, V., E. Bussière, P. Ludlow, F. Romero, D. Schlenker and A. Varsori (eds) (2019), *The European Commission 1986–2000: History and Memories of an Institution*, Luxembourg: Office for Official Publications of the European Communities.

Dumoulin, M. (2007a), 'From "Overseas Countries and Territories" to Development Aid', in M. Dumoulin (ed.), *The European Commission, 1958–72: History and Memories*, 377–90, Luxembourg: Office for Official Publications of the European Communities.

Dumoulin, M. (ed.) (2007b), *History of the European Commission 1958–1972: History and Memories*, Luxembourg: Office for Official Publications of the European Communities.

Dyson, K. (2017), 'Playing for High Stakes: The Eurozone Crisis', in D. Dinan, N. Nugent and W. E. Paterson (eds), *The European Union in Crisis*, 54–76, London: Palgrave.

Dyson, K., and K. Featherstone (1999), *The Road to Maastricht: Negotiating Economic and Monetary Union*, Oxford: Oxford University Press.

Dyson, K., and I. Maes (eds) (2016), *Architects of the Euro: Intellectuals in the Making of European Monetary Union*, Oxford: Oxford University Press.

Dyson, K., and L. Quaglia (2010), *European Economic Governance and Policies*, 2 vols, Oxford: Oxford University Press.

*Economist* (2022), 'Nein, danke! Why Germans Remain So Jittery about Nuclear Power', 8 January.

Edwards, G. (ed.) (2006), *The European Commission*, 3rd ed., London: John Harper.

Egan, M. (2001), *Constructing a European Market*, Oxford: Oxford University Press.

Ellinas, A., and E. Suleiman (2012), *The European Commission and Bureaucratic Autonomy: Europe's Custodians*, Cambridge: Cambridge University Press.

Ellison, J. (2000a), *Threatening Europe: Britain and the Creation of the European Community, 1955–58*, New York: St Martin's.

Ellison, J. (2000b), 'Accepting the Inevitable: Britain and European Integration', in W. Kaiser and G. Staerck (eds), *British Foreign Policy, 1955–64: Contracting Options*, 171–89, Basingstoke: Macmillan.

Erklärung (1978), 'zur Demokratie des Europäischen Rates in Kopenhagen', 7–8 April. Available online: https://www.cvce.eu/obj/erklarung_zur_demokratie_des_europaischen_rates_in_kopenhagen_7_und_8_april_1978-de-c054a cb7-0d62-466b-81ed-30c40f097567.html (accessed 18 February 2022).

Eurobarometer (2019), *Closer to the Citizens, Closer to the Ballot, Survey 91.1*, Brussels: European Parliament. Available online: https://www.europarl.europa.eu/at-your-service/files/be-heard/eurobarome ter/2019/closer-to-the-citizens-closer-to-the-ballot/report/en-eurobarome ter-2019.pdf (accessed 15 September 2022).

European Commission (1971), 'First Communication of the Commission about the Community's Policy on the Environment. SEC (71) 2616 final, 22 July 1971'. Available online: *Archive of European Integration*: http://aei.pitt. edu/3126/1/3126.pdf (accessed 26 March 2022).

European Commission (1972a), 'Communication from the Commission to the Council on a European Communities' Programme concerning the Environment (Submitted on 24 March 1972)', *Bulletin of the European Communities: Supplement*, 5 (5): 1–69.

European Commission (1972b), *First Report on Competition Policy*, Luxembourg: Office for Official Publications of the European Communities.

European Commission (1976), 'Draft First Annual Report on Consumer Protection and Information Policy, 27 August 1976', *Historical Archives of the European Commission*, BAC 153/1990 (74).

European Commission (1985), 'Completing the Internal Market: White Paper from the Commission to the European Council (Milan, 28-29 June 1985)'. Available online: https://op.europa.eu/en/publication-detail/-/publication/4ff49 0f3-dbb6-4331-a2ea-a3ca59f974a8 (accessed 13 February 2022).

European Commission (2000), 'Reforming the Commission: A White Paper'. Available online: https://op.europa.eu/en/publication-detail/-/publication/1b8f0 479-f395-43bd-8e29-be98955bd8a2 (accessed 15 September 2022).

European Commission (2010), 'The CAP towards 2020: Meeting the Food, Natural Resources and Territorial Challenges of the Future'. Available online: https://eur-lex.europa.eu/legal-content/EN/TXT/?uri=CELEX%3A5201 0DC0672&qid=1647899100200 (accessed 21 March 2022).

European Commission (2019), 'The European Green Deal: Communication from the Commission to the European Parliament, the European Council, the Council, the European Economic and Social Committee and the Committee of the Regions, Brussels, 11.12.2019, COM (2019) 640 final'. Available online: https://ec.europa.eu/info/sites/info/files/european-green-deal-communica tion_en.pdf (accessed 16 February 2021).

European Commission (2021), 'HR Key Figures: Staff Members'. Available online: https://ec.europa.eu/info/sites/default/files/european-commission-hr_key_ figures_2021_en.pdf (accessed 15 September 2022).

European Council (1980), *Conclusions*. Luxembourg, 1 and 2 December 1980. Available online: https://www.consilium.europa.eu/media/20730/luxembourg_ december_1980__eng_.pdf (accessed 19 February 2022).

European Council (1993), *Conclusions of the Presidency, Copenhagen, 21–22 June*, Brussels: General Secretariat of the Council. Available online: https://www.consilium.europa.eu/media/21225/72921.pdf (accessed 13 February 2022).

European Council (2001), *Presidency Conclusions, Laeken, 14–15 December*, Brussels: General Secretariat of the Council. Available online: https://www.consilium.europa.eu/media/20950/68827.pdf (accessed 13 February 2022).

European Council (2002), *Seville European Council 21–22 June 2002: Presidency Conclusions*, 13463/02, Brussels: General Secretariat of the Council. Available online: https://www.consilium.europa.eu/media/20928/72638.pdf (accessed 13 February 2022).

European Parliament (2019), 'Closer to the Citizens, Closer to the Ballot'. Available online: https://www.europarl.europa.eu/at-your-service/en/be-heard/eurobarometer/closer-to-the-citizens-closer-to-the-ballot (accessed 13 February 2022).

European People's Party Congress Document (2002), *A Constitution for a Strong Europe*, Estoril, 18 October.

European Union (2018), *The OLAF Report 2017*, Luxembourg: Publications Office of the European Union. Available online: https://ec.europa.eu/anti-fraud/sites/antifraud/files/olaf_report_2017_en.pdf (accessed 13 February 2022).

Eurostat (2018), *EU Mobile Citizens of Working Age*. Available online: https://ec.europa.eu/eurostat/statistics-explained/index.php?title=File:EU_mobile_citizens_of_working_age_(20-64)_by_country_of_citizenship,_%25_of_their_home-country_resident_population_2018.png (accessed 13 February 2022).

Federalist Letter to the Convention (2003), *The Convention Is Failing to Bring Democracy to the European Union*, Issue number 9, 12 June. Available online: https://federalunion.org.uk/federalist-letter-to-the-european-constitutional-convention-9/ (accessed 7 January 2022).

Federico, G. (2009), 'Was the CAP the Worst Agricultural Policy of the 20th Century?', in K. K. Patel (ed.), *Fertile Ground for Europe? The History of European Integration and the Common Agricultural Policy since 1945*, 257–71, Baden-Baden: Nomos.

Ferguson, N., C. S. Maier, E. Manela and D. J. Sargent (eds) (2010), *The Shock of the Global: The 1970s in Perspective*, Cambridge, MA: Harvard University Press.

Ferrari, L. (2016), *Sometimes Speaking with a Single Voice: The European Community as an International Actor, 1969–1979*, Brussels: PIE Peter Lang.

Final Communiqué (1969), 'Final Communiqué of the Meeting of Heads of State or Government of the Member States at The Hague, 1 and 2 December 1969'. Available online: http://www.cvce.eu/obj/final_communique_of_the_hague_summit_2_december_19 69-en-33078789-8030-49c8-b4e0-15d053834507.html (accessed 24 March 2022).

Fischer, C. (2012), 'The Failed European Union: Franco-German Relations during the Great Depression of 1929–32', *International History Review*, 34(4): 705–24.

Fischer, J. (2000), 'From Confederacy to Federation: Thoughts on the Finality of European Integration', Speech at the Humboldt University, Berlin, 12 May. Available online: https://ec.europa.eu/dorie/fileDownload.do?docId=192161&cardId=192161 (accessed 7 January 2022).

Flood, C. (2009), 'Dimensions of Euroscepticism', *Journal of Common Market Studies*, 47 (4): 911–17.

Fouilleux, E., and M. Ansaloni (2016), 'The Common Agricultural Policy', in M. Cini and N. Perez Solorzano Borragan (eds), *European Union Politics*, 5th ed., 308–22, Oxford: Oxford University Press.

Frank, R., H. Kaelble, M. Levy and L. Passerini (eds) (2010), *Building a European Public Sphere: From the 1950s to the Present*, Brussels: Peter Lang.

Frennhoff Larsén, M., and S. Khorana (2020), 'Negotiating Brexit: A Clash of Approaches', *Comparative European Politics*, 18 (5): 858–77.

Frey, J. E., and F. Warin (1974), 'European Consumer Protection: The Council of Europe Charter Initiative', *Law and Policy in International Business*, 6 (4): 1107–32.

Fritz, V. (2020), 'Activism on and off the Bench: Pierre Pescatore and the Law of Integration', *Common Market Law Review*, 57 (2): 475–502.

Garavini, G. (2006), 'The Battle for the Participation of the European Community in the G7 (1975–1977)', *Journal of European Integration History*, 12 (1): 141–58.

Garavini, G. (2012), *After Empires: European Integration, Decolonization, and the Challenge from the Global South, 1957–1986*, Oxford: Oxford University Press.

Garrett, G. (1995), 'The Politics of Legal Integration in the European Union', *International Organisation*, 49 (1): 171–81.

Garton Ash, T. (1990), *The Magic Lantern: The Revolution of '89 Witnessed in Warsaw, Budapest, Berlin, and Prague*, London: Random House.

Garzon, I. (2006), *Reforming the Common Agricultural Policy: History of a Paradigm Change*, Basingstoke: Palgrave Macmillan.

Gatrell, P. (2019), *The Unsettling of Europe: The Great Migration, 1945 to the Present*, London: Penguin.

Gaulle, C. de (1960), 'Press Conference 5 September', in *Discours et messages: Tome III: Avec le renouveau (1958–1962)*, 244-6, Paris: Plon. Available online: https://www.cvce.eu/en/obj/press_conference_held_by_charles _de_gaulle_5_september_1960-en-0993e4e3-896a-4c44-89c4-9de188c1d637. html (accessed 14 August 2022).

Gaulle, C. de (1963), 'Press Conference 14 January', in *Discours et messages: Tome IV: Pour l'effort (1962–1965)*, 66–71, Paris: Plon. Available online: https:// www.cvce.eu/en/obj/press_conference_held_by_general_de_gaulle_14_janua ry_1963-en-5b5d0d35-4266-49bc-b770-b24826858e1f.html (accessed 10 January 2022).

Gaulle, C. de (1970), *Discours et messages: Volume III: Avec le renouveau (1958–1962)*, 244–6, Paris: Plon (translated from the French original by KS). Available online: https://www.cvce.eu/en/obj/press_conference_held_by_charles_de_ gaulle_5_september_1960-en-0993e4e3-896a-4c44-89c4-9de188c1d637.html (accessed 21 March 2022).

Gavin Munte, V. (2008), 'A New Framework for Franco-German Relations through European Institutions, 1950 to 1954', in G. Germond and H. Türk (eds), *A History of Franco-German Relations in Europe: From 'Hereditary Enemies' to Partners*, 165–75, New York: Palgrave.

Geddes, A., L. Hadj-Abdou and L. Brumat (2020), *Migration and Mobility in the European Union*, London: Bloomsbury.

Gehler, M. (2016), '"Europe", Europeanizations and Their Meaning for European Integration Historiography', *Journal of European Integration History*, 22 (1): 141–74.

Georgakakis, D. (2017), *European Civil Service in (Times of) Crisis: A Political Sociology of the Changing Power of the Eurocrats*, Basingstoke: Palgrave.

George, G. (1994), *An Awkward Partner: Britain in the European Community*, Oxford: Oxford University Press.

Gerber, D. (2007), 'Two Forms of Modernization in European Competition Law', *Fordham International Law Journal*, 31 (5): 1235–65.

*German Politics & Society* (2013), 'The Elysée Treaty at Fifty', 31 (1) (Special Issue).

Germond, C. (2013), 'Dynamic Franco-German Duos: Giscard-Schmidt and Mitterrand-Kohl', in E. Jones, A. Menon and S. Weatherill (eds), *The Oxford Handbook of the European Union*, 193–205, Oxford: Oxford University Press.

Germond, C. (2022), 'Franco-German Relations and the European Integration Process since German Reunification', in K. Larres and H. Moroff (eds), *Oxford Handbook of German Politics*, 491–508, Oxford: Oxford University Press.

Germond, C., and H. Türk (eds) (2008), *A History of Franco-German Relations in Europe: From 'Hereditary Enemies' to Partners*, New York: Palgrave.

Geyer, M., and J. Paulmann (eds) (2001), *The Mechanisms of Internationalism: Culture, Society, and Politics from the 1840s to the First World War*, Oxford: Oxford University Press.

Gfeller, A. E. (2012), *Building a European Identity: France, the United States, and the Oil Shock, 1973–74*, New York: Berghahn.

Gfeller, A. E. (2014), 'Champion of European Rights: The European Parliament and the Helsinki Process', *Journal of Contemporary History*, 49 (2): 390–490.

Ghodsee, K., and M. Orenstein (2021), *Taking Stock of Shock: Social Consequences of the 1989 Revolutions*, Oxford: Oxford University Press.

Giauque, J. G. (2002), *Grand Designs and Visions of Unity: The Atlantic Powers and the Reorganization of Western Europe, 1955–1963*, Chapel Hill: University of North Carolina Press.

Gilbert, M. (2008), 'Narrating the Process: Questioning the Progressive Story of European Integration', *Journal of Common Market Studies*, 46 (3): 641–62.

Gilbert, M. (2021), 'Historicising European Integration History', *European Review of International Studies*, 8: 221–40.

Gilbert, M., and D. Pacquinucci (eds) (2020), *Euroscepticisms: The Historical Roots of a Political Challenge*, Leiden: Brill.

Gillingham, J. (1986), 'Zur Vorgeschichte der Montan-Union. Westeuropas Kohle und Stahl in Depression und Krieg', *Vierteljahreshefte für Zeitgeschichte*, 34: 381–405.

Gillingham, J. (1991), *Coal, Steel, and the Rebirth of Europe, 1945–55: The Germans and the French from Ruhr Conflict to Economic Community*, New York: Cambridge University Press.

Gilpin, R. (1987), *The Political Economy of International Relations*, Princeton, NJ: Princeton University Press.

Gram-Skjoldager, K., and H. Ikonomou (2019), 'Making Sense of the League of Nations Secretariat – Historiographical and Conceptual Reflections on Early International Public Administration', *European History Quarterly*, 49 (3): 420–44.

Gram-Skjoldager, K., H. Ikonomou and T. Kahlert (eds) (2020), *Organizing the 20th Century World: International Organizations and the Emergence of International Public Administration, 1920–1960s*, London: Bloomsbury.

Grant, W. (1997), *The Common Agricultural Policy*, Basingstoke: Palgrave Macmillan.

Greenwood, S. (1992), *Britain and European Cooperation since 1945*, London: Blackwell.

Greiner, F. (2014), *Wege nach Europa: Deutungen eines imaginierten Kontinents in deutschen, britischen und amerikanischen Printmedien, 1914–1945*, Goettingen: Wallstein Verlag.

Griffiths, R. T. (2000), *Europe's First Constitution: The European Political Community, 1952–1954*, London: Federal Trust.

Griffiths, R. T., and B. Girvin (eds) (1995), *The Green Pool and the Origins of the Common Agricultural Policy*, London: Lothian.

Grin, G. (2003), *The Battle of the Single European Market: Achievements and Economic Thought, 1985–2000*, London: Paul Kegan.

Guerrieri, S. (2015), 'The Genesis of Supranational Representation: The Formation of Political Groups at the Common Assembly of the ECSC', in L. Bonfreschi, G. Orsina and A. Varsori (eds), *European Parties and the European Integration Process, 1945–1992*, 393–410, Brussels: PIE Peter Lang.

Guieu, J. (2009), 'Introduction: Le Congres de La Haye (7–10 mai 1948), "porte-parole de l'Europe"?', in J. Guieu and C. Le Dreau (eds), *Le 'Congres de l'Europe' à La Haye (1948–2008)*, 15–42, Brussels: Peter Lang.

Guirao, F. (2020), *The European Rescue of the Franco Regime, 1950–1975*, Oxford: Oxford University Press.

Haas, E. B. ([1958] 2004), *The Uniting of Europe: Political, Social and Economic Forces, 1950–57*, Stanford: Stanford University Press.

Habermas, J. (2011), 'Wie demokratisch ist die EU? Die Krise der Europäischen Union im Licht einer Konstitutionalisierung des Völkerrechts', *Blätter für deutsche und internationale Politik*, 8: 37–48.

Haeussler, M. (2014), 'The Popular Press and Ideas of Europe: The *Daily Mirror*, the *Daily Express*, and Britain's First Application to Join the EEC, 1961–63', *Twentieth Century British History*, 25 (1): 108–31.

Haeussler, M. (2015), 'A Pyrrhic Victory: Harold Wilson, Helmut Schmidt, and the British Renegotiation of EC Membership, 1974–5', *International History Review*, 37 (4): 768–89.

Haeussler, M. (2019), *Helmut Schmidt and British-German Relations: A European Misunderstanding*, Cambridge: Cambridge University Press.

Haeussler, M. (2022), 'Don't Think Twice, It's All Right? A Historical Comparison of the 1975 and 2016 British Referendums', *Journal of European Integration History*, 28 (1): 37–56.

Haigh, N., and C. Lanigan (1995), 'Impact of the European Union on UK Environmental Policy Making', in T. S. Gray (ed.), *UK Environmental Policy in the 1990s*, 18–37, London: Macmillan.

Hall, R. (2014), 'The Development of Regional Policy in the Process of European Integration: An Overview', in G. Bischof (ed.), *Regional Economic Development Compared: EU-Europe and the American South*, 13–33, Innsbruck: Innsbruck University Press.

Hallstein, W. (1972), *Europe in the Making*, London: Allen and Unwin.

Hanhimäki, J. (2004), *The Flawed Architect: Henry Kissinger and American Foreign Policy*, Oxford: Oxford University Press.

Hansen, P., and S. Jonsson (2014), *Eurafrica: The Untold History of European Integration*, London: Bloomsbury Academic.

Harold D. Clarke, Matthew J. Goodwin and Paul F. Whiteley (2017), *Brexit: Why Britain Voted to Leave the European Union*, Cambridge: Cambridge University Press.

Hay, D. (1968), *Europe: The Emergence of an Idea*, Edinburgh: Edinburgh University Publications.

Heater, D. (1992), *The Idea of European Unity*, Leicester: Leicester University Press.

Hendriks, G., and A. Morgan (eds) (2001), *The Franco-German Axis in European Integration*, Cheltenham: Edward Elgar.

Hennock, E. P. (2007), *The Origin of the Welfare State in England and Germany, 1850–1914: Social Policies Compared*, Cambridge: Cambridge University Press.

Héritier, A., K. L. Meissner, C. Moury and M. G. Schoeller (2019), *European Parliament Ascendant: Parliamentary Strategies of Self-Empowerment in the EU*, Basingstoke: Palgrave Macmillan.

Hewitson, M., and M. D'Auria (eds) (2015), *Europe in Crisis: Intellectuals and the European Idea, 1917–1957*, New York: Berghahn.

Hirschhausen, U. v., and K. K. Patel (2010), 'Europeanization in History: An Introduction', in M. Conway and K. K. Patel (eds), *Europeanization in the Twentieth Century: Historical Approaches*, 1–18, Basingstoke: Palgrave Macmillan.

Hitchcock, W. (2010), 'The Marshall Plan and the Creation of the West', in M. Leffler and O. Westad (eds), *The Cambridge History of the Cold War*, 154–74, Cambridge: Cambridge University Press.

Hix, S., and A. Kreppel (2003), 'The Party System in the European Parliament: Collusive or Competitive', *Journal of Common Market Studies*, 41 (2): 309–31.

Hobolt, S. B. (2015), 'The 2014 European Parliament Elections: Divided in Unity?', *Journal of Common Market Studies*, 53 (Annual Review): 6–21.

Hobolt, S. B. (2016), 'The Brexit Vote: A Divided Nation, a Divided Continent', *Journal of European Public Policy*, 23 (9): 1259–77.

Höhler, S. (2015), *Spaceship Earth in the Environmental Age, 1960–1990*, London: Pickering & Chatto.

Hooghe, L., and G. Marks (2001), *Multilevel Governance and European Integration*, London: Rowman & Littlefield.

Hooghe, L., and G. Marks (2008), 'A Postfunctionalist Theory of European Integration: From Permissive Consensus to Constraining Dissensus', *British Journal of Political Science*, 39: 1–23.

Howorth, J. (2017), 'European Defence Policy between Dependence and Autonomy: A Challenge of Sisyphean Dimensions', *British Journal of Politics and International Relations*, 19 (1): 13–28.

Hugo, V. (1849), 'Speech to the Peace Congress at Paris', printed in *Sydney Morning Herald*, 26 December: 3.

Huysmans, J. (2006), *The Politics of Insecurity: Fear, Migration and Asylum in the EU*, Abingdon: Routledge.

Ireland, P. (1995), 'Migration, Free Movement, and Immigrant Integration in the EU: A Bifurcated Policy Response', in S. Leibfried and P. Pierson (eds), *European Social Policy: Between Fragmentation and Integration*, 231–66, Washington: Brookings Institution.

Jabko, N. (2006), *Playing the Market: A Political Strategy for Uniting Europe, 1985–2005*, Ithaca, NY: Cornell University Press.

Jackson, A. L. R. (2018), *Conserving Europe's Wildlife, Law and Policy of the Natura 2000 Network of Protected Areas*, Abingdon: Routledge.

James, H. (2012), *Making the European Monetary Union: The Role of the Committee of Central Bank Governors and the Origins of the European Central Bank*, Cambridge, MA: Harvard University Press.

James, H. (2016), 'The History of Economic and Monetary Union', in H. Badinger and V. Nitsch (eds), *Routledge Handbook of the Economics of European Integration*, 22–37, Abingdon: Routledge.

Johnson, J. (2016), *Priests of Prosperity: How Central Bankers Transformed the Post-Communist World*, Ithaca, NY: Cornell University Press.

Joint Declaration on European Defence (1998), Joint Declaration issued at the British-French Summit, Saint-Malo, 3–4 December.

Joint Franco-German Declaration (1963), Paris, 22 January. Available online: http://www.cvce.eu/obj/joint_franco_german_declaration_paris_22_j anuary_1963-en-5c771e9f-810d-426d-94ff- ee035b542a67.html (accessed 24 March 2022).

Jones, E., R. D. Kelemen and S. Meunier (2016), 'Failing Forward? The Euro Crisis and the Incomplete Nature of European Integration', *Comparative Political Studies*, 49 (7): 1010–34.

Josling, T., and S. Tangermann (2015), *Transatlantic Food and Agricultural Trade Policy: 50 Years of Conflict and Convergence*, Cheltenham: Edward Elgar.

*Journal of Modern European History* (2008), 'Technological Innovation and Transnational Networks: Europe between the Wars', Special Issue, 6 (2).

Judt, T. (2005), *Postwar: A History of Europe since 1945*, New York: Penguin.

Juncos, A. E., and N. Pérez-Solórzano Borragán (2016), 'Enlargement', in M. Cini and N. Pérez-Solórzano Borragán (eds), *European Union Politics*, 5th ed., 227–40, Oxford: Oxford University Press.

Kaelble, H. (2007), *Sozialgeschichte Europas 1945 bis zur Gegenwart*, Munich: C. H. Beck.

Kaiser, W. (1996), *Großbritannien und die Europäische Wirtschaftsgemeinschaft 1955-1961: Von Messina nach Canossa*, Munich: Oldenbourg.

Kaiser, W. (1999), *Using Europe, Abusing the Europeans: Britain and European Integration, 1945–63*, Basingstoke: Palgrave Macmillan.

Kaiser, W. (1997), 'Challenge to the Community: The Creation, Crisis and Consolidation of the European Free Trade Association, 1958–72', *Journal of European Integration History*, 3 (1): 7–33.

Kaiser, W. (2002), '"Überzeugter Katholik und CDU-Wähler": Zur Historiographie der Integrationsgeschichte am Beispiel Walter Lipgens', *Journal of European Integration History*, 8 (2): 119–28.

Kaiser, W. (2007), *Christian Democracy and the Origins of European Union*, Cambridge: Cambridge University Press.

Kaiser, W. (2008), 'History Meets Politics: Overcoming Interdisciplinary Volapük in Research on the EU', *Journal of European Public Policy*, 15 (2): 300–13.

Kaiser, W. (2021), 'Towards a European Constitution? The European Parliament and the Institutional Reform of the European Communities 1979–84', *Journal of European Integration History*, 27 (1): 79–97.

Kaiser, W., and J. Elvert (2004), *European Union Enlargement: A Comparative History*, London: Routledge.

Kaiser, W., S. Krankenhagen and K. Poehls (2016), *Exhibiting Europe in Museums: Transnational Networks, Collections, Narratives, and Representations*, New York: Berghahn.

Kaiser, W., B. Leucht and M. Rasmussen (eds) (2009), *The History of the European Union: Origins of a Trans- and Supranational Polity 1950–72*, London: Routledge.

Kaiser, W., and J.-H. Meyer (eds) (2017), *International Organizations and Environmental Protection: Conservation and Globalization in the Twentieth Century*, New York: Berghahn.

Kaiser, W., and K. K. Patel (eds) (2018), *Multiple Connections in European Cooperation: International Organizations, Policy Ideas, Practices and Transfers, 1967–1992*, London: Routledge.

Kaiser, W., and J. Schot (2014), *Writing the Rules for Europe: Experts, Cartels, and International Organizations*, Basingstoke: Palgrave Macmillan.

Kaiser, W., and A. Varsori (eds) (2010), *European Union History: Themes and Debates*, Basingstoke: Palgrave Macmillan.

Karamouzi, E. (2014), *Greece, the EEC and the Cold War, 1974–1979: The Second Enlargement*, Palgrave: Basingstoke.

Kassim, H., J. Peterson, M. W. Bauer, S. Connolly, R. Dehousse, L. Hooghe and A. Thompson (eds) (2013), *The European Commission of the Twenty-First Century*, Oxford: Oxford University Press.

Kelemen, R. D. (2020), 'The European Union's Authoritarian Equilibrium', *Journal of European Public Policy*, 27 (3): 481–99.

Kelemen, R. D., and D. Vogel (2010), 'Trading Places: The Role of the United States and the European Union in International Environmental Politics', *Comparative Political Studies*, 43 (4): 427–56.

Kennedy, J. F. (1962a), 'Special Message to Congress on Protecting Consumer Interest, 15 March 1962', *Papers of John F. Kennedy: Presidential Papers. President's Office Files. Speech Files*. Available online: https://www.jfklibr ary.org/asset-viewer/archives/JFKPOF/037/JFKPOF-037-028 (accessed 5 January 2022).

Kennedy, J. F. (1962b), 'Address at Independence Hall, Philadelphia, 4 July 1962'. Transcript available online: https://www.jfklibrary.org/learn/about-jfk/historic-speeches/address-at-independence-hall (accessed 21 March 2022).

Kleis, J. (2019), 'The European Consumer Organisation: Pioneer in Advocacy and Lobbying', in D. Dialer and M. Richter (eds), *Lobbying in the European Union: Strategies, Dynamics and Trends*, 239–50, Cham: Springer International.

Knill, C., Y. Steinebach and X. Fernández-i-Marín (2020), 'Hypocrisy as a Crisis Response? Assessing Changes in Talk, Decisions, and Actions of the European Commission in EU Environmental Policy', *Public Administration*, 98 (2): 363–77.

Knudsen, A. L. (2009a), *Farmers on Welfare: The Making of Europe's Common Agricultural Policy*, Ithaca, NY: Cornell University Press.

Knudsen, A. L. (2009b), 'Delegation as a Political Process: The Case of the Inter-institutional Debate over the Budget Treaty', in W. Kaiser, B. Leucht and M. Rasmussen (eds), *The History of the European Union: Origins of a Supranational Polity 1950–72*, 167–88, Abingdon: Routledge.

Knudsen, A. L. (2014), 'European Integration in the Image and the Shadow of Agriculture', in D. Dinan (ed.), *Origins and Evolution of the European Union*, 2nd ed., 189–216, Oxford: Oxford University Press.

Köhler, H. (1986), *Adenauer und die rheinische Republik: der erste Anlauf, 1918–1924*, Opladen: Westdeutscher Verlag.

Kopecký, P., and C. Mudde (2002), 'The Two Sides of Euroscepticism: Party Positions on European Integration in East Central Europe', *European Union Politics*, 3 (3): 297–326.

Krämer, L. (1985), *EWG-Verbraucherrecht*, Schriftenreihe Europäisches Recht, Politik und Wirtschaft, Baden-Baden: Nomos.

Krastev, I., and S. Holmes (2018), 'Explaining Eastern Europe: Imitation and Its Discontents', *Journal of Democracy*, 29 (3): 117–28.

Krastev, I., and S. Holmes (2019), *The Light That Failed: A Reckoning*, London: Penguin.

Kreppel, A. (2002), *The European Parliament and Supranational Party System: A Study in Institutional Development*, Cambridge: Cambridge University Press.

Krotz, U., K. K. Patel and F. Romero (eds) (2019), *Europe's Cold War Relations: The EC towards a Global Role*, London: Bloomsbury.

Krotz, U., and J. Schild (2013), *Shaping Europe: France, Germany, and Embedded Bilateralism from the Elysée Treaty to Twenty-First Century Politics*, Oxford: Oxford University Press.

Krotz, U., and J. Schild (2018), 'Back to the Future? Franco-German Bilateralism in a Post-Brexit Union', *Journal of European Public Policy*, 25 (8): 1174–93.

Krumrey, J. (2018), *The Symbolic Politics of European Integration: Staging Europe*, Basingstoke: Palgrave Macmillan.

Kuroda, T. (2019), 'EC–ASEAN Relations in the 1970s as an Origin of the European Union–Asia Relationship', *Journal of European Integration History*, 25 (1): 65–80.

Laczó, F., and L. Lisjak Gabrijelčič (eds) (2020a), *The Legacy of Division: East and West after 1989*, Budapest: CEU.

Laczó, F., and L. Lisjak Gabrijelčič (2020b), 'Introduction: The Legacy of Division: East and West after 1989', in F. Laczó and L. Lisjak Gabrijelcic (eds), *The Legacy of Division: East and West after 1989*, 1–10, Budapest: CEU.

Laffan, B. (2017), 'The Eurozone in Crisis: Core-Periphery Dynamics', in D. Dinan, N. Nugent and W. E. Paterson (eds), *The European Union in Crisis*, 131–48, London: Palgrave.

Lambert, J. (1972), 'Arming against Pollution: The Commission's Recommendations for Community-Wide Action to Protect the Environment Include a Proposal to Harmonize National Pollution Detection Methods, Punitive Measures, and Economic Incentives to Industrial Action', *European Community*, 157 (June–July): 14–15.

Langendijk, V., and J. Schot (2008), 'Technocratic Internationalism in the Interwar Years: Building Europe on Motorways and Electricity Networks', *Journal of Modern European History*, 6 (2): 196–217.

Larat, F., M. Mangenot and S. Schirmann (eds) (2018), *Les études européennes: Genèses et institutionnalisation*, Paris: L'Harmattan.

Laursen, F. (ed.) (2008), *The Rise and Fall of the EU's Constitutional Treaty*, Nijhoff: Brill.

Lawson, D. (1990), 'Saying the Unsayable about the Germans', *Spectator*, 14 July.

Le Boulay, M. (2010), 'Investir l'arène européenne de la recherche. Le « Groupe de Liaison » des historiens auprès de la Commission européenne', *Politix*, 89: 103–24.

Leconte, C. (2010), *Understanding Euroscepticism*, Basingstoke: Palgrave Macmillan.

Leruth, B., N. Startin and S. Usherwood (eds) (2018), *The Routledge Handbook of Euroscepticism*, Abingdon: Routledge.

Leucht, B. (2009), 'Transatlantic Policy Networks in the Creation of the First European Anti-trust Law: Mediating between American Anti-trust and German Ordo-liberalism', in W. Kaiser, B. Leucht and M. Rasmussen (eds), *The History of the European Union: Origins of a Supranational Polity 1950–72*, 56–73, Abingdon: Routledge.

Leucht, B. (2010), 'Expertise and the Creation of a Constitutional Core Europe: Transatlantic Policy Networks in the Schuman Plan Negotiations', in M. Gehler, W. Kaiser and B. Leucht (eds), *Transnational Networks in Regional Integration: Governing Europe, 1945–83*, 18–37, Basingstoke: Palgrave Macmillan.

Leucht, B. (2012), 'Actorness and Enlargement in Historical Perspective', in B. Arcidiacono, K. Milzow, A. Marion and P.-E. Bourneuf (eds), *Europe Twenty Years after the End of the Cold War: The New Europe, New Europes?*, 115–29, Brussels: PIE Peter Lang.

Leucht, B. (2017), 'Beyond Morgenthau: The Transnational Turn and the Potential of Interdisciplinary Approaches for International History', in B. Haider-Wilson, W. D. Godsey and W. Mueller (eds), *International History in Theory and Practice*, 289–309, Vienna: Austrian Academy of Sciences.

Leucht, B. (2022), 'Beyond 1973: UK Accession and the Origins of EC Consumer Policy', *Global Policy* 13(Suppl. 2), 20–9.

Leucht, B., and K. Seidel (2008), 'Du Traité de Paris au règlement 17/1962: Ruptures et continuités dans la politique européenne de concurrence, 1950–1962', *Histoire, économie et société*, 27 (1): 35–46.

Levi, G., and D. Preda (eds) (2019), *Euroscepticisms: Resistance and Opposition to the European Community/European Union*, Bologna: Il mulino.

Lezcykiewicz, D., and S. Weatherill (2016), *The Images of the Consumer in EU Law: Legislation, Free Movement and Competition Law*, Oxford: Hart.

Lindberg, L., and S. Scheingold (1970), *Europe's Would-Be Polity: Patterns of Change in the European Community*, Englewood Cliffs, NJ: Prentice-Hall.

Lipgens W. (1968), *Europa-Föderationspläne der Widerstandsbewegungen, 1940–1945: eine Dokumentation*, Munich: Oldenbourg.

Lipgens, W. (1977), *Die Anfänge der europäischen Einigungspolitik 1945–1950, Erster Teil: 1945–1947*, Stuttgart: Ernst Klett.

Lipgens, W. (1982), *A History of European Integration 1945–1947: The Formation of the European Unity Movement*, Oxford: Clarendon.

Lipgens, W. (ed.) (1986–8), *Documents on the History of European Integration*, Vols 1–3 (Vol. 3 ed. with W. Loth), Berlin: W. de Gruyter.

Lipgens, W. (1991), *Transnational Organizations of Political Parties and Pressure Groups in the Struggle for European Union*, Vol. 4: 1945–1950, Berlin: W. de Gruyter.

Loth, W. (ed.) (2001), *Crises and Compromises: The European Project 1963–1969*, Baden-Baden: Nomos.

Loth, W. (2012), 'Integrating Paradigms: Walter Lipgens and Alan Milward as Pioneers of European Integration History', in F. Guirao, F. Lynch and S. Ramirez-Pérez (eds), *Alan S. Milward and a Century of European Change*, 280–92, London: Routledge.

Loth, W., and M.-T. Bitsch (2007), 'The Hallstein Commission', in M. Dumoulin (ed.), *The European Commission, 1958–72: History and Memories*, 51–78, Luxembourg: Office for Official Publications of the European Communities.

Ludlow, N. P. (1997), *Dealing with Britain: The Six and the First UK Application to the EEC*, Cambridge: Cambridge University Press.

Ludlow, N. P. (2005), 'The Making of the CAP: Towards a Historical Analysis of the EU's First Major Policy', *Contemporary European History*, 14 (3): 347–71.

Ludlow, N. P. (2006), *The European Community and the Crises of the 1960s: Negotiating the Gaullist Challenge*, London: Routledge.

Ludlow, N. P. (2015), 'Safeguarding British Identity or Betraying It? The Role of British "Tradition" in the Parliamentary Great Debate on EC Membership, October 1971', *Journal of Common Market Studies*, 53 (1): 18–34.

Ludlow, N. P. (2016), *Roy Jenkins and the European Commission Presidency, 1976–1980: At the Heart of Europe*, Basingstoke: Palgrave Macmillan.

Ludlow, N. P. (2017), 'Not a Wholly New Europe: How the Integration Framework Shaped the End of the Cold War in Europe', in F. Bozo, A. Rödder and M. E. Sarotte (eds), *German Reunification: A Multinational History*, 133–52, London: Routledge.

Ludlow, N. P. (2019), 'Jacques Delors', in V. Dujardin, E. Bussière, P. Ludlow, F. Romero, D. Schlenker and A. Varsori (eds), *The European Commission, 1986–2000: History and Memories of an Institution*, 389–94, Luxembourg: Office for Official Publications of the European Communities.

Ludlow, N. P. (2020), 'A Double-Edged Victory: Fontainebleau and the Resolution of the British Budget Problem, 1983–84', in M. Gehler and W. Loth (eds), *Reshaping Europe: Towards a Political, Economic and Monetary Union, 1984–1989*, 45–72, Baden-Baden: Nomos.

Ludlow, N. P. (2021), 'Solidarity, Sanctions and Misunderstanding: The European Dimension of the Falklands Crisis', *International History Review*, 43 (3): 508–24.

Lundestad, G. (1998), *'Empire' by Integration: The United States and European Integration, 1945–1997*, Oxford: Oxford University Press.

Lynch, F. M. B. (2000), 'De Gaulle's First Veto: France, the Rueff Plan and the Free Trade Area', *Contemporary European History*, 9 (1): 111–35.

Maas, W. (2007), *Creating European Citizens*, Lanham, MD: Rowman & Littlefield.

Maes, I. (2006), 'The Ascent of the European Commission as an Actor in the Monetary Integration Process in the 1960s', *Scottish Journal of Political Economy*, 53 (2): 222–41.

Maes, I., and E. Bussière (2016), 'Robert Triffin: The Arch Monetarist in the European Monetary Integration Debates?', in K. Dyson and I. Maes (eds),

*Architects of the Euro: Intellectuals in the Making of European Monetary Union*, 30–50, Oxford: Oxford University Press.

Magnette, P. (2005), *What Is the European Union? Nature and Prospects*, Houndmills: Palgrave Macmillan.

Magnette, P. (2017), *CETA: quand l'Europe déraille*, Waterloo: Luc Pire.

Maier, C. S. (2010), '"Malaise": The Crisis of Capitalism in the 1970s', in N. Ferguson, C. S. Maier, E. Manela and D. J. Sargent (eds), *The Shock of the Global: The 1970s in Perspective*, 25–48, Cambridge, MA: Harvard University Press.

Mancini, F. (1988), 'Principi fondamentali di diritto del lavoro nell'ordinamento delle Comunità europee', in *Il lavoro nel diritto comunitario e l'ordinamento italiano*, 23–39, Padova: Cedam.

Manners, I. (2002), 'Normative Power Europe: A Contradiction in Terms?' *Journal of Common Market Studies*, 40 (2): 235–58.

Marelli, E., and M. Signorelli (2017), *Europe and the Euro: Integration, Crisis and Policies*, London: Palgrave Macmillan.

Marjolin, R. (1986), *Architect of European Unity: Memoirs 1911–1986*, London: Weidenfeld & Nicolson.

Mark, J. (2011), *Unfinished Revolution: Making Sense of the Communist Past in Central-Eastern Europe*, New Haven, CT: Yale University Press.

Mark, J., B. Iacob, T. Rupprecht and L. Spaskovska (2019), *1989: A Global History of Eastern Europe*, Cambridge: Cambridge University Press.

Marquand, D. (1978), 'Towards a Europe of the Parties?', *Political Quarterly*, 49: 425–45.

Martin, G., and J. Paulmann (eds) (2001), *The Mechanisms of Internationalism: Culture, Society, and Politics from the 1840s to the First World War*, Oxford: Oxford University Press.

Martin, A., and G. Ross (2004), *Euros and Europeans: Monetary Integration and the European Model of Society*, Cambridge: Cambridge University Press.

Masini, F. (2019), 'What Went Wrong. The Failure of the 1993 Delors' White Paper', *History of Economic Thought and Policy*, 8 (2): 85–100.

Mattli, W., and A.-M. Slaughter (1995), 'Law and Politics in the European Union: A Reply to Garrett', *International Organization*, 49 (1): 183–90.

McCormick, J. (2020), *European Union Politics*, London: Macmillan International.

McNamara, K. R. (1998), *The Currency of Ideas: Monetary Politics in the European Union*, Ithaca, NY: Cornell University Press.

Mechi, L. (2010), 'Formation of a European Society? Exploring Social and Cultural Dimensions', in W. Kaiser and A. Varsori (eds), *European Union History: Themes and Debates*, 150–68, Basingstoke: Palgrave Macmillan.

Mechi, L. (2012), *L'Organizzazione Internazionale del Lavoro e la ricostruzione europea: Le basi sociali dell'integrazione economica (1931–1957)*, Roma: Ediesse.

Mechi, L., G. Migani and F. Petrini (eds) (2014), *Networks of Global Governance: International Organisations and European Integration in a Historical Perspective*, Cambridge: Cambridge Scholar.

Melegh, A. (2005), *On the East-West Slope: Globalization, Nationalism, Racism and Discourses on Central and Eastern Europe*, Budapest: CEU.

Mény, Y. (2009), *Building Parliament: 50 Years of European Parliament History: 1958–2008*, Luxembourg: Office for Official Publications of the European Communities.

Mény, Y., and V. Wright (eds) (1987), *The Politics of Steel: Western Europe and the Steel Industry in the Crisis Years (1974–1984)*, Berlin: W. de Gruyter.

Merkel, A. (2011), 'If the Euro Fails, Europe Fails', *Der Spiegel*, 11 September. Accessible online: https://www.spiegel.de/international/germany/if-the-euro-fails-europe-fails-merkel-says-eu-must-be-bound-closer-together-a-784953.html (accessed 13 February 2022).

Meunier, S., and K. Nicolaïdis (2006), 'The European Union as a Conflicted Trade Power', *Journal of European Public Policy*, 13 (6): 906–25.

Meyer, J.-H. (2009), 'Tracing Transnational Communication in the European Public Sphere: The Summit of the Hague 1969', in W. Kaiser, M. Rasmussen and B. Leucht (eds), *The History of the European Union: Origins of a Trans- and Supranational Polity 1950–72*, 110–28, Abingdon: Routledge.

Meyer, J.-H. (2010a), *The European Public Sphere: Media and Transnational Communication in European Integration 1969–1991*, Stuttgart: Franz Steiner.

Meyer, J.-H. (2010b), 'Saving Migrants: A Transnational Network Supporting Supranational Bird Protection Policy', in W. Kaiser, B. Leucht and M. Gehler (eds), *Transnational Networks in Regional Integration: Governing Europe 1945–83*, 176–98, Basingstoke: Palgrave Macmillan.

Meyer, J.-H. (2013), 'Challenging the Atomic Community: The European Environmental Bureau and the Europeanization of Anti-Nuclear Protest', in W. Kaiser and J.-H. Meyer (eds), *Societal Actors in European Integration: Polity-Building and Policy-Making 1958–1992*, 197–220, Basingstoke: Palgrave.

Meyer, J.-H. (2017a), 'Who Should Pay for Pollution? The OECD, the European Communities and the Emergence of Environmental Policy in the Early 1970s', *European Review of History: Revue européenne d'histoire*, 24 (3): 377–98.

Meyer, J.-H. (2017b), 'From Nature to Environment: International Organizations and Environmental Protection before Stockholm', in W. Kaiser and J.-H. Meyer (eds), *International Organizations and Environmental Protection: Conservation and Globalization in the Twentieth Century*, 31–73, New York: Berghahn.

Meyer, J.-H. (2019), 'Environmental Policy', in V. Dujardin, E. Bussière, P. Ludlow, F. Romero, D. Schlenker and A. Varsori (eds), *The European Commission 1986–2000: History and Memories of an Institution*, 371–87, Luxembourg: Publications Office of the European Union.

Meyer, J.-H. (2020), 'Responding to the European Public? Public Debates, Societal Actors and the Emergence of a European Environmental Policy', in C. Wenkel E. Bussière, A. Grisoni and H. Miard-Delacroix (eds), *The Environment and European Public Sphere: Perception, Actors, Policies*, 221–40, Winwick: White Horse.

Meyer, J.-H. (2021), 'Pushing for a Greener Europe. The European Parliament and Environmental Policy in the 1970s and 1980s', *Journal of European Integration History*, 27 (1): 57–78.

Meyer, J.-H. (2022), 'Indispensable, Safe and Sustainable? How the European Parliament Debated Nuclear Energy Megaprojects in the 1970s Energy Transition', *Journal of Mega Infrastructure & Sustainable Development*, 2 (2): 187–205.

Meyer, J.-H. (forthcoming), 'Ludwig Krämer (*1939): Taking the Member States to Court', in P. R. Bajon and S. Vogenauer (eds), *Legal Biographies in European Integration*, Oxford: Hart.

Micklitz, H.-W. (2015), 'Norbert Reich, Gründer und Begründer des Verbraucherrechts 1937–2015 – ein Nachruf', *Verbraucher und Recht*, 30 (12): 443–5.

Migani, G. (2013), 'National Strategies and International Issues at the Inception of Community Development Aid: France, Sub-Saharan Africa and the Yaoundé Convention', in G. Bossuat and G. Cummings (eds), *France, Europe and Development Aid: From the Treaties of Rome to the Present Day*, 15–30, Paris: IGPDE. Accessible online: https://books.openedition.org/igpde/2938 (accessed 13 February 2022).

Migani, G. (2014a), 'Development Aid: Historic Priorities and New Dynamics', in E. Bussière, V. Dujardin, M. Dumoulin, P. Ludlow, J. W. Brouwer and P. Tilly (eds), *The European Commission, 1973–1986: Histories and Memories of an Institution*, 393–411, Luxembourg: Publications Office of the European Union.

Migani, G. (2014b), 'Lomé and the North-South Relations (1975–1984): From the "New International Economic Order" to a New Conditionality', in C. Hiepel (ed.), *Europe in a Globalising World: Global Challenges and European Responses in the 'Long' 1970s*, 123–46, Baden-Baden: Nomos.

Milne, R. (2014), 'Reinfeldt Aims for Unprecedented Third Term as Swedish PM', *Financial Times*, 2 September.

Milward, A. S. (1984), *The Reconstruction of Western Europe*, London: Routledge.

Milward, A. S. (1995), 'Allegiance. The Past and the Future', *Journal of European Integration History*, 1 (1): 7–19.

Milward, A. (2002), *The Rise and Fall of a National Strategy, 1945–1963: The UK and the European Community*, vol. 1, London: Whitehall History. In association with Frank Cass.

Milward, A., with the assistance of G. Brennan and F. Romero (1992), *The European Rescue of the Nation State*, London: Routledge.

Milward, A. S., F. M. B. Lynch, F. Romero, R. Ranieri and V. Sorensen (1993), *The Frontiers of National Sovereignty: History and Theory, 1945–1992*, London: Routledge.

Mittag, J. (2001), 'Die Politisierung der Gemeinsamen Versammlung der Europäischen Gemeinschaft für Kohle und Stahl: Anfänge transnationaler Fraktionsbildung im Europäischen Parlament', *Journal of European Integration History*, 17 (1): 13–30.

Möckli, D. (2008), 'The EC-Nine, the CSCE, and the Changing Pattern of European Security', in A. Wenger, V. Mastny and C. Nuenlist (eds), *Origins of the European Security System: The Helsinki Process Revisited, 1965–75*, 145–63, London: Routledge.

Monnet, J. (2015), *Memoirs*, London: Third Millennium.

Moore, C. (2019), *Margaret Thatcher: The Authorized Biography, Volume Three, Herself Alone*, London: Penguin.

Moravcsik, A. (1998), *The Choice for Europe: Social Purpose and State Power from Messina to Maastricht*, Ithaca, NY: Cornell University Press.

Moravcsik, A. (2007), 'The European Constitutional Settlement', in S. Meunier and K. R. McNamara (eds), *Making History: European Integration and Institutional Change at Fifty*, 23–50, Oxford: Oxford University Press.

Mourlon-Druol, E. (2012a), *A Europe Made of Money: The Emergence of the European Monetary System*, Ithaca, NY: Cornell University Press.

Mourlon-Druol, E. (2012b), '"Managing from the Top": Globalisation and the Rise of Regular Summitry, Mid-1970s–Early 1980s', *Diplomacy & Statecraft*, 23 (4): 679–703.

Mourlon-Druol, E. (2020a), 'European Monetary Integration', in S. Battilossi, Y. Cassis, and K. Yago (eds), *Handbook of the History of Money and Currency*, 809–32, Singapore: Springer.

Mourlon-Druol, E. (2020b), 'History of an Incomplete EMU', in F. Amtenbrink and C. Herrmann (eds), *EU Law of Economic and Monetary Union*, 13–36, Oxford: Oxford University Press.

Mourlon-Druol, E., and F. Romero (eds) (2014), *International Summitry and Global Governance: The Rise of the G7 and the European Council, 1974–1991*, London: Routledge.

Nocken, U. (1989), 'International Cartels and Foreign Policy: The Formation of the International Steel Cartel 1924–1926', in C. Wurm (ed.), *Internationale Kartelle und Aussenpolitik*, 33–82, Stuttgart: Franz Steiner Verlag Wiesbaden Gmbh.

Nugent, N. (2017), *The Government and Politics of the European Union*, London: Macmillan.

Nugent, N., and M. Rhinard (2015), *The European Commission*, 2nd ed., London: Palgrave Macmillan.

Nuttall, S. (1992), *European Political Co-operation*, Oxford: Oxford University Press.

Oberloskamp, E. (2016), ,'The European TREVI Conference in the 1970s: Transgovernmental Policy Coordination in the Area of Internal Security', *Journal of European Integration History*, 22 (1): 29–46.

Ophüls, C. F. (1951), 'Das Wirtschaftsrecht des Schumanplans', *Neue Juristische Wochenschrift*, 4(10): 381–4.

Organisation Charts of the Commission (2007), *The European Commission, 1958–72: History and Memories*, ed. M. Dumoulin, 565–76, Luxembourg: Office for Official Publications of the European Communities.

Orluc, K. (2007), 'Caught between Past and Future: The Idea of Pan-Europe in the Interwar Years', in H. Persson and B. Stråth (eds), *Reflections on Europe: Defining a Political Order in Time and Space*, 95–120, Brussels: PIE Peter Lang.

Pagden, A. (2002), *The Idea of Europe: From Antiquity to the European Union*, Cambridge: Cambridge University Press.

Palayret, J. M., and H. Wallace (2006), *Visions, Votes, and Vetoes: The Empty Chair Crisis and the Luxembourg Compromise Forty Years On*, Brussels: Peter Lang.

Paoli, S. (2010), *Il sogno di Erasmo: La questione educativa nel processo di integrazione europea*, Milano: FrancoAngeli.

Paoli, S. (2016), 'Migration in European Integration: Themes and Debates', *Journal of European Integration History*, 22 (2): 279–96.

Parr, H. (2005), *Britain's Policy towards the European Community: Harold Wilson and Britain's World Role, 1964–1967*, London: Routledge.

Parsons, C. (2003), *A Certain Idea of Europe*, Ithaca, NY: Cornell University Press.

Pasture, P. (2018), 'The EC/EU between the Art of Forgetting and the Palimpsest of Empire', *European Review*, 26 (3): 545–81.

Patel, K. K. (ed.) (2009a), *Fertile Ground for Europe? The History of European Integration and the Common Agricultural Policy since 1945*, Baden-Baden: Nomos.

Patel, K. K. (2009b), 'Europeanization a Contre-coeur: West Germany and Agricultural Integration, 1945–1975', in K. K. Patel (ed.), *Fertile Ground for Europe? The History of European Integration and the Common Agricultural Policy since 1945*, 139–60, Baden-Baden: Nomos.

Patel, K. K. (2009c), *Europäisierung wider Willen: Die Bundesrepublik Deutschland in der Agrarintegration der EWG 1955–1973*, Munich: Oldenbourg.

Patel, K. K. (2013), 'Provincialising European Union: Co-operation and Integration in Europe in a Historical Perspective', *Contemporary European History*, 22 (4): 649–73.

Patel, K. K. (2017), 'Who Was Saving Whom? The European Community and the Cold War, 1960s–1970s', *British Journal of Politics and International Relations*, 19: 29–47.

Patel, K. K. (2019), 'Widening and Deepening? Recent Advances in European Integration History', *Neue Politische Literatur*, 64 (2): 327–57.

Patel, K. K. (2020), *Project Europe: A History*, Cambridge: Cambridge University Press.

Patel, K. K., and C. Salm (eds) (2021a), 'Special Issue on the European Parliament', *Journal of European Integration History*, 27 (1): 1–156.

Patel, K. K., and C. Salm (2021b), 'The European Parliament during the 1970s and 1980s: An Institution on the Rise? – Introduction', *Journal of European Integration History*, 27 (1): 5–19.

Paterson, W. E. (2008), 'Did France and Germany Lead Europe? A Retrospect', in J. E. Hayward (ed.), *Leaderless Europe*, 89–110, New York: Oxford University Press.

Pedersen, J. (2016), 'Constructive Defiance – Denmark and the Effects of European Law, 1973–1993', PhD dissertation, Aarhus University.

Pedersen, S. (2015), *The Guardians: The League of Nations and the Crisis of Empire*, Oxford: Oxford University Press.

Petrini, F. (2013), 'Demanding Democracy in the Workplace: The European Trade Union Confederation and the Struggle to Regulate Multinationals', in W. Kaiser and J.-H. Meyer (eds), *Societal Actors in European Integration 1958–92: From Polity-Building to Policy-Making*, Basingstoke: Palgrave.

Petrini, F. (2014), 'Bringing Social Conflict Back In: The Historiography of Industrial Milieux and European Integration', *Contemporanea*, 17 (3): 525–42.

Pierson, P. (2004), *Politics in Time: History, Institutions, and Social Analysis*, Princeton, NJ: Princeton University Press.

Pinto, A. C., and N. S. Teixeira (eds) (2002), *Southern Europe and the Making of the European Union, 1945–1980s*, Boulder, CO: Social Science Monographs.

Piotrowska, K., and G. Rae (2018), 'Divergence Not Convergence. The Strengthening of the Post-Communist Welfare State Model in Central and Eastern Europe after European Union Expansion', *Polish Sociological Review*, 203 (3): 303–19.

Poidevin, R., and D. Spierenburg (1993), *Histoire de la Haute Autorité de la Communauté Européenne du Charbon et de l'Acier: Une expérience supranationale*, Brussels: Bruylant.

Pollack, M. (2003), *The Engines of European Integration: Delegation, Agency, and Agenda Setting in the EU*, Oxford: Oxford University Press.

Priestly, J. (2008), *Six Battles That Shaped Europe's Parliament*, London: John Harper.

Przeworski, A. (1991), *Democracy and the Market: Political and Economic Reforms in Eastern Europe and Latin America*, New York: Cambridge University Press.

Qvortrup, M. (2017), *Angela Merkel: Europe's Most Influential Leader*, London: Duckworth.

Raikes, P. (1988), *Modernising Hunger: Famine, Food Surplus & Farm Policy in the EEC & Africa*, Portsmouth: Catholic Institute for International Relations.

Ramírez Pérez, S. (2012), 'Conclusions and Perspectives for Future Research', in F. Guirao, F. Lynch and S. Ramírez Pérez (eds), *Alan S. Milward and a Century of European Change*, 499–525, London: Routledge.

Ramírez Pérez, S. (2020), 'Embedding the Market during Times of Crisis: The European Automobile Cartel during a Decade of Crisis (1973–1985)', *Business History*, 62 (5): 815–36.

Rasmussen, H. (1986), *On Law and Policy in the European Court of Justice: A Comparative Study of Judicial Policymaking*, Leiden: Brill Nijhoff.

Rasmussen, M. (2012), 'Establishing a Constitutional Practice of European Law: The History of the Legal Service of the European Executive, 1952–65', *Contemporary European History*, 21 (3): 375–97.

Rasmussen, M. (2014), 'Revolutionizing European Law: A History of the Van Gend en Loos Judgment', *International Journal of Constitutional Law*, 12: 136–63.

Rauh, C. (2016), *A Responsive Technocracy? EU Politicisation and the Consumer Policies of the European Commission*, Colchester: ECPR.

Reich, N., and H.-W. Micklitz (1980), *Consumer Legislation in the EC Countries: A Comparative Analysis; a Study Prepared for the EC Commission*, Consumer Legislation in the EC Countries, New York: Van Nostrand.

Rempe, M. (2012), *Entwicklung im Konflikt: Die EWG und der Senegal, 1957–1975*, Köln: Böhlau.

Reynolds, D. (1985), 'A "Special Relationship"? America, Britain and the International Order since the Second World War', *International Affairs*, 62 (1): 1–20.

Reynolds, D. (2000), *Britannia Overruled: British Policy and World Power in the Twentieth Century*, New York: Longman.

Risse-Kappen, T. (1995), 'Bringing Transnational Relations Back In: Introduction', in T. Risse-Kappen (ed.), *Bringing Transnational Relations Back In: Non-state Actors, Domestic Structures and International Institutions*, 3–33, Cambridge: Cambridge University Press.

Rittberger, B. (2005), *Building Europe's Parliament: Democratic Representation beyond the Nation State*, Oxford: Oxford University Press.

Rittberger, B. (2009), 'The Historical Origins of the EU's System of Representation', *Journal of European Public Policy*, 16 (1): 43–61.

Romano, A. (2009), *From Détente in Europe to European Détente: How the West Shaped the Helsinki CSCE*, Brussels: Peter Lang.

Romano, A. (2017), 'British Policy towards Socialist Countries in the 1970s: Trade as a Cornerstone of Détente', in J. Fisher, E. G. H. Pedaliu and R. Smith (eds), *The Foreign Office, Commerce and British Foreign Policy in the Twentieth Century*, 465–85, London: Palgrave.

Romano, A., and F. Romero (eds) (2020), *European Socialist Regimes' Fateful Engagement with the West: National Strategies in the Long 1970s*, London: Routledge.

Roos, M. (2021a), *The Parliamentary Roots of European Social Policy: Turning Talk into Power*, Basingstoke: Palgrave Macmillan.

Roos, M. (2021b), 'A Parliament for the People? The European Parliament's Activism in the Area of Social Policy: From the Early 1970s to the Single European Act', *Journal of European Integration History*, 27 (1): 37–56.

Rosen, M. J. (1958), 'The Brussels Entente: Export Combination in the World Steel Market', *University of Pennsylvania Law Review*, 106 (8): 1079–116.

Ruggie, J. G. (1982), 'International Regimes, Transactions, and Change: Embedded Liberalism in the Postwar Economic Order', *International Organization*, 36 (2): 379–415.

Rutten, M. (2001), 'From St Malo to Nice – European Defence: Core Documents', *Chaillot Papers*, 47, May, Paris: Institute for Security Studies. Available online: https://www.iss.europa.eu/sites/default/files/EUISSFiles/cp047e.pdf (accessed 13 February 2022).

Sandbu, M. (2015), *Europe's Orphan: The Future of the Euro and the Politics of Debt*, Princeton, NJ: Princeton University Press.

Sandholtz, W., and A. Stone Sweet (eds) (1998), *European Integration and Supranational Governance*, Oxford: Oxford University Press.

Sangar, E. (2020), *Diffusion in Franco-German Relations: A Different Perspective on a History of Cooperation and Conflict*, Cham: Palgrave Macmillan.

Saunders, R. (2018), *Yes to Europe! The 1975 Referendum and Seventies Britain*, Cambridge: Cambridge University Press.

Scepanovic, V., and D. Bohle (2018), 'The Institutional Embeddedness of Transnational Corporations: Dependent Capitalism in Central and Eastern Europe', in A. Noelke and C. May (eds), *Handbook of the International Political Economy of the Corporation*, 152–66, London: Edward Elgar.

Schenk, B. (2017), 'Eastern Europe', in D. Mishkova and B. Trencsényi (eds), *European Regions and Boundaries: A Conceptual History*, 188–209, New York: Berghahn.

Schimmelfennig, F. (2001), 'The Community Trap: Liberal Norms, Rhetorical Action, and the Eastern Enlargement of the European Union', *International Organization*, 55 (1): 47–80.

Schipper, F., and J. Schot (2011), 'Infrastructural Europeanism or the Building of Europe on Infrastructures: An Introduction', *History and Technology*, 27 (3): 245–64.

Schmidt, V. A. (2013), 'Democracy and Legitimacy in the European Union Revisited: Input, Output and "Throughput"', *Political Studies*, 61 (1): 2–22.

Schmitz, G. P. (2014), 'EU-Arbeitsprogramm: Juncker will Umweltschutzprogramme kippen', *Der Spiegel* (updated 16 December 2014). Available online: http://www.spiegel.de/politik/ausland/eu-kommission-jobs-und-nicht-so-viel-an-die-umwelt-denken-a-1008668.html (accessed 10 January 2022).

Schönwald, M. (2017), *Walter Hallstein: Ein Wegbereiter Europas*, Stuttgart: Kohlhammer.

Schrag Sternberg, C. (2013), *The Struggle for EU Legitimacy: Public Contestation 1950–2005*, Basingstoke: Palgrave Macmillan.

Schuman Declaration (1950), Paris, 9 May. Available online: http://www.cvce.eu/obj/the_schuman_declaration_paris_9_may_1950-en-9cc6ac38-32f5-4c0a-a337-9a8ae4d5740f.html (accessed 9 March 2022).

Schwarz, H.-P. (1995 [German 1986]), *Konrad Adenauer: A German Politician and Statesman in a Period of War, Revolution and Reconstruction*, vol. 1: 1876–1952, Providence: Berghahn.

Schwartz, T. (1991), *America's Germany: John McCloy and the Federal Republic of Germany*, Cambridge, MA: Harvard University Press.

Seefried, E. (2021), 'Developing Europe: The Formation of Sustainability Concepts and Activities', in A.-K. Wöbse and P. Kupper (eds), *Greening Europe: Environmental Protection in the Long Twentieth Century – a Handbook*, 389–418, Berlin: De Gruyter Oldenbourg.

Segers, M. (2020), *The Netherlands and European Integration, 1950 to Present*, Amsterdam: Amsterdam University Press.

Segers, M., R. Claassen, A. Gerbrandy and S. Princen (2019), 'Rethinking the European Social Market Economy: Introduction to the Special Issue', *Journal of Common Market Studies*, 57 (1): 3–12.

Seidel, K. (2010a), *The Process of Politics in Europe: The Rise of European Elites and Supranational Institutions*, London: I. B. Tauris.

Seidel, K. (2010b), 'Taking Farmers off Welfare: The EEC Commission's Memorandum "Agriculture 1980" of 1968', *Journal of European Integration History*, 16 (2): 83–101.

Seidel, K. (2016), 'Robert Marjolin: Securing the Common Market through Economic and Monetary Union', in K. Dyson and I. Maes (eds), *Architects of the Euro: Intellectuals in the Making of European Monetary Union*, 51–74, Oxford: Oxford University Press.

Seidel, K. (2019), 'The External Dimensions of the Common Agricultural Policy', in U. Krotz, K. K. Patel and F. Romero (eds), *Europe's Cold War Relations: The EC towards a Global Role*, 165–84, London: Bloomsbury.

Seidel, K. (2020a), 'The Challenges of Enlargement and GATT Trade Negotiations: Explaining the Resilience of the European Community's Common Agricultural Policy in the 1970s', *International History Review*, 42 (2): 352–70.

Seidel, K. (2020b), 'Britain, the Common Agricultural Policy and the Challenges of Membership in the European Community: A Political Balancing Act', *Contemporary British History*, 34 (2): 179–203.

Self, R. (2010), *British Foreign and Defence Policy since 1945: Challenges and Dilemmas in a Changing World*, London: Palgrave.

Servan-Schreiber, J. J. (1968), *The American Challenge*, New York: Atheneum.

Shaw, J. (2003), 'What's in a Convention? Process and Substance in the Project of European Constitution Building', in P. Magnette, L. Hoffmann and A. Verges Bausili (eds), *The Convention on the Future of Europe*, 51–2, London: Federal Trust.

Sierp, A. (2014), *History, Memory and Trans-European Identity: Unifying Divisions*, London: Routledge.

Slobodian, Q. (2018), *Globalists: The End of Empire and the Birth of Neoliberalism*, Cambridge, MA: Harvard University Press.

Smith, J. (2016), 'David Cameron's EU Renegotiation and Referendum Pledge: A Case of déjà vu?', *British Politics*, 11: 324–46.

Soldwisch, I. (2021), *Das Europäische Parlament 1979–2004: Inszenierung, Selbst(er)findung und politisches Handeln der Abgeordneten*, Stuttgart: Kohlhammer Verlag.

Spierenburg, D., and R. Poidevin (1994), *The History of the High Authority of the European Coal and Steel Community: Supranationality in Operation*, London: Weidenfeld & Nicholson.

Spinelli, A. (1972), 'A Fight to the Finish: The Community Must Continue Fostering Economic Development without Sacrificing Social Needs', *European Community*, 157 (June–July): 13.

Spinelli, A. (1991), *Diario europeo: 2, 1970–1976. A cura di Edmondo Paolini*, Milan: Il Mulino.

Spinelli, A., E. Rossi and E. Colorni (1941), *For a Free and United Europe: A Draft Manifesto (Ventotene Manifesto)*. Available online: https://www.federalists.eu/uef/library/books/the-ventotene-manifesto (accessed 7 January 2022).

Spoerer, M. (2015), 'Agricultural Protection and Support in the European Economic Community, 1962–92: Rent-Seeking or Welfare Policy?' *European Review of Economic History*, 19 (2): 195–214.

Spohr, K. (2019), *Post Wall, Post Square: How Bush, Gorbachev, Kohl, and Deng Shaped the World after 1989*, New Haven, CT: Yale University Press.

Statement (1972), Statement from the Paris Summit, 19–21 October 1972. Available online: http://www.cvce.eu/obj/statement_from_the_paris_summi t_19_to_21_october_1972-en-b1dd3d57-5f31-4796- 85c3-cfd2210d6901.html (accessed 24 March 2022).

Stein, E. (1981), 'Lawyers, Judges and the Making of a Transnational Constitution', *American Journal of International Law*, 75: 1–27.

Suzuki, H. (2020), *Japanese Investment and British Trade Unionism: Thatcher and Nissan Revisited in the Wake of Brexit*, Singapore: Palgrave Macmillan.

Szczerbiak, A., and P. Taggart (eds) (2008), *Opposing Europe? The Comparative Party Politics of Euroscepticism*, 2 vols, Oxford: Oxford University Press.

Taubman, W. (2017), *Gorbachev: His Life and Times*, New York: W. W. Norton.

Taylor, P. (2008), *The End of European Integration: Anti-Europeanism Explained*, Abingdon: Routledge.

Thatcher, M. (2007), *Internationalisation and Economic Institutions: Comparing the European Experience*, Oxford: Oxford University Press.

Ther, P. (2016), *Europe since 1989: A History*, Princeton, NJ: Princeton University Press.

Thiemeyer, G. (2009), 'The Failure of the Green Pool and the Success of the CAP: Long Term Structures in European Agricultural Integration in the 1950s and 1960s', in K. K. Patel (ed.), *Fertile Ground for Europe? The History of European Integration and the Common Agricultural Policy since 1945*, 46–59, Baden-Baden: Nomos.

Tiersky, P. (2001), *Euroskepticism: A Reader*, Lanham, MD: Rowan & Littlefield.

Tismaneanu, V. (1999), 'Understanding National Stalinism: Reflections on Ceauşescu's Socialism', *Communist and Post-Communist Studies, 32* (2): 155–73.

Tooze, Y. (2018), *Crashed: How a Decade of Financial Crises Changed the World*, New York: Viking.

Trachtenberg, M. (2012), 'The de Gaulle Problem', *Journal of Cold War Studies*, 14 (1): 81–92.

Tracy, M. (1989), *Government and Agriculture in Western Europe 1880–1988*, New York: Harvester.

Treib. O. (2020), 'Europescepticism Is Here to Stay: What Cleavage Theory Can Teach Us about the 2019 European Parliament Elections', *Journal of European Public Policy*, 21 (10): 1541–54.

Tulli, U. (2017), *Un Parlamento per l'Europa: Il Parlamento europeo e la battaglia per la sua elezione (1948–1979)*, Milan: Mondadori.

UNICE (1972), 'Avis de l'UNICE sur le Projet d'accord concernant l'information de la Commission en vue d'une harmonisation éventuelle à l'ensemble de la Communauté des mesures d'urgence en matière de l'environnement (Doc. COM (72) 334 du 22 mars 1972), 10 July 1972', *Archive of the Council of Ministers*, CM2 1973.529 (517).

Van Apeldoorn, B. (2003), *Transnational Capitalism and the Struggle over European Integration*, London: Routledge.

Van de Grift, L. (2018), 'Representing European Society: The Rise of New Representative Claims in 1970s European Politics', *Archiv für Sozialgeschichte*, 58: 263–78.

Van de Grift, L., and W. P. v. Meurs (2021), 'Europeanizing Biodiversity: International Organizations as Environmental Actors', in A.-K. Wöbse and P. Kupper (eds), *Greening Europe: Environmental Protection in the Long Twentieth Century – a Handbook*, 419–46, Berlin: De Gruyter Oldenbourg.

Van de Grift, L., H. Rodenburg and G. Wieman (2020), 'Entering the European Political Arena, Adapting to Europe: Greenpeace International, 1987–93', in C. Wenkel, E. Bussière, A. Grisoni and H. Miard-Delacroix (eds), *The Environment and European Public Sphere: Perception, Actors, Policies*, 147–64, Winwick: White Horse.

Van de Velde, C. (2014), 'Environmental and Consumer Protection', in E. Bussière, V. Dujardin, M. Dumoulin, P. Ludlow, J. W. Brouwer and P. Tilly (eds), *The European Commission 1973–86: History and Memories of an Institution*, 385–92, Luxembourg: Publications Office of the European Union.

Van der Harst, J. (2007), 'Enlargement: The Commission Seeks a Role for Itself', in M. Dumoulin (ed.), *The European Commission, 1958–72: History and Memories*, 533–56, Luxembourg: Office for Official Publications of the European Communities.

Van Hecke, S. (2012), 'Polity-Building in the Constitutional Convention: Transnational Party Groups in European Union Institutional Reform', *Journal of Common Market Studies*, 50 (5): 837–52.

Van Leeuwen, K., and M. Rasmussen (2021), 'A Political and Legal History of the Advisory Committee of Jurists and the Foundation of the Permanent Court of International Justice', in P. S. Morris (ed.), *Transforming the Politics of International Law*, 69–106, London: Routledge.

Van Middelaar, L. (2013), *The Passage to Europe: How a Continent Became a Union*, New Haven, CT: Yale University Press.

Van Middelaar, L. (2021), *Pandemonium*, Newcastle upon Tyne: Agenda.

Van Ouedenhove, G. (1962), *The Political Parties in the European Parliament: The First Ten Years (September 1952–September 1962)*, Leyden: A. W. Sijthoff.

Van Zon, K. (2020), 'A Consumers' Europe? Common Market Governance between Consumers and Commerce, 1960s–1990s', *Journal of European Integration History*, 26 (2): 203–28.

Van Zon, K. (forthcoming), 'Skincare, Health Scares and Animal Welfare: (De) politicising European Cosmetics Regulation in the Wake of Scandal, 1968–1986', in J.-H. Meyer and S. Vogenauer (eds), *Law and Policy in European Integration*, Oxford: Oxford University Press.

Van Zon, K., A. Schimmel and L. v. d. Grift (forthcoming), 'Vom Marktbürger zum Konsumbürger? Konsumpolitik und Verbrauchervertretung in den EWG in den 1960er und 1970er Jahren', in M. Reitmayer and S. Weispfennig (eds), *Konsum und Politik nach dem Boom*, Göttingen: Vandenhoeck & Ruprecht.

Vandenbroucke, F., C. Barnard and G. De Baere (2017), *A European Social Union after the Crisis*, Cambridge: Cambridge University Press.

Varsori, A. (ed.) (2006), *Inside the European Community: Actors and Policies in the European Integration 1957–1972*, Baden-Baden: Nomos.

Varsori, A., and G. Migani (eds) (2011), *Europe in the International Arena during the 1970s: Entering a Different World*, Brussels: Peter Lang.

Vassilou, G. (2007), *The Accession Story: The EU from 15 to 25 Countries*, Oxford: Oxford University Press.

Vauchez, A. (2010), 'The Transnational Politics of Judicialization: *Van Gend en Loos* and the Making of EU Polity', *European Law Journal*, 16 (1): 1–28.

Vauchez, A. (2015), *Brokering Europe: Euro-Lawyers and the Making of a Transnational Polity*, Cambridge: Cambridge University Press.

Vaughan-Whitehead, D. (2014), *European Social Model in Crisis: Is Europe Losing Its Soul?* Cheltenham: Edward Elgar.

Verdun, A. (2002a), 'Why EMU Happened: A Survey of Theoretical Explanations', in P. Crowley (ed.), *Before and beyond EMU: Historical Lessons and Future Prospects*, 71–98, London: Routledge.

Verdun, A. (ed.) (2002b), *The Euro: European Integration Theory and Economic and Monetary Union*, Boulder, CO: Rowman and Littlefield.

Verdun, A. (2010), 'Ten Years EMU: An Assessment of Ten Critical Claims', *International Journal of Economics and Business Research*, 2(1–2): 144–63.

Vick, K., and S. Schuster (2015), 'Person of the Year: Chancellor of the Free World', *Time*, December. Available online: https://time.com/time-per son-of-the-year-2015-angela-merkel/ (accessed 13 February 2022).

Villaume, P., and O. A. Westad (eds) (2010), *Perforating the Iron Curtain: European Détente, Transatlantic Relations, and the Cold War, 1965–1985*, Copenhagen: Museum Tusculanum.

Viñas, A., S. Ramírez-Pérez and E. Bussière (2014), 'Trade Policy and External Relations: New Dynamics', in V. Dujardin, E. Bussière, P. Ludlow, F. Romero, D. Schlenker and A. Varsori (eds), *The European Commission, 1973–1986: History and Memories of an Institution*, 413–28, Luxembourg: Office for Official Publications of the European Union.

Vogel, D. (2003), 'The Hare and the Tortoise Revisited: The New Politics of Consumer and Environmental Regulation in Europe', *British Journal of Political Science*, 33 (4): 557–80.

Wall, S. (2013), *The Official History of Britain and the European Community. Vol. II, From Rejection to Referendum, 1963–1975*, London: Routledge.

Wall, S. (2019), *The Official History of Britain and the European Community. Vol. III: 'The Tiger Unleashed', 1975–1985*, London: Routledge.

Warlouzet, L. (2011), 'De Gaulle as a Father of Europe: The Unpredictability of the FTA's Failure and the EEC's Success (1956–58)', *Contemporary European History*, 20 (4): 419–34.

Warlouzet, L. (2016), 'The Centralization of EU Competition Policy: Historical Institutionalist Dynamics from Cartel Monitoring to Merger Control (1956–91)', *Journal of Common Market Studies*, 54 (3): 725–41.

Warlouzet, L. (2018a), *Governing Europe in a Globalizing World: Neoliberalism and Its Alternatives Following the 1973 Oil Crisis*, London: Routledge.

Warlouzet, L. (2018b), 'Britain at the Centre of European Co-operation (1948–2016)', *Journal of Common Market Studies*, 56 (4): 955–70.

Warlouzet, L. (2018c), 'European Integration History: Beyond the Crisis', *Politique Européenne*, 44 (2): 98–122.

Warlouzet, L. (2019a), 'The EEC/EU as an Evolving Compromise between French Dirigism and German Ordoliberalism (1957–1995)', *Journal of Common Market Studies*, 57 (1): 77–93.

Warlouzet, L. (2019b), 'The Internal Market and Competition', in V. Dujardin, E. Bussière, P. Ludlow, F. Romero, D. Schlenker and A. Varsori (eds), *The European Commission, 1986–2000: Histories and Memories of an Institution*, 257–80, Luxembourg: Publications Office of the European Union.

Warlouzet, L. (2020), *Completing the Single Market: The European Parliament and Economic Integration, 1979–1989*, Brussels: European Parliament Research Service.

Warlouzet, L. (2021), 'A Social Europe with a Greener Perspective: The Evolution of the Delors Commission around 1989', *Studi Storici*, 62(1): 189–209.

Warlouzet, L., and T. Witschke (2012), 'The Difficult Path to an Economic Rule of Law: European Competition Policy, 1950-91', *Contemporary European History*, 21 (3): 437–55.

Warlouzet, L. (2022), *Europe contre Europe: Entre liberté, solidarité et puissance*, Paris: CNRS editions.

Warlouzet, L. (2023), 'A Flanking European Welfare State: The European Community's Social Dimension from Brandt to Delors (1969–1993)', *Contemporary European History*, online, to be published in print.

Wassenberg, B. (2013), *History of the Council of Europe*, Strasbourg: Council of Europe.

Wassenberg, B., and S. Schirmann (2019), *Political Culture and Dynamics of the European Parliament, 1979–1989*, EPRS-Study, Brussels.

Weatherill, S. (2013), *EU Consumer Law and Policy*, 2nd ed., Elgar European Law, Cheltenham: Edward Elgar.

Weatherill, S. (2021), 'Did Cassis de Dijon Make a Difference?', in A. Albors-Llorens, C. Barnard and B. Leucht (eds), *Cassis de Dijon: Forty Years On*, 119–38, London: Hart.

Weiler, J. H. H. (1994), 'A Quiet Revolution: The European Court of Justice and Its Interlocutors', *Comparative Political Studies*, 26 (4): 510–34.

Weiler, J. H. H. (1999), *The Constitution of Europe – 'Do the New Clothes Have an Emperor?' and Other Essays on European Integration*, Cambridge: Cambridge University Press.

Westad, O. A. (2005), 'Beginnings of the End: How the Cold War Crumbled', in S. Pons and F. Romero (eds), *Reinterpreting the End of the Cold War: Issues, Interpretations, Periodizations*, 68–81, London: Frank Cass.

Westlake, M. (1994), *The Commission and the Parliament: Partners in the European Policy-Making Process*, London: Butterworths.

Wille, A. (2013), *The Normalization of the European Commission: Politics and Bureaucracy in the EU Executive*, Oxford: Oxford University Press.

Winand, P. (1993), *Kennedy, Eisenhower, and the United States of Europe*, New York: St Martin.

Witschke, T. (2009), *Gefahr für den Wettbewerb? Die Fusionskontrolle der Europäischen Gemeinschaft für Kohle und Stahl und die «Rekonzentration» der Ruhrstahlindustrie 1950–1963*, Berlin: Akademie Verlag.

Wurm, C. (1995), 'Early European Integration as a Research Field: Perspectives, Debates, Problems', in C. Wurm (ed.), *Western Europe and Germany: The Beginnings of European Integration, 1945–1960*, 9–26, Oxford: Berg.

Young, H. (1998), *This Blessed Plot: Britain and Europe from Churchill to Blair*, Basingstoke: Macmillan.

Young, J. W. (1999), *Britain and European Unity 1945–1999*, 2nd ed., Basingstoke: Macmillan.

Zaccaria, B. (2021), 'Jacques Delors, the End of the Cold War and the EU Democratic Deficit', *Journal of European Integration History*, 26 (2): 285–304.

Zaiotti, R. (2011), 'Performing Schengen: Myths, Rituals and the Making of European Territoriality beyond Europe', *Review of International Studies*, 37 (2), 537–56.

Ziegenhofer-Prettenthaler, A. (2004), *Botschafer Europas: Richard Nikolaus Coudenhove-Kalergi und die Paneuropa-Bewegung in den zwanziger- und dreißiger Jahren*, Boehlau: Cologne.

Zito, A. R. (2000), *Creating Environmental Policy in the European Union*, Basingstoke: MacMillan.

Zito, A. R. (2002), 'Task Expansion: A Theoretical Overview', in A. Jordan (ed.), *Environmental Policy in the European Union: Actors, Institutions, and Processes*, 159–79, London: Earthscan.

Zito, A. R., C. Burns and A. Lenschow (2019), 'Is the Trajectory of European Union Environmental Policy Less Certain?', *Environmental Politics*, 28 (2): 187–207.

# INDEX